Islamic Futures and Policy Studies

Series editor, *Ziauddin Sardar*
Director, Center for Policy and Future Studies
East–West University, Chicago

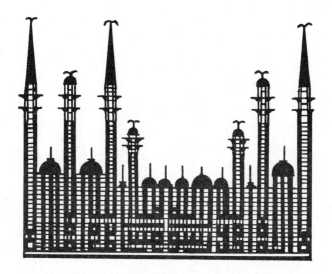

Islamic Futures

The Shape of Ideas to Come

Ziauddin Sardar

Mansell Publishing Limited

London and New York

First published 1985 by Mansell Publishing Limited
(A subsidiary of The H.W. Wilson Company)
6 All Saints Street, London N1 9RL, England
950 University Avenue, Bronx, New York 10452, U.S.A.

British Library Cataloguing in Publication Data
  Sardar, Ziauddin
    Islamic futures : the shape of ideas to come.—
    (Islamic futures and policy studies)
    1. Civilization, Islamic
    I. Title   II. Series
    909'.097671   DS35.62
    ISBN 0-7201-1731-3 hard cover
    ISBN 0-7201-1813-1 paper

Library of Congress Cataloging in Publication Data
  Sardar, Ziauddin.
    Islamic futures.

    (Islamic futures and policy studies)
    Companion vol. to: The future of Muslim civilisation.
  c1979.
    Bibliography: p.
    Includes index.
    1. Islam—20th century. I. Sardar, Ziauddin. The
  future of Muslim civilisation. II. Title. III. Series.
  BP163.S355   1985   909'.097671082   84-26179
  ISBN 0-7201-1731-3

Typeset by Spire Print Services Ltd, Salisbury, Wiltshire.
Printed and bound in Great Britain by Billing & Sons Ltd., Worcester

In the name of Allah, the Beneficient, the Merciful

'Has there come on man a while of time when he was a thing unremembered?' *The Qur'an: Surah Al-Insan 76:1*

for Maha

Contents

List of Figures and Table

Preface

In my previous work, *The Future of Muslim Civilization*, I explored viable future alternatives for Muslim societies using the methodology of systems analysis. The book presented an agenda for future orientated thought and action. Here, I continue with the same theme but the emphasis has now shifted to conceptual analysis and examination of the more important ideas that are now emerging in the Muslim world. As such, *Islamic Futures* is a companion volume to my earlier book.

In the wake of euphoria generated by the newly acquired wealth of certain Arab states, the Islamic Revolution in Iran, and the host of 'Islamization' programmes introduced from Morocco to Pakistan, from Malaysia to the Sudan, the belief that Muslim societies are being blown into the future by the uncontrollable, but benevolent, winds of 'Islamic resurgence' has become prevalent. My thesis in this book is exactly the opposite: the future is controllable, can be conceived and shaped according to the goals and desires of a society. The euphoria generated by the Islamic resurgence syndrome is somewhat dangerous in that it could lead to intellectual complacency and political day-dreaming. I argue that while there is no positive evidence that the Muslim world is going through a 'resurgence' or a 'revival', it is possible to conceive and plan a truly epochal Islamic resurgence and work towards its future realization.

I believe that Islam is perforce a future-orientated world-view. Its essential message concerns the shaping of a viable future both in this world and the hereafter. The irony is that contemporary Muslim societies are content to allow themselves to drift rather than actively to participate in designing their destinies. Moreover, events in the Muslim world, largely an outcome of an acute unrest produced by disillusionment with Western consumerism and cultural imperialism, have clearly overtaken Muslim scholars and intellectuals. Indeed, most of them have been reduced to making post-facto rationalizations of the emerging reality around them. Unless they prepare themselves to meet the future, respond to the challenge of time and develop an appropriate framework of thought and action, they would continue to be passed by. The chance to institutionalize the Islamic revival would then have been missed, and with it the prospect of enriching the dynamic Muslim civilization of the future.

It is my hope that this book will furnish Muslim scholars and intellectuals with preliminary ideas and the basic framework to meet the challenges that they are likely to face in the near future. If it only motivates them to examine viable Islamic futures and explore pragmatic alternatives it will have achieved its basic purpose. For Western readers it should provide an insight into some of the most exciting ideas and developments that are now being debated in the Muslim world—the emergence of 'Islamic science' and 'Islamic economics', the construction of theories of 'Islamization' and the Islamic environment, the rise of the Shariah as an integrative problem-solving methodology—developments that will eventually make an impact not just on Muslim societies but on the planet as a whole. The debate and discussion on Islamic futures, then, is just as important for concerned and enlightened Western readers as it is for the Muslim people.

Some of the chapters of *Islamic Futures* have appeared in various Muslim journals in abridged form. Chapter 1 appeared as 'The Other Side of History: Future in Contemporary Muslim Literature' in the *Muslim World Book Review* (*5* (1) 3–8 Autumn 1984). Chapters 2, 3, 4, 8 and 9 have appeared in *Inquiry:* 'Is there an Islamic Resurgence?' (*1* (1) 35–9 June 1984); 'Reconstructing the Muslim Civilization' (*1* (6) 39–44 November 1984); 'Islamisation of Knowledge, or the Westernisation of Islam?' (*1* (7) 39–45 December 1984); 'From Sweet Virtuosity to Domestic Self-reliance' (*2* (5) 39–45 May 1985); and 'Breaking Free from the Dominant Paradigm' (*2* (4) 40–7 April 1985). Chapter 10 appeared under the same title in *Arts and the Islamic World* (*3* (1) 12–23 Spring 1985). Chapters 13 and 14 appeared under similar titles in *Islamic Culture* (*58* (4) 307–26 October 1984 and *57* (3) 193–205 July 1983, respectively).

I would like to point out that many of the ideas expressed in the following text are the result of a group effort that spreads over time and space. I hope that my friends find in these pages my personal gratitude for all that they have contributed. I would like to thank Meredydd Davies who prepared the index. My special thanks go to Johanna Pool who compiled the bibliography and helped with the notes and to my wife Saliha who has for so long tolerated the ups and downs of my life.

Introduction

Islamic Futures:
Shaping a Synthesis

We are quite certain about our knowledge of the past. The past is the domain of the knowable fact: for example, I know that the Prophet Mohammad was born around 622 C.E. and that he was forty years old when he received the first revelation from God which asked him to 'Read, in the name of God, the Beneficent, and Merciful'. I also know that Abu Bakr was the first Caliph of Islam and that he was succeeded by Omar, Othman and Ali, respectively. We take such facts as given and assimilate them in our understanding of history. But I also know that after the four Rightly Guided Caliphs, the Muslim lands were ruled, in the name of Islam, by a series of dynasties: the Ummayids, the Fatimads, the Abbasids and so on. I regret that fact, but I am powerless to change it. The inability, indeed the fundamental impossibility of changing historical facts is a chief characteristic of the past. The past is not just the domain of knowable facts, it is also the domain over which mankind has no power.

In contrast, the future is a mine of uncertainty. My knowledge of the future cannot be tested or verified in the same way as my knowledge of the past. In fact, the very expression 'knowledge of the future' is a contradiction in terms. Only historical facts can be known; and we can only have positive knowledge of the past. While the future is the field of uncertainty, it is also a domain over which we can exercise some power. It is within the capabilities of individuals and societies to shape their own futures. Thus, our inability to know future facts or *futures* is balanced by our ability to make an input in the shaping of these facts.

Pragmatic individuals and societies exist in a world of futures because the only 'useful knowledge' we have relates not to the past but to the future. Historical facts are useful only as much as they affect our judgements concerning our present and future decisions. Known facts are the raw material we use to make estimates of the future. Because we are powerless to do anything about the past, it is the future that concerns us: we learn from our historical experiences and incorporate them in our present actions so that our future can be better. Our actions seek to enhance our present memories of our past and repeal all that is bitter and sorrowful in our history. We project into the future the glories of our past, the desirable present that we now contemplate, and the possible we wish to make real. Only in the future lies the solution to our past misfortunes and present agonies.

Imagine a devout Muslim whose only desire is to visit Makkah and perform the pilgrimage, or hajj. He knows how the hajj is performed but he has never been to Makkah and he is not in Makkah now. There is no room for this image in the past or the present; but there is room for his cherished image to perform the hajj in the future. Future time is the only domain where he is able to receive as 'possible' an image which is 'false' in the past and the present. And the future in which he now places his cherished image reaches out to him to make the image a reality.

Now imagine a society that is dependent for its economic survival on aid from developed countries. This society has known a historic time of wealth and prosperity, and now it wishes to shake off its economic dependency on aid. Its image of itself as a dynamic, prosperous society has a reality only in the future. It is powerless to go back in time to its former glory. It cannot conceive of itself as a wealthy, economically independent society in the present. Only in the future can this image be transformed into a reality: it is a future alternative. And the future in which this society now places its desirable image waits for pragmatic steps which can turn the image into a living, dynamic reality.

Future alternatives can only be realized if pragmatic steps are taken towards these alternatives in the present. We need to have some knowledge of the available options now, before the future arrives. We need to have some understanding of futures in the present so that we can take appropriate action to turn them into facts. The progress of time *per se* does not make a desired future into a reality; nor does it increase our knowledge of the future. The French scholar Bertrand de Jouvenel argues that in dynamic societies knowledge of the future is inversely proportional to the rate of change. In *The Art of the Conjecture* he writes:

> It would be naive to think that over-all progress automatically leads to progress in our knowledge of the future. On the contrary, the future state of society would be perfectly known only in a perfectly static society—a society whose structure would always be identical and whose 'Map of the Present' would remain valid for all time! All the traits of such a society at any future time could be foreknown. But as soon as a society is in movement, its familiar traits are perishable: they disappear, some more rapidly than others—though we cannot date their disappearance in advance—while new traits appear—traits not 'given' beforehand to our minds. To say the movement is accelerating is to say that the length of time for which our Map of the Present remains more or less valid grows shorter. Thus our knowledge of the future is inversely proportional to the rate of progress.[1]

Given the present rate of change, the future is becoming more and more uncertain. In contemporary societies the rate of change is itself changing: the paradox is that change is now the only constant. This acceleration in the rate of change is caused primarily by technological advances arising from scientific discovery, but manifested also in economic, political and social terms. In the Muslim world such changes are bringing about an upheaval through the rapid diffusion of uncertain and changing Western values and the consequent evaporation of Islamic norms and concerns. Almost overnight an integrated neighbourhood with established values and behaviour characteristics can be bulldozed and replaced by a concrete, perpendicular metropolis which then imposes its own value and behaviour patterns.[2]

While such trends make it increasingly difficult for us to acquire useful knowledge of the future, they also make it a necessity for us to study the future more systematically and rationally, to probe the consequences of contemporary events and trends, to foresee as far as possible the difficulties and problems ahead, and to make deliberate attempts to shape the future in accordance with our needs and desires. A society that is continuously reacting to one change after another will move from crisis to crisis until it reaches one from which there can be no escape. Consciously and rationally thinking and acting towards a desired future implies developing a *sense of direction*: behaving *in anticipation*. An aimless society drifts to an aimless future of stagnation and decay. A society with a sense of direction moves towards a planned future of desired goals and realizable visions.

The aimless and planned approaches to the future may be illustrated by the following analogy. An aimless society considers the future as a mighty river. The great force of history flows inexorably along, carrying everyone with it. Attempts to change its course amount to little more than throwing pebbles into the river: they cause a few ripples but have no real effect on the mighty river. The river's course can change but only by natural disasters such as earthquakes and landslides or by the will of God. This is fatalism in action. On the other hand, a society with a sense of direction sees the future as a great ocean. There are many possible destinations and many alternative paths to these destinations. A good navigator takes advantage of the main current of change and adjusts his course accordingly, keeping a sharp outlook for possible typhoons or changes in weather conditions, and moving carefully in fog or through uncharted waters. He will get safely to his intended destination.

Why Islamic Futures?

Islam perforce gives a sense of direction to a society.[3] Yet, ironically, Muslim societies show a conspicuous absence of a sense of direction. There are primarily two reasons for this: to a very large extent Muslim societies are still shaking off their colonial legacies and the contemporary accelerating rate of change has not permitted them to take stock of their present and plan for a viable, Islamic future. However, a number of recent events serve as indicators that future consciousness is emerging in the Muslim community, the *ummah*. One pragmatic indicator is the attempt over the past thirty or so years to unite the Muslims in one solid bloc and the consequent emergence of the Organization of Islamic Conference and its various subsidiary institutions such as the Islamic Foundation for Science and Technology for Development and the Islamic Educational, Scientific and Cultural Organization.[4] These organizations are trying to shape a common destiny for the Muslim *ummah*. An intellectual indicator is the emergence of Islamic economics as an independent discipline geared towards shaping an economic future for Muslim societies within an Islamic framework.

But these embryonic developments are isolated and unconscious attempts to shape the future of Muslim societies. Moreover, they are neutralized by a number of factors, some of which are outcomes of Muslim history while others are the products of contemporary reality. Let me mention a few of these forces:

(1) Beliefs in God and piety alone will ensure a revival of Islam. What matters is that our *aqidas* (beliefs) are correct: God will take care of the rest. As God has already ordained our destiny, we ought to concentrate on the proper observation of *salat* (prayer), *swam* (fasting) and *zakat* (poor-tax) to ensure our individual salvation. Individuals professing such fatalism are a dominant part of contemporary Muslim societies.

(2) *Homo righteous* exists side by side with *Homo modernus*. His views are at the other end of the spectrum: Islam has little to offer and modernism has answers to all our contemporary ills. This attitude is the result of physical and intellectual slavery that Muslim societies have experienced in the past three hundred years. It is the result of the lack of confidence we have in ourselves and our culture. It is a manifestation of our inferiority complex. The beliefs and values of *Homo modernus* are a serious threat not just to the survival of Muslim societies; they are threatening the very abode of their origin, the Western civilization. A vast body of literature has been produced describing how these beliefs and values are taking the Western societies and with them our terrestrial home, the earth, towards an impending crisis.[5] Ervin Laszlo describes the main traits of *Homo modernus* and the consequences

of his beliefs and values in these words:

> *Homo modernus* is a curious species. He lives in a jungle, benefits mankind by his pursuit of material gain, trusts invisible forces to right wrongs, worships efficiency, is ready to make, sell and consume practically anything (especially if it is new), loves today's children but is indifferent to the fate of the next generation, dismisses things that do not have immediate payoffs or are not calculable in money, and is ready to go and fight for his country because his country, too, must fight for survival in the international jungle.

> These curious traits of *Homo modernus* are now endangering his future. Belief in the law of the jungle encourages tooth-and-claw competitiveness which fails to make use of the benefits of cooperation—especially crucial in a period of reduced growth opportunities and frequent squeezes. Holding to the dogmas of the rising tide, the trickle-down effect, and the invisible hand promotes selfish behavior in the comforting—but no longer warranted—belief that this will be bound to benefit others. Faith in a perfectly self-regulating free-market system ignores the fact that in a laissez-faire situation those who hold the power and control the strings distort the operations of the market in their own favor and push the less powerful and clever partners into bankruptcy (a totally unacceptable situation when the less powerful and skilled comprise two-thirds of the world population). Efficiency without regard as to what is produced, by whom it is produced, and whom it will benefit can lead to mounting unemployment, a catering to the demands of the rich without regard to the needs of the poor, and a polarization of society in the 'modern' ('efficient') and the 'traditional' ('inefficient') sectors. The technological imperative becomes dangerous when economic growth curves are slackening, markets are becoming saturated, the environment is approaching the limits of its pollution absorption capacity, and certain energy and raw material resources are becoming scarce or expensive. Falling for the 'newer the better' ploy is merely being gullible. One day a product is 'improved' because it contains a certain ingredient (fluorocarbons, antihistamines, cyclamates, or whatever), and the next it is improved precisely because it does *not* contain it! Health and social benefit seem to get lost in the competition between artificially inculcated fads and desires.

> Living without conscious forward-planning may have been fine in the days of rapid growth when the future could take care of itself, but is not a responsible option at a time when delicate choices have to be

made with profound and far-reaching consequences for future generations.[6]

(3) We have inherited a way of thinking and solving problems from the Western intellectual tradition. The way of thinking in purely cause and effect terms is now totally inadequate in our present situation. We are faced with a whole complex of problems that are intricately interconnected—everything we do runs into everything else we do, and we cannot escape a whole array of interactions, non-linear effects and feedbacks. Moreover, in this great complex of problems any single problem is itself complex. For example, we may think the problem of providing food for Bangladesh is simple enough. But it is connected to the rising population of the country, the decreasing land that is available for growing food, the technologies available for increasing production, the social and economic systems that ensure a just and equitable system of distribution so that everyone has enough to eat, a governance structure that ensures that such a distribution system survives, and so on. In trying to solve any contemporary problems we find that we are hitting against the fringes of others. Thus we cannot solve problems in isolation: individual organizations and disciplines are inadequate for the task of solving contemporary problems.

(4) Stark, practical reality is forcing us to recognize the interdependence of Muslim countries with each other, as well as the interdependence of the Muslim world with the nations of the West and those of the Communist bloc. Every Muslim country is subjected to external forces which are beyond its control: monetary difficulties, contagious inflation, scarcity and high cost of imported raw materials and energy, social and societal disruptions caused by imported technologies. While the industrialized nations are dependent on Arab oil, Arab countries in turn are dependent on the technologies of the Western nations. While deforestation in Malaysia can bring financial rewards for the Malaysian timber industry, it can also bring climatic changes in the United States. The earth is a finite organic system: all of mankind is dependent on the actions of all people and all nations.

These factors suggest a new way of managing the diversity and complexity that confront the *ummah*—diversity that ranges from pure fatalism to beliefs and values that negate the very ideals of Islam. This diversity exists in a world whose dimensions have been shrunk by science and technology, and in which problems of scale compound with those of rapid change to generate a momentum and complexity which the existing institutions and policies cannot solve or manage. We need future-orientated approaches for the study of needs and desires of Islamic societies in order to end the present impasse.

However, it is not just external forces and contemporary factors that provide legitimacy for future-orientated thinking and action within an Islamic framework. Islam itself provides justification for a field of thought and inquiry which is concerned with the future of the *ummah*. The Qur'an describes itself as 'a Book of Guidance'—guidance that influences present individual and social actions to shape particular futures. Many of the dictates and principles of Islam can only be implemented in the future: for example, despite all the work on Islamic economics, the Qur'anic injunctions about *riba* (usury) can only be implemented fully in future time. The very fact that the Qur'an is eternal is enough to seek new and innovative ways of implementing its injunction in the future. This is why the idea of destiny runs throughout the Qur'an. Again and again the Qur'an tells us about the destinies of historic nations, and reminds us of the possibilities of our own destiny. Allama Muhammad Iqbal has beautifully captured the essence of the Qur'anic concept of *taqdir* (destiny):

> It is time regarded as an organic whole that the Qur'an describes as taqdir or the destiny—a word which has been so much misunderstood both in and outside the world of Islam. Destiny is time regarded prior to the disclosure of its possibilities. It is time freed from the net of causal sequence—the diagrammatic character which the logical understanding imposes on it . . . Time regarded as destiny forms the very essence of things. As the Qur'an says: 'God created all things and assigned to each its destiny'. The destiny of a thing then is not an unrelenting fate working from without like a task master; *it is the inward reach of a thing, its realizable possibilities which lie within the depths of its nature*, and serially actualize themselves without any feeling of external compulsion. (My italics)[7]

The life of the Prophet Mohammad is one continuous example of future-orientated actions and the shaping of destiny within the spectrum of 'realizable possibilities'. The Prophet anticipated future possibilities before taking an action: the *hijra* (migration) from Makkah to Medina was based on an anticipation of a more viable future for the then small Muslim community, it was planned and the path for the migration was systematically cleared; the Prophet anticipated the Quresh uprising against him, prepared and met the advancing Quresh army at Badr; he foresaw its future advantages and despite complaints from his companions concluded the Hudabiyah Agreement; months before the Battle of Trenches the Prophet was aware of the coming conflict and prepared to defend Medina by digging a trench around the city; and after the conquest the Prophet forgave his adversaries knowing full well that his action would produce future generals and leaders for the Muslim community.

And, after the Prophet, the Rightly Guided Caliphs continued the tradition of future orientated thinking and action. Abu Bakr foresaw the expansion of Muslim lands and began to develop a system of administration and management that could adjust to future needs. Umar realized that the future survival of the Muslim *ummah* was dependent on available resources, and that all resources must not be consumed by one generation. Against the explicit wishes of his companions and even at the risk of a conflict, he refused to distribute the conquered lands of Syria, Iraq, Iran and Egypt amongst the conquerors. Instead he set them aside as a future source of income for the succeeding generations.

Thus the very precepts of Islam are based on future orientated thought and action. Islam is a future orientated world-view: the real surprise is why Islamic history and tradition has not produced a systematic body of knowledge and fully developed methods of inquiry which concern themselves with the terrestrial future of the *ummah*.

The *ummah*, of course, can unwittingly become part of the future vision of another civilization: this is the ultimate justification for Islamic futures. To a very large extent, Muslim societies are already becoming part of the future of the Western, technological civilization. Such classical Muslim scholars as Ibn

Khaldun have identified a number of external features that shape a civilization: governance and political organization; cities, architecture and buildings; social organization; economic life; science and technology; education and learning; and art and culture. Judging by these parameters, the Muslim civilization exists only in name. Our governance and political organization are based on the Western model of the nation-state and bureaucratic structures; Islamic architecture has evaporated and our buildings and cities have no original or distinguishing features; our social structures have been destroyed by imported building technology and planning techniques; our economic life is dominated by usury and consumerism; our science and technology reflect the needs and requirements of Western societies and have the same priorities and emphasis; Muslim universities and institutions of learning have lost their original charcteristics and are now poor replicas of their Western counterparts; and, finally, even our art and culture has been assimilated and redirected towards the goals of the technological civilization. To a very large extent, we are already part of the future of another, alien civilization. The process of the colonization of the future has already begun: Western futurists never tire of repeating that we are heading towards one, global civilization with unmistakable Western traits and characteristics.[8] In this global civilization, non-Western societies will experience a kind of physical dependency and cultural slavery which has no counterpart in history.

A conscious, systematic effort to shape a viable future for the Muslim *ummah* will ensure that the possibility of intellectual and physical colonization of future Muslim societies is checked. A growing and perceptive body of knowledge on and methods of inquiry for Islamic futures will not only enable us to shape a more desirable destiny for ourselves but also provide insight and guidance for those Western futurists who are looking for alternative values and norms to shape a more enlightened future for their own societies. Islamic futures, then, is not just a theoretical field with some pragmatic possibilities: it is an extension of the Islamic principle of *dawa*, inviting others to all that is good and enlightened.

The Paradigm

In this book Islam is perceived not as a religion with a set of rituals, nor as a body of law with a catalogue of dos and don'ts, but as a total, systematic holistic *world-view*. Religion, as commonly understood, is only one part of this world-view. Islamic futures is a rational and systematic exploration of alternatives that can be realized in the long-range future within the framework of the world-view of Islam. This exploration is carried out within a defined boundary provided by a conceptual field consisting of a whole range of pure Islamic concepts to be found in the Qur'an and the Sunnah. Such concepts as *tawhid* (unity of God), *khilafah* (trusteeship of man), *adl* (justice), *ilm* (knowledge), *ijma* (consensus of the community), *istihsan* (public interest), *ibadah* (worship), *iman* (enlightened belief), *zulm* (tyranny), *halal* (praiseworthy), *haram* (blameworthy), *riba* (usury), etc., are the territory within which future alternatives are sought. This conceptual matrix describes the systematic nature of reality to which future thinking, planning and actions are applied; delineates the boundaries of all that is desirable in a Muslim society; and distinguishes the desirable from the undesirable. Within this matrix, restrictions to narrow angles of view—looking separately at economic, political, social, scientific, technological and urban aspects of the future—clearly become absurd. The conceptual field demands a systematic, integrative study of the future, cutting across all dimensions and disciplinary boundaries.

Here, Islamic futures are explored within a civilizational perspective. The dominant image of Islam in the future is of a dynamic, thriving civilization with unique traits and characteristics. These traits manifest themselves in the governance and political structure, social and economic organization, scientific and technological priorities and emphasis, architecture and town planning, education and learning and arts and crafts—the external parameters of the Islamic civilization. The emphasis is placed on the major theoretical and pragmatic parameters of a possible Muslim civilization of the future. However, certain contemporary issues, such as development, the degradation of the hajj environment, and the development of Islamic studies, all of which will have a major impact on the re-emergence of the Muslim civilization, are also studied in some detail. The entire approach is normative and teleological: it is a basic assumption of this study that the direction of events towards a perceived final goal—a dynamic, thriving Muslim civilization—can be expressed as if the present behaviour were dependent on the final state. However, the final state is never reached: it is a goal that is continuously sought and is the essence of the study of the future of Muslim civilization.

In contrast to the macro-approach adopted in this study, Islamic futures can also be explored on a micro-level. For example, the future of a particular Muslim group, such as the Arabs, Afghans or the Malay, can be studied from the perspective of cultural anthropology. Within the purview of Islamic civilization, local cultures are a form of group self-actualization which enables the group to shape its environment and control its destiny. Individual Muslim societies and groups can work out their own pragmatic routes, using their cultural strengths and considering their particular situations, to put into operation their individual models of Islamic futures. Similarly, Islamic futures can be explored from the perspective of a single vision: for example, an architect and town planner, like Gulzar Haider, can construct his particular utopia, a future city of Islam, and suggest in conceptual and practical detail how this vision can be made a reality.[9]

These various approaches to the study of the future of Muslim societies are equally valid. While I emphasize and argue for a civilizational approach to the study of Islamic futures, I place an equal importance on diversity of approaches, for this diversity of approaches, opinions, thoughts and ideas is the corner-stone of Islamic futures. Notice the emphasis on the plural *futures*: we are seeking alternatives, possibilities, options, not one single, all-embracing, final way of expressing our Islamic identity in the future. There is no place in exploring the future for the tyranny of the Righteous or the fanaticism of the Revolutionary, because monocultures in human life and behaviour, thought and opinion are just as dangerous as they are in agriculture. In the domination of one single mode of thought or behaviour there is a real danger of total collapse, simply because every complex system has some probability, however small, of moving into unfamiliar and improbable states which can bring about 'system death'. Variety is the essence of long-term survival, which is the reason the beloved Prophet Mohammad has said that differences of opinion are a blessing for the Muslim *ummah*. And variety is also the essence of studying alternative Islamic futures.

However, diversity does not imply incoherence. While internally there is a whole array of routes to the realization of viable Islamic futures, the world-view of Islam and its conceptual field ensure that there are civilizational coherence and spiritual unity externally—a manifestation of the *ummah*'s unique historical characteristic. Throughout history, Islam has managed to maintain its spiritual unity within a great cultural diversity.

There are also a number of other factors that generate coherence in the Muslim civilization and must be examined in the study of Islamic futures.

Besides unity within diversity, or complementarity, interconnectedness is a strong feature of the world-view of Islam. Everything in Islam is connected to everything else; nothing exists in isolation. The whole earth is a mosque, everything is sacred. In Islamic futures, the principle of interconnectedness manifests itself in the conceptual field, serving as the basic tools for shaping the future. Each concept in the field is connected to every other concept: for example, *tawhid* (unity of God) can only be fully expressed when *adl* (justice) is totally established, and *zulm* (tyranny) is checked in all its multidimensional (social, economic, political, scientific, technological) facets. *Ilm* (knowledge) is *ibadah* (worship) only if it leads to the distribution of *adl*, promotes *istislah* (public interest) and does not promote *zulm*. Thus the study of Islamic futures, based as it is on contemporary elaboration of the concepts found in the Qur'an and the Sunnah, emphasizes the interconnectedness of the Islamic world-view.

To diversity and interconnectedness we must also add that redistribution is a basic tenet of the Islamic world-view. Muslim societies are like living ecological systems: the beloved Prophet Mohammad implied this when he said that the believers are like a body, that if one part of the body catches an infection, the whole body suffers. If the Muslim world is like a body, a holistic system, then it must behave according to the principles of nature. One of the basic features of an ecosystem is that it periodically redistributes energy, materials and structures through biochemical and geophysical processes and cycles. Human societies that live in harmony with nature 'also conform to the principles of redistribution of these same resources that they use and transform, whether primary energy and materials or derived "wealth" (capital, money, structures, means of production and "power") as well as continually changing institutions'.[10] That Islam emphasizes redistribution of wealth and power can be seen in such institutions as *zakah* (Islamic laws of inheritance) and the injunctions against usury, hoarding and monopolies. These and numerous other principles and injunctions of the Qur'an have not been appreciated from the perspective of the concomitant ecological reality that they represent: redistribution is the essence of *adl* and survival.

The principles of complementarity, interconnectedness and redistribution are the basis of all natural, evolving systems; and they form the pillars on which Islamic futures are to be built. The task of the student of Islamic futures is to elaborate the worldview of Islam, within a macro- or micro-perspective, using the conceptual matrix to build models of viable futures and develop pragmatic routes to put these models into, while being guided in this endeavour by the natural principles of complementarity, interconnectedness and redistribution.

It is quite evident that the study of Islamic futures is essentially interdisciplinary. There is no place here for the purely artificial phenomenon of the division of reality into independent disciplines. Indeed, our growing understanding of complementarity and interconnectedness of problems facing contemporary societies, as well as the linkages and interactions between diverse fields of learning and approaches to the discovery of new knowledge, has forced us to adopt a holistic and dynamic approach: in essence this amounts to returning to the Islamic principle of the unity of all knowledge. It was this principle that gave rise to polymathy, the major manifestations of Islamic scholarship. Muslim futurists have to be the counterparts of such polymaths of classical Islam as al-Beruni and ibn Sina, al-Ghazzali and ibn Rushd, ibn Tufail and ibn Bajjah. In this spirit, Islamic futures ought to be regarded as the foci of advancing knowledge, the field of study which can be consolidated only by contributions from many other fields and techniques.

To appreciate fully the interdisciplinary approach to Islamic futures, let us examine the four disciplinary approaches in common use today. A *mono-disciplinary* approach is very sectoral and partial, implying a study involving only one discipline. Such an approach is unsatisfactory for the study of the future because, to use the words of Kenneth Boulding, while the universities are administratively divided into departments, nature is not. The universe does not have an 'economic department' working separately from its 'physics' department. A *multidisciplinary* approach involves parallel inputs from different fields, is unintegrated and is not of much use because the interconnectedness of all phenomena is not recognized. An *undisciplined* approach is completely meaningless, and while a *cross-disciplinary* approach, involving the marriage of two or three disciplines, is a step forward, it nevertheless falls short of a completely integrated method of study.

In contrast, an *interdisciplinary* approach is more like an 'intellectual commune' in which many disciplines cross-interact. The interaction may range from simple communication of ideas to the mutual integration of organizing concepts, methodology, procedures, epistemology, terminology, data and organization of research in a fairly large field. Such an approach calls for the unification of all knowledge. Here existing disciplines are integrated into a unified body of knowledge which is then used to study complex reality.[11]

In Islamic futures, it is the complex conceptual field of the world-view of Islam which enables various disciplines to come together and be integrated into a coherent whole. The conceptual framework also furnishes us with a language for this field of study; a language that is both distinctively Islamic yet adoptable to a futuristic mode of inquiry. The ultimate aim of Islamic futures is to forge a synthesis that leads to a recognition that Islam, as a holistic world-view, can generate a whole array of alternative routes for the re-emergence of a dynamic, thriving Muslim civilization in our time. A framework of the methodology of Islamic futures is presented in Figure 1.

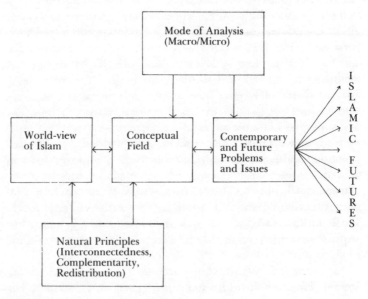

Figure 1. *The Methodology of Islamic Futures*

There are numerous ways this methodology can be used to produce images of viable futures for the Muslim civilization. A purely speculative approach would yield many useful intuitive and imaginative elements that could influence general thinking about Islamic futures. Most utopias are the result of speculative thinking; but here, the methodology ensures that the speculation remains within the relevant boundaries and has some policy significance. Existing trends within Muslim societies can be projected to form both utopian and dystopian scenarios. Similarly, individual concepts can be developed into fully-fledged scenarios: for example, an entire political structure can be developed, in a purely speculative way, around the concept of *Shura* (counsel).

The construction of such utopias and scenarios, or designing of desirable futures, is extremely productive, not only stimulating the mind to think of what is possible, but also forcing the attention of scholars and intellectuals towards micro-futures—discovering ways and means, routes and policy alternatives, which can lead society towards the imagined goals.

In contrast to the speculative and scenarist approach, the methodology can also be used for prospective planning. By taking account of present trends and their interactions, including the working out of the probable consequences of different possible decisions, truly Islamic alternative policies and strategies can be developed to meet the more likely contingencies. By studying contemporary problems and issues with Qur'anic and Sunnah concepts as basic tools, and working within the natural principles of interconnectedness, complementarity and redistribution, Muslim futurists will be well prepared to meet future dangers. They will be able to introduce deliberate changes to avoid serious consequences and to ensure that Muslim societies move towards a healthier and healthier Islamic environment.

Islamic futures, then, is both a visionary and pragmatic field of inquiry. It is an attempt to create new visions of a better Muslim world—visions that will motivate the myriads of Muslim communities to set aside their political and parochial differences and move on with the task of shaping a more enlightened society. Islamic futures invite the *ummah* to consider the future as something that can be moulded, a field of power that can be grasped. To bring a system of concepts, ideas and values that germinate from the world-view of Islam into play in an effective, rational and creative way, and to put it into a framework of thinking and action that can cope with a high degree of diversity, is what the emerging field of Islamic futures is all about. And this, in essence, is the message of this book.

Notes

1. Bertrand de Jouvenel, *The Art of the Conjecture*, Basic Books, New York, 1967, p. 175.

2. For a good account of what is happening to Muslim cities, *see* G. H.

Blake and R. I. Lawless (eds.), *The Changing Middle Eastern City*, Croom Helm, London, 1980; for more specific case studies of Muslim holy lands in Saudi Arabia, *see* Ziauddin Sardar and M. A. Zaki Badawi (eds.), *Hajj Studies*, Croom Helm, London, 1979.

3. For a good, general introduction to Islam, *see* Khurshi Ahmad (ed.), *Islam: Its Meaning and Message*, Islamic Council of Europe, London, 1975; and for a modern interpretation of how Islam gives societal directions, *see* Salem Azzam (ed.), *Islam and Contemporary Society*, Longman, London, 1982.

4. For a descriptive account of the Organization of Islamic Conference and its various subsidiary organizations, *see* Hamid H. Kizilbash, 'The Islamic Conference: Retrospect and Prospect', *Arab Studies Quarterly*, 4 (1–2) 138–57 (1982).

5. This point is made particularly strongly by Theodore Roszak in *Person/Planet: The Creative Disintegration of Industrial Society*, Victor Gollancz, London, 1979; by Hazel Henderson in *The Politics of Solar Age*, Anchor Books, New York, 1981; and by Alexander King in *The State of the Planet*, Pergamon, Oxford, 1980.

6. Ervin Laszlo, 'The obsolescence of modernism', in Frank Feathers (ed.), *Through the '80s: Thinking Globally, Acting Locally*, World Future Society, Washington, 1980. p. 283.

7. Alama Mohammad Iqbal, *Reconstruction of Religious Thought in Islam*, Ashraf, Lahore, 1971 (reprint), pp. 49–50.

8. Most notable of these is Alvin Toffler, *The Third Wave*, Bantam Books, New York, 1980. Most futurists see Islam as a threat to the full future flowering of Western civilization and its technological dream. For example, in their 308-page study, *Encounters with the Future: A Forecast of Life into the 21st Century* (McGraw-Hill, New York, 1982), Marvin Cetron and Thomas O'Toole find Islam worthy of only three pages; moreover, they pack in almost every classical stereotype and misrepresentation. Here, in its entirety, is what they have to say about Islam:

> The fastest-growing religion in the world today is Islam, whose conservative appeals to ancient values are fueled in the oil-rich Islamic countries of the Middle East. There are now 450 million men and women of every race representing every one of the six continents who call themselves Moslems and who follow the Prophet. Islam is the dominant faith in a broad swath of the earth that runs from Morocco in the west to Pakistan and across India to Malaysia and Indonesia in the east. Islam doubles itself in Africa every 25 years. The number of Moslems making the *hadj*, the holy pilgrimage to Mecca, increases by

100,000 every year. There are no signs this surging growth will slacken. The way the Moslem faith is spreading, the way the Moslem populations are growing, Islam may embrace almost one billion people by the year 2000.

Why in this age of spiritual doubt should Islam be so vibrantly alive? Where in this time of religious confusion is Islam getting its astonishing vitality? In part, Islam has caught fire for some of the same reasons that cults and Mormonism are heating up. Islam is a fundamentalist religion, a church that teaches basic tenets, has only two affirmations (there is no God but Allah, Mohammed is his prophet) where Christianity has as many as fourteen. In return, Islam offers the answers without doubt or contradiction. Its ethical doctrines are austere and simple, something similar to what the Quakers believe. Its universal appeal has also let it cut across barriers of race, tribe and caste, which is another reason for its rapid growth in places like black Africa and black America.

Ironically, Islam is the religion most akin to Christianity and Judaism, the two religions Islam seems to have gone to war with. The late Professor Philip Hitti, one-time head of the Semitic Literature Program at Princeton University told us that the alienation between Islam and the Judeo-Christian worlds is more one of politics and economics than it is of ideology. In a sense, Hitti said, Judaism is the essence of the Old Testament, Christianity of the New and Islam of a Third Testament, enshrined in the Koran. If the New Testament reads like the life of Christ, Hitti went on, the Third Testament is the life story of Mohammed, the Prophet. People tend to think of Islam as an Arabian culture, a notion Hitti said is not correct. 'Except for the Arabic language through which it was disseminated, the Arabians contributed almost nothing', Hitti said. 'Islam is a compound of ancient Semitic, classic Greek and medieval Indo-Persian.'

One reason Westerners find it so hard to understand and accept Islam is that it has always threatened and challenged the West. Christianity doesn't challenge the West because Christianity is a part of the West. Judiasm is too small and too tribal to pose any challenge to the West. Hinduism and Buddhism don't challenge the West because they've too ethereal. Only Islam is a threat, as it has been economically for the last 20 years, politically for the last 180 years and militarily for the last 1,500 years. Islam is confronting us again, in Iran calling us Satan for supporting the shah and challenging us in the rest of the Moslem world for supporting Israel. Think back to the hostages. No swami, no Dalai Lama, no guru and no rabbi ever threatened us the way the madjis and the Ayatollah did.

Another reason Islam is so inscrutable to Western eyes is that it runs on what we feel are outdated practices and principles. The whippings, the stonings, the mutilations and the executions meted out for violations of Islamic law are anathema to the Western mind. Why are bribes a way of life in the Moslem world? Why must women wear veils? Why can't women take jobs? Why must Moslem women walk behind Moslem men? Why can't they change? Why can't the Moslems be like us? There's a third reason why the West finds it so hard to accept Islam. There is no separation of church and state in the Moslem world. The state is the church. For Islam, God is Caesar and Caesar is God. There can be no distinction between church and state in the Moslem world, where criticism of Islam is seen as an injury against the state and society. Criticism of society is a criticism of the Moslem faith. It's more than criticism, it's treason. For this reason alone, there can be no easy accommodation between the West and a large segment of the Moslem world. The Moslem challenge to the West will continue as long as Islam's oil riches fuel its growth, which will last for at least another 15 years.

9. See his excellent essay, 'Habitat and Values in Islam: A Conceptual Formulation of an Islamic City', in Ziauddin Sardar (ed.), *The Touch of Midas*, Manchester University Press, 1984.

10. Hazel Henderson, 'Identifying the planetary coalition for a just New World Order', in Frank Feather (ed.), *Through the '80s: Thinking Globally, Acting Locally*, World Future Society, Washington, 1980, p. 53.

11. This topology of disciplinary approaches is after Kimon Valaskakis, 'Eclectrics: Elements of a transdisciplinary methodology for future studies' in *The Future as an Academic Discipline*, Ciba Foundation Symposium 36, Elsevier, Amsterdam, 1975.

Part One

Moving Towards a Planned Future

I

The Future in Contemporary Islamic Literature

Islam is perforce a future-orientated world-view. A system of thought and action that has eternal validity must have inherent components designed to meet future challenges. A universal ideology strives continuously for a full realization of its basic precepts: it must always concern itself with shaping the future. A civilization with a golden history must look to the future to recapture its past glories. As a religion, ideology and civilization, Islam, therefore, presents a world-view that is concerned primarily with improving the future: both in this world and in the hereafter.

The basic concepts of Islam, such as *tawhid* (unity of God), *khilafah* (the trusteeship of man) and *akhirah* (accountability on the Day of Judgement), force Muslims to think about their individual and collective future. In fact, a true understanding of such basic concepts is not really possible without appreciating their future components. Consider, for example, the concept of *akihrah* which is a basic tenet of Muslim belief. *Akihrah* is normally translated as 'life after death', but to have any significant understanding of *akihrah* one has to relate it to time. In a rationalist world-view, time is a linear progression: for a particular individual, time ends with his life. Beyond his life there is no time, at least as far as his own individual life is concerned. In some religions, only some kind of belief in life after corporeal death makes life on this earth meaningful. But the concept of *akihrah* goes much beyond that: it connects this life to the life after death by presenting time as a tapestry in which time and eternity are woven together. This life is life in time, while the hereafter is the life in eternity, where we are able to pass beyond the limits of space, time and causality. But the life in eternity is a function of life in time: the hereafter is shaped on this earth. Thus the concept of *akihrah* makes Muslims aware of their long-term future; and a true believer would always be working for his and his community's future interests.

Similarly, the concept of *khilafah* is intrinsically future orientated. If man is the *khilafah*, trustee or steward of Allah's estate, then he has no absolute right to anything. The natural resources of this earth are the property of God and no individual or generation has an absolute monopoly over them. Future generations have just as much right over them as the present; and the present generation must conserve and preserve God-given resources for the future generations. With the authority of a trustee goes the responsibility—and that responsibility belongs to the future.

Considering the importance of the future for a contemporary understanding of the basic precepts of Islam and the inherent future orientation in the world-view of Islam, one should expect a whole body of literature and organized knowledge on the Muslim approach to the future. The reality, however, is somewhat tragic: in the last fifty years no more than half-a-dozen books and less than twenty articles have been published, which concern themselves directly or indirectly with the future. And much of this literature is of rather poor quality.

Of course, if Muslims are not concerned with studying their own future, there are others who are all too willing to shape their future for them. Exactly a hundred years ago, Wilfrid Scawen Blunt, an admirer and friend of the noted Muslim revivalist Jamaluddin Afghani, found it necessary to give some serious thought to the future of Islam.[1] He was concerned about a number of trends which were pointing towards a particular future: 'the French, by their invasion of Tunis, have precipitated the Mohammedan movement in North Africa; Egypt has roused herself for a great effort of national and religious reform; and on all sides Islam is seen to be convulsed by political portents of ever-growing intensity'.[2] Blunt foresaw the decline of the Ottoman Empire and the emergence of a 'progressive thought in Islam' and an 'Arabian theology' based at al-Azhar. He was basically concerned with 'liberalising' Islam and argued: 'if, as now seems probable, a liberal Mohammedan Government by a free Mohammedan people should establish itself firmly on the Nile, it is beyond question that the basis of a social and political Reformation for all Islam has been laid'.[3]

Blunt wrote *The Future of Islam* as a series of essays for the *Fortnightly Review* in the summer and autumn of 1881 and published them as a book in the following year. Considering the period when these five assays were written, he reveals a great deal of insight of his subject and a genuine futuristic understanding of the political and intellectual trends of the time. He starts by studying the hajj and uses it to estimate the 'total census of Islam': 175 million. He describes various groups of pilgrims and thus delineates various sects and schools of Islamic thought. Blunt believes that the future belongs to liberal Muslims, and in his next assay, entitled 'the Modern question of the Caliphate',[4] he skilfully presents the Ottomans as the arch villians: 'Turkey, I have shown, and the Hanefite school, are far from being the whole of Mohammedan world; and side by side with the fanatical obduracy of the Ottoman State party and the still fiercer puritanism of the Melkites there exists an intelligent and hopeful party favourable to religious reforms. Shafite Egypt is its stronghold, but it is powerful too in Arabia and further East. With it a first article of faith is that the House of Ottoman has been and is the curse of Islam, and that its end is at hand.' Blunt predicts the end of the Ottoman Empire with ferocity and repeatedly, knowing that 'such prophecies often work their own fulfilment'.

The future of Islam, Blunt argues, depends on a general reform in Islamic political and moral life; on the decline and eventual break-up of the Ottoman Empire, the transfer of Islam's 'metropolis' from Constantinople to Mecca, and to a certain 'triumph of her arms'. But above all Islam's survival depends on an internal reform of law and ethics. Blunt has enough insight to argue that this reform is best carried out by Muslims themselves: 'in considering its future it [is] easy for a candid English mind to escape the admission that, for all purposes of argument, the

Mohammedan creed must be treated as no vain supersititution but a true religion, true inasmuch as it is a form of the worship of that one true God in whom Europe, in spite of her modern reason, still believes . . . I would urge that it is to Mohammadans themselves that we must look to work out their ultimate regeneration according to the rules of their own law and conscience.'[5] He outlines two possible Muslim scenarios: a Christian–Muslim accord similar to the principles laid down in 'the Prophet's first treaty with the Christians of Arabia' which would given Islam a legal *modus vivendi* with Europe and hence enable Muslim societies to absorb all that is good and healthy in Western society; and the emergence of a Mahdi who would introduce a moral and political reformation.

Is all of Blunt's futuristic analysis solely for the benefit of his Muslim friends? On the contrary, like a good futurist, Blunt translates his analysis into policies for the English government: England's interest, he shows, is distinct from the 'Crusading States of Europe' and she should not ally herself with them. England should prepare for the fall of the Ottoman Empire and the general disruption which will follow; and the British government should prepare to give political guidance to the various nations of Islam. After the Ottomans, the Muslims of the Indian subcontinent, being the wealthiest and most numerous, will become the most important segment of Islam. Their newly-acquired position should be used to strengthen the British Empire. The political future of Egypt will be linked with the future of Britain and its goodwill towards the British Empire should be ensured. And, 'the Caliphate—no longer an empire, but still an independent sovereignty—must be taken under British protection, and publicly guaranteed its political existence, undisturbed by further aggression from Europe'.[6]

Within the next fifty years many of Blunt's predictions became realities: the Ottoman Empire did disintegrate, a Mahdi did appear in the Sudan, liberal reforms were taken by the Egyptian *ulemas*, and Islam even won new converts in Africa and South Asia. His recommendations became part and parcel of British foreign policy. Blunt envisaged a particular future for the Muslim world and produced a mechanism to shape it according to the dictates of his vision.

Today, Blunt's modern counterparts continue to colonize the future of Muslim societies. In *Images of the Arab Future*,[7] Ismail-Sabri Abdalla, Ibrahim S. E. Abdalla, Mahmoud Abdel-Fadil and Ali Nassar examine, on behalf of the United Nations University, how the Arab future is perceived in modern future studies and global models. Since the publication of the *Limits to Growth* in 1972, several global models have been developed and used to study alternative futures. Abdalla and colleagues examine the roles assigned to the Arab region in six such models: the 'World Model' developed by Meadows and the MIT team in the *Limits to Growth*;[8] the more enlightened Mesarovic-Pestel model presented in *Mankind at the Turning Point*;[9] the Latin American world model built by Fundacion Bariloche in the Argentine;[10] the Leontief model of the world economy;[11] the SARUM model constructed by the UK Department of the Environment; and the Interfutures study commissioned by the Organisation for Economic Cooperation and Development (OECD).[12] The basic findings of Abdalla and colleagues' survey is that most global models extrapolate the present structures of advanced industrial nations onto the future of Arab countries.[13] The authors complain that the Arab region is regarded in these models as a long-term oil and fuel depot and its social and political significance is inappropriately represented. On the whole, global modellers are reluctant to address the region as a 'distinct entity' in total disregard of social, cultural, religious, economic and political realities and of 'the recognition by the international community of the potential and aspirations of the Arab nation'.

With the sole exception of the Latin American model which is concerned with proving that the basic needs of the Third World can easily be met in the foreseeable future, the other models are concerned with protecting the interests of the industrialized countries while maintaining an open dialogue with the Third World nations. Some models go to incredible lengths to divide the Arab region into arbitrary fragments: the United Nation's model for the future produced by Leontief, for example, divides Arab countries between two of the fifteen regions of the world covered by the model. Only the Interfutures study acknowledges that the Arab world has a distinct entity based on a cultural homogeneity and a political awareness of the 'Arab nation' but ignores the importance of this identity in its analysis. All this is hardly surprising: global models are trying to colonize the future and find strategies and mechanisms to preserve the contemporary exploitative international structures for the future. In such schemes the Arab region can only play the secondary role of the resource depot.

Now, if the images and predictions put forward in the global models are not very assuring or appealing, are there any alternative and feasible images of the Arab future? Abdalla and his colleagues argue that an alternative 'future outlook and strategic visions' exist in key documents prepared for various conferences by specialized Arab agencies. They examine seven such documents only to discover that the vision of the Arab future presented by them is often inarticulate and incomplete.[14] The Arab political and intellectual leadership seems to be suffering from an acute lack of 'strategic thinking' which is obscuring their paths to viable alternative futures. Abdalla *et al.* confess that 'it is hard to see how the strategic visions and outlooks contained in these documents can be effective and positive without a clear understanding of the *transitional paths* and *mechanisms*. The absence of any vision of these mechanisms and their functions implies the continuation of existing mechanisms, and, accordingly, the perpetuation of all the manifestations of backwardness and crisis, making the desired goals more remote than ever.'

To overcome these shortcomings, Abdalla and his colleagues call for a more comprehensive approach to Arab future studies based on a 'thorough knowledge of the present and its problems, of the historical and cultural evolution of the Arab nation, of the prevailing socio-economic pattern of relations, of the economic, social and cultural structures, of the processes of change, both conscious and unconscious and of their mutual effects and interrelations within the framework of the dynamics of the Arab socio-economic-cultural order and its links with the various components of the outside world'. Only by pursuing such an approach can the Arab world choose the safest and optimum path to the future.

The call of Abdalla and his colleagues for the development of Arab futures studies is both timely and important. The resources and potentials of the Arab region are unique; and so are its needs and requirements. Regional futures studies, therefore, have a vital role to play in shaping a viable and constructive future of the local environment. However, regional futures which overlook the important global connections cannot produce positive results. Despite the insistence on pan-Arabism and cultural identity, the work of the Arab Alternative Futures group is very nationalistic and narrow-minded. There is, for example, no awareness of the role Islam plays in Arab culture and conscience in *Images of Arab Future*; nor is there any acknowledgement of the political importance of Islam for the region or of the Islamic awakening the region is going through. In fact, the *only* mention of Islam occurs in *one* sentence right at the end of the study: 'the region is in the centre of the new wave of Islamic revival'. As such, Abdalla and his colleagues are guilty of exactly the same crime of which they accuse the authors of global models: they are projecting the alien future of Arab nationalism on a region that has a distinct Islamic identity and needs and aspirations which have to be fulfilled not within a nationalistic Arab outlook but within the world-view of Islam. The development of Arab futures studies must be part of the development of the theories and methodologies of Islamic futures.

Much of the Muslim literature on the future does not have the contemporary awareness of the study produced by Abdalla and his colleagues. This literature can be divided into three categories: the prophetic, the explorative and the reconstructive.

The prophetic literature is mostly concerned with the prophecies of the Qur'an and Hadith. It has no methodology and no real standards of scholarship. However, it is extremely popular amongst Muslim audiences. Q. I. Hingora's *The Prophecies of the Holy Qur'an*[15] and K. M. Islam's *Spectacle of Death Including Glimpses of Life Beyond the Grave*[16] are good examples.

Hingora attempts to give a 'fairly composite picture of the major prophecies and promises of the Holy Qur'an'. Each of the seventy-nine sections in the book contains verses from the Qur'an followed by interpretative commentary. On the whole the commentary is extremely naive. Prophecies contained in over half the verses quoted by Hingora have already been proved true and he is on safe ground in commenting upon them. For example, for the verse 'if any think that God will not help him [His Apostle] in this world and the Hereafter, let him stretch out a rope to the ceiling and cut [himself] off: then let him see whether his plan will remove that which enrages [him]!' he gives the following commentary: in this verse, 'definite victory is promised to Muhammad. And history shows that this promise was fulfilled when the Children of Unity carried the banner of Islam right through the whole of Arabia, in the Mediterranean regions and finally in the then known world. Within a short period, Islam reached the peak of glory which has no precedent in history.' But when it comes to the future, Hingora is clearly out of his depth. He quotes some twenty verses from the Qur'an dealing with the cosmos and asks the question whether man will be able to reach the moon or any other planet. His interpretation of the Qur'anic verses is that man is doomed to live and die on earth and cannot leave the bounds of his terrestrial journey. Moreover, 'man's attempt to take control of any other planet would mean transgression on his part'. He considers the moon to be part of the 'lower heaven' (the Qur'an; 37: 6–10) and states that 'the lowest heaven is too well guarded to be penetrated either by man or jinn'. A few sections later, Hingora tells us that the deaf and blind cannot be cured by modern medicine; Neither can there be any cure for heart attack!

Spectacle of Death is even more absurd. By the use of Qur'anic verses, a variety of *ahadith* (saying of the Prophet Mohammad) ranging from *sahih* (correct) to *zaif* (weak) to downright fabricated, anecdotes of known and unknown men, and a powerful imagination, the learned author paints a chilling picture of hell. The book is divided into six parts: the fearful sight of death; the conditions of *barzakah* (the interval between death and the Day of Resurrection); the accounts of the Day of Resurrection; description of hell; glimpses of paradise; and the impact of moral offences on faith. The methodology of the book is illustrated by the following anecdote:

> There was a man who had accumulated huge wealth and there was left nothing which he had not purchased . . . he was saying to himself that he had collected all sorts of things and there was left no need to buy

anything for years to come. Hardly had he thought of it, when a beggar dressed in rags and a bowl slung round his neck came outside and began to knock at the door violently. When the servants heard the noise, they ran out to see the foolish intruder. They asked him what the matter was? The beggar said to them to send for their master. The servants wondered if their master would like to meet him. He assured them that the master would come out. They came back and narrated the whole story to their master who said they should have given a lesson to the beggar. In the meantime the beggar again started knocking at the door violently. The guards ran and reached the door. The beggar asked the servants to tell their master that he was the angel of death. On hearing that, they were confounded and conveyed the message to their master. He also lost his senses and said in a humble tone that they should request the angel of death to substitute another person in his place. Meanwhile, the beggar entered into the house and told the wealthy man to do whatever he liked because he could not return without extracting his soul. He heaped all things at one place and cursing them said that his indulgence in those riches had prevented him from offering prayers and he could not spare time to remember God and full devotion. The Almighty God gave those riches the power of speech who said: 'why do you curse us. It was due to us that you could have an access to the kings at a time when the pious were driven out. It was because of us that you derived sexual pleasures from the beautiful women and led your life like a king . . .'

After the taste of death, there is a graphic description of hell: its depth ('if a stone is thrown into hell, it will take seventy years to reach its bottom'); its walls ('hell has been encircled by four walls and the breadth of each wall covers a period of four years'); its darkness ('the flames of hell do not illuminate, it always remains dark'); its fire ('the fire of hell is seventy degrees hotter than the worldly fire') and its rage and fury. Then follow pages and pages of description of the tortures of hell and of the various implements of such tortures. All this is contrasted with the pleasures of paradise. Quite apart from the rivers of milk and honey, there will be a bazaar, each inmate will have seventy-two houris in attendance, there will be cupfuls of pure wine and people will go about wearing crowns of pearls and diamonds. The men of paradise will have extraordinary virility and would be able to cope with seventy-two women!

After the accounts of hell and paradise, we come to the prophecies. Islam devotes some seventy pages to the signs of doom according to which we should see the end of the world before the turn of the century. The followers of Muhammad will imitate the deeds of the Jews, Christians and the magicians; false prophets would appear; people shall 'refrain from calling a spade a spade'; naked females shall lay snares of temptations for men; homicide will become the order of the day; new beliefs and new practices will gain currency; infidelity will be widespread; and the birth rate of illegitimate children will increase, and so on. The final message of the book is that there is no future; the doom is already here.

I have described the contents of Hingora and Islam's books in detail because they have a powerful hold on the minds of the Muslim masses. The first edition of Hingora's book was published in 1964 and has been reprinted continuously, without modifications, ever since. *Spectacle of Death* is a runaway best seller in the Indian subcontinent. Despite considerable assistance that Maulana Islam gets from the Qur'an and *ahadith*, an objective mind would only believe his graphic accounts of experiences beyond the grave if he produced *bona fide* credentials of having been there and returned. Hingora's absurd prophecies can only be believed by someone who lived in the Middle Ages. Yet, both books are taken seriously by perfectly intelligent Muslims. This is partly because their arguments, such as they are, are given apparent legitimacy from the Qur'an and the *ahadith*. Partly it is because of their hallucinating effect: both books promote fatalism, lethargy and a sense of helplessness about the future. The message of Hingora and Islam is simple and direct: be good and virtuous and you do not need to do anything else. They make a supreme virtue out of fatalism and a state of complete ignorance.

Coming to explorative literature, we find that most of it comes in the form of articles and research papers. A few of these articles are to be found in *The Muslim World and the Future Economic Order* which is based on an international conference organized by the Islamic Council of Europe in July 1977.[17] Of the contributions which deal with the various aspects of the future, the essays of

A. M. Hegazy, Khurshid Ahmad, Ahmed S. Heiba and Ahmad Mohammad Ali are specifically concerned with the future aspects of their chosen theme. But all four articles suffer from the common shortcomings of Muslim explorative literature on the future: complete absence of futuristic framework and thinking. In fact, critical readers can easily be forgiven for regarding these contributions as pious diatribes aimed more at proving the superiority of Islam than coming to grips with contemporary and future problems.

Hegazy's article, 'The Promotion of an Equitable World Order—the Muslim Role and Contribution', illustrates the point well.[18] He starts by describing the problems of capitalism and socalism and then makes the offering which has become a standard feature of contemporary Muslim scholarship; an equitable world order will come about, almost as if by magic, if we could 'develop and effectively distribute more information and knowledge concerning Islam', make the 'message of Islam clear to the world' and so on. One is naturally led to ask about countries where Islam is dominant, where knowledge of Islam is widely available: are these countries models of equitable societies? Is this the ideal future for all the countries of the planet to adopt? In the next essay in this volume, 'Islam and the New World Order', Khurshid Ahmad tackles the same issue from the perspective of the New International Economic Order (NIEO).[19] He argues, with some force, for a New World Order and not just NIEO, because 'the real problem is more basic and covers a vaster area than that of mere economic crisis'. The global economic crisis, he argues, 'deserves to be examined in the wider context of the overall human crisis—of the crisis of civilization'. Agreed. But how do we do that? With some real insight, Khurshid Ahmad argues that we can move towards the New World Order by taking full cognizance of the 'Islamic approach to social changes'. This means: (1) change has to be planned and engineered and be purposeful; it must not only be external, it must also come about 'within the heart and soul of man'; and change must be balanced and gradual and evolutionary. Good. How do we go about introducing this change? Here, unfortunately, the author is at a loss. He is content with giving the standard account of 'Islamic approach of life' and asks for zakah, *tazkiyyah* (purification) and the principles of *tawhid* to be adopted.

The contributions of Ahmed S. Heiba, 'Agricultural Resources in the Muslim World—Capacity and Future Growth',[20] and Ahmad Mohamed Ali, 'The Role of the Islamic Development Bank in the Future Economic Order',[21] contrast sharply. Heiba shows a real awareness of the future; Ali has no idea what will happen tomorrow. Heiba describes the world food crisis and discusses the extent to which the Muslim world is subject to it. He relates food production to population increase and estimates the expected demand for the year 2000. He then examines the present trends and shows the shortfalls that can arise. Finally, he argues that the overall situation for the year 2000 can be improved by preparation of integrated agricultural projects and conversion from rain-fed agriculture to continuous irrigation by storing the floods of rivers. There is a methodology at work in his essay. Ali, on the other hand, is content with describing the functions of his bank and its loaning policies. And on the basis of his description, it is quite evident that the Islamic Development Bank has no role to play in the future economic order.

The contributions to *The Muslim World and the Future Economic Order* and a handful of other papers which have been published in the last few years indicate that Muslim scholars are now beginning to treat the future with some seriousness.[22] However, with the exception of my *The Future of Muslim Civilization*, there has not been any systematic attempt to explore the future within the framework of Islam in recent times. Yet, way back in the thirties and forties, two authors tried to lay the foundation for just such an exercise.

Allama Muhammad Iqbal's *The Reconstruction of Religious Thought in Islam*[23] and M. Rafi-Ud-Din's *Ideology of the Future*[24] are two of the most neglected works of modern Muslim scholarship. Both authors were years ahead of their time and have produced books which constitute the backbone of the Muslim reconstructive literature on the future. This literature derives its inspiration from the celebrated work of al-Ghazzali, *The Revival of Religious Sciences*, published towards the end of the eleventh century. In *Revival*, al-Ghazzali sought to reconstruct the Muslim civilization on what he saw as the true spiritual and moral basis of Islam. The monumental work, consisting of forty volumes, starts with a new and dynamic exposition of the epistemology of Islam and goes on to give extensive treatment to social behaviour and the Islamic way of life. During the life and times of al-Ghazzali, the Muslim civilization, despite its internal moral and ethical problems, was the dominant civilization. It was, therefore, natural for him to concentrate on spiritual and social matters. But Iqbal and Rafi-Ud-Din are writing for Muslims who have lost the very foundations of their societies: they operate in alien political structures, social organizations, cultural environment and a mode of production that bears no relationship to anything in Muslim history. Their task, then, is considerably more difficult than that of al-Ghazzali.

In his preface to *Reconstruction*, Iqbal touches on the task that he is trying to tackle. The contemporary religious scholars,

owing to their ignorance of the modern mind, have become absolutely incapable of receiving any fresh inspiration from modern thought and experience. They are perpetuating methods which were created for generations possessing a cultural outlook differing, in important respects, from our own. 'Your creation and resurrection', says the Qur'an, 'are like the creation and resurrection of a single soul'. A living experience of the kind of *biological unity*, embodied in this verse, requires today a *method* physiologically less violent and psychologically more suitable to a concrete type of mind. In the absence of such method the demand for a scientific form of religious knowledge is only natural . . . I have tried to meet, even though partially, this urgent demand by attempting to reconstruct Muslim religious philosophy with due regard to the philosophical tradition of Islam and the more recent developments in the various domains of human knowledge.[25] (my emphasis)

Iqbal wants to reconstruct Muslim epistemology, and hence lay the basis for the reconstruction of Muslim civilization, on a purely ecological basis: words like 'biological unity' and 'organic whole' occur throughout the book. He sees time in an ecological perspective, arguing that 'pure time, as revealed by a deeper analysis of our conscious experience, is not a string of separate, reversible instants; it is an organic whole in which the past is not left behind, but is moving along with, and operating in, the present. And the future is given to it as lying before, yet to be traversed; it is given only in the sense that it is present in its nature as an open possibility'.[26] Thus for Iqbal the future is an *open possibility* and not closed and predetermined. He defines 'taqdir' as 'time regarded as prior to the disclosure of its possibilities'. The destiny of a thing 'is not an unrelenting fate working from without like a task master; it is the inward reach of a thing, its realizable possibilities which lie within the depths of its nature'. Destiny is shaped, it is made by effort, and does not consist of 'fully-fledged events' that are lying in the future, as it were, 'in the womb of Reality' dropping 'one by one like the grains of sand from the hour-glass'. Iqbal wants the efforts towards the reconstruction of Muslim civilization to begin with the appreciation of 'life as an organic unity' thus introducing the contemporary idea of interdependence and 'a keen sense of the reality of time'. A civilization based on such a concept of life and time would naturally reconcile the categories of permanence and change. Permanence is brought about by external principles which regulate the collective life of that civilization and give a foothold in the world of perpetual change. And adjustment to change is made by continuously striving to understand the dynamic nature of the Qur'an and such basic concepts of Islam as *ijtihad*. Within this futuristic framework, Iqbal wants to re-examine everything. His arguments for looking at the Shariah in a futuristic perspective, for example, lead him to say some very interesting things. Taking his cue from Shah Waliullah, Iqbal states that the prophetic method of teaching takes special notice of the habits, ways and peculiarities of the people to whom he is specifically sent.

> The prophet who aims at all-embracing principles, however, can neither reveal different principles for different peoples, nor leave them to work out their own rules of conduct. His method is to train one particular people, and to use them as a nucleus for the building up of a universal *Shariat*. In doing so he accentuates the principles underlying the social life of all mankind, and applies them to concrete cases in the light of the specific habit of the people immediately before him. The

Shariat values (*Ahkam*) resulting from this application (e.g. rules relating to penalties for crime) are in a sense specific to that people; and, since their observance is not an end in itself, they cannot be strictly enforced in the case of future generations.[27]

In other words, various generations in various epochs have to reconstruct the *Shariah* from the basic principles to fulfil their particular needs and requirements. Iqbal cites the example of Abu Hanifa who had to introduce the principle of *istihsan* (juristic preference) to meet some of the challenges he faced in his time. On the basis of this analysis much of the contents of the traditional schools of thought become irrelevant in the strict sense of the word. Iqbal is fully aware of this and points out that from the first century to the beginning of the fourth, no less than nineteen schools of law and legal opinion appeared in Islam. 'This fact alone is sufficient to show how incessantly our early doctors of law worked in order to meet the necessities of a growing civilization.' Iqbal expects and demands just such an effort; the full import of his analysis and demands of his futuristic thinking have yet to be appreciated by Muslim minds.

Rafi-Ud-Din approaches his effort at reconstructing Islamic thought from a quite different route. His book is partly a critique of Marxism, one of the most powerful and comprehensive that one is likely to find, and partly an attempt at re-understanding Islam from the theories of human nature and contemporary psychology. His basic thesis is that the urge for ideals is the real, the ultimate and the sole dynamic power of human action and any ideology that can meet the demands of the future must be based on this axiom. This 'urge for ideals is neither derived from nor subserves any of those human impulses, known as the instincts, the object of which is the maintenance of life. On the other hand, it is man's natural and independent urge for Beauty and Perfection which rules and controls all such impulses, in spite of their biological compulsion, for the sake of its own satisfaction.[28] Although Rafi-Ud-Din never actually says so, it is strongly implied throughout the book that the ideal man continuously strives for is Islam. He presents this ideal as a *weltanschauung* and within its frameworks 'reconstructs the philosophies of politics,

ethics, economics, history, law, education and art and the individual and social psychologies on a single basis' and presents it in
'the shape of a single Science of Man'. At every step of realizing
this ideal, argues Rafi-Ud-Din, man faces resistance. But, 'man
will evolve by action and effort in future as the animal evolved by
action and effort in the past. Resistance is a blessing for us as it
quickens our progress. When a man acts for the Right Ideal, he is
consciously and directly evolving himself.' In this framework the
ideal is never reached but is continuously strived for in the future.
Each conscious step into the future, that is each time 'resistance'
is overcome, man reaches closer to his destiny: the state of total
Islam. And each step is a step up the ladder of evolution which is
leading man towards Islam, the primordial religion of man.
Rafi-Ud-Din relates this process of evolution to 'the ideology of
the Last Prophet' which 'divides itself into four natural periods'.
'During the first period the community of believers spread from
one man to a considerable section of humanity. Their general level
of self-consciousness is very high and their actions *exemplify* the
process of actual, conscious evolution of humanity.' During the
second period, wrong ideals have gained in power but in spite of
this the ideology is able to resist total disintegration because of its
internal dynamics which became operational in the first period.
These two periods of the ideology of the Prophet occurred in the
past. The future offers two more stages of growth: the third period
where the ideology becomes an important political power; and
the fourth period 'when it has conquered all wrong ideals and
united the whole of the human race'. This is the destiny that the
Muslims have to shape for themselves. Rafi-Ud-Din wants Muslim societies to perceive this ideal as the only viable and natural
course and work from this normative position to realize the ideology of the future.[29]

For several decades the seeds sown by Rafi-Ud-Din and Iqbal
lay dormant. In 1974, the Muslim Institute for Research and
Planning in London took it upon itself to push forward ideas and
thought on Muslim Futures and work towards the reconstruction
of a Muslim civilization of the future. The result was *Towards A
New Destiny* in which Kalim Siddiqui examines the status of Muslim intellectual thought by reviewing the proceedings of the Inter-

national Islamic Youth Conference which met in Tripoli in July 1973.[30] This brief volume contains an important insight which deserves serious attention from Muslim scholars concerned with the future: 'the conceptual framework of Islam has for too long existed in isolation from an operational social order or a living civilization based on it' and as such 'there is an urgent need to revive a tradition of Muslim scholarship to produce a philosophical framework which is at least as articulate and rationally satisfying as all the other traditions of knowledge that are current today' and 'that no meaningful action to reorder Muslim societies is possible without the prior emergence of a new framework of knowledge'. Later on, these insights were articulated more carefully and in a little more detail in the *Draft Prospectus* of the Muslim Institute.[31] The present situation of the Muslim civilization is summed up in the last prognosis of this document: 'the damage to (contemporary) Muslim societies is so extensive that it may not be possible, or even desirable, to *repair* and *restore* their existing social orders; the only viable alternative is to *conceive* and *create* social, economic and political systems which are fundamentally different from those now prevailing in Muslim societies throughout the world'.

And this is where the whole futures debate stood until the fateful day, on 16 January 1979, when Ayatollah Khomeini arrived in Tehran to make the official declaration that the Iranian revolution was here to stay. Much of the discussion about the development in the Muslim world, in the early eighties, has concentrated on 'Islamic resurgence' and the role the Iranian revolution is playing in promoting a revival of Islam in our time. The revolution itself has provided a vision of the future: the general thesis propagated by many Muslim scholars is that the Iranian revolution will spread like fire and engulf the rest of the Muslim world. Mashi Muhajeri, a leader of the Jihad-e Sazandegi (Struggle for Construction), one of the most practical and positive outcomes of the revolution, argues in his *Islamic Revolution: Future Path of the Nation*[32] that the conditions prevailing in much of the Muslim world are similar to those of pre-revolutionary Iran, and Muslim people, inspired by the example of Iran, will force events to take a similar turn. Indeed, it is a moral duty of the Iranian people to export their revolution. Muhajeri writes:

> the export of the revolution simply means the introduction of the spiritual values and achievements attained in the course of the Islamic revolution. The deprived people who are suffering under the domination of exploiters, many who are dying daily because of hunger or military aggression, should come to know the valuable experience that the Iranian nation has gained in the course of its struggle against the exploiters. It is incumbent on the Iranian people to furnish the exploited nations with their own accomplishments and to help them liberate themselves from the grip of the exploiters.[33]

Indeed, while the Islamic revolution in Iran is a major accomplishment which has changed the course of contemporary Muslim history, it is by no means clear that it is an exportable commodity. On the other hand, there are serious indications that the revolution itself can do with some sustained long-range planning. The post-revolutionary events show that it has moved forward in a haphazard fashion; and if it were to sustain its impact, serious attention has to be given to solving the present and future problems of the Iranian society in an Islamic perspective. Even revolutions, it seems, cannot do without studying the future.

Meanwhile, much of the euphoria about 'Islamic resurgence' generated by the Islamic revolution in Iran has evaporated. Muslim scholars and intellectuals have now begun to question whether the Muslim world is *really* going through a contemporary revival.

Notes

1. Wilfred Scawen Blunt, *The Future of Islam*, London, 1882. Reprinted by Sind Sagar Academy, Lahore, 1975. All the citations are from the Lahore edition.
2. *Ibid*. Preface: v.
3. *Ibid*. vii.
4. *Ibid*. p. 88.
5. *Ibid*. p. 142.
6. *Ibid*. p. 204.

7. Translated from the Arabic by Maissa Taldat, Francis Pinter, London; and the United Nations University, 1983.

8. Potomac Associates, New York, 1972.

9. Hutchinson, London, 1974.

10. Described in Amilcar O. Herrera *et al.*, *Catastrophe or a New Society? A Latin American World Model*, International Development Research Centre, Ottawa, 1976.

11. W. Leontief *et al.*, *The Future of the World Economy*, Oxford University Press, 1977.

12. Interfutures, *Facing the Future: Mastering the Probable and Managing the Unpredictable*, OECD, Paris, 1979.

13. For a summary and analysis of global models from the Muslim perspective, *see* Ziauddin Sardar, *The Future of Muslim Civilization*, Croom Helm, London, 1979, Chapter 4.

14. The documents are: (1) a strategy for securing food supplies in the Arab countries issued by the Arab Organisation for Agricultural Development, 1977; (2) a strategy for industrialization based on self-reliance and aimed at basic needs sponsored by the Industrial Development Centre for the Arab States, 1977–8; (3) documents of the first Arab Energy Conference sponsored by the Organisation of Arab Petroleum Exporting Countries (AOPEC) and the Arab Fund for Economic and Social Development, 1979; (4) a strategy to develop Arab education issued by the Arab Organisation for Education, Culture and Science, 1979; (5) alternative patterns of development and lifestyles in the Arab region, study commissioned by the UN Economic Commission for West Asia and the UN Environmental Programme, 1979; (6) working paper prepared by a three-man committee selected by the committee of experts on a strategy for joint Arab economic action submitted to the first pan-Arab conference on a Joint Arab Economic Strategy, 1978; (7) towards developing joint Arab economic action, the principle document presented to the eleventh Arab summit in Amman, 1980.

15. Ashraf, Lahore, 1964.

16. Tablighi Kutub Khana, Lahore, 1976.

17. Islamic Council and Europe, London, 1979.

18. *Ibid*. pp. 123–37.

19. *Ibid*. pp. 138–54.

20. *Ibid*. pp. 296–315.

21. *Ibid*. pp. 336–42.

22. These include: Anis Ahmad, 'The future of Jihad Movement in

Afghanistan—A Review Article', *Al-Ittihad*, **17** (3), 23–29 (1980); M. A. H. Ansari, 'The Future of Islamic Mission', *Islam and the Modern Age*, **13** (1), 56–9 (1982); S. Ismael, 'Thoughts for the Education of Muslim Planners of the Future', *Ekistics*, No. 285, 428 (1980); E. Maula, 'On the impact of the Past upon the Future of Islamic Science', *Journal of Central Asia*, **3**, 77 (1980); I. H. Qureshi, 'Islam and the West: Past, Present and the Future', in Altaf Gauhar (ed.), *The Challenge of Islam*, Islamic Council of Europe, London, 1978; and Fazlur Rahman, 'Islamic Studies and the Future of Islam', in Malcolm Karr (ed.), *Islamic Studies: A Tradition and Its Problems*, Undena Publications, Malibu, California, 1980.

23. Ashraf, Lahore, 1936; reprinted 1982. All quotes from the 1982 edition.

24. Ashraf, Lahore, 1946; reprinted 1970. All quotes from the 1970 edition.

25. Iqbal, *op. cit.* p. i.

26. *Ibid.* p. 49.

27. *Ibid.* p. 172.

28. Rafi-Ud-Din, *op. cit.*, p. vi.

29. The theory of the ideology of the Last Prophet is well summarized towards the end of the book, pp. 473–80.

30. Open Press, Slough, 1974.

31. Open Press, Slough, 1974.

32. External Liaison Section, Central Office of Jihad-e-Sazandegi, Tehran, 1982.

33. *Ibid.* p. 175.

2

The Dialectics of Islamic Resurgence

Nothing has generated more passion and heated debate, both in the West and the Muslim world, than the alleged 'resurgence' and 'revival' of Islam. In the West, 'Islamic resurgence' has generated a positively mediaeval preoccupation with the Muslim world. 'The hordes are again at the gates of Vienna, holding civilization hostage, menacing our energy as they once menaced our faith.'[1] Western fundamentalism about Islam has taken vivid forms. A *Time* magazine cover shows a fully-costumed Mulla, complete with turban, calling the faithful to, presumably, *jihad*. Adjacent, the cover-line: 'Islam—the Militant Revival'. Another *Time* cover carries a grim portrait of Ayatollah Khomeini gazing threateningly, like Eisentein's Ivan the Terrible, over an insert photograph of a cool, collective President Carter. The flame coloured heading reads: 'The Test of Wills'.

The words accompanying these banal icons have been equally insulting and mundane. Consider, for example, the diatribe of *Washington Post* columnist, Joseph Kraft:

Who would want to kill the Pope? . . . In fact the gunman was the crazed product of a notorious cultural milieu. I speak of the milieu of Islamic fundamentalism . . . At the root of the assassination attempt is a turbulent Islamic society. It is a society pregnant with nasty surprises, and the large lesson is that those who look to the Muslim world as a sure supplier of oil or a steady ally against Moscow do so at their peril.[2]

And impressions of G. H. Jansen, the 'Lavant' correspondent of the *Economist*, who proudly declared to have visited Makkah, Medina and Karbala (disguised as a Muslim?):

> The image that the Western observer could take away from his contemplation of this vast, turbulent unsettled area is one of precarious unease and violence—of strange, bearded men with burning eyes, hieratic figures in robes and turbans, of blood dripping from the stumps of amputated hands and from the striped backs of malefactors, and piles of stones barely concealing the battered bodies of adulterous couples.[3]

An image which this former diplomat reinforces in his hastily completed, blindly written *Militant Islam*.[4]

Within the Muslim scholarly and intellectual circles, there are two divergent views about the movement and events sweeping through the Muslim world. The first interpretation holds that 'Islamic revivalism, reassertion, revitalisation, renewal, fundamentalism, neo-fundamentalism, reawakening and resurgence' is largely a creation of people like Kraft, modern-day devotees of such medieval bigots as Dante who portrayed Muslims as apostates, violent, lecherous, economic exploiters,[5] and Jensen, successors to eighteenth- and nineteenth-century European imperial travellers such as Giovanni Finati, J. L. Burckhardt, Bayard Taylor and Richard Burton, who visited the holy cities disguised as Muslims and returned to paint fantastic pictures of the Muslim infidels in their savage existence. It is in fact a reaction to the loss of empire, to the causes of the West's economic and political crisis.

While there is every sign that Islam is coming back to its own as a force in world affairs and as a power in Muslim societies itself, it is incorrect to call this a revival or a resurgence. Islam has always been there: it has always been a force; and it has always fought, in the form of massive protest movements, against internal despotism and dictatorship and external domination. Only when some short-sighted regime has tried to suppress the religious feeling of a Muslim society and impose a value system alien to the people have the resultant eruptions appeared to the

outside world as some form of resurgence. Essentially, such eruptions are in keeping with the traditions of Islam, and the saying of
the Beloved Prophet Mohammad that 'there will come in every
century a reformer who shall revive my faith in my people'. M.
Manazir Ahsan presents this view cogently:

> It is true that much of current Islamic resurgence can be seen as a
> quest for stability and revival of past Islamic heritage inspired by a
> disdain for western values, secular nationalism, socialist materialism
> and western consumerism that have exasperated economic and social
> problems in many Muslim countries. However, it will be naive as well
> as misleading to say that the present wave of Islamic resurgence is a
> strange phenomenon which has come suddenly out of nothing.
> Whenever in Muslim history Islam was befogged by *jahili* or pagan
> practices, and the influence of un-Islamic culture became dominant in
> society, people with revivalist spirit appeared on the scene and
> brought about the intellectual, moral and political revolution, making
> once again the Islamic ideal supreme. The conflict of Islam and *jahiliya*
> is not something peculiar to this century. It has been an integral part
> of Islamic history ever since its early phase. The conflict has had of
> course different dimensions at different periods, as every age has its
> own peculiar features and problems. Not all the revivalist movements
> in the past were able to bring about the ideal and complete transfor-
> mation of society as desired by them. Some achieved only a little, some
> went half-way, some went even further and some succeeded in reach-
> ing their destination with glory. The activities of Imam Husain, Umar
> bin Abdul Aziz, the Abbasid Caliph Al-Muhtadi Billah, Al-Ghazzali,
> ibn Taiymiyya, Imam Sirhindi, and Shah Waliullah of India, Imam
> Shamil of Russia, Shayku Muhammad ibn Abdul Wahhab of
> Arabia, Usman Dan Fodio of Nigeria and many others represent the
> different stages of success and glory. Islamic revivalism and
> resurgence is a continuous process which runs like an unbroken thread
> through the different phases of Muslim history.[6]

On purely historical ground, it is tempting to accept this interpretation. The last century, for example, provides ample evidence of
the ceaseless activity and vitality of Islam. The struggle against
imperial powers, the work of Jamaluddin Afghani, Mohammad
Abduh and Rashid Rida in Egypt,[7] the rise of the Mahdi in the
Sudan, the Pakistan Movement in the Indian subcontinent,[8] the

tobacco crisis in Iran (in which the *ulama* led a popular movement and forced the Shah of the day to withdraw the lucrative financial concession he had made to an European imperialist),[9] the revolt against a modernist monarch in Afghanistan, the rise of various Islamic Conferences for Muslim unity, are just a few, and randomly chosen, examples of Muslim efforts to assert their political identity. The present upturn in the Muslim World is a continuation of the aspirations of Muslims, from the days when the Muslim civilization was at its zenith, for political power and cultural expression. All that is different now is that some Muslim countries possess huge oil revenues which enable them to exert certain influences on world affairs.

However, the rich historical and, to some extent, religious support for this interpretation does not completely diminish the validity of the second interpretation. This view is essentially focused around the Islamic revolution in Iran. It is argued that the overthrow of the Shah by a popular uprising is such a unique event that it constitutes a civilizational upturn. Iran is a watershed for all Muslims who desire an Islamic state. As a first victory of Islam against despotism, neo-imperial dictatorship and the forces of *kufr* (non-believers), the Iranian revolution provides a reality to which all Muslims can relate their ideals, their histories and the development of the entire *ummah*. We are, therefore, in a new phase of Muslim history: Islamic revolution will spread from Iran, almost like a fire, and will engulf Muslim societies and people, thus taking the process which began with the return of Ayatollah Khomeini to Tehran to its logical and natural conclusion. Kalim Siddiqui, for example, has argued and developed a number of somewhat convoluted and turgid theories around this assertion.[10]

Those who do not support the Iran revolution unconditionally, but are forced to subscribe to this interpretation by the fact of the actual *event* of the revolution, argue that Iran is just one manifestation of the contemporary resurgence of Islam. The emergence of the Organisation of the Islamic Conference and the development of a somewhat united Muslim political front is another indication; the various 'Islamization' programmes of Pakistan, Sudan, Malaysia, Morocco are still others. These events are not unconnected: they are interlinked with a new cultural and political awareness within Muslim societies all over the world.

The late Hamid Enayat, the noted Iranian political scientist, argued that the process of cultural re-discovery sweeping through Muslim societies is a result of a chain of *humiliating* experiences. The failure of democracy in Turkey, the defeat of the Arabs in the Six Day War in 1967, Pakistan's defeat in its war with India in 1971, the Arab–Israeli war of 1973—all have contributed and are major landmarks in the contemporary revival of Islam. Far from undermining the validity of Islam as the legitimate ideology for Muslims, these failures have fostered and nourished visions of a return to Islam. The sudden arrival of oil revenues in Iran, Saudia Arabia, Libya and the Gulf and the consequent process of acute modernization and rapid industrialization at all costs introduced by the governments of these states made the political expression of this desire by the masses a necessity. Islamic resurgence had arrived.[11]

Contemporary Events: a Unique Phenomena

Whether one fully subscribes to the Islamic resurgence theory or not, it is difficult to maintain that contemporary events in Muslim countries are not much different from what has happened in Muslim history in different epochs. Since the fifteenth century, the Muslim world has continuously lost political power to Western nations. However, for the first time in almost five centuries, the Muslim people are now asserting their political identity instead of apologizing for their existence. Both the unique event of the Islamic revolution in Iran and the formation of the Organisation of Islamic Conference are responsible for this newly-discovered assertion of Muslim identity. Moreover, the hard-won independence of Malaysia, Sudan, Algeria, Egypt and the creation of Pakistan are events of considerable significance: they represent a reverse process to colonization which was, up to thirty years ago, the norm in the Muslim world. The political dynamism and unceasing perseverance of the traditional leadership, combined with the unreservedly mass support they have received, has to be admired: it is something unique in recent Muslim history and gives this epoch an unparalleled dimension.

From failure after failure, the Muslim societies now have not one but two success stories to talk about. Both the roots of the revolution in Iran and the efforts to create a global Muslim forum go back in history to the beginning of this century. The *ulama* in Iran have opposed the monarchy since the pre-First World War days. Qajar dynasty's centralizing policies and westernizing tendencies were fiercely resisted by the *ulama* and led to the so-called tobacco rebellions at the end of the nineteenth century and the 1905–11 constitutional crisis. In 1906, the constitution gave the senior *ulama* a veto over legislation: the *ulama* in the 1905 constitutional movement campaigned for the same demands as Ayatollah Kashani in the Musaddiq period and Ayatollah Khomeini in the time of Reza Shah Pahlavi. Moreover, by the nineteenth century most senior ayatollahs normally lived in exile outside Iran, in the holy cities of Najaf and Karbala, mainly to be independent of the ruling monarchs. The exile since 1963 of Ayatollah Khomeini, first in Iraq and then in Paris, was in keeping with the tradition.[12] But whereas the efforts of earlier *ulama* had failed, Ayatollah Khomeini has succeeded. This is a major departure from tradition.

He had no arms and no real means of communication, from his refuge in Najaf and then from his suburban maisonette at Neuf-le-château, with his people. Only smuggled tape-recordings of his speeches linked him with the Iranian people. Yet, he turned this disadvantage into a major gain and brought the Peacock Throne, supported by major Western powers, one of the most powerful armies in the world, and a savagely ruthless secret police, crumbling down. For Muslims everywhere, this had universal significance—a clear demonstration that Islam can stand against imperial powers and oppression and *win*. A whole generation of radicals brought up to believe that Islam was a reactionary force, an enemy of change, and forced to look towards alien ideologies for liberation from oppression and exploitation, witnessed the fall of a mighty kingdom at the voice of an aging *alim*, like the walls of Jericho at the sound of Joshua's trumpet. When they looked closer at this figure they discovered a man with an unswerving integrity of purpose, fearlessly opposed to tyranny, living the simplest of lives with only a rug to sit on and a daily diet of lentil soup and prayer. Whether they support the post-revolutionary developments in Iran or not, Muslims everywhere have learned the unique lessons that traditional leadership is not *passe*: it can lead revolutions and win.

The importance of this lesson is brought sharply into focus when one considers the *failure* of the Islamic movements of our time. The most important of these are undoubtedly *Ikhwanul Muslimeen* or the Muslim Brotherhood of Egypt and the *Jamaat-e-Islami* of Pakistan. In the last fifty years or so of their chequered history, both *Ikhwan* and *Jamaat* have won many Muslim intellectuals and scholars to their cause: but in the political field, they have not gained a single victory.

The influence of *Ikhwanul Muslimeen* can be found over the entire Middle East. It was founded by the celebrated Egyptian teacher and scholar Hasan al-Banna who instilled a disciplined devotion and ethics of hard work in his followers. However, the organization was administratively centralized, and the assassination of Hasan al-Banna on 12 February 1949 dealt it a serious blow. The movement further suffered serious setbacks when it was ruthlessly and inhumanly crushed in 1954 and its most articulate and intellectually bold advocate, Sayyid Qutb, was executed by Nasser on 29 August 1966. The savage oppression of the *Ikhwan* by Nasser failed to arouse the outrage of Egyptian people, indicating that the influence of the movement was limited to the universities and the middle classes. However, the quality of the writings of its leadership, particularly Sayyid Qutb, has developed a strong following in Sudan, Syria, Kuwait, Lebanon, Jordan and Libya. The *Ikhwan* has also gained influence and protection from the ruling elites of Saudi Arabia, Jordan and the Sudan. But their influence has not reduced, let alone eliminated, oppression and despotism in these countries.

Like the *Ikhwan*, *Jamaata-e-Islami* has also inspired and motivated intellectuals and scholars throughout the Muslim world. Tightly centralized like the *Ikhwan*, it is, however, much less militant. While the Islamic stance, and the influence of the vast intellectual output of its founder and life-long president, the late Maulana Abul 'ala Maududi, cannot be doubted, *Jamaat*'s tinkerings with Pakistani politics have spelled disaster for the movement. In coalition after coalition—from the opposition alliance against the military government of Ayub Khan, to its tragic cooperation with General Yahya Khan, its grouping with the opposition against the corrupt rule of Zulfiqal Ali Bhutto, its participation in the 'Islamization' programme of General Ziaul Haq and its regrouping with its former enemy, the People's Party of the executed Mr Bhutto, against the 'Islamization' of Gen. Ziaul Haq—the *Jamaat* has compromised itself repeatedly. Moreover, the death of its charismatic leader, Maulana Maududi, has left the *Jamaat* in complete limbo; its post-Maududi leadership inspires little confidence.

Thus the major Islamic movements—*Ikhwanul Muslimeen* and the *Jamaat-e-Islami*—contrast sharply with the Iranian revolution.[13] While the Islamic movements are largely elitist, the Iranian revolution draws its strength from the masses. Maududi and Hasan al-Banna could not motivate over a million people to fill the streets on the basis of a single directive. While the Islamic movements are personified with failure and compromise, the Islamic revolution in Iran is manifestly successful. In the long, agonizing Muslim history of continuous decline, Iran marks a first upturn. That's why Iran is unique in the recent epochs of Muslim history.

The establishment of the Organisation of Islamic Conference is also a somewhat unique event: it marks the culmination of over sixty years of effort that has its origins in the last days of the Caliphate. For the Muslim world, the significance of the First World War lies in the fact that the demise of the Ottoman Empire also ended the 1300 years' old institution of Caliphate. Under the leadership of Mustafa Kemal Attaturk, the Young Turks wanted to build a modern, Westernized state. The Caliphate was identified with 'old values' and a declining civilization; and, therefore, it had to be abolished. On 3 March 1924, the Turkish Grand National Assembly did just that by passing a law, Article One of which reads: 'The Caliphate is deposed. The office of the caliphate is abolished, since the caliphate is essentially comprised in the meaning and signification of the words Government (*hukumah*) and Republic (*jumhuriyyah*).'[14]

The Caliphate, despite its numerous weaknesses, had an emotional hold on the Muslim *ummah* and provided a platform for the Muslim countries to speak with an unified voice. Since the twenties, the search for an alternative platform which would bring Muslim countries together and provide them with a powerful, united voice had led to numerous conferences and summits: the Islamic Caliphate Congress in Cairo in 1926; the World Muslim Congress in Makkah, also in 1926; the Al-Aqsa Islamic Conference in Jerusalem in December 1931; the Second International Islamic Conference in Karachi in 1949; the Third International Islamic Conference, again held in Karachi, in 1951; the Islamic Summit in Makkah in August 1954; and the World Muslim Congress in Mogadishu in 1964. Whatever the historical value of these meetings, they all failed in providing a united platform for Muslim nations. It was the Malaysian initiative in 1968 to establish a 'Muslim Commonwealth' to promote solidarity and cooperation which eventually produced some positive results in the shape of the 1969 Kuala Lumpur conference of Muslim foreign ministers where a platform to discuss political problems facing Muslim countries and promote economic cooperation between them was developed. The burning of al-Aqsa mosque in August 1969 precipitated the Islamic Summit in Rabat in setting up the Organisation of the Islamic Conference, with a permanent secretariat in Jeddah.

Because of a whole string of failures, the creation of an intragovernmental Muslim forum in itself is an achievement. Like the United Nations, the Organisation of Islamic Conference suffers from serious shortcomings, not least the inability of its members to take the institution seriously. Nevertheless, it is a unique institution for it has the ability to bring all the nations of the Muslim world, even those who have openly declared war on each other, under one roof, and to promote cooperation and communication between Muslim people that has not been possible in recent history. Moreover, it has the potential of becoming a powerful institution capable of articulating Muslim anger and aspiration with clarity and force. This potential alone makes the Organisation of Islamic Conference a unique, but qualified, success.

The creation and development of the Organisation of Islamic

Conference and the reaction to the Islamic revolution in Iran throughout the Muslim world, indicates that the movement of a return to Islamic roots is a transnational phenomena. It is not limited to a single country or community; it has, in fact, been occurring in virtually every Muslim society regardless of size or political, economic and cultural environment. Indeed, as Hrair Dekmejian writes,

> the quest for a new Islamic identity is discernible not only in the Arab sphere, but also in Nigeria, Turkey, Pakistan and Indonesia. It is manifest not only in countries where Muslims are numerically domin- ant, but also among Islamic minorities in India, the Philippines, the Soviet Union and the Western countries. Nor is the Islamic revival limited to particular social and economic classes or occupations. While much of its grass roots support has come from the lower middle clas- ses, there is increasing evidence of widespread emulation of Islamic lifestyles among the middle and upper middle classes in such relatively advanced countries as Egypt, Turkey and Tunisia.[15]

The yearning among Muslim people for self-expression has con- tinuously been increasing since the abolition of the Caliphate. The belated discovery of its existence in the West notwithstand- ing, the tendency towards a cultural re-discovery has persisted in the last century. But the tendency towards self-assertion, expressed in its most profound and explosive form in the Islamic revolution in Iran, does not constitute a systematic, coherent Islamic resurgence. The yearning for cultural expression and political assertion by themselves not to justify such hyperbole as 'resurgence', 'renaissance', 'recovery of identity' or 'critical power shift'. There is no evidence to suggest that the Muslim countries, individually or collectively, have acquired any *real* political clout in the international arena. The political expression of Muslim identity should not be confused with *real* political power. That lies in economic independence and the indigenous ability to generate and maintain a coherent system of appropriate knowledge, including a modicum of science and technology. The Organisation of Islamic Conference has manifestly not made any move in this direction. And only rabid believers in a flat earth would argue that Iran today possesses *real* political and intellectual power. Contemporary Iran has gone through a massive spiritual and political transformation; whether it can be translated into an all-round intellectual, cultural, social, economic, scientific and technological change remains to be seen. While the Islamic revolution is unique, there is nothing unique about the Iranian state: its economic and social policy, urban development framework, science and technology policy—institutions which shape contemporary society—are exactly the same as those of any Muslim country. Declaring a state to be 'Islamic' and actually creating an 'Islamic state' are two quite different enterprises.

An Islamic resurgence, with a critical shift in economic, political and intellectual power, truly epochal in nature can be identified, as Ralph Braibanti has pointed out, by three characteristics: (1) although it may rise from a restricted national or regional base, it must be global in scope or have the clear potential of global influence; (2) it must overturn certain fundamental assumptions about the relationship of man to man or nation to nation or man to natural resources and establish new equations for these relationships; (3) it must be irreversible in its effects; that is, granted moderate oscillations characteristic of all change, there can be no return to the *status quo ante*.[16] The industrial revolution in Europe and the emergence of the post-colonial era after the Second World War certainly meet these criteria. However, the developments in the Muslim world in the last two decades fail to come up to these criteria. This is largely because the political and economic changes ushered by the Iranian revolution, the emergence of Organisation of Petroleum Exporting Countries (OPEC) and the establishment of the Organisation of Islamic Conference, do not have a well-defined, concrete *knowledge* base: the gains accomplished by Muslim societies in recent times do not have indigenous *intellectual* roots and, far from having lasting, global impact, they can easily evaporate.

Without a knowledge base that produces real wealth and political clout, it is premature for Muslim intellectuals to believe that there *is* an Islamic resurgence. The Muslim world is going not through a resurgence but an unrest—an unrest that is the product of its acute disillusion with capitalism and Communism, development and modernization, instant answers and political expediency. It is an unrest that has fermented a feeling of global Islamic community, deposed monarchs and military regimes, and produced transnational Islamic activities and institutions. It is an unrest based on a deep anxiety about the future of the Muslim societies; one that is heading towards a search for genuine solutions.

The Reacting Syndrome

The quest for Islamic solutions to contemporary and future problems has been thwarted in the last three centuries by two major factors: the poverty of the intellectual thought and insight of Muslim people and their love–hate relationship with Western civilization. The closing of the gates of *ijtihad* (reasoned struggle) during the fourteenth and fifteenth centuries by the learned scholars of the community who feared unethical innovation in religion, and the consequent emergence of *taqlid* (passive imitation) as the dominant mode of thought in all spheres of life provided the first impetus for the intellectual decline of the Muslim civilization.[17] It is not possible for an intellectually superior people to be politically and physically subjugated by a civilization that does not have the same intellectual resources at its disposal. The political decline of the Muslim civilization immediately followed the loss of its intellectual leadership. When the Muslim world met Western civilization in the battlefield in the eighteenth century, its fate had already been sealed.

At the beginning of the European imperial adventure, the Muslim hatred of Western powers was almost total. But European military superiority meant that the Muslims were obliged to acquire their military technology. The Ottomans, for example, both hired European technicians and sent their technologists to be trained in Europe. While conscious efforts were made to keep the influence of Western technology to the military sphere, the transfer of technological hardware and technicians nevertheless had a certain social and economic impact on Muslim lands. European technology was responsible for inducing the Western mode of thought and behaviour in Muslim societies. It was also responsible for the realization that Western superiority went far beyond military technology and organization. It presented an intellectual domination.

At the beginning of the twentieth century, when the process of colonialization was completed and Muslim minds finally conquered, the Muslim hatred of Western civilization was transformed into total love. This phase of history was summed up by the Egyptian modernist scholar Taha Hussain when he said, 'let us adopt western civilization in its totality and all its aspects, the good with the bad and the bitter with the sweet'. Even the traditionalist scholars lost faith in their intellectual heritage, and Muslim societies pursued Western ideologies and ways of life under the guiding principle of modernization with a mix of nationalism.

Modernization was seen to be synonymous with Westernization. In Turkey, for example, nationalism was combined with modernization by Kemal Ataturk, and the Young Turks were proud of being Turks and of imitating Europe. 'There is only one civilization', Ataturk used to say, 'and Turkey must imitate it in all its aspects.' In Iran, Reza Shah Pahlavi propagated a Persian nationalism that based itself on ancient Persian culture and introduced patterns and strategies of development *a la occident*. In the Indian subcontinent, nationalism emerged in the form of a demand for a separate homeland for the Muslims, and modernization was introduced by efforts of such scholars as Sir Syed Ahmad Khan and establishments such as the Aligarh Muslim University.[18]

In the fifties, when many Muslim countries had gained their independence, the love affair of Muslim societies with Western civilization reached a new peak. The post-independence days, characterized by imitation, dependency, dissension and political despotism, have seen three decades of development strategies designed to modernize Muslim lands.[19] These strategies were based on the principles of 'economic development', 'advancement', 'progress', 'industrialization'—in short, the Western model of state and society—and constituted an all-out effort to turn Muslim societies into plastic replicas of the Anglo-Saxon world.

However, these experiments in Western reforms have had

some serious side-effects in the form of cultural tension, the domination of Westernized elites, dislocation of agriculture, the destruction of rural areas and a sense of dispossession that dominates the Muslim world. Against this background, the frustrations of Muslim masses have built up to such a pitch that they now find any talk of Westernization and modernist reforms repugnant.

So the Muslim societies have turned a full circle. Once again they have come to hate the West; and yet intellectually their position is no better than at the beginning of the eighteenth century. Are we going to see the cycle repeated again?

Love and hate are powerful emotional forces: they allow little time for intellectual pursuits, cool reasoning, long-range planning and chartering a journey towards a desired future. These emotions have ensured that the history of Muslim decline has been dominated by reaction. Muslim societies are constantly *reacting* to Western civilization: 'catching up', ogling at the wonders of modern technology, gasping at the achievements of Western science, forcing a traditional people to conform to Western economic models, turning serene urban and natural environments into poor replicas of Western ones; Muslim intellectuals and writers are always attacking the Western media for its bias, writing manic scribblings about the moral decay and social disintegration of Western society, denouncing political and economic hegemony of the West. The existence of Muslim societies is defined by their reactions to external stimuli which has its origins in Western intellectual, social and political institutions. The Muslims are thus a *re*-acting people who have become almost incapable of taking initiatives, original thinking and planned action.

The re-acting syndrome has had profound effects on contemporary Muslim scholarship and intellectual efforts. The 'Islamic literature' of the colonial period—works of Jamaluddin Afghani, Mohammad Abduh, Syed Ameer Ali and colleagues—was pure apologia. The post-independence scholarship too is conservative and preservative: the works of Maulana Maududi, Abul Hasan Ali Nadwi, Syed Qutb, Beruizaman Said Nursi and, indeed, Ali Shariati are little more than sermons—morals, after all, are nothing more than a poor man's substitute for powers.[20] The works of these and other contemporary scholars and *ulama* are not scintillating with ideas and intellectual boldness or show relevance to contemporary or future reality: they have performed a vital role in inspiring and equipping an entire generation, but from an intellectual viewpoint they have failed to motivate their readers to think. It is as though they were deliberately holding themselves back: they fear *adventurous thinking* and show no *intellectual joy* of being a Muslim.

It is difficult to perceive that there can be an Islamic resurgence without an intellectual base, a solid foundation of contemporary ideas and analysis, a futuristic synthesis of epistemology and philosophy that is derived from the primary source of Islam: the Qur'an and the *Sunnah* of the beloved Prophet Mohammad. Islamic resurgence cannot be brought about by haphazard gains, a random, often mindless reaction, to external stimuli, a revolution here, an Islamization programme, which often legitimzies oppression, there. It has to be a planned, systematic and coherent endeavour of thought and action that leads to real political and intellectual power and indigenous scientific, technological and economic capability.

Thinking about Islamic Resurgence

Islam is a multi-dimensional world-view. There is an Islamic perspective on every human endeavour. Moreover, Islam is concerned with a complete human being and, as such, it expresses the states of being characteristic of humans by offering an impressive repertoire of values: instrumental, ethical, aesthetic, eschatological—all of which reflect and recapitulate the variety of aspects of man's existence. These values knit together the vast array of human activities and concern, giving them an organic shape and connecting every Islamic perspective with every other. Thus, Islam is an holistic enterprise. In planning for Islamic resurgence, then, due emphasis has to be given to all aspects of society: *ijtihad* (intellectual struggle) must go hand in hand with *jihad* (all out effort), allowances must be made for both unity of goals and diversity of actions, history has to be given due recognition but the future too has to be emphasized. The recent history of Muslim revivalist movements demonstrates that social action and political activism on their own do not produce long-lasting gains: it was the weakness of *ijtihad* that led to the failure of the *jihad* movements in India, the Sudan, the Arabian peninsula and other places. As Fazlur-Rahman has argued, 'the survival of the Islamic world as Islamic is conditioned not only on activist ferment, but on patient and complex intellectual labour which must produce the necessary Islamic vision'.[21] But more than that, both 'intellectual labour' and political activism must make allowances for diversity and dissension. The purview of Islam is vast: there is place here for diverging political views, dissenting interpretations, and ethnic norms and customs—the intellectual foundations of Islamic resurgence need an ibn Taymiyyah as well as an al-Ghazzali, an ibn Rushd as well as Mulla Sadra, an ibn Sina as well as al-Razi. It needs an entire cosmos of thought and opinion.

The true solutions to contemporary, and even more frightening future, political, social, economic, technological and scientific problems of Muslim societies must emerge from *within* the unified yet diverse intellectual heritage of Islam. Cultural authenticity, being true to ourselves, must be the starting-point of this quest, which means that Muslim societies cannot use the West as a yardstick, neither can they adopt an emotional attitude towards it: Muslims must take a neutral stand, synthesizing what is beneficial for their societies and rejecting what is harmful. Moreover, Muslim societies need to build, in some cases rebuild, Islamic institutions and seek indigenous solutions to pressing problems. No one can solve the problems of Muslim societies; or can offer ready-made solutions. An Islamic perspective on every outlook on life has to be sought and an intellectual edifice on which a viable future can be built has to be constructed with indigenous ideas and resources. A civilization devoid of original intellectual content, which borrows concepts and ideas from other cultures and stops seeking indigenous solutions to its problems, is doomed to be marginalized.

The Beloved Prophet Mohammad is reported to have said: 'the latter days of this *ummah* would be improved only by what improved its beginning'. And what improved the beginnings of the Muslim civilization and took it, in a matter of decades, to the zenith? It was more than just religious piety and a love for the

Qur'an and the *Sunnah*; or a willingness to sacrifice life for trans-cendental goals. It was also an intellectual and realistic under-standing of the dictates, injunctions and concepts of the Qur'an and the *Shariah*. It was also intellectual boldness and an ability to synthesize productive ideas from other cultures within the framework of Islamic norms and values. The unrest and the 'activist ferment' in the Muslim world is a good indication that the Muslim love of the Qur'an and the *Sunnah* has not diminished. And the willingness to sacrifice their lives for higher goals is amply demonstrated by the Islamic revolution in Iran. The West has destroyed the intellectual integrity and political sovereignty, and made deep in-roads in the cultural authenticity of Muslim societies, but it has not, and it could not, destroy the Muslim identity. And the works of concerned Muslim scholars and *ulamas* have ensured that the moral fibre of Muslim societies is more or less intact. What is now required is the development of Muslim intellectual integrity and the discovery of boldness and courage needed to find authentic solutions to present and future prob-lems.

The Muslim societies face a formidable intellectual agenda. Yet, unless it is tackled head on, the aspirations of truly epochal Islamic resurgence will remain a pious hope. The Muslim destiny will be shaped by the quality of our intellectual effort: by our contemporary and futuristic understanding of the concepts and principles of the Qur'an and by developing, analysing and synth-esizing new ideas. The road to Islamic resurgence, then, will be determined by the shape of ideas to come.

Notes

1. Michael Gilsenan, 'The Spectre of Islam', *Issues*, April 1980. Gilse-nan, an anthropologist, provides a fascinating analysis of Western para-noia about 'Islamic resurgence'.

2. *Washington Post*, 19 May 1981.

3. 'Muslims in the modern world', *The Economist*, 3 January 1981.

4. G. H. Jansen, *Militant Islam*, Harper and Row, New York, 1979.

5. In the *Inferno*, Dante Meets Mohammad in the eighth of the nine circles of Hell. So before he reaches Mohammad, he passes through circles containing people whose sins are less heinous, i.e. the lustful, the

avaricious, the gluttonous, the heretics, the wrathful, the suicidal and the blasphemous, and after Mohammad there are only the falsifiers and the treacherous before Dante arrives at the bottom of Hell where Satan resides. See Edward Said, *Orientalism*, Routledge and Kegan Paul, London, 1978, for a criticism of Dante and other orientalists.

6. M. Manazir Ahsan, 'Islamic Resurgence: An Unbroken Thread', *Inquiry*, 1 (4), 53–5 (1984).

7. For a detailed account of works of these revivalists, *see* M. A. Zaki Badawi, *The Reformers of Egypt*, Croom Helm, London, 1979.

8. See Istiaq Hussain Qureshi, *Ulama in Politics*, Ma'aref, Karachi, 1976.

9. See Hamid Algar, 'The Oppositional Role of the Ulama in Twentieth-Century Iran', in Nikki R. Keddie (ed.), *Scholars, Saints and Sufis: Muslim Religious Institutions since 1500*, University of California Press, Berkeley, 1972.

10. See Kalim Siddiqui (ed.), *Issues in Islamic Movement: 1980–81*, Open Press, London, 1982; and subsequent volumes in the *Issues* series: the theories are developed in the introduction to each volume. See also his pamphlet, 'The state of the Muslim world today', Open Press, London, 1980; and my analysis of his theories and ideas, 'Islamic Resurgence', *Muslim World Book Review*, 2 (4), 13–18 (1982).

11. Hamid Enayat, 'The Resurgence of Islam: the Background', *History Today*, 30 February 1980, 16–22.

12. See Hamid Algar, *The Roots of Islamic Revolution*, Open Press, London, 1980.

13. For a comparative bibliography of the Muslim Brotherhood, *Jamaat-e-Islami* and the Iranian revolution, *see* Asaf Hussain, *Islamic Movements in Egypt, Pakistan and Iran: An Annotated Bibliography*, Mansell, London, 1983.

14. *Qawanin Mejmuasy* 1924/1340, No. 431, Ankara Press of the Grand National Assembly of Turkey. English translation in *Survey of International Affairs*, 1 (3), 575 (1925).

15. R. Hrair Dekmejian, 'The anatomy of Islamic revival: legitimacy crisis, ethnic conflict and the search for Islamic alternatives', *The Middle East Journal*, 34 (1), 1–12 (Winter 1980).

16. Ralph Braibanti, 'The recovery of Islamic identity in global perspective', in Bruce Lawrence (ed.), *The Rose and the Rock: Mystical and Rational Elements in the Intellectual History of South Asian Islam*, Carolina Academic Press, Durham, North Carolina, 1979, p. 159.

17. For an account of the closing of the gates of *ijtihad*, *see* Kemal A. Faruki, *The Evolution of Islamic Constitutional Theory and Practice from 622 to*

1926, National Publishing House, Karachi, 1971; see also his *Islamic Jurisprudence*, Pakistan Publishing House, Karachi, 1962.

18. For the emergence of the Kamalist ethics in Turkey, *see* David Kushner, *The Rise of Turkish Nationalism*, Frank Cass, London, 1977; for the background to Aligarh Muslim University and the teachings of Sir Syed Ahmad Khan, *see* B. A. Dar, *Religious Thought of Sayyid Ahmad Khan*, Institute of Islamic Culture, Lahore, 1971.

19. For a detailed account of the role of 'development' and 'modernization', *see* Ziauddin Sardar, *Science, Technology and Development in the Muslim World*, Croom Helm, London, 1977.

20. Each one of these scholars, of course, has a substantial following in the Muslim world. Often criticizing the 'guru' solicits the charge that the criticism is not 'based on any thorough study of their writings and research. It is unfortunate that only a trickle of their writings is available in English, depriving people not familiar with Arabic and Urdu from appreciating the proper contribution these scholars have made' (M. Manazir Ahsan, *op. cit.*). A poor apology that also insults the capability of the critic.

21. Fazlur-Rahman, 'Roots of Islamic neo-fundamentalism', in Philip H. Stoddard, David C. Cuthell and Margaret W. Sullivan, *Change and the Muslim World*, Syracuse University Press, New York, 1981, p. 25.

3

Reconstructing the Muslim Civilization

When thinking and writing about Islam, most Muslim intellectuals, both modernists and traditionalists, work within a very narrow and confining canvas. Islam is often presented as a religious outlook: the modernists are happy to confine Islam to the boundaries of personal piety, belief and rituals; while the traditionalists always describe Islam as 'a complete way of life'. What is meant by this phrase is that Islam touches all aspects of human living—particularly social, economic, educational and political behaviour of man.

However, while these approaches to the study of Islam are extremely useful, they are restrictive. Each approach itself determines the boundary of exposition: note that in their monumental output, both Maulana Abu Ala Maududi and Syed Qutb, two of the most articulate traditionalists of our time, find no space for discussing epistemology and science, technology and environment, urbanization and development—all burning, indeed pressing, issues for contemporary Muslim societies as well as the dominant West. Moreover, the picture of the 'Islamic way of life' that emerges from these authors is a very atomized and segregated one. While Islam is presented as a complete way of life, the various aspects of human living, economic activity, political behaviour and educational development, are treated in isolation from each other. There is no integrated methodology in action in Maulana Maududi or Syed Qutb's works. The result is that while it is repeatedly emphasized that Islam is a 'complete way of life', nowhere is it really represented as an integrated, holistic world-view.

More recently, Sayyid Muhamad Baqir al-Sadr and Sheikh Murtada Mutahhari showed much promise in developing an interdisciplinary methodology from within the realms of traditional scholars. Sayyid Baqir al-Sadr did much work on an integrated Islamic political economy. Sheikh Mutahhari, with his strong background in philosophy and *irfan* (gnosis), tried to apply these to contemporary socio-political realities. Both these scholars were killed in their forties, cutting short their promising initiatives.

In a different vein, this time from the ranks of modern scholars, Ali Shariati devoted much effort to developing a multidisciplinary base for an Islamic world-view. His early death, however, did not allow him to systematize his thoughts into a theory and his ideas remain scattered in numerous articles and lectures.

The more *avant-garde* Muslim intellectuals—the most noteworthy among them being Syed Muhammad al-Naquib al-Attas, representing the traditional sufi outlook, and Shaikh Parvez Manzoor, representing a more contemporary interpretation—have sought to project Islam as an ethical system. For example, in his brilliant essay, 'Islam: the concept of religion and the foundation of ethics and morality',[1] Naquib al-Attas argues that *din* of Islam can be reduced to four primary significations: indebtedness, submissiveness, judicious power and natural inclination. He then proceeds to present Islam as a 'natural' social and ethical system. Parvez Manzoor equates the *Shariah* to an ethical system and has used his analysis to develop a contemporary Islamic theory of environment.[2]

The exposition of Islam as an ethical system takes us a step further. An underlying ethical system can permeate all human endeavour, and questions of ethics can be raised in all contemporary situations whether they involve the impact of science on Muslim societies or technology on natural environment or planning on the built-environment. And, because everything is examined from the perspective of a total ethical system, a more integrated and coherent exposition of Islam comes to the fore.

However, reducing Islam to one demoninator, namely ethics, is still very confining. The excessive concern with ethics generates an illusion of moral superiority and ignorance of power realities. In Islam, ethics is a pragmatic concern: it *must* shape individual and social behaviour.[3] But methodologically, discussion and analysis of ethical criteria—what ought to be, what is right and wrong, what is our duty and obligations—produces a strange mirage. It leads to the erroneous belief that just by doing right, by being righteous, fulfilling our duty, Muslim societies and hence Islam will triumph and become dominant. Ethical analysis substitutes piety for pragmatic policy, morality for power, and righteousness for bold and imaginative planning. Piety, morality, righteousness are the beginning of Islam: they are not an end in themselves. Ethics is our navigational equipment; it is not the end of our journey. Ethics ensures that we tread the right path, avoiding pitfalls and quicksands, and reach our intended destination. But within the ethical geography, there are no limitations to where we take ourselves and our societies. Our destinations and goals are limited only by our imagination and naivety, our confining outlooks and our lack of understanding of the richness and the vast panorama of Islam.

The Civilization of Islam

We can only give our imagination and intellect full reign, something that is demanded of us by God, if we think, conceive and study Islam as a living, dynamic civilization of the future. Only by approaching Islam as a civilization can we really do full justice to the *din* of Islam. It is worth noting that when Naquib al-Attas discusses the many manifestations of *din*, he stops short of noting that one connotation of it is *medina*, the city-state which marked the beginning of Islamic civilization. From Medina onwards, Islam ceased to be just a religion, or an ethical system, or even a political institution—it became a civilization. And, it has continued to be a civilization since then.

However, whenever Muslim writers and intellectuals have discussed Islam as a civilization, it has always been as a *historic* civilization, never as a contemporary or a future civilization. By limiting the civilizational aspects of Islam to history, they have negated its future. Moreover, they have concentrated discussion on either the self-evident aspects of Islam such as ethics and beliefs or further increased the fossilization of an already stagnant body of jurisprudence, legal thought and scholastic philosophy. Unless we break this suffocating mould, Muslim societies are doomed to a marginalized existence.

Furthermore, only by presenting Islam as a living, dynamic civilization, and all that it entails, can we really meet the challenge that comes to us from the West. Encounters in the arena of religion and theology, philosophy and ethics, may generate good intellectual writings but, essentially, they are meaningless.[4] But an encounter of two civilizations, seeking reapproachment as well as asserting their own identities, is a completely different phenomenon. Only such an engagement can produce a beneficial dialogue and mutual respect between two equals.

At this juncture of our history, however, we are not in a position to present Islam as a *total* civilization. Having failed to do our homework in this area, we find ourselves as a rather truncated and limping civilization. Many of our essential civilizational features, having been neglected for over four centuries, are dormant and in urgent need of serious surgery. Islam and Muslim societies are like a magnificent but old building on which time, and years of oversight, have taken their toll. The foundations are very solid, but the brickwork needs urgent attention; the plaster needs to be replaced, the façade needs to be redecorated and made much more exciting. Inside, the building needs to be brought into tune with contemporary living, present and future needs and requirements. We need to reconstruct the Muslim civilization: if not brick by brick, then to a very considerable scale.

The reconstruction of Muslim civilization is essentially a process of elaborating the world-view of Islam. The 'complete way of life' group of scholars are content with re-stating the classical and traditional positions as if the old jurists and scholars had solved all problems of mankind for all time! The *avant-garde* seem to believe that casting contemporary concerns in ethical moulds is enough. We need to go beyond all this and produce distinctively Islamic alternatives and solutions to the vast array of problems faced by our societies. We need to do this by producing a whole array of theoretical alternatives and by demonstrating them practically. I am talking not of abstract, metaphysical theories: we have enough of these. I am talking about a pragmatic theoretical edifice that gives contemporary meaning to the eternal guidelines laid down in the Qur'an and the Sunnah. I am talking about a body of theory that can be translated into policy statements and produce practical models that could guide us towards a complete state of Islam. I am talking about theories that produce distinctive methodologies which ensure that both ends and means of human enquiry are within the precepts of the ethical system of Islam. The reconstruction of Muslim civilization is both a theoretical and practical process, each feeding on the other, theory shaping practice and behaviour, and practice polishing the theory.

As reconstruction is both a theoretical and practical process, and involves elaboration of the world-view of Islam, we simply cannot rely on our normal crop of scholars and intellectuals. The days of the individual Muslim scholar working in isolation on metaphysical issues, writing an odd commentary on the Qur'an, are numbered. Reconstruction is a group process: it requires the effort of a multitude of scholars, coming from different educational backgrounds and disciplines, all concentrating and focusing their talents on the interdisciplinary endeavour of reconstructing the Muslim civilization. A global quest requires, naturally, a global effort. It is an effort which, of necessity, must involve all the thinking and working elements of the *ummah*.

But even before we taken the initial steps towards reconstruction of our civilization, we must begin to *think*, individually and collectively, like a civilization. Our commitment and aspirations should be directed not towards some parochial objectives, but towards a civilizational plane. We, the Muslim *ummah*, are an holistic aggregate: despite the fact that we at present live in different polities, come from a kaleidoscope of ethnic backgrounds, hold and express a complex array of opinions and ideas, we are united by a single world-view, the hallmark of our civilization. That means our political differences are only temporary; and we should behave as though they are temporary. It also means that the old differences of opinions and expressions between us—such as the dissension between shias and sunnis, whabbis and sufis—should be placed where they belong: on the dirt heap of history.[5] While history should always be with us, we should not live in it.

In general, civilizations have been studied in terms of large historic units. For example, in his *A Study of History*, A. J. Toynbee points to twenty-one civilizations in the known history of the world, each with distinctive characteristics, but all sharing certain features or qualities which enable them to be distinguished as members of the same category.[6] Sociologists speak of modern civilizations, by which is meant contemporary urban and industrialized societies. These approaches to the study of civilizations 'fix' them to a particular historic epoch. Thus, by definition, civilization becomes a historic entity with a finite life-time. Ibn Khaldun spoke of the rise and fall of civilizations, thus presenting a cyclic view of history.[7]

But Muslim civilization is no more fixed to a particular historic epoch or geographical space than the teachings of the Qur'an and the Sunnah. The Muslim civilization is a historic continuum: it has existed in the past, it exists today, and will exist in the future. But each step towards the future requires a further elaboration of the world-view of Islam, an invocation of the dynamic principle of ijtihad which enables the Muslim civilization to tune in to the changing circumstances. Whether it is raising or declining, or indeed purely static, depends on the effort exerted by the Muslim *ummah* to understand and elaborate the teachings of Islam to meet the new challenges.

Challenges Before Us

There are essentially seven major challenges before us. However, none of these can be tackled in isolation: they are all interlinked and each has a bearing on the other. If we were to describe the Muslim civilization as a flower-shaped schema, then we can identify the seven areas which need contemporary elaboration (*see* Fig. 2). The centre of the flower, the core, represents the world-view of Islam: it produces seeds for future growth and development. The core is surrounded by two concentric circles representing the major manifestations of the Islamic world-view: epistemology and the *Shariah* or law. The four primary petals represent the primary external expressions of the *weltanschauung*: political and social structures; economic enterprise; science and technology; and environment. The flower also has a number of secondary petals representing such areas as architecture, art, education and community development, social behaviour and so on, but here we will limit our discussion to primary petals.

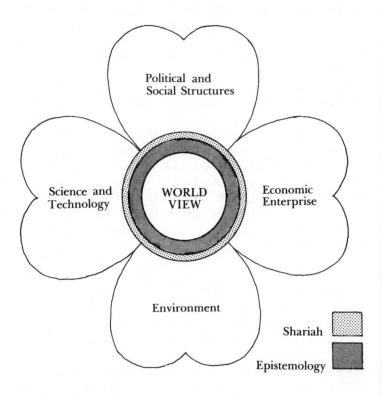

Figure 2. *The Challenges before us*

A detailed elaboration of the 'flower', and hence the development of a theoretical edifice, practical models and distinctive methodologies is an essential prerequisite for the reconstruction of Muslim civilization. For example, the world-view of Islam needs to be continuously elaborated so that we can understand new developments vis-à-vis Islam. Essentially, the world-view of Islam consists of a few principles and a matrix of concepts to be found in the Qur'an and the Sunnah. The principles outline the general rules of behaviour and development and chalk out the general boundaries within which the Muslim civilization has to grow and flourish. The conceptual matrix performs two basic functions: it acts as a standard of measure, a barometer if you like, of 'Islamicness' of a particular development or institution; and it serves as a basis for the elaboration of the world-view of Islam.

The principles of the world-view of Islam, largely relating to social, economic and political behaviour, have been well discussed in Islamic literature. For example, the principle forbidding *riba* (all forms of usury) has been written about extensively. However, to turn it into a fully-fledged theory, and develop working models from it, we need to operationalize and develop a contemporary understanding of the relevant concepts from the conceptual matrix. For example, we need to have a detailed and analytical understanding of the concepts of *shura* (cooperating for the good), *zakah* ('poor-tax') and *zulm* (tyranny). In fact, to a certain extent, that is how the contemporary theory of Islamic economics has developed over the last two decades. But each of these and many other concepts need to be elaborated to a fully-fledged body of knowledge; only from further theoretical understanding can we develop practical models and apply them to real situations.

The most interesting feature of the world-view of Islam is that it presents an interactive and integrated outlook. The various elements of the conceptual field, therefore, all have a bearing on each other. Qur'anic and Shariah concepts are not unidisciplinary; that is, a single concept does not only have relevance to one discipline but is, in fact, applicable to a whole range of disciplines. Therefore, a contemporary understanding of one concept, say *istislah* (public interest), may lead to a theoretical understanding of economics, science, technology, environment and politics. Similarly, lack of understanding of a key concept may thwart developments in all these fields.

The Qur'an and the Shariah contains numerous concepts that have been dormant for centuries. I have extracted over a hundred key concepts (Table) that need the urgent attention of Muslim scholars. They are our basic tools for the elaboration of the world-view of Islam and hence reconstruction of a dynamic, thriving Muslim civilization of the future.

Table.　*Some Key Concepts of the Civilizational Framework*

Allah	God, the Supreme Being
Adab	Culture, virtue, equilibrium
Adl	Justice
Ajal	Haste
Akhlaq	Ethics, manners, good behaviour (*see*, Adab)
Akhirah	The Hereafter, Beyond
Alam	World, cosmos, creation
Alim	Scholar, scientist, savant, expert
Aman	Peace, protection, tranquility
Amanah	Trust, entrustment
Amin	Trustworthy, reliable, true
Amir	Commander, ruler, in-charge, chief
'Aql	Reason, intellect, intuition
Ard	Earth, globe
Bai'ah	Formal allegiance, acquiescence, political loyalty
Bait-al-Mal	Public treasury
Bidah	Heresy, deviation, innovation
Dar-al-Islam	Peace zone, the House of Islam
Dar-al-Harb	War zone, the Abode of Un-Islam
Da'wah	Calling, vocation, mission, propagation
Din	Religion, ethics, morality, faith, the Ultimate Orientation, world-view
Divan	Institution, dossier
Dhikr	Remembrance of God
Du'a	Prayer, supplication, submission, request
Dunya	World, expediency, the Immediate Orientation
Fard	Obligation, duty, statutory act
Fatwa	Legal verdict, moral guideline

Fiqh	Jurisprudence, derivatory stipulation
Ghaib	Non-empirical reality
Hadd	Limit, parameter, degree
Hajj	Pilgrimage, pan-Islamic assembly
Halal	Permissible, rightful act, lawful, abiding
Haqiqah	Reality, verity, 'true facts'
Haram	Forbidden, wrong act, unlawful, violation
Hidayah	Moral guidance
Hijra	Migration, estrangement, re-focusing, regrouping, revival, transition, collective struggle
Hikmah	Wisdom, discretion
Hukm	Order, rule, arbitration
Ibadah	Worship, devotion, service, dependence
Ihsan	Kindness, ecological compassion
Ijma	Consensus, accord, agreement
Ijmal	Synthesis, summation, Holism
Ijtihad	Intellectual struggle
Ilm	Knowledge, science, discipline
Imam	Leader, guide, authority
Iman	Faith, belief, acceptance of God (Ultimate Reality)
Infaq	Spending for public good
Insan	Man, mankind, humanity
Islah	Reform, setting aright
Israf	Excess, extravagance, waste
Istihsab	Moral and civilizational self-review
Istihsan	Custom and practice
Istiqlal	Civilizational autonomy
Istislah	Public interest, welfare, common good
Jahiliyah	The Age of Ignorance, state of Un-Islam
Jihad	Righteous struggle, all-out effort
Khalq	Creation, nature
Khilafah	Vicegerency, stewardship, caliphate, guardianship
Kitab	Book, scripture, revelation, law, writing
Kufr	Ungratefulness, denial of God's mercy
Madraba	Sharing, equal participation
Maut	Death, transition, inevitability
Nafs	Individual soul, human person
Niyyah	Intention, commitance
Qalam	Pen, knowledge, reason, intellect, civil authority
Qibla	Cardinal point, point of convergence, reference
Qiyas	Analogy, deduction

Riba	Unearned income, superfluous riches
Risalah	The Message and Mission of the Prophet
Sabr	Patience, fortitude, dependence on God
Shahadah	Testimony, martyrdom, attestation (of the Ultimate Truth)
Shariah	The Normative Code of Islam
Shirk	Denial of Unity, antithesis of *tawhid*
Shukr	Gratefulness, acceptance of God's mercy
Shura	Consultation, debate, assembly
Sunnah	Pattern, model, paradigm, tradition
Taubah	Repentence, return
Tafsir	Exegesis, explanation, interpretation
Tasawwuf	The Internal Way, the path of personal development
Tawhid	Affirmation of Unity, the cardinal Islamic concept
Tazkiyah	Social welfare through *zakah*, development through purification
Thawab	Moral recompense, reward
Ummah	Muslim body-politic, the totality of *Muslim* reality (as opposed to the *Islamic* reality), the Ultimate Community based on faith
Urf	Custom, legal precedent
Usul	Principles, primary disciplines
Waqf	Public welfare institution
Yaqin	The certainty of faith
Zakah	Economic obligation, institution of alms tax
Zulm	Injustice, tyranny, oppression

A primary task without which all future work will be hampered is the development of a contemporary theory of Islamic epistemology. Epistemology, or theory of knowledge, is in fact nothing more than an expression of a world-view. All great Muslim scholars of the 'Golden Age' devoted their talents and time to this task: for epistemology permeates all aspects of individual, societal and civilizational behaviour.[8] Without a distinct epistemology, a distinct civilization is impossible. Without a way of knowing, that is identifiably Islamic, we can neither elaborate the world-view of Islam nor put an Islamic stamp on contemporary issues. For the Muslim scholars of the past, an Islamic civilization was inconceivable with a fully-fledged epistemology; hence their preoccupation with the classification of knowledge. Without the same concern among contemporary Muslim scholars and intellectuals, there is little hope of a Muslim civilization of the future.

Why is epistemology so important? It is vital because it is the major operator which transforms the vision of a world-view into reality. When we think about the nature of knowledge, what we are doing is indirectly reflecting on the principles according to which society is organized. Epistemology and societal structures feed on each other: when we structure knowledge, we tacitly manipulate images of society; when we develop and erect social, economic, political, scientific and technological structures, we are taking cue from our conception of knowledge.[9] This is why the Islamic concept of knowledge, *ilm*, is so central to the Muslim civilization.

What reasons can one give for the intimate connection between epistemology and society? The answer is deceptively simple. When people think about common problems or speculate about social and political concerns, the material they use are ideas, mental images or representations of what they perceive may (or may not) exist in the world around us. Their perceptions, and hence their ideas and mental images, are shaped by epistemology. This becomes obvious when rival claims to provide knowledge are offered by different social groups such as institutionalized religion and structured mysticism, the scientist and the layman, the specialist and the generalist, the powerful and the weak, the established and the dissenting. Indeed, there are many intuitive connections between epistemology and society. Knowledge has to be gathered, selected, organized, sustained, transmitted and disseminated. These are all processes visibly at work in established institutions: the banks, the laboratories, the school, the religious seminary. The mind thus registers an unconscious connection between social institutions and knowledge; and by extension, between knowledge and authority and power. The connection between epistemology and society cannot be emphasized more.

For some reason, thinking about the nature of knowledge in Western societies has been an abstract and obscure endeavour: it has led the Western philosophers to a paralysis of mind. But as the history of Islam demonstrates so clearly, issues of Islamic epistemology are pragmatic issues; and we need to develop a highly pragmatic, contemporary epistemology of Islam. Classical scholars like al-Ghazzali, al-Baruni, al-Farabi, al-Khwarizmi *et al.* have laid a solid foundation for a practical epistemology of Islam. Their work has to be dragged from history and given a dynamic, modern form. It is one of the most urgent tasks awaiting the attention of Muslim scholars.

The Shariah, or Islamic law, too, is a pragmatic concern. Shariah, rather than theology, has been the main contribution of Muslim civilization to human development. Like epistemology, the Shariah touches every aspect of Muslim society; it is law and ethics rolled into one. As Parvez Manzoor says,

> all contradictions of *internalised* ethics and *externalised* law, of concealed intentions and revealed actions are resolved in the all-embracing actionalism of Shariah because it is both a *doctrine* and a *path*. It is simultaneously a manifestation of divine will and that of human resolve to be an agent of that will. It is *eternal* (anchored in God's revelation) and *temporal* (enacted in human history); stable (Qur'an and Sunnah) and dynamic (*ijma* and *ijtihad*); *Din* (religion) and *Muamalah* (social interaction); divine gift and human prayer all at once. It is the very basis of the religion itself: to be Muslim is to accept the injunctions of Shariah.[10]

Yet, we have allowed such a paramount and all-pervasive manifestation of the Islamic world-view to become nothing more than an ossified body of dos and don'ts. Without a deep and detailed contemporary and futuristic understanding of the Shariah. Muslim societies cannot hope to solve their local, national and international problems. The belief that the four classical schools of Islamic law have solved all societal problems is dangerously naive. We need to go *beyond* the classical Hanafi, Maliki, Shafi'i, Hanbali and Jafari schools and build a contemporary structure on the foundations laid down by earlier jurists. What is needed is not re-working of the classical works in the realm of prayer and ritual, personal and social relations, marriage and divorce, dietary laws and rules of fasting: these have been taken care of admirably. What is needed is the *extension* of the Shariah into contemporary domains such as environment and urban planning, science policy and technology assessment, community participation and rural development. In many instances this amounts to reactivating hitherto dormant Shariah concepts and institutions and giving them a contemporary life. For example, the Shariah injunctions about water laws need to be studied from the perspective of modern environmental problems and such Shariah institutions as *harim* (inviolate zones of easement), *hima* (public reserves) and *hisbah* (office of public inspection) have to be given a living form.

Moreover, the Shariah needs to be extended beyond law and turned into a dynamic problem-solving methodology. Most jurists would agree that the chief sources of the Shariah are the Qur'an, the Sunnah, or the authentic traditions of the Prophet Mohammad; *ijma* or the consensus of opinion; and *qiyas*, or judgement upon juristic analogy. The supplementary sources of the Shariah as *istihsan*, that is prohibiting or permitting a thing because it serves a 'useful purpose'; *istislah* or public interest; and *urf* or custom and practice of a society. Classical jurists used *ijma*, *qiyas*, *istihsan*, *istislah* and *urf* as methods of solving practical problems.[11] It is indeed tragic that their followers have abandoned the methods and followed the actual juristic rulings despite the fact that their benefits were obviously limited to a particular historic situation. The blind following of these rulings, *taqlid*, has not only turned the body of the Shariah into a fossilized canon but now threatens to suffocate the very civilization of Islam. Elevating the pronouncements of classical jurists into eternal principles and rules is not only insulting to the Shariah, it is detrimental to the Muslim societies as well. The reconstruction of Muslim civilization begins by setting the Shariah free from this suffocating hold and giving it the status it truly deserves in the Muslim civilization: a dynamic problem-solving *methodology* which touches every aspect of human endeavour.

We now come to the four external manifestations of the Islamic *weltanschauung*. For each of the four petals of the flower that represents the Muslim civilization—political and social structures, economic enterprise, science and technology, and environment—the theoretical basis is provided by Islamic epistemology, the methodological guidelines by the Shariah, and the conceptual matrix of the world-view of Islam gives us the basic working materials, that is concepts and ideas. All four areas have received attention in modern Islamic literature: political theory and economics for almost thirty years now; science, technology and environment have only recently begun to be studied from the Islamic perspective. Thus, there is plenty of original scholarship here to build upon and to streamline within a civilizational framework.

Islamic economics, in particular, has developed considerably in the last decade. However, much of modern work in Islamic economics has been descriptive; and most of it has been trapped in Western epistemological concerns and economic framework. Indeed, with the sole exception of Nawab Haider Naqvi's *Ethics and Economics: An Islamic Synthesis*,[12] works on Islamic economics have used description (excessive in the work of Nejatullah Siddiqui)[13] and reduction (overdone in the writings of Monzer Kahf)[14] as the dominant methods. Moreover, Islamic economics has developed as a 'discipline' (a shadow of Western economics, perhaps?) and not as an integrated field destined to become a pillar of the Muslim civilization. Note that Nejatullah Siddiqui's Faisal Prize-winning book, *Muslim Economic Thinking: A Survey of Contemporary Literature*[15] does not contain a single citation linking economics to political theory, science and technology or the environment. Considering that technology is the backbone of modern economics, information a prime commodity, environmental degradation a major outcome, it is indeed surprising that the advocates of Islamic ecnomics are silent on these issues. The atomized development of Islamic economics as a unitary discipline, an obsessive concern of Western epistemology, has relegated it to a marginalized existence. Perhaps this is an unfair criticism. But the fact remains that any major advances in Islamic economics can only be made if it becomes a truly interdisciplinary field of endeavour pursued within a civilizational framework.

Much the same criticism can be made of the recent works on Islamic political structures and social organizations. Many of the writings here are trapped in the mould cast by the nation-state and such concepts of Western political theory as nationalism, democracy, socialism, bureaucracy and the like. Such works as *The Nature of Islamic State* by M. Hadi Hussain and A. H. Kamali[16] beg the obvious question: is Islam a state? Is the nation-state the only expression of an Islamic polity? When it comes to the issue of governance, Muslim political scientists reveal themselves to be true victims of history: only monarchy or Caliphat (best exemplified by Maulana Maududi's, as yet untranslated but controversial urdu treatise, *Caliphat or Mulakiat* (Caliphate or Kingship?))[18] appear to be the viable options: in the vast universe of ideas that is Islam, is there no other method of governance? Apart from political theory, social structures have also received little interdisciplinary attention. Only Syed Qutb seems to have realized that social exploitation is a dominant theme in Muslim society (an excellent treatment of which is to be found in his *Social Justice in Islam*).[19] The related issues of population and urban decay, the blatant exploitation of women, community development and cultural awareness are conspicuously absent from the social analysis of modern Muslim writers.

Both in the fields of political and social structures and economics we need interdisciplinary theories, models and methodologies which synthesize these fields with Islamic epistemology and the *Shariah* as well as with other external expressions of the world-view of Islam: science and technology and the environment.

Very little has been written about the environmental perspective of Islam. However, the few works on the subject are of exceptionally good quality and concentrate on conceptual analysis. For example, various papers of Othman Llewellyn on 'Desert reclamation and Islamic law'[20] (one of which appeared in the *Muslim Scientist*, **11** (1), 9–30 (1982)) and Parvez Manzoor's 'Environment and Values: The Islamic Perspective'[21] provide good indication that a totally contemporary, conceptual as well as pragmatic Islamic theory of environment can be developed relatively easily, and translated into pragmatic policy statements. Similarly, Waqar Ahmad Husaini's attempt to develop a modern theory of *Islamic Environmental Systems Engineering*,[22] although deeply flawed, proves that the conceptual matrix of the world-view of Islam can be fruitfully used for analytical purposes.

Science and technology, on the other hand, have not fared so well. In this field, the hold of Western epistemology and social models on the minds of Muslim scientists and technologists is almost total. The link between what purports to be a scientific 'fact' and epistemology is not easy to grasp. The point that 'scientific facts' are not something we can take for granted or think of as solid rocks upon which knowledge is built is, to a modern scientist working in Western paradigms, slightly mind-boggling. The epistemological and methodological point is that facts, like cows, have been domesticated to deal with run-of-the-mill events. Hence, the connection between facts and values is not always obvious; and the notion that knowledge is manufactured and not discovered is not appreciated by many Muslim scientists. Thus, the bulk of the literature on 'Islam and science' is pretty naive; and some works like Maurice Bucaille's *The Bible, the Quran and Science*,[23] are highly dangerous (what can be proved by science and also be disproved by the same science; where does that leave the Qur'an).

However, some constructive, conceptual studies, within a civilizational framework, have recently appeared on Islamic science. For example, Munawar Ahmad Anees' attempts to show that both reduction *per se* and modern bio-engineering[24] raise serious questions of values for Muslim societies, and the work of various scholars attached to the 'Science in Islamic Polity' unit of the National Science Foundation of Pakistan, and writers at the Centre for Science Studies in Aligarh, indicate that serious attention is being given to this area.

In Part Two, I discuss in some detail, from a futuristic and civilizational perspective, the work that is being done and that which needs to be done on the seven major challenges which together constitute the process of reconstruction of the Muslim civilization. My main thesis in this chapter has been that Muslim societies have to think and study their future not in terms of a resurgence, but a planned and continuous process of reconstruction of their civilization. This process does not involve 'Islamizing' this or that discipline, but casting the external expressions of Muslim civilization in the epistomology of Islam and the methodology of the Shariah. It involves elaborating the world-view of Islam and using the conceptual matrix that is at the heart of the Qur'an and the Sunnah. The mental outlook of this process is based on synthesis and interdisciplinarity. What relevance is there of Islamic economics without a viable, contemporary Islamic polity? Or of an Islamic science which does not shape the environment according to the dictates of the Shariah? Thus, the world-view of Islam has to be extended within a framework that emphasizes that relationships exist between all theoretical and physical manifestations of Muslim civilization. It is an outlook that does not confine Islamic epistemology or the Shariah to particular areas, but combines future consciousness with open-mindedness and a spirit of adventure and discovery.

The process of restructuring the Muslim civilization is something that is not learnt; it is discovered and practised as the fruits of continual transformation, while systematically working towards finer and finer synthesis. This process is rather like giving form to the act of living itself: breathing epistemological consciousness to every act of life which is itself part of a larger effort of converting facts into values, actions into purposes, hopes and plans into consummation and realizations, so eventually the *ummah* itself becomes a living, dynamic, thriving civilization. It is therefore not only a question of research and study: it is a process of making and shaping the Muslim himself as the work of art the process ultimately seeks to transform.

Notes

1. Published as a pamphlet by the Muslim Youth Movement of Malaysia, Kuala Lumpur, 1976; and included in his *Islam, Secularism and the Philosophy of the Future*, Mansell, London, 1985.

2. In Ziauddin Sardar (ed.), *The Touch of Midas*, Manchester University Press, 1984.

3. On this theme, *see* the excellent work of B. Dar, *Qur'anic Ethics*, Institute of Islamic Culture, Lahore, 1960.

4. A case in point is *Christian Mission and Islamic Dawah*, Islamic Foundation, Leicester, 1982, in which both sides try to patronize each other and generally avoid crucial issues of power and territory.

5. Some contemporary Shai scholars are moving towards a Shai-Sunni

synthesis. For example, Hamid Enayat, *Modern Islamic Political Thought*, Macmillan, London, 1982, takes pains to show the convergence of Shi'i and Sunni political thought and on the debate on the nature of Islamic state.

6. London, 1933–54.

7. Ibn Khaldun, *The Muqaddimah*, translated by Franz Rosenthal, Routledge and Kegan Paul, London, 1967.

8. For al-Ghazzali's classification of knowledge, *see* his *Book of Knowledge*, translated by Nabih Amin Faris, Ashraf, Lahore, 1962. For ibn Khaldun's approach to knowledge, *see The Muqaddimah*, *op. cit.* Both have been admirably discussed in some detail by Waqar Ahmed Husaini. *Islamic Environmental Systems Engineering*, Macmillan, London, 1980, chapter 3. Seyyed Hossein Nasr, *Science and Civilization in Islam*, Harvard University Press, Cambridge, Massachusetts, 1968, provides a good general introduction to Muslim classifications of knowledge (chapter two). F. Rosenthal, *Knowledge Triumphant*, Brill, Leiden, 1970, discusses numerous definitions and classification schemes.

9. For a detailed discussion of the connection between epistemology and society, *see* David Bloor, *Knowledge and Social Imagery*, Routledge and Kegan Paul, London, 1976.

10. Parvez Manzoor, 'Environment and Values: The Islamic Perspective', in Ziauddin Sardar, *The Touch of Midas*, *op. cit.*, p. 157.

11. *See* Said Ramadan, *Islamic Law: Its Scope and Equity*, Geneva, 1970; Muhammad Khalid Masud, *Islamic Legal Philosophy*, Islamic Research Institute, Islamabad, 1977; and Anwar Ahmad Qadri, *Islamic Jurisprudence in the Modern World*, Ashraf, Lahore, 1973.

12. Islamic Foundation, Leicester, 1981.

13. *See* his *Banking Without Interest*, Islamic Foundation, Leicester, 1983; and *Issues in Islamic Banking*, Islamic Foundation, Leicester, 1983.

14. *See* his *The Islamic Economy*, MSA, Plainsfield, Indiana, 1978.

15. Islamic Foundation, Leicester, 1981.

16. National Book Foundation, Karachi, 1977.

18. Delhi, 1967.

19. Octagon Books, New York, 1971.

20. This paper has appeared in a number of forms in several places. *See The Muslim Scientist*, **11** (1), 9–30 (1982); and *Journal of Research in Islamic Economics*, **1** (2), 25–50 (1984).

21. *Op. cit.*

22. Macmillan, London, 1980.

23. American Trust Publications, Indianapolis, 1981.

24. 'Islamic Values and Western Science: A Case Study of Reproductive Biology', in Ziauddin Sardar (ed.), *The Touch of Midas*, *op. cit.*

Part Two

The Shape of Ideas to Come

4

Rediscovering the Epistemology of Islam

Epistemology, or theory of knowledge, is the central core of any world-view. It is the parameter which delineates what is and what is not possible within the purview of Islam: what is possible to know and ought to be known, what is possible to know but is better avoided, and what is simply not possible to know. Epistemology seeks to define knowledge, distinguish its principal varieties, identify its sources and establish its limits. 'What can we know, and how do we know?' are questions central to epistemology. But these are not merely philosophical questions. They have a strong bearing in concrete reality: the response to these questions has implications for every aspect of human activity; the kind of society we build is a direct outcome of this response.

Indeed, the Qur'anic concept of *ilm*, commonly translated as 'knowledge', originally shaped the main features of Muslim civilization and guided it towards its zenith.[1] Then, as it should be now, *ilm* shaped the Muslim mode of thought and inquiry. It determines how Muslims can best perceive reality and shape and develop a just society. *Ilm* is the glue that binds the *Muslim society* with its *environment*, hence giving Islam a dynamic, living form. However, while the scholars and intellectuals of the classical period recognized that *ilm* was the concept on which rested the very foundations of the Muslim civilization, and that it was an all-pervasive *value*, contemporary scholars, both modernists and traditionalists, are largely oblivious to the key role that epistemology plays in shaping a society.[2]

The neglect of epistemology in contemporary Muslim writings and the consequent lack of appreciation of the true significance of the concept and value of *ilm*, is largely a result of a dominant way of knowing that has assumed a universal role. The epistemology of Western civilization has now become a dominant mode of thought and inquiry to the exclusion of other, alternative ways of knowing. Hence, the totality of Muslim societies, indeed the planet as a whole, is being shaped in the image of Western man.

This epistemological imperialism has deep roots going back over 300 years. Its origins lie in the beginnings of the European colonial adventure and the emergence of scientific rationality as the only legitimate method for understanding and controlling nature. It is the epistemology of modern science which characterizes the way in which individuals in industrialized societies think about their world, seek to know, understand and control it. This epistemology emphasizes the distinction between objective and subjective, between the observer and an external world, between subjective states of emotion and a 'reality' which lies outside the observer and which can be known only by observation and reason. The dichotomy between 'facts' and 'values', 'objective reality' and 'subjective emotions' is a main characteristic of the epistemology of modern science. It is a way of knowing that contrasts sharply from that which is prevalent in many societies where knowledge and wisdom are seen as residing in a state of inner consciousness. The dominant method of inquiry produced by Western epistemology is reduction: the true nature of reality is 'discovered' by digging deeper and deeper beneath the surface to analyse the forces and structure underlying appearances. The success of reduction and the epistemology of modern science lies in its pragmatic value. It has yielded knowledge which can be checked with reference to a separate reality and which has brought unimagined dividends for mankind.

However, the epistemology of modern science has also produced some bitter fruits. Its insistence on rejecting all considerations of value from the pursuit of knowledge means that it treats its object of inquiry (both human and non-human) as mere stuff that can be exploited, manipulated, dissected and generally abused in the name of science. Its overall emphasis on control and domination has produced an ecological crisis that threatens to destroy the very abode of man's terrestrial journey.[3] Its methodology has reduced science to an endless process of solving problems, of freezing or 'fixing' a subject for study and of placing it at a 'distance' to evaluate. In its more extreme forms, for example in biological reductionism, it has become what Fromm calls necrophilia, the passion to kill so as to freeze and love. That science is inescapably linked to repression and domination is no accident: it is a direct product of a rationalistic epistemology, just as Newton, Darwin, Freud, B. F. Skinner and Edward Wilson are the product of the same epistemology. Social Darwinism, sociobiology, stockpiles of nuclear weapons that could destroy the earth several times are a logical outcome of the epistemology of instrumental rationality. Positive knowledge allows no escape: it yields inexorable laws and imperatives with no place for human will or values.

This pathological epistemology has now become the basis of Occidental civilization. Moreover, as it pursues its quest to control nature and understand reality with more and more vigour, it takes an even more frightening pathological shape. In the mid-nineteenth century, Darwin proposed a theory of natural selection and evolution in which the unit of survival was either the family line or the strongest species or sub-species. Today, sociobiologists are suggesting that the inequalities of wealth and power, violence and aggression, competitiveness and xenophobia, far from being socially and politically determined, are merely the inevitable products of the human genome and the process of biological evolution. Weapons of terror and destruction, end-products of some three-quarters of research and development work in modern science, have lost all sense of reality: they continue to get more destructive, more accurate, more lethal, more lasting in their destructive impact. There seems no end to the incessant epistemological madness.

More radical Western scholars are well aware of the problems of the epistemology of Western science. The confession of Gregory Bateson is typical of the attitudes of concerned thinkers:

> It is clear now to many people that there are many catastrophic dangers which have grown out of the Occidental errors of epistemology. These range from insecticides to pollution, to atomic fallout, to the

possibility of melting the Antarctic ice cap. Above all, our fantastic compulsion to save individual lives has created the possibility of world famine in the immediate future.

Perhaps we have an even chance of getting through the next twenty years with no disaster more serious than the mere destruction of a nation or group of nations.

I believe that this massive aggregation of threats to man and his ecological systems arises out of errors in our habits of thought at deep and partly unconscious levels.[4]

However, the awareness that there are serious faults in Western epistemology is not altogether new. The theory of Objective Knowledge, as developed by such diverse figures as Descarte and Popper, has been under attack for over 200 years. What makes a piece of knowledge 'objective' is decided by a set of criteria; and it is this 'criteria of objectivity' which has been systematically attacked, most notably by David Hume and, more recently, by T. S. Kuhn.

What is the criteria of objectivity? Essentially, for a piece of knowledge to be accepted as objective in Western epistemology, it must have five basic features. Robert Brownhill describes these as follows:

1. The knowledge must refer to a reality which is separate from ourselves, and this entails that a distinction has to be drawn between what the world is and what we happen to say about it. All of us could believe a certain thing about reality but we could all be mistaken, as our beliefs cannot change reality. Likewise it is possible for a certain person to have a belief about reality which is in conflict with all other people's beliefs but if his belief coincides with what reality is then his belief is correct.

2. As there is an independent reality we can test our beliefs by reference to this reality and without this possibility of testability there can be no objectivity. For instance, Sir Karl Popper would argue that for a theory to be classed as a scientific theory it must be put in a testable form. The idea here is that nature itself is a judge of a belief's validity.

3. In referring to the objectivity of science we are talking about the ideas of science as being objective. We are concerned with theories about facts, theories about the relationship of one set of facts to

another, theories about the relationship of our beliefs to other beliefs and their relationship to the original facts. We test theories rather than for the existence of the original facts themselves. We are concerned with such things as measurement, relationship and prediction. Michael Polanyi brings out this point when he argues that scientists considered the Copernican theory to be more objective than Ptolemaic cosmology as they attributed greater objectivity to theoretical knowledge than that gained through the senses. Theoretical knowledge is not tied to our senses but must stand on its own feet.

4. A theory must be able to stand on its own feet like a map with its own independent status and rationality. The objective status of a theory has nothing to do with our commitment to it, as our own personal tastes are irrelevant to its truth. For instance, a person who gets lost when he correctly follows a map will attribute the mistake to the map and not to himself. The point being that in the case of a scientific theory it is not the person putting forward the theory who is proved wrong when the theory fails but the theory. In order to achieve this status of independence a theory must have an explicitness as a system of rules, which is separate from sense experience. Ideally it should be in a mathematical form which can be understood by and demand acceptance from other rational beings.

5. This brings out another aspect of an objective theory. It has to have public communicability so that we can understand it whatever our location or situation. It should not depend on our own situation but be an independent form of public knowledge. Polanyi again indicates this when he points out that the Ptolemaic system depended for its rationality on our earthbound situation but the Copernican system commended itself to dwellers on any planet.[5]

In his *Treatise on Human Nature*, Hume attacked this criteria vigorously and questioned the justification of postulating a world outside ourselves, or indeed a self for it to be outside (as against a mere set of experiences).[6] He declared that repetition has no power whatever as an argument, although it plays a key role in our 'understanding' of things. Indeed, Hume was convinced that reason and arguments play only a small role in our understanding; knowledge was nothing more than belief which could not be defended.

More recently, Kuhn has taken the arguments further to a position where any objective stance is completely denied. Kuhn's work, based on the examination of the role of discovery in the history of science, suggests that scientists work within belief systems or paradigms from which they seldom depart.[7] Science is essentially problem-solving within paradigms. Nature does not describe itself: it does not perform according to mathematical formulae and equations. It is the scientists who give meaning to her messages by determining how they should be fitted into existing concepts and beliefs, and how far our existing concepts and beliefs should be modified and extended to accommodate them. In other words, there is no relevant difference between 'theoretical' and 'factual' concepts in science: both kinds of concept are our *inventions*. The consensus among scientists about the paradigm within which they operate is the basis of *normal science*. The manufacture of modern scientific knowledge—including its pedagogy and training, research and development, and new discoveries—all takes place within normal science. In agreeing upon a paradigm, scientists do not accept a finished product: rather, they have agreed on a basis for future work and to ignore all apparent inadequacies of the paradigm. In normal science, paradigms are refined and elaborated and used for the development of further problems and solutions. Where attempts to find a solution fails, or the evidence does not fit the paradigm, it is the scientist, or the apparatus, or simply misfortune, that must take the blame: to blame the paradigm itself would mean a break with normal science. Although scientists often claim that their concepts and theories in some sense apply to the whole of nature, what they effectively do within normal science is actively to arrange phenomena under concepts, instance by instance. It is the activity of normal science that gives concepts significance, not the inherent significance of concepts that determines the activity. Thus the scientist is constructing reality to fit preconceived notions.

Breaks with normal science, however, do sometmes occur. This happens when the paradigm itself ceases to pose interesting questions and anomalies are discovered that resist all attempts to incorporate them within the accepted framework. A crisis begins to develop within normal science which can reach a stage where certain scientists are forced to question the paradigm itself. Alternative paradigms mushroom which threaten to cast much of the work done under normal science into oblivion: this is revolutionary science. But the period of revolutionary science is short-lived as eventually an alternative paradigm becomes dominant and the whole process of normal science is repeated.

However, the new paradigm that becomes dominant is not selected on a purely objective basis. Its selection is not free from personal influence, partisan considerations, social outlooks of the scientists. Kuhn believes that in the last analysis there is no unambiguous scientific test that enables individual scientists to choose between competing scientists. Thus, in Kuhn's epistemology, an objective, value-free, neutral science does not exist.

Kuhn's arguments have been taken a step further by Paul Feyerabend.[8] He argues that competing paradigms are chosen, as indeed preference for one scientific theory over another is made, on the basis of purely aesthetic appreciation. So what theory one supports, what paradigm one fights for, simply depends on one's taste!

Attacks on Western epistemology from within the scientific community—particularly from Whitehead,[9] Kuhn, Polanyi,[10] Feyerabend, Mitroff[11] and Ravetz[12]—has opened up a debate on alternative epistemologies and non-Western styles of thought. Criticism from outside the scientific community—notably by Roszak,[13] Nasr[14] and Illich[15]—has shown that viable alternatives are indeed available (Fig. 3).

The Islamization of Knowledge

On the whole, the Muslim reactions to Western epistemological imperialism has been slow. Considering the strong tradition of epistemological criticism in classical Islam—almost every renowned scholar of this period produced a classification of knowledge and elaborated the concept of value of *ilm*—this is rather surprising. In the sixties and early seventies, Syed Hossein Nasr was the sole scholar who presented an overtly Sufi perspective, in such works as *Encounter of Man and Nature*, on the crisis of epistemology in Western civilization. In the last ten years, however, a more concerted effort has been made to rediscover the major elements of an Islamic epistemology.

	Objective	Subjective
	Reductionist	*Sensate*
Separation	analysis (linear, deductive)	mysticism
	cognition	sensation
	properties of parts explain whole	reality of inner world of mind: consciousness determines existence
	mediation of measuring instruments	opening mind to direct consciousness
	quantitative	
	abstract thought	escape from constraints of external world
	universal laws	
	Holist	*Romantic*
Integration	synthesis (lateral, inductive)	intuition
	cognition	understanding
	whole is greater than sum of parts	integration of thought and feeling, fact and value
	models and analogues	immediate experience
	quantitative	qualitative
	abstract thought	concrete examples
	universal laws	unique instances

Figure 3. *Some Styles of Thought*   Source: Stephen Cotgrove, *Catastrophe or Cornucopia?*, Wiley, Chichester, 1982.

This effort centres around the issue of 'Islamization' of knowledge. Two notable scholars have made a distinctive contribution to the field, Syed Mohammad al-Naquib al-Attas and Ismail Raji al-Faruqi.

In his paper 'The Dewesternisation of Knowledge', al-Attas has produced one of the most devastating criticism of Western epistemology.[16] He argues that the *all-pervasive* scepticism, which knows no ethical and value boundaries, of the Western system of knowledge is the antithesis of Islamic epistemology. Now, al-Attas is not arguing against doubt and scepticism *per se*; indeed, he agrees with the celebrated Muslim philosopher and epistemologist al-Ghazzali (d. 1111), who said that 'nobody really believes until he has doubted' and that healthy scepticism is essential for intellectual progress. He is arguing against a framework of knowledge that sacrifices social and cultural values at the altar of scepticism.

> It seems to be important to emphasize that knowledge is not neutral, and can indeed be infused with a nature and content that masquerades as knowledge. Yet it is in fact, taken as a whole, not true knowledge but its interpretation through the prism, as it were, the world-view, the intellectual vision and psychological perception of the civilization that now plays the key role in its formulation and dissemination. What is formulated and disseminated is knowledge infused with the character and personality of that civilization—knowledge presented and conveyed as knowledge in that guise so subtly fused together with the real so that others take it unaware *in toto* to be the real knowledge *per se*.[17]

Al-Attas, in common with other contemporary Muslim critics of Western epistemology, identifies the values of the Enlightenment, the seventeenth-century French philosophical movement, as the root values of modern science and technology. He admits that Islam made a very significant contribution, at the early stage of its evolution, to Western science and technology, 'but the knowledge and the rational scientific spirit have been recast and remoulded to fit the crucible of Western culture so that they have become fused and amalgamated with all the other elements that form the character and personality of Western civilization'.[18]

This fusion and amalgamation has produced a characteristic dualism in the world-view and values of the Occidental system of knowledge: 'a dualism that cannot be resolved into a harmonious unity, for it is formed of conflicting ideas, values, cultures, beliefs, philosophies, dogmas, doctrines and theologies altogether reflecting an all-pervasive dualistic vision of reality and truth locked in despairing combat'.[19] This dualism has produced an eternal inner tension in Western culture and civilization, which in turn produces the insatiable desire to seek and embark on a perpetual journey of discoveries. 'The quest is insatiable and the journey perpetual because doubt ever prevails, so that what is sought is never really found, what is discovered never really satisfied its true purpose.'[20] 'Change', 'development' and 'progress', al-Attas asserts, are results of this insatiable quest and perpetual journey spurred on by doubt and inner tension.

The essence of al-Attas's argument is this: working within the Occidental system of knowledge, Muslim scholars and scientists can only promote the values and inner tensions of Western culture and civilization. Such a body of scholarship and science cannot really serve the needs of Muslim societies or indeed take social root within the Muslim world.

Al-Faruqi has taken the whole process several steps forward by suggesting a systematic plan for discovering a contemporary epistemology of Islam. His programme for the Islamization of knowledge is the result of several years of effort as well as debate and discussion of a number of international seminars that he organized. *Islamisation of Knowledge*[21] presents a step-by-step process for Islamizing knowledge.

Al-Faruqi argues that the 'malaise of the ummah' can only be cured by an epistemological injection. The task before the ummah is to solve the problem of education:

There can be no hope of a genuine revival of the ummah unless the educational system is revamped and its faults corrected. Indeed, what is needed is for the system to be formed anew. The present dualism in Muslim education, its bifurcation into an Islamic and secular system must be removed and abolished once and for all. The two systems must be united and integrated; and the emergent system must be infused with the spirit of Islam and function as an integral part of its ideological program.[22]

Moreover, Muslim youth should be instilled with the vision of Islam by introducing compulsory study of Islamic civilization. Numerous other Muslim scholars have made the similar point, and in some cases much more strongly than al-Faruqi. But it is in the 'Islamization of modern knowledge', which is part of the whole scheme of 'revamping' the Muslim educational system, that al-Faruqi's contribution comes to the fore:

> The task of Islamizing knowledge (in concrete terms, to Islamize the disciplines, or better, to produce university level textbooks recasting some twenty disciplines in accordance with the Islamic vision) is also the most difficult. No Muslim has yet contemplated it enough to discern its prerequisites, or to articulate its constitutive steps and measures. All that our previous reformers had thought of was to acquire the knowledge and power of the West. They were not even aware of the conflict of Western knowledge with the vision of Islam. It is our present generation that first discovered the conflict as we lived it in our own intellectual lives. But the spiritual torture the conflict has inflicted upon us caused us to wake up in panic, fully aware of the rape of the Islamic soul taking place before our very eyes in the Muslim universities.[23]

Al-Faruqi, then, wants nothing less than to 'recast the whole legacy of human knowledge from the standpoint of Islam'. He offers a methodology and a programme of action to do just this.

Unfortunately, al-Faruqi's methodology amounts to very little. He prefers to describe only the 'first principles' of his methodology and these are essentially pious statements of belief. Saying that Islam asserts the unity of God, His creation and mankind hardly sheds new light on the vast array of methodological problems that confront the Muslim scholars. The one interesting statement of al-Faruqi's 'first principles' is not really developed enough to provide guidance in the thorny terrace of the epistemological landscape. This concerns the assertion of 'the unity of Truth and the unity of Knowledge'. If 'Truth' and 'Knowledge' are indeed one and the same, as many Muslim scholars apart from al-Faruqi have argued, then we are in trouble. As most self-respecting scientists will admit, there is a great deal of knowledge that could easily be proved false in the near future. If 'knowledge' is 'truth', then the pursuit of knowledge is the pursuit of truth. So is one chasing truth while researching the techniques of torture, seeking new ways of making anthrax and more and more sophisticated weapons of mass destruction, for it is all knowledge, and useful knowledge for those who desire it? And even 'truth' does not come in singular units: what is true in the behaviour of a light photon as a wave or as a particle? Both are manifestations of reality which al-Faruqi also equates with truth. Al-Faruqi asserts that if God is *Al-Haqq* ('the truth'), which is one of the names of Allah, and if God is indeed God, as Islam affirms, then the truth cannot be many. But the argument is not quite correct: if God is the Absolute Truth, then it follows that there is only one Absolute Truth. It does not necessarily follow that 'truth cannot be many'. Indeed, the entire spectrum of modern physics is full of 'truths' some of which are logically inconsistent, relativity and quantum mechanics being the obvious examples.

But the real point is that the sort of arguments which seeks to equate truth, knowledge and reality are superfluous and do not help us in developing a pragmatic epistemology. Indeed, to claim that the purpose of knowledge is to seek the truth, while noble, is basically misleading. In its original form, this propensity for simplistic, linear, teleological reasoning is a mere extension of the naivete of the child who asks 'what are the trees for?' and is answered 'the trees are to provide shelter from the sun', or 'to decorate the footpaths', or 'to provide us with mangoes'. Voltaire captured the quality of this egocentricism when he had Pangloss observe that noses were obviously made for spectacles in this best of all possible worlds.

Al-Faruqi's workplan for the Islamization of knowledge has five objectives:

(1) To master the modern disciplines.
(2) To master the Islamic legacy.
(3) To establish the specific relevance of Islam to each area of modern knowledge.
(4) To seek ways for creative synthesis between the legacy and modern knowledge.
(5) And to launch Islamic thought on the trajectory which leads it to fulfillment of the divine pattern of Allah.[24]

These objectives are to be achieved by twelve systematic steps which would eventually lead to the Islamization of knowledge.

Step 1: Mastery of the modern disciplines. Al-Faruqi asserts that modern disciplines have to be broken down into categories, principles, methodologies, problems and themes—the breakdown reflecting the 'table of contents' of the classical textbook.

Step 2: Discipline survey: once the categories of the disciplines have been broken down, a state-of-the-art survey should be written on each discipline. This is necessary to ensure that Muslim scholars have mastered each discipline.

Step 3: Mastery of the Islamic legacy. Islamic legacy has to be mastered in the same way. But here what is needed is anthologies on the Muslim heritage pertaining to each discipline.

Step 4: Mastery of the Islamic legacy. Once the anthologies are prepared, the Islamic legacy has to be analysed from the perspective of the problems of the present.

Step 4: Establishment of the specific relevance of Islam to the disciplines. This relevance, asserts al-Faruqi, can be established by posing three questions:

> The first is, what did the legacy of learning, from the Qur'an to the modernists, contribute to the whole range of issues envisaged by the discipline? The second is, how does the Islamic legacy's contribution to the discipline compare or contrast with the achievement of the discipline? Where has the legacy fulfilled, fallen short of, or transcended the vision and scope of the discipline? The third is, given the areas or issues in which the Islamic legacy has given little or nothing, in which direction may Muslim effort be henceforth exerted in order to fill the discrepancy, to reformulate the problem, to enlarge the vision?[25]

Step 6: Critical assessment of the modern discipline. Once the relevance of Islam to each discipline has been made, it should be assessed and analysed from the standpoint of Islam.

Step 7: Critical assessment of the Islamic legacy. Similarly, Islamic legacy's contribution in each field of human activity must be analysed and its contemporary relevance discovered.

Step 8: Survey of the ummah's major problems. A systematic study must be made on the political, social, economic, intellectual, cultural, moral and spiritual problems of the Muslim people.

Step 9: Survey of the problems of mankind. A similar study, this time concentrating on the whole of humanity, should also be made.

Step 10: Creative analysis and synthesis. At this stage, Muslim scholars would be ready to synthesize the Islamic legacy and modern disciplines and to 'bridge over the gap of centuries of non-development'. From here on the legacy of Islamic learning would 'become continuous with the modern achievements and start to move the frontiers of knowledge to more distant horizons than the modern disciplines have envisaged'.

Step 11: Recasting the disciplines under the framework of Islam. Once a parity between Islamic legacy and modern disciplines has been achieved, university textbooks should be written to recast modern disciplines into Islamic moulds.

Step 12: Dissemination of Islamic knowledge. The intellectual work produced from the previous steps should be used to awaken, enlighten and enrich the humankind.

Al-Faruqi's workplan for Islamization of knowledge, summarized in Figure 4, has received considerable support: indeed, it has led to the establishment of the International Institute of Islamic Thought in Washington, devoted exclusively to implementing the twelve-step programme. In Pakistan, it has the complete backing of the newly established Islamic University in Islamabad. It is to al-Faruqi's credit that he has the vision to conceive and carry out such an ambitious, but nevertheless vital, programme. It is, therefore, rather unfortunate that his programme for the Islamization of knowledge is fundamentally flawed and somewhat naive.

Let us first examine some glaring omissions in his programme. Al-Faruqi essentially wants to 'Islamize' Western social sciences: economics, political science, sociology, psychology and anthropology. He rightly asserts that these disciplines are Eurocentric and promote the Western notions of nation-state and ethnic identity. While the world may be structured according to how

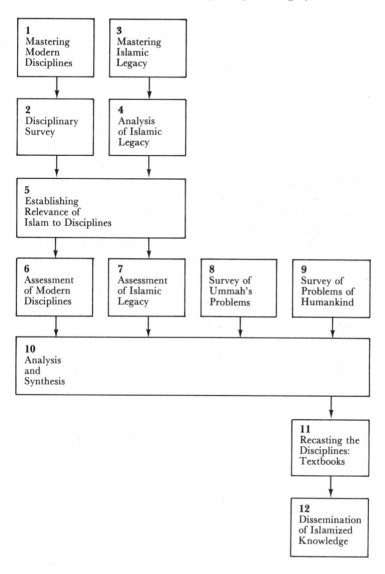

Figure 4. *Al-Faruqi's Programme for the Islamization of Knowledge*

Western social sciences perceive human reality, it is *not* main-tained and developed by them. It is science and technology that maintains the social, economic and political structures that dominate the globe. Contemporary society is being shaped by science; and scientific and technological knowledge are the prime tools of Western epistemological imperialism. Like the proverbial ostrich, al-Faruqi chooses to ignore the stark reality that it is the epistemology of Western science which has created the modern world and it is primarily this which any programme on the Islam-ization of knowledge has to tackle.

For the major part of the twentieth century, the 'criteria of objectivity' that I described above has provided the epistemologi-cal basis for both natural and social sciences. But today the pre-tence of social sciences to have anything in common with natural sciences lies exposed. In the debate on the values and objectivity in social sciences, the so-called idealist tradition is clearly sup-reme. It is now taken *a priori*: (1) that perception, rather than being conceptually neutral, is structured by both linguistic categories and the mental attitudes and interests of the observers; (2) the categories in terms of which experience is organized and, in turn, known, as well as canons of truth and validity, reflect the values and interests of different groups at different times in his-tory; and (3) that man does not encounter reality as an uninter-preted given but rather something mediated or constructed by conceptual schema (Kant), ideologies (Marx), language games (Wittgenstein) or paradigms (Kuhn). What purpose, then, is served by breathing Islamic spirit into disciplines that are shaped by other people's perceptions, concepts, ideologies, languages and paradigms? Does that constitute 'Islamization of knowledge' or the Westernization of Islam?

For a Western social scientist, his disciplinary activities are carried out within what he considers to be normal science. Any-one coming from outside, therefore, has to conform, like him, to the dominant paradigm. Otherwise the activity does not make sense to him. However, how are Muslim social scientists, who ought to be working in radically different paradigms, supposed to synthesize their disciplines with the Western social scientists? It is a synthesis of concepts, values, ideologies, languages or paradigms? These elements are not so much the point of departure but the parameters within which the arguments have their life. We can only argue from within our own world-view, and the arguments we may use will not necessarily be acceptable or understandable to a person with another world-view. Reasons that seem imperative to us are good reasons with particular commitments, and if we support an alternative paradigm, an alternative world-view, then we can only resort to persuasion.

To a very large extent the problem lies with the very notion of discipline. Disciplines, contrary to what al-Faruqi may have us believe, are not made in heaven. Neither nature nor human activities are divided into watertight compartments marked 'sociology', 'psychology' and 'political science'. Disciplines are born within the matrix of a particular world-view and are always hierarchically subordinated to that world-view. Disciplines do not have an autonomous existence of their own: they develop within a particular historical and cultural milieu and only have meaning within the world-view of their origin and evolution. The division of knowledge into various disciplines as we find today is a particular manifestation of how the Western world-view perceives reality and how the Western civilization sees its problems. For example, the discipline of orientalism evolved because Western civilization perceived Islam as a 'problem' to be studied, analysed and controlled. Thus to accept the disciplinary divisions of knowledge as they exist in Western epistemology is to make the world-view of Islam subordinate to the Western civilization.

This is certainly not what al-Faruqi seeks to achieve. But when he states that one of the objectives of his programme for the Islamization of knowledge is 'to establish the specific relevance of Islam to each area of modern knowledge', it does seem as though he is putting the cart before the horse. It is not Islam that needs to be made relevant to modern knowledge; it is modern knowledge that needs to be made relevant to Islam. Islam is *a priori* relevant for all times.

The discovery of contemporary epistemology of Islam cannot begin by focusing on already established disciplines but by developing paradigms within which the main external expressions of the Muslim civilization—science and technology, politics and international relations, social structures and economic activity, rural and urban development—can be studied and developed in relation to contemporary needs and reality. Essentially, we need two types of paradigms: knowledge paradigms and behavioural paradigms. Knowledge paradigms focus on the main principles, concepts and values of Islam pertaining to a particular field of inquiry. Behavioural paradigms determine the ethical boundaries within the scholar and the scientists can freely operate. Of course, the main body of the principles, concepts and values are to be found in the Qur'an, the life of the Beloved Prophet and the intelletual heritage of Islam. But these have to be studied from the perspective of contemporary reality.

Disciplines, like paradigms, also come in two types: disciplines as knowledge, such as mathematics, grammar, sociology and physics; and disciplines as the shaping of human behaviour—persons or groups—towards orderly self-controlled conduct such as parental rearing of children, team development for complex tasks in medicine and science, and cultural saturation process in foreign language eduction. If inquiry is pursued within fully developed Islamic paradigms, both kind of disciplines will emerge according to the needs of Muslim society. Specific needs, specific problems, specific tasks will focus the attention of scholars and scientists on specific fields of inquiry, thus generating disciplines that are both subordinate to the world-view of Islam and geared to meeting the material, cultural and spiritual needs of the *ummah*.

Thus paradigms are prerequisites for rediscovering the epistemology of Islam. Essentially, these paradigms have to emphasize the areas of knowledge that need the urgent attention of Muslim scholars and scientists, emphasize the main features of the world-view of Islam, and chalk out the moral and ethical parameters to guide disciplinary inquiry.

Classically, the epistemology of Islam has furnished Muslim scholars with just such paradigms. Islamic epistemology emphasizes the totality of experience and reality, and promotes not one but a number of diverse ways of studying nature. The concept of *ilm* incorporates almost every form of knowledge from pure observation to the highest metaphysics. Thus *ilm* can be acquired from revelation as well as reason, from observation as well as intuition, from tradition as well as theoretical speculation. While the various diverse ways of studying nature and reality are equally valid in Islam, all are subservient to the eternal values of the Qur'anic revelation. As such, Islamic epistemology emphasizes the pursuit of all forms of knowledge within the framework of eternal values which are the corner-stone of the Muslim civilization.

Besides diversity of ways of knowing, the Islamic epistemology also emphasizes interconnectedness. All forms of knowledge are interconnected and organically related by the ever-present spirit of the Qur'anic revelation. Thus, Islam does not only make the pursuit of knowledge obligatory but also connects it with the unique Islamic notion of worship: *ilm* is a form of *ibadah* (worship). As such, knowledge is pursued in obedience to, and for the pleasure of, Allah. Moreover, *ilm* is not just connected to *ibadah*; it is also connected to every other Qur'anic value such as *khilafah* (trusteeship), *adl* (justice) and *istislah* (public interest). While the connection between *ilm* and *ibadah* means that knowledge cannot be pursued in open transgression of Allah's commands, the connection between *ilm* and *khilafah* transforms nature into the realm of the sacred. Man as the trustee of God, as the custodian of his gift, cannot pursue knowledge at the expense of nature. On the contrary, as the guardian of nature he seeks the understanding of nature not to dominate it but to appreciate the 'signs' of God. The study of nature, therefore, leads to two outcomes: an understanding of the material world as well as reflection of spiritual realities. The interconnection of *ilm* and *adl* and *istislah* ensures that knowledge is pursued to promote equality, social justice and values that enhance the well-being of Muslim society and culture.

Its emphasis on diversity and interconnectedness gives a unique character to the epistemology of Islam. It provides a middle path for the pursuit of knowledge, ensuring that no individual form of knowledge or method of knowing becomes the sole criteria of truth or is pursued to the exclusion of others. It is for this reason that a predilection for systematic classification of knowledge is so noticeable in Muslim civilization. The classification of knowledge into various branches was the prime occupation of many Muslim scholars of classical age. It provided both an overall paradigm within which appropriately relevant knowledge was sought and a method indispensable to genuine scholarship that proved extremely fertile in the history of Muslim intellectual endeavour. Moreover, the insistence of Islamic epistemology on giving equal status to all forms of knowledge within a single matrix of values meant that no particular branch of knowledge developed at the expense of another. Furthermore, it brought to the fore disciplines, such as astronomy and agriculture, medicine and mathematics, theology and taxonomy, which were most needed for the development of Muslim civilization.

In each area of knowledge, Muslim scholars of classical age worked in clearly defined knowledge and behavioural paradigms. Thus, they were able to synthesize the science of other civilizations which they inherited. Once these sciences came under the paradigms developed by the Muslim scholars they were transformed into a new substance.

This is exactly how contemporary Muslim scholars and scientists have to approach the crucial issue of the Islamization of knowledge. By divorcing ethics and morality from its epistemology, Western civilization has produced a body of knowledge that does not concern itself with the Islamic concerns of trusteeship of man, sacredness of nature, social justice, public interest and seeking the pleasure of Allah. This body of knowledge and its associated disciplines promote the interests and well-being of Western civilization and cannot by Islamized. The task before Muslim intelligentsia, then, is to develop, using the epistemology of Islam, alternative paradigms of knowledge for both natural and social sciences and to conceive and mould disciplines most relevant to the needs of contemporary Muslim societies. Only when distinctive Islamic paradigms and associated bodies of knowledge have evolved can Muslim scholars contemplate achieving synthesis on an appropriate footing with knowledge created by Western civilization.

This is quite a formidable, but not an impossible, task. In their respective ways, both al-Attas and al-Faruqi have shown that Muslim scholars are gearing up to meet the challenge.

Notes

1. For a detailed discussion of *ilm* and its various definitions, see F. Rosenthal, *Knowledge Triumphant*, Brill, Leiden, 1970.

2. Consider, for example, the role epistemology plays in the works of ibn Khaldun and al-Ghazzali. See ibn Khaldun's *The Muqaddimah: An Introduction to History*, trans. by F. Rosenthal, Routledge and Kegan Paul, London, 1967; and al-Ghazzali's *The Book of Knowledge*, trans. by Nabih Amin Faris, Ashraf, Lahore, 1962.

3. A whole body of environmental literature cataloguing the environmental hazards of contemporary science and technology has now been produced. A critical assessment of this literature is provided by Stephen Cotgrave, *Catastrophe or Cornucopia: The Environment, Politics and the Future*, Wiley, Chichester, 1982.

4. Gregory Bateson, *Steps to an Ecology of Mind*, Paladin, 1973, p. 463.

5. Robert Brownhill, *Education and the Nature of Knowledge*, Croom Helm, London, 1983, pp. 11–12.

6. David Hume, *Treatise on Human Nature*, Selby Bigge edn, Oxford, 1906.

7. T. S. Khun, *The Structure of Scientific Revolution*, Chicago University Press, Chicago, 1962.

8. Paul Feyerabend, *Against Method*, New Left Books, London, 1975.

9. A. N. Whitehead, *Science and the Modern World*, Free Association Books, London, 1984 (reprint).

10. M. Polanyi, *Personal Knowledge*, Oxford University Press, Routledge and Kegan Paul, London, 1958.

11. Ian Mitroff, *The Subjective Side of Science*, Elsevier, Amsterdam, 1974.

12. J. R. Ravetz, *Scientific Knowledge and its Social Problems*, Oxford University Press, Oxford, 1972.

13. T. Roszak, *Where the Wasteland Ends*, Doubleday, New York, 1972; and *Person/Planet*, Gollancz, London, 1979.

14. S. H. Nasr, *Encounter of Man and Nature*, Allen and Unwin, London, 1968.

15. I. Illich, *Celebrations of Awareness*, Calder and Boyars, London, 1971; *Energy and Equity*, Calder and Boyars, London, 1971; and *Tools for Conviviality*, Calder and Boyars, London, 1975.

16. In *Islam, Secularism and the Philosophy of the Future*, Mansell, London, 1985.

17. *Ibid.* pp. 127–8.

18. *Ibid*. p. 128.

19. *Ibid*. p. 128.

20. *Ibid*. p. 130.

21. Ismael R. al-Faruqi, *Islamisation of Knowledge: General Principles and Workplan*, International Institute for Islamic Thought, Washington, 1982.

22. *Ibid*. pp. 8–9.

23. *Ibid*. p. 14.

24. *Ibid*. p. 38.

25. *Ibid*. p. 41.

5

The Shariah as a Problem-solving Methodology

The Shariah is the core of the world-view of Islam. It is that body of knowledge which provides the Muslim civilization with its unchanging bearings as well as its major means of adjusting to change. Theoretically, the Shariah covers all aspects of human life: personal, social, political and intellectual. Practically, it gives meaning and content to behaviour of Muslims in their earthly endeavours.

Normally, the Shariah is described as 'Islamic law'. But the boundaries of Shariah extend beyond the limited horizons of law. The Shariah is also a system of ethics and values, a pragmatic methodology geared to solving today's and tomorrow's problems. Literally, the Shariah means 'way to water'—the source of all life. For a Muslim civilization, the Shariah represents that infinite spiritual and worldly thirst that is never satisfied: a Muslim people always seek better and better implementation of the Shariah on their present and future affairs. The Islamic nature of the Muslim civilization is measured by its success in its quest for the Shariah: how close it has got to the 'well of water' in its adherence to the legal, ethical and the methodological principles of the Shariah. The outward form of a Muslim civilization depends on the actual scientific, technological and economic conditions prevailing in a particular epoch. These forms are obviously different from epoch to epoch and illustrate the dynamic nature of the world-view of Islam. But internally, the fixed principles of the

Shariah ensure that Muslim civilizations of different epochs always seek the same ethical goals. As such, the 'Islamic civilization' would be that civilization in which the values of the Shariah have reached their highest expression.

In the entire history of Islam, the Shariah has not been more abused, misunderstood and misrepresented than in our own epoch. It has been used to justify oppression and despotism, injustice and criminal abuse of power. It has been projected as an ossified body of law that bears little or no relationship to modern times. It has been presented as an intellectually sterile body of knowledge that belongs to distant history rather than the present and the future. All this has been to the deteriment of the Muslim people; and has suffocated the true revival of Islam and a genuine emergence of a contemporary Muslim intellectual tradition.

Many of the problems of the contemporary Muslim societies arise from the fact that the Shariah has been limited to the domains of 'law'. Thus it has been the exclusive concern either of traditional scholars who have been too preoccupied with legal rulings passed hundred of years ago by classical *ulamas* and Imams or of modern lawyers who have tried to understand the Shariah with the tools of Western legal systems. Either way the values that the Shariah seeks to promote and the real issues to which it should be addressed are virtually ignored. Moreover, the Shariah is not just forced into the narrow constraints of law, but limited even further to only one or two segments of its legal precepts. Thus, those aspects of the Shariah which deal with crime and punishment and social behaviour figure a great deal in the work and thoughts of contemporary traditional and modern scholars. By fragmenting the Shariah in this way, and by ignoring its overall ethical goals, Muslim scholars and lawyers destroy its essential holistic nature and present it in a grotesque manner. While the Shariah emphasizes mercy, balance and equilibrium, today's exponents of the Shariah emphasize extreme punishments without due regard to social or political environment. While the Shariah is inherently against all forms of despotism, contemporary saviours of the Shariah impose it by despotic means. While the Shariah promotes political and social justice, and equality of all before the law, modern practitioners seek to impose its ruling on the downtrodden, the under-privileged or the minorities and foreign expatriots for whom the Shariah has no meaning. While one aspect of the Shariah is suppressed because it does not go down well with the ruling oligarchy or Western mores, another is over-emphasized to dupe the populace that 'Shariah law' is in operation.

If the Shariah is to become the dominant guiding principle of behaviour of contemporary Muslim societies, then it must be rescued from the clutches of fossilized traditional scholars and over-zealous Westernized lawyers. The legalistic rulings of the classical Imams, and their associated schools of thought—five of which are now predominant: the Hanafi school in the Indian subcontinent, West Asia and Egypt; the Maliki in North and West Africa; the Shafi'i in Malaysia and Indonesia; the Hanbali in Arabia; and the Ja'feri in Iran and Iraq—were space and time bound. They were concerned with solving the problems of their societies and examined these problems in the light of the available knowledge. They gave their judgements without bias or fear and were concerned only with the truth as they saw it. This is why most of their legal judgements went against the rulers of their time and for which they were persecuted by these rulers. However, these rulings were never meant to be the final word, or the ultimate understanding of a particular precept of the Shariah. The great Imams never intended that their judgements should become eternal law: that would amount to claiming divine authority; this is why they all, without exception, emphasized that their rulings were their own opinions, derived from the sources of the Shariah, and should not be accepted uncritically. And that is why they loathed the idea that a 'school of thought' should be formed around their juristic judgements. The fact that Muslims today give their rulings eternal validity, and seek answers to modern problems in their judgements and thought, rather than looking to the sources of the Shariah, is a sign of Muslim intellectual lethargy. Even though it is conceived as a compliment to the work of the great Imams, it is in fact an insult to their achievements. Of course, contemporary Muslim societies have a great deal to learn from their experience and work of which we should make full use. In particular, the judgements of classical

Imams on theological matters, beliefs and prayers, cannot be surpassed. And there is certainly no need for us to do that. But Shariah is not theology: it is an amalgam of law, ethics and methodology. We could draw lessons from how the Imams applied this amalgam to the particular situation of their time; but there is no substitute for us than doing our own homework and seeking our own contemporary solutions to our own problems. Indeed, this exercise of going back to the sources of the Shariah to find solutions to new, different and emerging problems must be applied in every epoch; for every century produces radically different and new problems which cannot be foreseen and which are not amenable to traditional solutions.

While the Shariah has to be rescued from the weight of fossilized traditional scholarship, it must also be protected from the onslaught of modern apologia. In trying to impose a 'modern', Westernized framework on the Shariah, Muslim lawyers have undermined its integrity. The Shariah does not need to be 'modernized' but understood on its own terms. Even the use of Westernized terminology becomes a hurdle in gaining a contemporary understanding of the Shariah. For example, the Shariah deals with the entire span of human life and interactions, and as such in traditional Muslim sources there is no term to denote what in Western legal framework is called 'personal law'. By labelling a segment of the Shariah as such, it is divorced from the social and economic aspects of human behaviour—thus the interconnections that the Shariah is trying to emphasize are undermined. Similarly, one cannot ignore and underplay certain aspects of the Shariah, while giving undue importance to certain others. For example, in societies where the dowry is used to acquire wealth, and thus make it difficult, indeed impossible, for the vast majority of young men to get married, it makes little sense to hand out extreme punishments for sexually frustrated behaviour. Neither does it make much sense to apologize, and sweep under the carpet, those aspects of the Shariah which are designed to cater for the special circumstances and diversity of human needs. Polygamy is a good example: most Westernized Muslim lawyers find the Shariah injunction on polygamy embarrassing and try to underplay it at every opportunity. Hossein Nasr makes an apt comment in this regard:

> Many modernised Muslims feel embarrassed by this feature of the Shariah for no other reason than that Christianity eventually banned it and in the West today it is forbidden. The arguments against it are not so much logical as sentimental and carry the weight and prestige of the modern West with it. All the arguments given, based on the fact that polygamy is the only way of preventing many social ills of today, have no effect on those for whom the fashion of the day has replaced the Sunnah of the Prophet. One wonders if modernism had originated in the Himalayan states rather than in Europe, whether the modern Muslim apologists would have tried to interpret the teachings of the Shariah as permitting polyandry, as today they interpret its teaching only in the monogamous sense which is current Western practice.[1]

The point is that Western custom and practice should not dictate our approach to the Shariah. We cannot take the world as it exists today as the sole reality and judge the relevance or non-relevance of various aspects of the Shariah according to its degree of conformity to this world. Similarly, we cannot take the historical experience of classical authors as the sole arbitrator and exposition of the Shriah. Muslim scholars and intellectuals must gain contemporary understanding of the Shariah on its own terms, treating it as an integrated whole and using its own methodology. That means not moulding the Shariah into alien frameworks or giving undue importance to the opinions and judgements of classical jurists. And that requires going back to the original sources of the Shariah.

The Sources of the Shariah

Traditionally, the sources of the Shariah have been divided into two basic categories: the chief and supplementary sources. The chief sources of the Shariah are universally recognized to be the Qur'an and the Sunnah of the Prophet Mohammad. During the lifetime of the Prophet, the Qur'an was given a practical shape by his words and deeds. The Muslim community needed nothing else to understand the legal boundaries and ethical precepts of Muslim behaviour. The Prophet himself tackled problems faced by the community and provided the necessary answers. However, direct explanation of the legal injunctions of the Qur'an was not available after his death; thus general consensus or the *ijma* of the companions of the Prophet took its place next to the Qur'an and the Sunnah as a major source of the Shariah. The reason for the emergence of *ijma* as a major source of the Shariah is simple: it was natural for the Muslims to assume that after the Prophet himself, the understanding of the Qur'an of those who were with him during his lifetime must be the most thorough and deep. It was therefore natural that in legal matters which needed clarification the *ijma* of the then Muslim community was followed. A tradition of the Prophet legitimized *ijma* as a chief source of Islamic law: 'My people will never agree on a lie.'

As the Muslim community grew, newer and newer problems surfaced, many of which were quite unique in their character. Muslim scholars and jurists solved these problems by making deductive analogical parallels from the Qur'an and the Sunnah. Analogy, or *qiyas*, assured them that two different cases could be solved by the same divine injunction. Moreover, judgements reached by the use of *qiyas* obtained the general approval of the entire Muslim community; it thus had the *ijma* of the believers. *Qiyas*, or analogical reasoning, therefore became the fourth chief source of the Shariah. To these four main sources, some Muslim scholars also add *ijtihad*, or 'individual reasoning', which has its basis both in the Qur'an and the traditions of the Prophet Mohammad as a major source of the Shariah.

Ijtihad is defined as 'the putting forth of every effort in order to determine with a degree of probability a question of the Shariah'. 'Every effort', of course, includes reasoning by analogy, and this is why many scholars regard *qiyas* as a special form of *ijtihad*. While the Qur'an and the Sunnah provide the Shariah with its immutable laws, *ijtihad* together with *ijma* provides the Shariah with its dynamic base. The use of *ijtihad* involves focusing the legal and ethical precepts of the Qur'an, together with its pragmatic formulation given in the Sunnah, on the practical and ethical problems of today. But before the results of *ijtihad* can have validity in the Shariah, they must have the *ijma* of Muslim scholars and intellectuals. In this way the Shariah is added to and develops, and adjusts to continuous change.

To these chief sources of the Shariah—the Qur'an, the Sunnah, *ijma* and *ijtihad*—three further supplementary sources are added. In the words of Said Ramadan, these are:

(a) *Al-Istihsan*, or the deviation, on a certain issue, from the rule of a precedent to another rule for a more relevant legal reason that requires such deviation.
(b) *Al-Istislah*, or the unprecedented judgement motivated by public interest to which neither the Qur'an nor the Sunnah explicitly refer.
(c) *Al-Urf*, or the custom and the usage of a particular society, both in speech and action.[2]

These secondary sources of the Shariah make 'rigid laws' more flexible and further illustrate the adoptable and amenable character of the Shariah. Muslim jurists have given particular attention to the institution of *istislah* or public interest, arguing that it is a valuable source of legislation and a viable means by which the Shariah meets the challenge of change.

Traditionally, Muslim scholars have focused not on *istislah*, but its more general form, *maslaha*, which means a cause, a means, an occasion, or a goal which is good. It is also used for an affair or a transaction which is good or has the potential of promoting good. In its Arabic usage, it is often encountered in the form *nazara fi masalih al-nas*: 'he considered the things that were for the good of the people'. Its use as a principal tool of promoting the Shariah is based on the argument that 'good' is 'lawful' and that 'lawful' must be good. On the basis of such reasoning, traditional Muslim scholars developed a whole array of *maslaha* categories, some of which required direct evidence from the Qur'an and the Sunnah while others could lead to binding legal sanctions on the basis that they clearly promote a noted ethical critera—such as preservation of life and property, promotion of Islamic morals and sound reasoning—of the Shariah.

Maslaha has been used as guiding principle of law-making in recent Muslim history. In 1857, *maslaha* was used as basis for reforms in Tunisian law. The preamble to the 1860 Constitution stated 'God . . . has given justice as a guarantee of the preservation of order in this world, and has given the revelation of law in accordance with human interests (*masalih*)'. It listed three basic components of *maslaha*: 'liberty, security and equality'.[3] The noted Muslim scholar Muhammad Abduh stressed the use of *maslaha* in the reforms of the court system in Egypt and Sudan. More recently, the use of *maslaha* in gaining a contemporary understanding of the Shariah has been urged by a number of scholars including Abd al-Razzaq Sanhuri,[4] Maruf Dawalibi[5] and Muhammad Khalid Masud.[6]

When taken in totality, the primary and secondary sources of the Shariah provide a body of law and ethics, and a methodology for solving contemporary problems, that is at once deeply grounded in eternal values and completely open to change and adjustment. At the apex of the Shariah are the Qur'an and the Sunnah—these are eternal and provide the absolute reference frame for Muslim behaviour. All other sources of the Shariah are subordinate to the Qur'an and the Sunnah: they do not and cannot challenge the authority of the absolute reference frame, but enhance its understanding and appreciation. While the Qur'an is the very basis of legality and legal injunctions in Islam, it does not issue a command on every legal possibility or on every foreseen and unforeseen circumstance of human situation. It is essentially a book of guidance, not a classification of legal prescriptions. And as a book of guidance, it lays down in general terms the minimum and maximum parameters within which a Muslim society must pursue its legal and ethical activities. The legal parameters which the Qur'an actually lays down are remarkably few: only seventy injunctions regarding family affairs, seventy on civil matters, thirty on penal law, thirteen on jurisdiction and procedure, ten on constitutional law, twenty-five on international relations, and ten on economic and financial matters.[7] (An enumeration such as this, as Said Ramadan points out, can only be approximate. The legal bearing of some injunctions can be disputed, while others clearly apply to more than one sphere of human endeavour.) The Sunnah of the Prophet Mohammad illustrates how these few injunctions can best be actualized in a community. Thus, the legal and ethical parameters, together with the best example of how they can be turned into living reality, form the unchangeable core of the Shariah. Beyond these limited parameters, the Shariah is completely open: it can be developed and shaped according to the needs of society and time by any number of its other sources: *ijma*, *qiyas*, *ijtihad*, and *istislah*. The sources of the Shariah that supplement the Qur'an and the Sunnah are problem-solving tools; they provide a methodology for adjusting to change. It is indeed tragic that Muslim societies have chosen to ignore them. The path towards the Shariah adopted by some Muslim countries in recent decades negate one of the basic ethical principles that the Shariah seeks to promote: the end does not justify the means. In the pursuit of the Shariah, both the ends and the means must themselves be derived from the Shariah.

The Shariah in Contemporary Muslim Societies

While the Shariah provides guidance on every aspect of human behaviour, its practical use in the Muslim world, as I argued above, has been limited to conventional law. But even in this area, the implementation of the Shariah has been fragmented and presented as an absurd caricature. The responsibility for this lies not only with zealous dictators and monarchs who have used the Shariah to legitimize their own power base, but also with Muslim scholars and intellectuals who have failed to carry out the *ijtihad* so badly needed to gain a contemporary understanding of the Shariah, and with Islamic activists who, in their eagerness to see the Shariah implemented, have cooperated with all types of demented politicians and power-hungry demagogues. The way to the Shariah in the future has to be through the drawing board.

One of the fundamental features of the Shariah is that it is an integrated and interconnected whole: every aspect, every law, every injunction of the Shariah is connected, in a hierarchical and horizontal relationship, to every other. The Shariah cannot be understood, let alone implemented, without appreciating its holistic nature.

The intrinsic holistic character of the Shariah means that one or two aspects of 'Islamic law' cannot be imposed on a society at the expense of others or at the expense of the basic ethical principles which the Shariah aims to promote. Thus, it makes no real sense for a military regime which has itself required power by illegal means to introduce the 'criminal law' element of the Shariah. Neither does it make much sense in a society where poverty is prevalent and wealth and power is accumulated in a few hands to dish out the *hudud* (boundary, outer limit) punishments on petty thiefs, while the real criminals sleep soundly in their bungalows and palaces. As the Shariah itself declares that 'there is no compulsion in religion', it cannot be imposed on an unwilling people; it has to be desired and admired and adopted by a people out of their own free will.

But the adoption of the Shariah by contemporary Muslim societies cannot be a sudden, overnight affair. Neither can the 'minor' themes of the Shariah be introduced before its dominant concerns.

The Qur'anic approach to change is gradual: it allows the believer ample time to adjust to oncoming change. The best example of this are the Qur'anic injunctions prohibiting the use of alcohol. The first revelation warned that the evils of alcohol outweigh its good effects; the second asked the believers not to pray while under the influence of alcohol. The complete ban on drinking was finally made in the third revelation:

> First stage: 'They question thee about strong drink and games of chance. Say: in both is great sin, and (some) utility for men; but the sin of them is greater than their usefulness.' (The Qur'an: 2:219).
> Second stage: 'O ye who believe! Draw not near unto prayer when ye are drunken, till ye know that which ye utter . . .' (The Qur'an: 4:43).
> Third stage: 'O ye who believe! Strong drink and games of chance and idols and divining arrows are only infamy of Satan's handiwork. Leave it aside in order that ye may succeed.' (The Qur'an: 5:90).

History records that by the time the third stage was reached, despite the fact that the Arabs were great drinkers and wine played a major part in their social customs and literature, the Muslim community was well prepared: wine flowed in the streets of Medina as every member of the community threw out his/her reserves.

The principle of gradual change is fundamental to the Shariah. The gradual introduction of the Shariah in a Muslim society not only provides the society with an opportunity to adjust to changes introduced by it, it also enables it to get the emphasis and priorities of the Shariah correct. The prime aim of the Shariah is to promote the interests and benefits of the people. Muslim jurists have classified people's interests and benefits into three main categories:

(1) Those benefits which meet an absolute necessity—for example, the preservation of life, protection of property, and the protection of physical and mental health.
(2) Those benefits which meet no absolute necessity but are generally useful, promote social welfare and make life easy for members of society, such as the provision of public amenities such as a roads and parks.
(3) Those benefits which serve a particular end like the promotion of Islamic morals and culture.[8]

It is obvious that a society has to focus on absolute benefits before it promotes benefits which are generally useful. The development of parks in a city where the life of man and his family is not safe makes little sense under the Shariah. Similarly, under a dictatorship, where the entire population is at the mercy of a despot and the life and property of anyone who opposes him is not safe, projects which promote 'Islamic culture' appear positively perverse. The first goal of the exponents of the Shariah must be to ensure a system of government based on popular consensus, the *ijma* of the people. Only under a system of government that comes into being on the basis of the principles of the Shariah can the implementation of the injunctions of the Shariah have a true meaning.

All this does not mean that under a non-Islamic government certain general goals of the Shariah cannot be pursued. However, this has to be done in a manner which does not link the Shariah in any way with the dominant unjust system. Under an un-Islamic government, fighting for the Shariah means fighting against *all* injustice: political, economic, social, educational and technological. But under such systems, which are prevalent all over the Muslim world, the scholars and intellectuals have another, equally important, duty: to illustrate the contemporary relevance of the Shariah and demonstrate how it can actually solve the problems of Muslim societies and hence usher in a superior, just order.

Seeking the Contemporary Relevance of the Shariah

A fresh, contemporary understanding of the Shariah is crucial for the emergence of a Muslim civilization of the future. To a very large extent the exercise demands the use of those tools of the Shariah which have hitherto remained unexplored by Muslim scholars and intellectuals. *Ijtihad*, *ijma* and *istislah* have to be used to invoke the Shariah as a problem-solving methodology. The scope of the Shariah beyond the confines of 'Islamic law' must be realized by Muslim scholars and intellectuals, and its techniques must be used to develop viable alternatives for Muslim societies and individuals to pursue.

The Shariah is *the* Islamic problem-solving methodology has not been recognized by many contemporary muslim scholars. Parvez Manzoor is a notable exception:

> Sharia is ... the *methodology of history* in Islam. By its application temporal contingencies are judged by eternal imperatives, moral choices are transformed into options for concrete action and ethical sentiment is objectified in law. It is in fact the *problem-solving* methodology of Islam *par excellence*. Any practical Muslim thinking, as for example our search for an environmental ethics, must pass through the objective framework of Sharia in order to become positive and be part of Muslim history. Sharia thus provides both the ethical norms and the legal structure within which Muslim state(s) may make actual decisions pertaining to concrete ... issues.[9]

Thus many contemporary problems can be studied using the Shariah and policy alternatives developed that could become an integrated part of Islamic law if they obtained the *ijma* of Muslim scholars and intellectuals. In fact, this is exactly how the Shariah developed in the early part of Islamic history. The ultimate aim of classical jurists when they developed *Usul al-Fiqh*, the science of approaching and appreciating the Shariah, was the establishment of a methodology through which the learned and the lawyers could make practical decisions about emerging problems. Similarly, the painstaking classifications that the classical jurists developed were designed to guide action, to highlight the essential from the merely necessary, to enable the society to set its priorities and consciously pursue them.

Contemporary Muslim scholars and intellectuals have to perform similar tasks today. However, the development of the Shariah as a problem-solving methodology requires focusing not at the specifics but at the general principles of the Shariah. Going back to the example of alcohol quoted above, it is evident that this is a specific category derived from a more general and universal rule. That the Shariah bans not only alcohol but all types of intoxicants, including narcotics, would be readily admitted by most Muslim scholars. But even the prohibition of all intoxicants is only a specific case of the general rule that all those things in which the bad is greater than the good ought to be prohibited from society. Now if we applied this general rule of the Shariah to nuclear energy, we can draw certain conclusions that would become, if they had the consensus of Muslim scholars and intellectuals, the basis of nuclear policy of a Muslim state. It is indeed possible for us to prove that the bad elements of nuclear power, its potential dangers to present the future life-forms, far outweigh its good factors, its ability to provide cheap energy. It is at this level of practical policy-making that the Shariah must be used to shape the destiny of Muslim societies.

Apart from focusing on the general principles of the Shariah, Muslim intellectuals must also rediscover its *norms*. The fragmented and abnormal imposition of the Shariah in various Muslim countries has led many to believe that the Shariah, almost always, takes the extreme position on every issue. This image is projected by *hudud* punishments—so beloved of dictators and others seeking expedient 'Islamic' legitimacy for their rules. The Shariah is like a spiral, confined by its limits but moving with time, with its norm requiring a fresh effort to understand by Muslims of every epoch (see Fig. 5). It limits the maxima and minima of human behaviour by erecting a clear-cut boundary, the *hudud*, outside which all actions are categorically unIslamic.

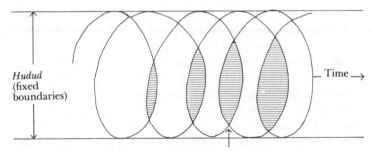

Norm of the Shariah that changes and expands with time

Figure 5. *Continuity and change in the Shariah*

These *hudud* represent the outer limits of human actions and not the norm. Within these limits all actions are permissible but the best actions are those which meet the dictate of time and preserve the equilibrium and balance of the Shariah. Thus while acknowledging the fact that human beings have a tendency to seek retribution (*qisas*) for their ills, the Shariah puts a limit beyond which retribution cannot be sought. Thus the principle of 'an eye for an eye, a tooth for a tooth' implies the maximum retribution that anyone can exact. It is not the norm of the Shariah but the outer limit allowed by the Shariah. The norm of the Shariah is mercy and forgiveness as examplified in the Sunnah. Throughout his life, Prophet Mohammad always forgave his adversaries, to the extent that after the final capture of Makkah when the Prophet became the undisputed political leader of Arabia, he issued a general amnesty for all his adversaries and declared that not only his arch enemy Abu Sufyan, who had persecuted and led armies against him for decades, was perfectly safe but anyone taking refuge in his house was also safe from advancing Muslim army. This, according to the Shariah, is the pattern of behaviour that Muslims seeking retribution have to follow; while the Shariah allows just and exact retribution, it makes mercy and forgiveness and not revenge the dominant norm. In trying to make the *hudud* elements of the Shariah into the norm, Muslim scholars and lawyers risk sacrificing the spirit of the Shariah at the altar of expediency.

The undue emphasis on the outer limits of what the Shariah does and does not permit has led Muslim scholars and intellectuals to see things only in terms of black and white. The fact that a great deal of contemporary moral and ethical problems occur in the hazy overlap that is a shade of grey has meant that many pressing problems of Muslim societies have not been solved. Consider, for example, the problem of population policy: whatever one may say about the causes and nature of underdevelopment, the fact that galloping population is undermining the economic prosperity and efforts for self-reliance in such countries as Bangladesh, Pakistan, Turkey, Egypt and Morocco cannot be denied. However, the vast majority of Muslim scholars take the extreme position and reject birth control, the basis of any population policy, outright. The case against birth control is based on the argument that the Shariah regards human life as sacred and that God has promised to sustain those on whom He bestows the gift of life. Maulana Abul Ala Maududi, for example, argues that birth control 'violates the laws of nature and the Guidance God has given for individual and social life'. What laws of nature? Maulana Maududi quotes the following verses from the Qur'an to substantiate his case:

> And who goeth farther astray than he who followeth his lust against guidance from Allah. (28:50)
> He said: Our Lord is He Who gave unto everything its nature, then guided it right. (20:50)
> And whoso transgresseth Allah's limits, he verily wrongeth his soul. (65:1)[10]

Although he marshalls his arguments from a number of Western sociological studies, and alleges that birth control leads to numerous social evils (some real, some imagined), in essence

Maulana Maududi's conclusion that birth control is against Islam is based only on the above verse. Thus birth control is envisaged by him to be a 'lustful desire' which transgresses the limits of human actions set by God. Hence a couple overburdened by numerous children and engaged in family planning is acting out of 'lust'. Or a state faced by a runaway population and promoting family planning is transgressing the established boundaries of God. Such arguments are not just based on dubious logic, but also insult the vast majority of Muslim people who face a real need and promote an attitude of fatalism.

In contrast, the people who argue that birth control is not against the principles of Islam point out that the Prophet permitted *azal* (withdrawal) and *ghayl* (coitus with a lactating women). An authentic tradition of the Prophet, attributed to a close companion, states: 'we used to have recourse to *azal* in the Prophet's age. He came to know of it but did not prevent us from doing so. If it were something to be prevented, the Qur'an would have prohibited it'. This tradition, together with sundry arguments, is used by many scholars to declare that birth control is permitted by the Shariah. However, just because the Prophet allowed the practice of particular methods of birth control does not mean that the Shariah sanctions birth control *per se* and permits the use of *all* types of contraceptives.

Somewhere between these two extreme positions lies the true Shariah norm: the Shariah neither completely bans birth control, as Maulana Maududi argues, nor does it promote it as a general principle. The Shariah allows individuals and societies to practise family planning if they have a clearly defined need to do so but it does not permit the use of *all* kinds of contraceptives.

Up to the twentieth century there was no real need for birth control in Muslim societies, hence its complete absence from Muslim societies of other epochs. Now that it clearly fulfils a need, both for individual families and certain over-populated Muslim states, it becomes a necessity under the Shariah. However, it would not permit the use of those contraceptives which violate certain ethical principles of Islam. Considering the stand of the Shariah on abortion, intra-uterine devices (IUDs) which are abortive would be *haram* (not permitted), but other devices which simply prevent gametic union by mechanical means would be *halal* (permitted). While a Muslim state can make birth control a basis for its population policy, it cannot impose it on individuals: the Shariah does not permit interference in individuals' personal lives.

This type of analysis which seeks the norms of the Shariah, rather than simply makes declarations based on its outer limits, actually provides practical answers to contemporary problems. But it also demands serious work from Muslim scholars and intellectuals. For example, in the case of birth control, Muslim scholars would be required to study every type of contraceptive in minute detail to discover whether it violates any of the ethical principles of the Shariah. Similarly, population policies would have to be carefully confined within parameters acceptable to the Shariah.

Apart from seeking the norms of the Shariah and focusing on its general principles, it is also necessary to develop certain secondary sources of the Shariah as fully-fledged methodologies. Methodologically, the question of how to apply and extend the Shariah to contemporary needs and new situations has been hampered by over-reliance on narrow specifics, legal formalism, literalism and outdated legal texts. To break away from this straitjacket, Muslim scholars and intellectuals have to concentrate on the *conceptual basis* of the Shariah.

As I have argued in *The Future of Muslim Civilization*, adjusting to change requires that we gain a fresh understanding of and operationalize such Shariah concepts as *ijma*, *shura*, *ijtihad* and *istislah*. This has also been the position of those classical scholars who focused on the question of continuity and change in Islam. For example, the fourteenth-century Muslim jurist, Abu Ishaq al-Shatabi, believed that social change and legal change were interrelated. He differentiated between two types of change: *bida* and *ada*. *Bida* is change in religious practices, a type of change that the Shariah does not permit. For example, no new forms of worship can be introduced nor any changes be made in the basic beliefs and tenets of Islam. *Ada* is change in habits, behaviour and custom of people introduced by new factors of production or the emergence of a new type of technology. Shatabi argued that the

Shariah not only acknowledges such types of change but 'the Shariah can change *ada* in certain cases, and *vice versa*, but more important is the fact that when change takes place within an *ada*, it also effects the rule of Shariah. A thing which was relatively good becomes evil and vice versa; the Shariah has to adjust itself accordingly.' Shatabi recognizes both 'horizontal' and 'vertical' changes in *ada* and argues that the Shariah, so far as it is related to *ada*, must also admit change.

Shatabi focused on *maslaha*, the general variant of *istislah*, as the major concept and methodology by which the Shariah could be adjusted to change and used to solve new and emerging problems. He defined *maslaha* as follows: 'I mean by *maslaha* that which concerns the subsistence of human life, the completion of man's livelihood, and the acquisition of what his emotional and intellectual qualities require of him, in an absolute sense.[1] He divides *maslaha* into *daruri* (necessary), *haji* (needed) and *tahsini* (commendable). He uses these categories to show how the methodology of *maslaha* can be used to derive new legislations from the Shariah to meet the changing needs of a society. It is interesting to note that Shatabi does not consider *maslaha* to be an individual or fanciful criteria, but justifies its use on the basis of the preservation of life and property of individuals, and the values and mental health of a society.

In our own time, such examination of concepts like *istislah* can lead to Shariah legislations on the preservations of environment, conservation of cultural property, health regulation in industry and the power and the role of the media. Similarly, the analytical study of other Shariah concepts can lead to useful legislation on the abuse of natural resources, the destructive use of technology, the social and cultural parameters of urban planning, research on genetic engineering, and Islamic stands on such international issues as law of the sea, peace and disarmament, and the new international economic order.

To some extent this is already happening. Muslim scholars are moving away from the confining limitations of the classical texts and beginning to focus on the general principles of the Shariah as is evident from the 'Model Islamic Constitution' produced by the Islamic Council of Europe (see Appendix). Shariah is being extended, at least theoretically, into areas where it has hitherto been dormant for several centuries as our discussion on Islamic science, Islamic economics and Islamic theory of environment (Chapters 7, 9 and 10 respectively) shall demonstrate. But all this is only the beginning: the full realization of what the Shariah offers Muslims, as well as non-Muslims, is still some way into the future.

Notes

1. Seyyed Hossein Nasr, *Islamic Studies*, Librairie du Liban, Beirut, 1967, p. 31.

2. Said Ramadan, *Islamic Law—Its Scope and Equity*, Geneva, 1970, p. 33.

3. Quoted by Muhammad Khalid Masud, *Islamic Legal Philosophy: A Study of Abu Ishaq al-Shatibi's Life and Thought*, Islamic Research Institute, Islamabad, 1977, p. 173.

4. Abdul al-Razzaq Sanhuri, 'Wujub tanqih al-qanun al-madani al-Misri', *Majallat al-Qanun wa'l Iqtisad*, **6** (3–144) (1963).

5. Maruf Dawalibi, *al-Madkhal ila ilm usul al-fiqh*, Dar al-ilm l'il-malain, Beirut, 1965.

6. Muhammad Khalid Masud, *op. cit.*

7. Said Ramadan, *op. cit.*

8. Anwar Ahmad Qadri, *Islamic Jurisprudence in the Modern World*, Ashraf, Lahore, 1973 (2nd edn), p. 224.

9. S. Parvez Manzoor, 'Environment and Values: the Islamic Perspective' in Ziauddin Sardar (ed.), *The Touch of Midas*, Manchester University Press, 1984, p. 158.

10. Abul Ala Maududi, *Birth Control*, Islamic Publications, Lahore, 1978 (13th edn), p. 74. Much of Maulana Maududi's book is devoted to Western approach and attitudes to birth control; the discussion on Islam's stand on birth control occurs only on pp. 72–92, but even here Maulana Maududi depends more on Western sources to make his case.

11. Masud, *op. cit.* p. 225.

6

Islamic State in the Post-industrial Age

The establishment of an 'Islamic state' in our time has been the goal of all Islamic movements. The ideal cherished by most devout Muslims is to live in a modern 'Islamic state' which provides an environment conducive to the healthy spiritual and material growth of the Muslim community. Almost all political ideals and ideas which have currency in the Muslim world are directly or indirectly related to the notion of an 'Islamic state'.

However, as the Qur'an does not provide a clear theory of state, there is a considerable amount of debate and discussion on the nature of an 'Islamic state' and a whole body of literature on the political theory of Islam has been produced. Apart from such obvious and basic questions as whether the Islamic state is a democratic welfare state or a one-party dictatorship, what is the nature of the political process by which authority to administer the state is constituted, what role does the government and political parties play in an Islamic state, to whom is the government or political leadership ultimately responsible, some even more fundamental questions have come to the fore. For example, given the fact that Islam promotes an uncompromisingly universalist worldview, can it be confined to the geographical boundary of a state? Are not the terms 'Islam' and 'state' contradictory? Is an Islamic state, on the lines of a modern nation-state, possible? Indeed, desirable?

While there is no consensus on the answers to these and many other similar questions, Muslim scholars and intellectuals agree on the general outlines of an Islamic state. In his treatise on the Islamic government, Ayatullah Khomeini summarizes the essential nature of an Islamic state as follows:

> The Islamic state bears no resemblance to any existing system of government. The Islamic state is neither autocratic nor does it make its head the repository of all powers so as to let him play with the life and property of the people. The Islamic state is free of all despotism. It is a constitutional state but not in the modern sense where the constitution is interpreted by parliament or public representative bodies. The Islamic state is a constitutional state in the sense that those charged with running it are bound by the rules and conditions laid down by the Qur'an and the Sunnah.[1]

That the Islamic state is some kind of a constitutional state is now accepted by the vast majority of Muslim scholars. Moreover, most writers also agree that the Islamic state is based on the consent and cooperation of the people. For example, Abd al-Rahman Azzam makes consultation a basic tenet of the Islamic state. Islam, he writes,

> has made consultation a general principle whose application is mandatory and whose observance is to be respected by all Islamic states and communities at all times. Human experience has demonstrated the continuous character of this principle and its uses. However, Islam avoided defining a single method for consultation or specifying certain forms from which we were to select whatever might be suitable at a given time or place, for such particulars would have caused us hardship; the choice of the rules regulating consultation was left to us, with trust in our loyalty to our religion and to ourselves . . . It has been left to us to decide, within the scope of this principle, the forms of consultation and the manner in which it should be conducted with a view to meeting our needs and securing general stability and the consent and satisfaction of the people.[2]

Along with consultation, that is the principle of Shura, Muslim writers have also argued that justice, freedom and equality are essential tenets of an Islamic state. Muhammad Asad considers that it is in these principles that the Islamic state finds its true *raison d'être*:

To make the Law of Islam the law of the land in order that equity may prevail; to arrange social and economic relations in such a way that every individual shall live in freedom and dignity, and shall find as few obstacles as possible and as much encouragement as possible in the development of his personality; to enable all Muslim men and women to realise the ethical goals of Islam not only in their beliefs but also in the practical spheres of their lives; to ensure to all non-Muslim citizens complete physical security as well as complete freedom of religion, of culture, and of social development; to defend the country against attack from without and disruption from within; and to propagate the teachings of Islam to the world at large: it is in these principles, and in these alone, that the concept of an Islamic state finds its meaning and justification.[3]

However, while there is consensus on the fundamental nature and principles of the Islamic state, by and large Muslim scholars have failed to produce a contemporary methodology by which such a state can be created and run. Indeed, it has not even been possible to produce a modern mechanism by which the all-important principles of Shura or consultation can be put into practice in an Islamic society. The more profound issues of how a modern state can work towards a just and equitable order, how strong yet caring political leadership can emerge in Muslim societies, how a socially responsible administration which serves the true interest of the people can evolve, have not only been ignored but some authors are not even aware of their existence.

The Paradigm of Medina State

On the whole the focus of attention and analysis has been the 'ideal' and the 'first Islamic state' created by the Prophet Mohammad after his migration from Makkah to Medina. However, the emphases have been on descriptive analysis: the Medina state has been described not in terms of how it functioned as a state and polity, but largely in terms of actions that the Prophet Mohammad himself and his companions, particularly the four Rightly Guided Caliphs, Abu Bakr, Omar, Othman and Ali, undertook. Thus the best picture we have of the Medina state consists of a series of events. It is hardly surprising that such an analysis fails to provide the depth and level of insight that contemporary political scientists need to evolve a model of a contemporary Islamic state. Moreover, the Medina state model is never studied with reference to contemporary reality; it is almost always projected as an historical ideal that needs to be implemented in its totality.

The Medina state was established by the Prophet Mohammad in the first year of the *hijra*, or 622. Its basis and the major instrument of its creation was the constitution of Medina which was drawn up by the Prophet himself.[4] This constitution united three groups of people: the Prophet's followers who came with him from Makkah (the Muhajirun); his followers who belonged to Medina (the Ansars); and the friends, allies and followers of these two groups including several Jewish tribes. The document declared that the three groups of people constituted a 'single *ummah* (or community) distinct from other people'. Thus the document brought together both Muslims and non-Muslims, local population and immigrants, for mutual protection against external aggression, adjudication for inter-tribal disputes and feuds, and for administration of legislative and judical activities.

The main thrust of the Medina constitution, as Hussain and Kamali point out, was 'voluntary association and cooperation'. When the constitution was first framed, the Prophet Mohammad had no political power; he was simply the leader of the Muhajirun who were themselves dependent on the support of Medina's indigenous population. As such, there was 'no question of his using coercion in any shape or form to make the different sections of Medina's population accept a system of political inter-relationships which, while it promised them certain collective advantages, involved the abandonment of their long-established and dearly cherished tribal customs and traditions'. Moreover, 'it would not have helped him in establishing the kind of society it was his endeavour to establish—a society of free men voluntarily holding values like justice, equality, brotherhood, peace'.[5]

As the Medina state was founded and governed by the Prophet Mohammad, and as its laws were enacted by him, it is rightly regarded as the model Islamic state—one based on the injunctions of the Qur'an and the practice of the Sunnah. After the death of the Prophet, the state was consolidated and governed by the four Rightly Guided Caliphs—their practices and methods are also considered to be part of the ideal model of the Islamic state. In particular, the manner in which they assumed power has been a focus of attention.

The Prophet left the question of who should succeed him as the ruler of Medina open for his followers to decide. Immediately after his death, the Ansars gathered in the Saqifa of Bani Saida where they used to meet to discuss community affairs. They were joined by Abu Bakr, Umar bin al-Khattab and Abu Ubaida bin al-Jarrah in the decision-making meeting. Many scholars consider this meeting to be a constituent assembly which laid the political foundation of the *ummah*. The meeting presented three points of view. The Ansars argued that since they had rendered a major service to the Prophet by inviting him to Medina, and by defending Islam with their lives and property, the Khalifah, the office of successor to the Prophet, ought to be theirs by right. Abu Bakr acknowledged the contribution of the Ansars in helping the Prophet and shaping the Medina state, but argued that this did not give them any privileges over others. He argued that the Muhajirins were among the first to accept Islam and shared in the sufferings and injuries that the Quraysh inflicted on the Prophet. He also argued that the Arabs only recognized authority in the clan of the Quraysh—the best of the Arabs in blood and country. The third view presented at the meeting in Saqifa suggested that there should be two rulers—one each from the Ansars and the Muhajirins.

After these views were discussed, and Umar and Abu Ubaida had sworn allegiance to Abu Bakr, the gathering at Saqifa decided to accept Abu Bakr as the first Caliph of Islam.

Before his death, Abu Bakr, in consultation with other companions of the Prophet, nominated Umar to succeed him as Caliph. The nomination was embodied in an ordinance which Abu Bakr dictated to Othman. The ordinance was read out to a gathering of Muslims at the Prophet's mosque, after which Abu Bakr sought the approval of the gathering to his nomination. The approval was readily granted; and Umar became the second Caliph to hold office after the death of Abu Bakr.

When Umar was mortally stabbed, he was approached by his companions to nominate his successor. But Umar chose to nominate an Electoral Council of seven companions who were to decide on his successor from among themselves. He ordered them to consult the Ansars, the Muhajirins and the chiefs of clans present in Medina and reach a decision within three days. As one member of the Electoral Council was away from Medina, and it was not certain that he would return in time, the Council decided that in the event of a tie, the proposal supported by Abd al-Rahman would prevail. Hussain and Kamali take up the story of Umar's successor as follows:

The councillors were unable to reach a decision within the time prescribed. Meanwhile Umar had died. Therefore, Abd al-Rahman, declaring that he for one was not a candidate, took it upon himself to get one of the others agreed upon. With this objective in view he held consultation not only with his fellow councillors, but also with other leading Companions and dignitaries. Ultimately, by a process of self-elimination, the choice boiled down to one between Ali and Uthman, representatives, respectively, of the houses of Hashim and Umayya, both leading branches of the Quraysh. Abd al-Rahman decided to put the matter to the believers' congregation in the Prophet's mosque. But when he did so, an altercation arose between the supporters of the two candidates. Abd al-Rahman thereupon informed the congregation that the determination of the matter rested with him by virtue of the authority given to him by Umar. He, however, added that he will take his decision in the presence of the congregation. He first asked Ali whether he, if appointed khalifa, would bind himself to do everything in accordance with the Qur'an, the Sunnah of the Prophet and the precedents of his two predecessors. 'I hope', replied Ali, 'that I shall do so within the bounds of my knowledge and ability'. Uthman's reply was unconditional. 'Yes', he said, 'I will act accordingly'. On hearing this reply, Abd al-Rahman rendered baia to Uthman, and the other people followed his example.[6]

Thus Uthman became the third Caliph of Islam. However, when he was assassinated, he left the question of his successor completely open. During Uthman's era a number of political groups had emerged, and among these a group of rebels who controlled the city of Medina made their support for Ali common

knowledge. Indeed, they put pressure on Ali to accept the respon-
sibilities of being the fourth Caliph. However, despite the fact
that Ali was ready to swear allegiance to either Talha or Zubair,
both of whom could be considered for election, he was persuaded
to accept the office of the Caliph. Ali was thus duly elected and
Talha and Zubair were among the first to accept his appointment. The rest of the Muslim community followed suite.

The state evolved by the Prophet Mohammad and ruled after
him by the four Rightly Guided Caliphs, together with the system
of government that they produced, is the basic paradigm of an
Islamic state. The simplicity of the Prophet's political arrangements for conducting the affairs of the state and his refusal to
leave behind a detailed set of administrative directives is an indication of the fact that he did not wish to closely associate his
Prophethood and his message with the art of statecraft. He thus
left it for the future generations of Muslims to evolve political
structures that best suited their needs and requirements, and
provided the best platform for the optimum realization of his
message.

It is, therefore, not surprising that the paradigm of Islamic
state is based on a very simple structure of 'state' and that it does
not represent any definite form of government. It is an open
paradigm which provides the bare bones, the minimum of
guidelines, a few basic principles, such as the strong emphasis on
consultation and consensus of the community in arriving at political leadership, which can be used to develop a model of an
Islamic state in tune with contemporary reality. However, the
contemporary mapping of the paradigm cannot be carried out
using non-Islamic tools; it has to be based on concepts and ideas
that are unquestionably authentic.

The Modern Understanding of Islamic State

The founding theoretician of modern notions of Islamic state is
the Egyptian scholar, Muhammad Rashid Rida (d. 1935), the
spokesman of the Salafiyyah school of Egypt. His ideas have had
a profound influence on the major elements of contemporary
Islamic movements such as the Muslim Brotherhood and the

Jama't-e-Islami. Rashid Rida, like his teacher and mentor, Mohammad Abduh, was concerned with the reinterpretation of Islam in the light of modern thought. His political thought is to be found in *The Caliphate and the Great Immamate* published in Cairo in 1930. In the study, Rida reviews the theories and ideas of early scholars such as Mawardi and Taftazani, analyses the historical role of Caliphate and finally offers his guidelines for the restoration of the true Caliphate. Rida had an unending desire to see the restoration of the Khilafate after the disintegration of the Ottoman Empire and worked for the creation of a state that was truly based on the principles of the Qur'an and the Shariah.[7]

Rashid Rida saw the creation of a modern Islamic state as the nearest alternative to the restoration of the Caliphate. However, the terms he uses for the Islamic state, *ad-dawlah* or *al-hukumat al-Islamiyyah*, do not exist in the Qur'an and cannot be found in classical Arabic. Although his plan for the construction of an Islamic state is offered in the name of the reorganization of the Caliphate, as Hamid Enayat points out, it actually proposes a new entity and makes a direct assault on two vital issues: 'the principle of popular sovereignty, and the possibility of man-made laws'.[8]

On the principle of sovereignty, Rashid Rida argues, along with most traditionalist and modernist Muslim scholars, that once the principle of consultation between the ruler and the ruled and consensus of the people are implemented, an Islamic state will automatically become a democratic state. Rashid Rida also argues that the *ulama*, who are the natural and genuine representatives of the people, will also ensure that democracy prevails and cites the example of the *ulama* in Iran during the Tobacco Rebellion of 1892 and the Constitutional Revolution of 1906.

Rashid Rida also argued that Shariah must be given its rightful place in the Islamic state, it must be revived in its proper form and adapted to meet the needs and requirements of modern society. Taking the cue from Abduh, Rashid Rida argued that the Shariah's boundless resources for legal renovation would ensure a dynamic body of legislation that would cope more than adequately with the growing complexities of modern life. He compared the legal system of every society to its language: 'just as no language should allow the grammatical rules of another language to govern its syntax and modes of expression, if it wants to keep its identity, no nation should adopt the laws of another nation without exercising its independent judgement and power of adaptation for adjusting them to its beliefs, mores and interests, otherwise it will fall prey to mental anarchy, and forfeit its solidarity and independence'.[9] The methodology for renovating the Shariah are the principles of *ijtihad* or reasoned struggle and *istislah* or public interest.

While Rashid Rida argued for the Shariah as the supreme law of the Islamic state, he also allowed for a body of 'positive law' (*qanun*) which is subordinate to the Shariah and is accepted as religiously binding. Moreover, the political leader, Caliph or Imam of the state, Rida argued, should be someone who has the capability of performing *ijtihad* in which he would be aided by a Council of Jurists. Indeed, the head of the state is elected from this Council, modelled after the Electoral Council set up by Umar to find his successor, which itself represents all groups of Muslims. The head of the state thus has both political and religious authority and is one of the main spirits behind the legislative process of the country. Furthermore, he is the head of all Muslims who are to obey him as long as his decisions conform to the principles of Islam and are in the public interest.

Rashid Rida's model of a modern Islamic state has been adopted by various Islamic movements fighting to establish Islamic states throughout the Muslim world. The Muslim Brotherhood, based in Egypt, Sudan and elsewhere in the Middle East, has taken over the model with one modification: in the Brotherhood perspective, the Islamic state is to be created by a militant and armed movement which is charged with a burning mission to establish the rule of the Shariah on earth. In Iran, the same goal was achieved by a violent revolution which overthrew the Shah and gave an opportunity to the *ulama* to test out their theories. But it was in Pakistan where the first experiment to set up an Islamic state was made.

Pakistan as an Islamic State

Pakistan is the first state in contemporary history to be created solely for the sake of Islam. It was to be a separate home for the Muslims of the Indian sub-continent—a home where the rule of the Shariah was supreme, the basic principles and concepts of Islam were fully operationalized, and social justice and equity were dominant. When, on 14 August 1947, Pakistan became established, these were the sentiments and the hopes of millions who sacrificed their property and endangered their lives to make the mass migration from India to the new state; indeed, countless people lost their lives in the process. And the parallels with the historical *hijra*, the migration of the Prophet from Makkah to Medina where he created the first Islamic state, were there for all to witness.

Mohammad Iqbal, the poet-philosopher of the East, who conceived the idea of Pakistan, and Mohammad Ali Jinnah, who turned the idea into reality, were visionaries who really belonged to a future age. Iqbal saw that within a Hindu-dominated India, Muslims would have little chance of cultural and physical survival. A glance at today's India confirms the worst of Iqbal's fears. His achievement was a brilliant synthesis of authentic metaphysical philosophy and sublime poetry into a political vision that was capable of practical realization. But Iqbal's vision of 'a homeland for the Muslims of North-Western India' was only a first step towards the realization of a bigger dream: the reconstruction of the intellectual and philosophical tradition of Islam. In his Presidential Address, delivered at the Annual Session of the All India Muslim League at Allahabad on 29 December 1930, Iqbal pointed out that his vision of Pakistan is based on the premise that Islam is 'an ethical ideal plus a certain kind of polity'. And that polity, he argued, can only become functional in the framework of a 'Muslim national state'.[10]

It was left to Mohammad Ali Jinnah to take Iqbal's embryonic vision to its logical conclusion. Jinnah saw all too clearly that without a separate homeland, the Muslims of India could not put all the dictates of the Qur'an and Shariah into practice. All around him he saw the liberty and faith of Muslims under attack:

internally, atrocities against them both by the British and the Hindus continued to multiply; externally, the Ottoman Empire and the Khilafate had crumbled. So Jinnah had no other choice but to fight for 'a consolidated Muslim State'. It was his genius, commitment and shear hard work that ensured the creation of a homeland for the Muslims of India.

However, while Jinnah rescued the Muslims for British as well as Hindu imperialism, he did not deliver them to Islam. He couldn't really do that for a number of reasons. He had a love–hate relationship with the West: he knew that Western ways of being and doing were not healthy. Listen to him on his death bed:

> The economic system of the West has created almost insoluble problems for humanity, and to many of us it appears that only a miracle can save it from the disaster that is now facing the world. It has failed to do justice between man and man and to eradicate friction from the international field. On the contrary, it was largely responsible for the two world wars in the last half-century. The Western world, in spite of its advantages, of mechanization and industrial efficiency, is today in a worse mess than ever before in history. The adoption of Western economic theory and practice will not help us in achieving our goal of creating a happy and contented people. We must work our destiny in our own way, and present to the world an economic system based on the true Islamic concept of equality of mankind and social justice. We will thereby be fulfilling our mission as Muslims and giving to humanity the message of peace which alone can save it and secure the welfare, happiness and prosperity of mankind.[11]

He said this on 1 July 1948, before it was fashionable to talk about Islamic economics or worry about a New International Economic Order. Yet, Jinnah was very much a product of the Western system. Despite the existence of the Rashid Rida model, he saw Pakistan as a Western type 'nation-state'. While he was very conscious of the fact that an 'Islamic state' had its own distinct identity, not surprisingly he was not sure what this identity really was.

Moreover, Jinnah did not receive any support from those who

could have helped him in shaping a truly distinct and Islamic identity for the new state. A few traditional scholars who could provide him with fresh ideas were too astonished with the speed with which things happened to have full control of their intellectual faculties. Consider, for example, the confusion in Maulana Abul Ala Maududi's mind: first he thought Pakistan was a bad idea, but when it became a reality he changed his view; he was originally of the opinion that constitutional reform was the way to an Islamic state, then he opted for democracy and when that did not work either, he thought that working with a benevolent military dictatorship may be a way forward. Maulana Abu Kalam Azad, perhaps the most intellectually powerful of the traditional scholars, simply sold out: he preferred the company of Gandhi and Nehru to that of Jinnah. And an assortment of other *ulamas* were too busy arguing over the translation of 'Bismillah' and how the constitution of the new state would guarantee that sovereignty belongs to Allah (as if it could belong to anyone else!) to worry about the formidable intellectual agenda of the new country.

Given the status of the traditional scholars, it was natural that the modernist leadership would take over the running of Pakistan. Jinnah had more confidence in the bureaucracy than the politicians or the *ulama*. He thus placed Pakistan in the hands of a civil service which was originally trained to administer the Raj. And this bureaucracy did what it was programmed to do—it turned Pakistan into a replica of a colonial state. In this task the bureaucracy was amiably assisted by the Government of India Act 1935, a product of the British parliament designed to give dictatorial powers to a provincial governor, which became the basis of Pakistan's constitution.

In the early days of Pakistan, the civil service scored a few initial victories: it ensured the survival of Pakistan in its infancy against enormous political and economic pressures from India. It even believed in the goals of Pakistani nationhood. What Liaquat Ali Khan, the first Prime Minister of Pakistan, told the Constituent Assembly of Pakistan in early 1949 echoed not only the thoughts of the politicians but also the sentiments of the bureaucracy:

> The State is not to play the part of neutral observer, wherein the Muslims may be merely free to profess and practice their religion, because such an attitude on the part of the State would be the very negation of the ideals which promoted the demand of Pakistan and it is these ideals which should be the corner-stone of the state which we want to build. The state will create such conditions as are conductive to the building up of a truly Islamic society, which means that the state will have to play a positive part in this effort.[12]

But how was the state to do this? Liaqat Ali Khan did not live to tell us. But the civil service and those who followed him certainly did not have a clue.

But the bureaucracy did know how to bulid a state. After all, its sole function is to run the apparatus of the state; and without a state it has no function. So, while the politicians fought it out among themselves and debated the pros and cons of an Islamic constitution, the civil service set out to build a modern state. And they adopted the only model they understood and the only model they could work: the model of a Western nation-state.

The civil service took the initiative to turn Pakistan into a Western nation-state largely because no one really knew how to go about creating a modern Islamic state. Although there was some consensus among the Pakistani *ulama* and intellectuals that an Islamic state is a constitutional state, that Shariah must become the basis of Pakistan's constitution, no one had the remotest idea what followed afterwards. How was the political leader of the country to be elected? What would be an Islamic solution to many of the pressing economic, social and legal problems of the newly created state? Mohammad Asad, who was the first Director of the Department of Islamic Reconstruction in Punjab, admits that just after its birth no one in Pakistan had the foggiest idea about what constituted an Islamic state, how it could come about and indeed be recognized when it arrived:

> What was needed was the outline of a constitution which would be Islamic in the full sense of the word and would also take the practical requirements of our time into consideration: a demand that was justified by our conviction that the social scheme of Islam supplies valid answers to problems of all times and all stages of human development.

Nevertheless, the existing Islamic literature offered no guidance in our difficulty. Some Muslim scholars of earlier centuries—especially of the Abbasid period—had bequeathed to us a number of works on the political law of Islam; but their approach to the problems had naturally been conditioned by the existing cultural environment and by the sociopolitical requirements of their time, and the result of the labours were therefore inapplicable to the needs of the Islamic state of the twentieth century. The available modern Muslim works on the same subject, on the other hand, suffered as a rule from too great a readiness to accept the political concepts, institutions, and governmental methods of modern Europe as the norm to which (in the opinion of these authors) a modern Islamic state should conform: an attitude in many cases resulted in the adoption by these authors of many concepts which are diametrically opposed to the true demands of Islamic ideology. Thus, neither the works of our predecessors nor those of our contemporaries could furnish a satisfactory conceptual basis on which the new state of Pakistan could be built.[13]

Not much has changed since Mohammad Asad wrote these lines. Numerous attempts at constitutional reforms have been thwarted by the combined might of the bureaucracy, military and opportunistic politicians. However, under General Zia a number of traditional and modern scholars have produced a new theoretical model of an Islamic state.

The new model is a product of the Ansari Commission's Report published in early 1984. The report represents the essence of the constitution-making carried out in Pakistan since its creation and is based on the Objective Resolution 1949, the guiding principle for all constitution-making in Pakistan. The Commission was chaired by a leading Pakistani lawyer and *alim*, Maulana Zafar Ansari, a close companion of Mohammad Ali Jinnah.[14]

The report argues that the goals and objectives of an Islamic state are clear: to seek the pleasure of Allah by implementing the principles and injunctions of the Qur'an and promoting justice in all its multidimensional manifestations. However, as there is a complete consensus in an Islamic society on Qur'anic injunctions, the Ansari Commission argues that there is no need for different political groups and entities to seek alternative targets and goals. In Western secular states, the goals and objectives of the society are by no means defined. As such, different political parties can seek power from different perspectives and for different purposes. Elections can be fought on different ideological platforms, each party wishing to take society in a different direction. As an Islamic state does not permit an ideological change or shift, there is no need for different political parties presenting varying ideological perspectives.

The Commission further argues that in party politics, members are loyal to their particular parties, irrespective of moral considerations or interests of the country. This makes the individual member a prisoner of party policies and restricts his freedom of expression. Moreover, the *raison d'être* of any political party is to secure power which becomes an all-consuming objective in itself. In order to secure power, political parties do not hesitate to play on people's sentiments and emotions, and downgrade and ridicule their opposition. Furthermore, party politics and parliamentary democracy allow access to power only to those who have the financial muscle to contest expensive elections. Often, it is a powerful minority that rules the majority in the name of democracy. Party politics is based on short-term expedient goals to the detriment of the long-term perspectives and the future interests of the society and state.

The Commission takes *shura*, the Qur'anic principle of consultation and cooperation, as the foundation of the political system of an Islamic state like Pakistan. In a system based on *shura*, party politics would divide the consultative body into warring groups: the ruling party and the opposition. The Islamic tradition, on the other hand, suggests that people should give allegiance to a single ruler. Thus the Islamic state is a one-party state based on the principles of *shura*.

In this state, anyone can stand for election, from any constituency, for central or regional Majlis-e-Shura. The central *shura* is divided into an upper house, which represents the state, and the lower house, which represents the people. The head of the state is elected by an electoral college comprising members of the central and regional Majlis-e-Shura. He is duty bound to accept any decisions of the *shura* if it has a two-thirds majority in the Majlis.

He has no power to dissolve the *shura* or to change or abrogate the constitution fully or partly.

In the Ansari Commission's model of an Islamic state, the judiciary is completely independent of the President or the Amir as well as the Majlis-e-Shura—neither have any power to interfere with the process of justice. The Supreme and High Courts have complete power to abrogate any law which they consider to be repugnant to the principles of the Qur'an and the Shariah.

The Ansari model has not been adopted in Pakistan: that there are considerable difficulties with it can be readily seen, a point to which I shall return later. However, it is fair to say that despite the fact that Islam was the underlying motivation for Pakistan, it has never been an Islamic state. Indeed, the tragedy of Pakistan is that it is 'Islamic' only in name. This has led many scholars to argue that Pakistan has failed as an Islamic state, an argument that assumes that throughout its history Pakistan has indeed been functioning as an Islamic state. Those who are disillusioned with Pakistan's experiment often look to Iran as the prototype of the Islamic state of the future.

The Iranian Model of Islamic State

Like the creation of Pakistan, the Iranian Revolution was also undertaken in the name of Islam. The end-product of that revolution, by definition, is an Islamic state. The Iranian *ulama* turned to revolution as a legitimate means of establishing an Islamic state after several decades of struggle for constitutional reforms. However, Iranian *ulama*, being mostly Shia, sought somewhat different reforms than those sought by the Islamic elements in Pakistan. Shia policy is based on the belief in a succession of twelve Imams after the Prophet Mohammad. The last of these is said to be in *ghayba* (occultation) and will appear towards the end of time. The dominant political theme for Iranian Muslims has been the shape of government during the occultation of the twelfth Imam.[15]

Under the Safvid dynasty, Iran progressively moved towards despotism. The *ulama* sought to limit the authority of the monarch to put checks on tyranny and foreign domination. They sought to supervise the constitution and all legislation to ensure that it adhered to Islamic principles. However, the efforts of the constitutional reform movement of the late nineteenth and early twentieth centuries did not produce positive results: the Pahlavi dictatorship and despotism became the dominant political order for Iran. This experience had a profound affect on the thinking of the *ulama* who concluded that constitutional limitation of power was not sufficient to ensure justice and equity in society. As the guardians of the people in the absence of the twelfth Imam, they were duty bound to oversee the whole political process.

Charged with this outlook, the Iranian ulama *threw* themselves into an armed struggle against the Shah. However, unlike the *ulama* elsewhere in the Muslim world, the Shia *ulama* have always had a popular base backed by a strong organizational and institutional structure. The revolution that culminated in the overthrow of the Shah in 1979 thus had mass support.[16]

The model of Islamic state that has emerged in the post-revolution Iran is distinctively Shia. It revolves around the concept of Vilayat-e-Faqih, the Guardianship of the Jurisconsult, which is the supreme authority of the state. Vilayat-e-Faqih, the spiritual and political leader of the state, need not be an individual but can consist of a Leadership Council. In the absence of the twlefth Imam, the Vilayat-e-Faqih is given wide-ranging and decisive powers including the power to declare war, appoint the commanders-in-chief of the army, navy and airforce, appoint the Chief Justice and Prosecutor General, approve presidential elections, and appoint six *Fuqaha* (jurists) of the Shura-e-Nigahban or the Guardianship Council.

The Guardianship Council is the second most powerful body in the state and consists of twelve members—six jurists and six lawyers. The six jurists are nominated by the Vilayat-e-Faqih and the six lawyers are elected by the Majlis (the Parliament) from among those introduced by the Supreme Judicial Council. Matters of Islamic principle are determined by a majority vote of the six jurists and those of constitutional compliance by a majority vote of the whole body. The Council approves all the candidates proposing to stand for presidential and parliamentary elections. It also approves all the legislation passed by the

Majlis-e-Shura-e-Islami, the Islamic Consultative Assembly or the Parliament. Indeed, without its approval any leglislation passed by the Majlis is void.

The third non-elective body is the Supreme Judicial Council. It sits at the apex of the independent judiciary of the state. It includes the Chief Justice and the Prosecutor General and three jurists elected from among the judges throughout the country.

Among the elected bodies, the Majlis-e-Khubragan (the Assembly of Experts) comes into existence by a popular ballot and consists of over eighty jurists and scholars well versed in Islamic law. Its specific task is to fill in any vacancy in the post of the Vilayat-e-Faqih by selecting an individual or a group of three or five. Moreover, it can also dismiss the Vilavat-e-Faqih, whether the office is occupied by an individual leader or Leadership Council.

The second elected institution is the Majlis-e-Shura-Islami. It consists of 270 elected deputies and is the main legislative organ of the state. It is also responsible for approving the President's nominee for Prime Minister and Prime Minister's choice of ministers.

The final elected institution is the office of the President who is elected by a direct ballot, but this must be ratified by the Vilayat-e-Faqih. The President nominates a Prime Minister but this nomination has to be approved by a clear majority of the Majlis-e-Shura. In its turn, the nomination of the Council of Ministers, the cabinet, by the Prime Minister, has also to be approved by the Majlis-e-Shura.

On the surface this governance structure, consisting as it does of three elected and five nominated or indirectly approved institutions, appears to be a theocracy. Indeed, the Shia *ulama*, with their highly structured and organizational institutions, do behave as though they were an organized church. However, the Muslim belief that no man, class of people or sect has any special relationship with God means that Vilayat-e-Faqih does not have any particular spiritual powers, neither is he a viceroy of God. He is not like the Pope of the Catholic Church issuing decrees which become religious law. On the contrary, he rules under the law; and not above it. Moreover, he does not have absolute powers; he can be dismissed by the Shura-e-Nigahban, if he, in their opinion, acts contrary to Islamic law.

Indeed, no single institution seems to have absolute power: each institution is responsible to some other institution, the system of checks and balances ensuring that the final decision that emerges has had an input from all sides. As the core of Islam consists of law rather than theology, the various non-elected and *ulama*-dominated bodies of the state are primarily concerned with the implementation of the Shariah and with ensuring that innovations in law are in accordance with the principles of Islam. The system gives ample freedom to the President, the Prime Minister and the cabinet as the chief executives to look after the other main functions of the state.

Perhaps the most intriguing and successful aspect of this political structure has been the flow of legislation from the Majlis to the Shura-e-Nighaban and back to the Majlis. It is here that new and innovative legislation has been introduced to build a modern Islamic society. Legislation like the one providing for land reform or nationalization of certain sectors of the economy or the Islamization of the banking system, which will have a far-reaching impact on the future shape of Iranian society, has been debated and introduced.

It has been argued that the concept of Vilayat-e-Faqih approximates closely in its political impact to the institution of Khilafat in Sunni political theory.[17] Moreover, it provides an important bridge to transcend the historical divide between the two major groups of Muslims. While it is true that Sunni and Shia political thought has been coming closer and closer over the last decades, it is difficult to demonstrate that the notion of Khilafat and Vilayat-e-Faqih are similar. One of the main difficulties here is the fuzziness that surrounds the modern understanding of Khilafat and its contemporary role.

State and Ideology

There are considerable difficulties with the whole notion of 'Islamic state'. Indeed, even the term itself is self-contradictory: Islam is uncompromisingly universal; state is unquestionably parochial. An Islamic state with its fixed boundaries and allegiance to a particular nation, undermines both the universality of Islam and the notion that the Muslims are one *ummah*, a single global community which shares common political, intellectual and spiritual goals.

The Western concept of state has its origins in the city-states of Greece. The modern Western state is a direct descendant of the Socratic theory of a 'just state'. For Socrates, and the Greek philosophers who followed him, an ideal state is organized into three types of citizens. First there are the common people, artisans and merchants who provide the material wealth for the state's existence. Next came the military who had the responsibility of protecting the state and keeping internal law and order. Finally, there is the class of rulers and guardians, who govern and legislate. To ensure the stability of the state, the three orders are kept separate. To make everyone feel contented with his role in society, the 'rule of, and by, the people', or democracy, was introduced. However, in the Greek states, the 'people' and the 'citizens' are synonymous: democracy for Greeks implied a strictly oligarchic form of government. The 'people' were the free-born inhabitants of the state, who were rarely more than one-tenth of the total population. The majority for whom democracy had little meaning were the serfs and slaves who actually oiled the wheels of the state—the working classes in Marxist jargon.

The modern state contains many of the trappings of its Greek counterpart. But the rise of the nation-state has added a few new dimensions to the classical Greek notion of the state. Two separate but nevertheless interrelated historical forces have been responsible for the changes—the French and the industrial revolutions. The French Revolution challenged the long existing rigid, exploitative social hierarchies of Europe by preaching equality of the individual. But at the same time it promoted the sentiments of nationalism which raised the nation to a new exalted level. It thus freed the individual only to make him the slave of the nation. The industrial revolution introduced new modes of production which brought with it a relentless linear logic of mass production, standardization and vast economic units. The state was thus transformed into a factory, where economic forces and industrial technology worked to create a 'mass society'. Thus the modern state not only has the class structure of its Greek counterpart, but also merges individual identity into larger units and expects the individual to defend the state according to the dictum, 'my country, right or wrong'.

All these shortcomings of modern nation-state are demonstrated, for example, by Pakistan which has adopted the model well; the only difference being that the military, in its zeal to maintain law and order, has become part of the ruling oligarchy.

Moreover, the ideology of Pakistan ensured the legitimacy of such a state. The founding fathers envisioned the Muslims of India as a 'separate nation'. In the pre-independence days, and to some extent in the early stages of Pakistan, this 'nation' was said to embrace the 'ideology of Islam'. Later on, the 'ideology of Islam' became synonymous with the 'ideology of Pakistan'. In either case, this ideology was not seen as a system of ideas and concepts, but as a catalogue of dos and don'ts whose only binding force was emotion. However, with Pakistan standing for Islam it was natural for some people to confuse national emotions with Islamic sentiments. Almost every Pakistani leader, from Sikendar Mirza to Ayub Khan, Zulfiqar Ali Bhutto and Ziaul Haq, has used 'Pakistan's ideology', and the arch spokesman of this ideology, Mohammad Ali Jinnah, as an excuse to legitimize their abhorrent actions. Perhaps the most notorious example of this was Bhutto's attempt to introduce 'Islamic socialism'. He justified it by saying that Jinnah himself supported the idea and talked about it, as could be easily confirmed by examining his speeches!

Ideology, like state, is a western notion. And here too, just as in the case of 'state', the logic and grammar of the notion remains paramount. Indeed, it transforms the Muslim mind and moulds it into strange new shapes. As originally conceived by the French philosopher Destutt de Tracy, ideology was meant to denote a 'science of ideas' which revealed one's biases and prejudices. De Tracy believed only in sense perception and was an empiricist; thus ideology for him was a kind of secular religion. The concept soon gained wide currency signifying not a science of ideas, but a set of beliefs, ideas, values and emotions. Marx and Mannheim gave the concept their individual colour. In Marx's hand, ideology became associated with vested interests of a ruling class or the aspirations of petty bourgeoisie. It is something that is by its nature anti-people. Marxists, therefore, are always 'unmasking' and 'exposing' ideology. Mannheim used the term to present all thought distorted by the passion to conserve the *status quo* or restore the past. For him, ideology represents the programme of action of a vested group; it is reactionary and conservative.

And if the pursuit of an Islamic state becomes an ideology itself, then reason and justice are readily sacrificed at the alter of emotions. And there are always those who take upon themselves the role of the guardians of the ideology, who regard themselves more equal than others and are ever ready to prove it. In revolutions, ideology plays a key role: it is used to arouse emotions of the masses and produces ideologues who assume the leadership of the revolution. Every revolution in history has led to the strengthening of the state and dictatorship in the name of ideology. A small group of ideologues is necessary to carry the revolution through; then the surrounding insecurity becomes so overwhelming that the small group has to consolidate its power to preserve the ideas of the revolution. Dictatorship thus emerges. This is exactly what happened in the early stages of the revolution in Iran.

Ideology is the antithesis of Islam. It is an enterprise of suppression and not a force for liberation. Islam is an invitation to thought and analysis, not to imitation and emotional and political freebooting. Ideology ensures that mistakes and errors are perpetuated; Islam requires an open attitude where mistakes are freely admitted and efforts made to correct them. Islam is not, and cannot be, moulded into ideological boundaries.

By equating Islam with ideology, Muslim intellectuals have presented Islam as a reactionary force, the concern of various vested groups such as the *ulamas* and the *mullahs*, and against the interest of the vast majority. The traditional sector provides ample illustrations to ensure that this image is crystalized. Their ready support for dictators and despots who promise to turn their country, almost overnight, into an Islamic state is truly appalling. It is an undeniable fact that, perhaps apart from Iran, traditional leaders in almost every Muslim country, from Nigeria, Sudan, Egypt, Saudi Arabia, Pakistan, Bangladesh to Malaysia, are among the most narrow-minded, bigoted, antiquated, thoroughly chauvinist and opportunistic group in society. For them, Islam is a personal property to be rented out and leased, hired and sold.

No wonder, then, that the average Muslim cringes with fear at the mention of 'Islamic rule'. And every time an attempt is made to turn a country into an 'Islamic state', as in Pakistan, Libya or Sudan, their worst fears are realized. The picture is always the same: a dictator sits on the throne charged with the belief that he has a divine mandate to impose Islam on the masses.[18] His first actions are to introduce 'Islamic punishment'—as if Islam begins and ends with them—and various public floggings take place to convey the message that he means business. Various groups of *ulamas* and Islamic parties seek appointments in his government and applaud his actions. He declares women to be non-entities, establishes a 'Council of Islamic Ideology' and various 'Shariah courts' where summary justice is seen to be done. Can there be a better invitation to Islam than this?

From Islamic State to Ummah State

The desire of many Muslim countries to become an 'Islamic state' should not become an end in itself; only a means to make Islam the dominant order of the country. Instead of seeking the grand goal of becoming an Islamic state, perhaps administrators and Islamic activists could concentrate on such simple, and admittedly boring, issues as justice and fair play, tolerance and social equality, a more even distribution of wealth, freedom of expression and creativity. 'Islamic state', if it has a meaning, is a process of becoming; not an instant product that is imposed from above irrespective of ills and injustices that are dominant in a society. Muslim intellectuals and *ulamas* owe it to their integrity to articulate such basic notions of Islam as justice and equity, brotherhood and political consent in accordance with contemporary reality and to fight for policies through which these principles can be integrated within the fabric of society. The state will then automatically become 'Islamic'.

However, the days of individual 'Islamic state', akin to the Western nation-state, are limited. This is not just because the concept of 'state' is the antithesis to Islamic universalism, but also for a number of compelling ecological reasons. In the contemporary world, the nation-state has become a dangerous institution. Apart from its divisive and chauvinist nature, it is too small to play a real role at the global level. No individual Muslim state, on its own, can assure its military defence and its prosperity, develop its technological resources or prevent environmental catastrophes. Indeed, the imbalances introduced by the dictates of maintaining what is seen as an adequate defence budget and meeting the basic needs of food and shelter of the people, threatens to tear many Muslim states apart. Moreover, the economic interconnections between nations makes it impossible for any individual government to manage its own economy independently. Individual states cannot meet the demands of employment or control inflation. Furthermore, the global communication system and the accompanying information revolution threatens to remove all frontiers which have hitherto been jealously guarded. Thus the nation-state is splitting at the seams, growing arthritic and crotchety, and progressively becoming less able to cope with the accelerated pace of change.

Given the fact that the nation-state has a limited life, what can take its place? In a Muslim context, the concept of 'one *ummah*, one state' seems the natural candidate to replace the ailing and divisive notion of nation-state. A global *ummah* state may emerge in the future, not only because Muslims desire it, but also because the future dictates it. It is the only guarantee for the physical, cultural and spiritual survival of the *ummah* as a whole. And it is the only conceptual solution that removes all the dichotomies inherent in transforming a nation-state into an 'Islamic state'.

The evolution of a universal *ummah* state with global boundaries is the logical conclusion of the Medina state established by the Prophet. The Medina state was not modelled on the nation-state of today: it incorporated the entire *ummah*. It just so happened that the entire *ummah* of that period was in the city of Medina. That state, in various non-ideal forms, lasted as a legal entity for over 1300 years, until 1922, when it was divided into fragments by European powers. Apart from religious reasons, practical necessity will ensure that various Muslim nation-states are synthesized into one unit. The fear that the creation of one Islamic state will necessarily involve practical uncertainty and extensive warfare is not justified. If in Europe, sheer necessity and practical demands can lead a group of perpetually warring nations to rise above their national interests, develop a European consciousness and work as a unit, what earthly reasons can prevent a spiritually similar people, with a single body of law, from integrating politically?

Political unity is, of course, an outcome of common political consciousness. There is ample evidence to support, as I argued in Chapter 2, that such a consciousness is growing throughout the Muslim world and is manifesting itself in the form of an unrest that covers the region from Morocco to Indonesia. The rise of Islamic awareness is a very powerful force in the growth of political consciousness. Leaving aside the fact that in Islam, the individual, social, political and spiritual consciousness is welded together, even a partial political analysis irresistibly leads to a common political entity. Moreover, given the convergence of Sunni and Shia political thought, the emergence of a state that encompasses the entire *ummah* seems a natural development for the future.

However, certain barriers to this political unity will remain in the next few decades. Monarchs and despots, Westernized elites and ruling classes, will not be easily persuaded to give up their interests. And superpowers will naturally perceive the emergence of a *ummah* state as a threat to their dominance. But the very momentum of history, the dictates of necessity, will sweep these hurdles aside.

The creation of a universal, global *ummah* state is not an exercise in imperialism: it does not involve territorial expansionism or subjugation of one group of people by another. It simply requires internal readjustments in the political organization of Muslim countries and the linking of these independent and autonomous republics into a single state. The unifying factor, the glue that will bind all Muslim republics throughout the globe is the Shariah. It is the Shariah which provides the basis for a *ummah* state and which can ensure its practical realization.

The nature of a universal, global *ummah* state must reflect the nature of Islam itself. Thus it is not a monolithic state with a vast bureaucracy reminiscent of Kafka's *The Castle*. What logic is there in replicating at the global levels the formulae that are failing to cope with complexity at the level of the nation-state? The global state based on a world-view which unites people on the basis of common values and spiritual concerns and a body of law, while promoting diversity in all human expressions must externally present a unified front and internally encourage cultural pluralism and ethnic expression. Nature does not allow monocultures to survive; and monolithic states are not exempt from the laws of nature. *Ummah* state, therefore, must be a decentralized state where individual Muslim communities, ethnic groups and republics must have an autonomous local rule to ensure their full cultural and ethnic flowering. It is rather like the numerous varieties of plant and wild life in a forest which give it its overall integrity and ensure its survival.[19]

While the *ummah* state would guarantee the autonomy of individual Muslim communities, what benefit would it bring them? First of all it will preserve valuable resources which individual Muslim countries allegedly waste on their military and national defence. The *ummah* state, by its very nature, will incorporate a much wider concept of defence, concentrating not just on military defence but also considering such important areas as energy, balance of payments, environmental risks and preservation of religious and cultural identity. It will free individual Muslim countries from superpower bullying and lead to a state of superpower parity. Because it will have a large base, it will be able to promote viable scientific and technological solutions to urgent problems. It will replace 'demand pull' migration with 'supply push' migration leading to purposeful growth with equity and social justice.

All this means that individual Muslim communities will be free to concentrate their energies and resources on fulfilling the basic requirements of an Islamic society. The ultimate goal of any Muslim community is the creation of an order where at least a few basic principles of Islam are clearly paramount. These principles are best expressed in terms of such Islamic concepts as *adl* (justice), *khilafah* (trusteeship), *shura* (consultation) and *istislah* (public interest). No society, however many devout and pious Muslims it may contain, has the right to categorize itself as Islamic if it does not fulfil these minimum conditions.

Justice, in all its multidisciplinary facets, is the ultimate social, economic and political goal of Islam. Without justice, a Muslim community becomes a pathetic caricature. Islamic ideals of justice), *khilafah* (trusteeship), *shura* (consultation) and *istislah* (public equity, individual freedom and social dignity. To achieve these goals, national economic and political affairs have to be arranged in such a way that every member of society is able to fulfil his physical needs, and finds a few hurdles and as much encouragement as possible in the development of his potential and personality. Everyone is equal before the law and every man and woman has the opportunity to realize the ethical goals of Islam in the practical spheres of their lives. It is obvious that such a notion of justice cannot permit wealth to be concentrated among a few families, a rural population that is largely landless, a social structure that reserves unfair advantages and privileges for a certain class (including the military) and oppressive social customs that aggravate the miseries of the poor. Neither can it allow the aggregation of political power in a single class or individual.

When the concept of *adl* is combined with the ideas of *khilafah*, *istislah* and *shura*, the true nature of social, economic and political goals of a Muslim community come to the fore. As a Khilafah, or trustee, of Allah, man is accountable for his trust. This accountability is not just for the Hereafter (*akhrah*); but accountability is sought here and now. This accountability is sought in terms of *istislah*, or public interest. *Istislah* has to be the guiding principle for all public policy, social development and economic reforms. Thus a feudal lord who owns more land than he obviously needs for his family is clearly violating the dictates of *istislah*. Or putting up a factory that will pollute the environment and kill off the fish in the local river is going against the dictates of both *khilafah* and *istislah*. Finally, the principle of *shura* presupposes that the government which is making policies based on the dictates of justice, trusteeship and public interest and undertaking urgent needed reforms has come into existence on the basis of the community's free choice and is fully representative of this choice. *Shura* does not mean hand-picking a group of your pyschophants and seeking their approval; it means consulting the community as a whole. Acquisition of power without the consent of the whole community amounts to, as Mohammad Asad points out, the 'conquest' of the Muslim community. Those who seek to impose Islam by such means, no matter how sincere their intentions, are only worthy of the community's contempt.

No Muslim would disagree with the fact that unlike democracy, where sovereignty belongs to the people, in Islam it belongs to God. However, this does not mean that Islam requires that people should be excluded from the political processes. Or because the people completely agree that the Qur'an and Sunnah are their guide, they do not have different opinions or ideas about how to make Islam the dominant order of the community. Why should an individual group have the monopoly of ideas on how best to implement the principles and injunctions of Islam? Just because two groups of people share a set of goals does not mean that they cannot develop two alternative, and equally valid, approaches to achieve them. And why shouldn't the community as a whole be given the choice of selecting which group has the best policy and therefore the best chance of realizing the goals that every one cherishes? The rejection of democracy as an ideology, where sovereignty is handed over to the people, does not mean the rejection of democracy as a principle for the participation of people in the political process. The principles of *shura* and *ijma* dictate that the people must be allowed to participate fully in the shaping of a political structure and selection of the leadership of a community.

The task before Muslim scholars and intellectuals, therefore, is to ensure that the basic principles of Islam are paramount in their community and to do the intellectual spadework needed for a smooth transition from the present situation of numerous Muslim nation-states in mutual conflict to the *ummah* state which brings together Muslim countries and communities throughout the globe into a integrated whole yet preserves their individual autonomy. In particular, there are certain issues which need urgent attention:

1. Since the emergence of the *ummah* state is a necessity for the political and cultural survival of the Muslims, what attitudinal and institutional changes—with and among Muslim countries—are needed, and how might they be brought about?

2. Interdependence and autonomy: how can the dictates of interdependence and autonomy be realized in an Islamic framework? What criteria must the *ummah* state fulfil before it becomes a viable, integrated state? How can its individual constituents ensure that they have full autonomy? What areas ought to be the exclusive preserve of local community; and what areas should be handled by the *ummah* state?

3. Synthesis of political thought. How can we synthesize current modes of political thought in the Muslim world? How can we generate a unified political outlook that individual countries can believe in and work towards? How will this synthesis lead to a common polity?

4. Science and technology. What science and technology policies will bring Muslim countries together and demonstrate the benefits of cooperation and a unified approach? How can scientific and technological cooperation between Muslim states be increased to a level where pooling of resources becomes a natural process? What role can science and technology perform in the creation of a global *ummah* state?

5. The role of communication. How can computers, satellites and modern communication techniques be best used for promoting integration and cooperation in the Muslim world and used to usher in a common polity that eventually leads to the creation of a *ummah* state? How can a proper balance be struck between the centralizing and pluralizing effects of modern communication technology? How can Muslim communities use this technology to maximize human choices without infringing on diversity, creativity and freedom of flow of information between and among Muslim countries?

These and other equally important questions need to be answered both to prepare the ground for a *ummah* state and to act as a catalyst for its realization. An Islamic society, let alone a global universal *ummah* state, cannot occur in the absence of proper intellectual homework. As long as intellectuals and *ulamas* have no real answers but only slogans, as long as Western concepts and notions shape the thought of Muslim thinkers, as long as Islam remains the business of a few and not the purview of the vast majority, opportunist politicians and the military will continue to exploit the unrest that is paramount in Muslim countries.

Notes

1. Ayatollah Khomeini, *Islamic Government*, trans. by Hamid Algar, Mizan Press, 1982.

2. Abd'al-Rahman Azzam, *The Eternal Message of Muhammad*, Quartet, London, 1979, p. 113; originally published in 1964.

3. Muhammad Asad, *The Principles of State and Government in Islam*, Dar al-Andalus, Gibraltar, 1980, p. 33; originally published in 1961.

4. For a detailed account of the Median constitution, see Muhammad Hamidullah, *The First Constitution in the World*, Ashraf, Lahore, 1970. See also A. A. Kurdi, *The Islamic State: A Study Based on the Holy Constitution*, Mansell, London, 1985, who uses the Medina constitution to develop a contemporary model of an Islamic state which aims to secure 'freedom from outside invasions, the security of domestic tranquillity and the provision of justice, equality and personal security for its people'.

5. M. Hadi Hussain and A. H. Kamali, *The Nature of the Islamic State*, National Book Foundation, Karachi, 1977, p. 4.

6. *Ibid.* pp. 10–11.

7. For a detailed account of the thought of Mohammad Abduh and Rashid Rida, see M. A. Zaki Badawi, *The Reformers of Egypt*, Croom Helm, London, 1979.

8. Hamid Enayat, *Modern Islamic Political Thought*, Macmillan, London, 1982, p. 77.

9. *Ibid.* p. 78.

10. M. H. Saiyid, *Mohammad Ali Jinnah: A Political Study*, Elite Publishers, Karachi, 1962, p. 153.

11. M. Quoted by Hector Bolitho *Jinnah: Creator of Pakistan*, John Murray, London, 1954, pp. 217–18.

12. *Constituent Assembly of Pakistan Debates*, vol. 5, 7 March 1949; quoted by Syed Abdul Quddus, *Pakistan: The Task Before Nation*, S. I. Gillani, Lahore, 1980, p. 18.

13. Mohammad Asad, *ibid*. p. x.

14. For a summary of the Ansari report, see 'Pakistan: A blueprint for return to civilian rule', *Afkar: Inquiry*, **1** (1), 13–15 (June 1984).

15. For an introduction to Shia theology, see S. M. Jafary, *Sh'ite Islam*, Longman, London, 1979.

16. For an account of the Iranian Revolution, see Hamid Algar, *The Islamic Revolution in Iran*, Open Press, London, 1980.

17. For example, by Hamid Enayat, *op. cit.*

18. In contrast to modern dictators and despots intent on foisting their versions of Islam on the people, consider this speech by Caliph Yazid III (d. 744) delivered immediately after his election: 'O people, I pledge myself to erect no buildings, to let out on lease none of your rivers, to build no palace, to hoard up no riches, to enrich neither wife nor child. From me is due to you your annuity year by year, and provisions month by month, so that prosperity among Muslims may increase, and those who live far away may participate in it just as well as those living near. Should I keep my promise, you are duty bound to listen to me and cheerfully obey me to support and protect me. If, on the other hand, I do not keep my word, you are at liberty to depose me; only you should give me timely warning, and where I do amend my ways, then you should accept my apology. Should you, however, know a man of tried temper who willingly offers what I have offered to you, choose, then, such a one, and, if you so desire, I shall be the first to do him homage and render him obedience.' Quoted by Khuda Bakhsh, *Orient Under the Caliphs*, Calcutta, 1920, p. 250.

19. A number of authors have argued that the Muslim world should be integrated into a 'commonwealth'. See, for example, Manzooruddin Ahmed, *Islamic Political System in the Modern Age*, Saad Publications, Karachi, 1983, where he proposes a federal structure for the integration of the Muslim world.

7

Islamic Science:
Reclaiming a Heritage

Science is the basic problem-solving tool of any civilization. Without science a civilization cannot maintain its political and social structures or meet the basic needs of its people and culture. As an external manifestation of an epistemology, science shapes physical, intellectual and cultural environment and promotes the chosen economic mode of production of a civilization. In short, science is the tool which ultimately moulds a civilization: it is a physical expression of its world-view.

Modern science has evolved and matured in the bosom of the Western civilization. It is an expression of the Western mode of thought which isolates what belongs to God and what belongs to Caesar. It is a legacy of the Judaeo-Christian intellectual heritage and the ultimate manifestation of the world-view of this tradition. As a product of Western culture and intellectual tradition, modern science is distinctively occidental. In the words of Lynn White Jr, all 'around the globe, all significant science is western in style and method, whatever the pigmentation or language of the scientist'.

When Francis Bacon said that 'nature gives up her secrets under torture', he summed up the basic axioms on which the foundations of modern science are built. Torture, and its natural corollary domination, has been the central theme of occidental science. It is not an accident that much of contemporary science is intrinsically linked with the war machine; that fundamental biological research inevitably leads to torture of animals; the genetic manipulation and control of individuals is an explicit goal of such emerging fields as socio-biology; and most of the products of modern science are used for domination of the vast majority of humankind, the Third World, by a select minority—the industrialized countries.

The intellectual and scholarly tradition which is responsible for the present status of science has its roots in the Enlightenment which is considered by many to be the beginning of modern times.

> The Enlightenment was the work of the *philosophes*, the intellectuals who conceived and perfected it. The *philosophes* looked at science and exploration not just for new knowledge but also for new attitude towards knowledge. From science they acquired the sceptical attitude of systematic doubt, and from exploration a new relativistic attitude towards belief and used them as ammunition against traditional norms and values. Montesquieu's tolerant Persians, Voltaire's sage Chinese, Diderot's virtuous Tahitians, coming after Fountenelle's plurality of worlds, that was designed to reduce man in his pride, all served excellently as weapons to knock down European society and for suggesting a better one. Curiously, the effect of such scepticism and relativism was to glorify and magnify man in general and European man in particular. When the Enlightenment wanted to characterise its power in one word it called it 'Reason'. 'Reason' became the verifying force of the eighteenth century, expressing all it strives for and all that it achieves.[1]

However, reason was not the discovery of the intellectual spokesmen of the Enlightenment or of Bacon and Descartes. What the Enlightenment did was to raise reason to a level where it became the sole arbitrator of all human thought and actions, values and norms. Reason, therefore, replaced the Christian God. Its use was thus not limited to mathematical and physical knowledge, but was used to dissect all branches of human endeavour. Such traditional disciplines as politics, ethics, metaphysics and religion were analysed on the basis of reason and logic with a view to ending their perplexities once and for all. The principles which the *philosophes* attempted to apply became the new cannons of science: there was to be no *a priori* deduction from 'natural' principles without concrete experimental evidence. Anything that did not submit to the tyranny of the new methodology was dismissed and discarded as unintelligible and meaningless.

The seventeenth-century philosophical struggle for a new epistemology involved, besides the proponents of the Enlightenment, two other groups. Against the 'mechanical' world-view presented by the Enlightenment was the 'organic' world-view of the Aristotelians who were mainly university-based, and the 'magical' world-view of practising alchemists. But the opponents of the Enlightenment were swept aside; its world-view became paramount and its epistemology has dominated science for the last 300 years.

In the epistemology of the Enlightenment, knowledge and values are kept in isolated, watertight compartments. The pursuit of knowledge *per se* becomes *the* arch value to which all other values, including the sacredness of life itself, are sacrificed. Bacon gave the pursuit of knowledge a specific direction with his aphorism, 'knowledge and power meet in one'. The power, secular as well as material power operating socially, became the dominant value replacing the personal, intuitive and contemplative value which had for generations emphasized the cultivation of nature. The social legitimation of this epistemology, relentless pursuit of knowledge for the sake of material and political power, was provided by the expectation that it will lead to happiness and improve the conditions of human life.

However, the expectations of the early 'heroic' ages have not been fulfilled. As Ravetz argues,

the style of Occidental science and technology which suppressed and ignored the questions of values, which was based on the faith that all problems could be decided 'scientifically', now finds enmeshed in even deeper contradictions. (A) category produced by Alvin Weinberg, that of 'trans-science', describes the problems that we face. It is impossible to calculate the risks and the environmental impact through the future life of any major technological development. Our science is totally inadequate to such a task, and even if it were better developed would probably not be good enough. And so when we decided on some major innovation, be it a concentrated unit like a nuclear power station or a diffused technology like the automobile or the microchip this has been done not on the basis of science but on the basis of guesses, speculations, commitments, values ... Our Occidental science, then, has given us paradoxes and contradictions all round; and this is the present state of knowing and doing and being based on a certain restricted contact with the world of reality, and whose intellectual faith involved the relegation of the realm of values to another irrelevant and impotent sphere. The triumphs of this Occidental system are all around us but its perils are crowding in upon us at an increasing rate ...[2]

The 'perils' of occidental science manifest themselves in the form of frightening arsenals of nuclear, chemical and biological weapons; an environmental *Gotterdammerung*; through fears of potential scientific advances in such fields as genetic engineering and socio-biology leading to new forms of control and domination; the explicit use of science for the purpose of imperialism as is evident from the absorption of university science into secret research funded by defence departments; the alienation of man and nature; the computer invasion of privacy; and a runaway technology that is leading humankind by the nose towards a massive pileup on the highway to the future. Collectively, these not so inviting outcomes of the epistemology of science are threatening the very existence of mankind and the very abode of our terrestrial journey.

These developments are the result not so much of a science that is 'neutral' and 'value-free', but a science that is explicitly seeking out values which form its basic foundations: separation of 'knowledge' from social, moral and ethical concerns, and the pursuit of this knowledge for the sake of secular and material power and control over man and nature. The belief that scientific knowledge, based on observation and theory, and the assessment of what is true and what is probable, is totally 'objective', not concerned with human values and social issues, is at best naive and at worse highly dangerous. Far from being independent of values, scientific knowledge is shaped by values and constructed by the dominant social and cultural themes of the Western civilization.

Science and Values

Science is not just the collection and analysis of data and the construction of theories based on this analysis. It is an activity of human beings, acting and interacting, and thus a social activity. Science involves peoples and values. As David Morley writes,

> the pure scientist does not exist in isolation from the rest of society: he spends its money, educates its children, heals its sick and feeds its hungry, develops its consumer products—indeed, there is almost no aspect of modern life which is untouched by science and the scientist. He is also a human being and a citizen, who makes mistakes, collaborates and competes with his scientific colleagues, tries to persuade others to do what he thinks is right; who, in short, displays all the qualities and failings of the human race. Man is an ethical animal, and so is the scientist.[3]

If scientists are mortal human beings and science is what they do, how is it possible for them to focus upon nature to the virtual exclusion of themselves? How is it possible for scientists to exclude their values, biases and preferences from what they do?

The conventional answer to such questions is that sicentific discovery is a product of detached, rational inquiry; it is a process on which human emotions and values cannot play any part. A discovery is something unmasked and revealed for the first time. Unlike an invention which has to be constructed, a discovery is simply encountered. And what is discovered is already there: it is an integral part of the world. As such one cannot discover falsehood or untruths as reality does not correspond to them. As scientific discovery reveals the truth, brings some hitherto hidden aspect of reality to the fore, science is the pursuit of truth. And as truth, aspects of material reality do not take sides: science and scientific discoveries are neutral and value-free.

The flaws in this ideal picture of science have now been thoroughly exposed. There is the obvious criticism of selection of areas deemed important and worthy of scientific investigation: both the priorities and emphasis of science, which lead to certain discoveries being made and certain others *not* made, are determined by cultural and political criteria such as where are the funds coming from, which areas would lead to possible profitable discoveries and what areas are culturally beneficial to pursue. Hence the emphasis on cancer research rather than finding cures for diarrhoea, obesity rather than malnutrition, high-rise buildings rather than mud dwellings. But the criticism of science goes much beyond the questions of emphasis and priorities. It goes right to the heart of the nature of science itself.

The methodology of science aims at proving theories by gathering experimental evidence. However, Popper has shown that tis key element of scientific method is based on a logical fallacy. No matter how large a number of experiments and observations confirm a particular proposition, they cannot *prove* that the next one will not threaten all those that went before. This illogicality of the inductive leap undermines the notion of science as a rational enterprise. Popper's face-saving solution to get around this inherent illogicality in the methodology of science was to propose a 'technical fix': the driving force behind science is no longer to be confirmation but refutation. Scientists would proceed and develop their hypothesis by a series of tests that would prove them to be false and would apply these tests until the theory fell, giving rise to a new one with greater powers of explanation and prediction which would be tested in a similar way.[4]

While Popper's criticism of a logical fallacy at the heart of scientific method reduces science's claim to be the arch mode of rational inquiry, and his hypothetical-deductive method avoids some of the pitfalls of theory development, it does not highlight the values inherent in modern science. That task was accomplished by Thomas Kuhn.

The conventional explanation of discovery relates scientific knowledge entirely to nature, truth and reality and not at all to culture. Kuhn examines the role of discovery in science by analysing concrete case studies. For example, the discovery of oxygen is identified with the experiments carried out by Priestley in 1775, or another done by Lavoisier in 1776. Kuhn asks: is the discoverer of oxygen the first person to obtain a sample of a gas? If this were so, then Hales in the 1730s would be the discoverer or, failing that, Bayen in the early 1770s, as both did what is required to produce the gas as a new kind of substance. However, neither knew what he had, and accordingly is not recognized as the discoverer of oxygen. Having a vessel full of oxygen did not make Hales its discoverer, any more than having a lung-full of oxygen made Adam its discoverer. In discovery, possession is not nine-tenths of the law. To be recognized as a discoverer, one has to change one's thinking—to know what one is in possession of. Thus, if discovery is an event, it is a psychological event: a new perception, a flash of insight, a change of *gestalt*. Priestley was able to make the necessary change in perception to realize that he had made something new. But his awareness grew slowly; it was not a single psychological event. Moreover, Priestley changed this thinking the 'wrong' way. He thought that the new gas was common air with less than the normal amount of 'phlogiston', a substance that burning material gave off. When air became saturated with 'phlogiston', materials ceased to burn as there was no room for any more. Materials burned more vigorously in the new gas because it had less than the normal amount of 'phlogiston'.[5]

Scientific discoveries, then, are not 'events' at which nature's secrets are laid bare by some highly motivated searcher for the truth. If it is an event at all, it is a psychological event which produces a new realization in the scientist. This can be illustrated further with a more recent example: the discovery of pulsars. Pulsars are stars which emit pulses with the precision of a cosmic clock. Since they existed out there, waiting to be discovered, one would have thought that simply pointing a radio telescope towards them would have been enough to detect the pulses and produce the 'event' of discovery. However, nothing of the sort happened.

In August 1967, Anthony Hewish and his assistant Jocelyn Bell, while probing the sky with their radio telescope, came across some very peculiar radio signals. On amplified recording, these signals appeared as little flickers. Hewish thought that they were no more than interference signals from a passing car or an aeroplane. This idea was abandoned when it was established that the signals always originated from the same celestial coordintes. The signals disappeared for four weeks and reappeared again as extremely sharp bursts regularly spaced with an interval of approximately 1.3 seconds. Now Hewish thought that the signals were coming from a space probe secretly sent by the Russians. However, calculations showed that the signals were coming from outside the solar system and their source was the size of a small planet. The next thought was that they were being sent by 'little green men', intelligent beings on a small planet. But the 'Doppler effect' test revealed that the source of the signals was not a planet. Observations and theoretical calculations involved many astronomers and when all those involved concluded that the signals were coming from some sort of a 'collapsed star', discovery claims were published.

The discovery of pulsars (apart from the controversy that the credit should have gone to Jocelyn Bell, who feels cheated, rather than Anthony Hewish) was a long drawn-out process. And as Barry Barnes writes, it was

> a process of cognitive change, initially within a small group of scientists. This is the typical pattern. However clear nature's communications might be, they are not encoded in language: nature does not describe itself. It is we who give meaning to her messages by determining how they should be fitted into existing concepts and beliefs, and how far our existing concepts and beliefs should be modified and extended to accommodate them. Another way of putting this is to say that there is no relevant difference between 'theoretical' and 'factual' concepts in science: both kinds of concepts are our *inventions*—'star' and 'pulsar' as much as 'phlogiston' and 'oxygen'. And from this it follows that to 'discover' corresponding entities of either kind involves processes of cognitive orientation.[6]

The assimilation of a 'discovery' within a rigid framework of accepted beliefs and practices is the conventional methodology of science. Kuhn termed this 'normal science': this is what the vast majority of scientists do. They solve problems within the existing framework, refine ideas and make discoveries that fit the accepted notions. The framework of fundamental beliefs and practices, the paradigm, determines what problems are to be investigated, the style in which solutions of these problems are offered; and the criteria of acceptability which these solutions have to meet. Science continues along this course, argues Kuhn, until the paradigm itself becomes fossilized, ceases to pose interesting questions, and various anomalies which cannot be fitted into the paradigm come to the fore. A crisis now engulfs normal science and eventually leads individual scientists to question the fundamental framework of beliefs and practices which constitute the paradigm. From now on 'revolutionary science' takes over. Numerous alternative paradigms emerge, all questioning the legitimacy of the hitherto dominant paradigm which is vigorously defended by those whose life's work is threatened by the emergence of a new paradigm. The period of revolutionary science is short-lived as eventually scientists gather around one of the alternative paradigms which now assumes the role of orthodoxy; and normal science begins life once again.[7]

The new paradigm is not selected on a neutral or rational basis; it is not free from personal or partisan influence of scientists. Indeed, Kuhn argues that there is no clear scientific test that enables individual scientists to choose between competing paradigms. However, if paradigms are not chosen on the basis of some objective, universal criteria, then what of the objectivity and neutrality of science? The belief in science as an objective, neutral and value-free enterprise simply collapses. And science loses all its alleged claim to be unique and universal.

Kuhn's work has been taken further by a number of people. For example, Ravetz has argued that science is 'industrialized',[8] Feyerabend has argued that science is dominated by anarchy,[9] Rose and Rose proclaim that there is ideology in and of science,[10] Mitroff has demonstrated that the subjective elements of science far outweigh the alleged objective criteria;[11] and most critics inside and outside the scientific community now argue that scientific knowledge is socially constructed. The new starting-point for anyone who is aware of the vast literature on 'science and society' that has accumulated over the last decade[12] is the recognition that science is not inevitably progressive, nor even a neutral set of facts, theories and techniques which can be used for good or evil. Nor are the scientists highly righteous individuals accumulating abstract knowledge for the benefit of the entire humankind. Science and its practitioners are locked into a social and cultural order: the oppressive and anti-human technologies they generate are not merely accidental abuses or unwanted spin-offs of beneficial research. They are part and parcel of the total system of

Western science, which itself is an integral component of the Occidental civilization.

Approaches to Science within Islam

The work of Kuhn and other critics of science is just beginning to have an impact on Muslim scientists and intellectuals. Although the belief in the objective and neutral nature and science is paramount, the awareness of the fact that scientific knowledge is socially constructed is beginning to dawn in many Muslim academic and intellectual circles. A series of conferences over the last decade, on various aspects of science and Muslim societies, has further enhanced interest in the concept of an 'Islamic Science', a socially concerned science set within the world-view of Islam.

The interest in discovering a contemporary style of doing science which fully incorporates the ethical dictates of Islam and is an embodiment of Islamic culture and tradition is particularly strong among the young scientists and intellectuals. Mashhood Ahmed's study on 'Islamic ethos and Muslim scientists' provides some evidence for this.[13] The study examines the attitudes and motivations of seventy Muslim scientists (professors, readers and lecturers) at the Chemistry, Zoology, Botany, Geology and Physics Departments of the Aligarh Muslim University, Aligrah, India. Ahmed finds that younger scientists tend to be more aware and critical of the value orientation of science. Moreover, while only 50 per cent of the older generation admits that Islamic values and ethos could play a part in their scientific activities, over 71 per cent of young Muslim scientists *insist* that Islamic values can and should be made the basis of scientific enterprise. I found similar generational differences, with older scientists clinging to the 'international culture of science' with its alleged claims to all-pervasive neutrality and younger ones arguing for a science based on the world-view of Islam, when I visited university campuses throughout the Muslim world for the British science journal *Nature*.[14]

The different attitudes of the young and the more senior Muslim scientists have produced distinctively different approaches to the issue of science and Islam. Apart from those scientists who dismiss the whole question of Islamic science as irrelevant, arguing that science is neutral and universal and hence the same for all cultures, there is another group of scientists which seeks to legitimize modern science by equating it with the Qur'an. This is done by pointing out that the Qur'an places great emphasis on the pursuit of knowledge and use of reason: some 750 verses, almost one-eighth of the Qur'an in contrast to only 250 legislative verses, exhorts the believers to study nature, reflect, make the best use of reason, and make scientific enterprise an integral part of the community life. It is further pointed out that the Qur'an mentions several scientific facts and theories all of which are supported by recent discoveries and advances. The influence drawn from this is two-fold: if the facts and theories mentioned in the Qur'an, which was revealed 1400 years ago, are supported by modern science, the divine nature of the Qur'an is confirmed, if confirmation is indeed needed; and if modern scientific facts and theories find a reflection in the Qur'an, then modern science must have the same universal and eternal validity as the Qur'an.

The standard reference work which propagates this type of approach to science and Islam is *The Bible, the Qur'an and Science* by Maurice Bucaille, a French surgeon.[15] After a thorough and detailed analysis of the 'holy scriptures in the light of modern knowledge', Bucaille, whose book has been translated into most Muslim languages and enjoys a huge following in Muslim intellectual circles, concludes that

> the Qur'an most definitely did not contain a single proposition at variance with the most firmly established modern knowledge, nor did it contain any of the ideas current at the time of the subjects it describes. Furthermore, however, a large number of facts are mentioned in the Qur'an which were not discovered until modern times. So many in fact, that on November 9, 1976, the present author was able to read before the French Academy of Medicine a paper on the 'Physiological and Embryological data in the Qur'an'. The data—like many others on differing subjects—constituted a veritable challenge to human explanation—in view of what we know about the history of the various sciences through the ages. Modern man's findings concerning the absence of scientific error are therefore in complete agreement with the 'Muslim exegetes' conception of the *Qur'an as a*

Book of Revelation. It is a consideration which implies that God could not express an erroneous idea.[16]

The Bible, of course, did not meet the stringent criteria of modern knowledge, and the 'clear-cut' conclusion of Bucaille that 'it is impossible not to admit the existence of scientific errors in the Bible' simply confirms the Muslim belief that the Bible, as it exists today, is not true divine revelation.

Bucaille's study has motivated numerous Muslim scientists and scholars to look further for scientific facts and theories in the Qur'an. Thus Shamsul Haq, for example, manages to find the 'seeds of the theory of relativity and quantum mechanics in the Qur'an' and produces Qur'anic evidence to support the Big Bang theory.[17] M. Manzoor-i-Khuda manages to find the theory of the development of the biosphere, the water cycle of life on earth, and even a justification for the geological development of earth in the Qur'an![18] Numerous scholars have looked for 'embryology in the Qur'an'. The most noted effort is by Keith L. Moore whose 'Highlights of human embryology in the Koran and the Hadith', which when it was first presented at the Seventh Saudi Medical Meeting, caused excitement similar to an earth-shattering discovery.[19] Moore simply illustrates the Qur'anic verses describing the development of a foetus with clinical drawings and textbook descriptions.

Bucaillism appeals particularly to the older generation of Muslim scientists because of its psychological message value. It reinforces their faith in the Qur'an and Islam, on the one hand, and confirms their belief in the superiority and universal validity of Western science, on the other. Their naivete is well reflected by Candide: all is well in this best of all possible worlds.

However, the dangers inherent in Bucaillism are very grave. There is the obvious fact that it generates a strangely dumbfounding theology—as all scientific knowledge is contained in the Qur'an, simply studying it from a scientific perspective will reveal all and lead to new theories and discoveries. While the Qur'an obviously contains some passing references to natural facts, it is not a textbook of science. It is a book of guidance: it provides motivation, and only motivation, for the pursuit of

knowledge. Knowledge begins with the Qur'an and does not end
with it.

But more important, by equating the Qur'an with science,
Bucaillism elevates science to the realm of the sacred and makes
divine revelation subject to the verification of Western science.
Apart from the fact that the Qur'an needs no justification from
modern science, Bucaillism opens the Qur'an to the counter-
argument of Popper's criteria of refutation: would the Qur'an be
proved false, and written off just as Bucaille writes off the Bible, if
a particular scientific fact does not tally with it or if a particular
fact mentioned in the Qur'an is refuted by modern science? And
what if a particular theory, which is 'confirmed' by the Qur'an
and is in vogue today, but is abandoned tomorrow for another
theory that presents an opposite picture? Does that mean that the
Qur'an is valid today but will not be valid tomorrow?

Moreover, by raising science to the level of sacred knowledge,
Bucaillism effectively undermines any criticism of science.
Because the pursuit of knowledge is so strongly emphasized in the
Qur'an, most Muslim scientists already possess a sense of reverence towards modern science. Bucaillism takes this reverence to a
new level: a whole generation of Muslim scientists do not just
accept all science as good and true, but attack anyone who shows
a critical or sceptical attitude towards science. Furthermore, the
belief in a universally beneficial science leads to a pestiferous kind
of fatalism: since it is universal and for the benefit of all humankind, it will eventually make its way to Muslim societies and serve
their needs!

In contrast to Bucaillism, a second approach to Islam and
science takes a more critical attitude towards the latter. While
still preserving the belief in the neturality and universality of
science, the proponents of this approach argue that when science
is pursued within an Islamic polity its functions are modified to
serve Islamic ideals and Muslim societies. The consciousness of
devout Muslims and the dynamic principles of movement in
Islam, *ijtihad*, ensures that science is put to proper social use and
given a new cultural and intellectual boost. The cause of 'science
in Islamic polity' has been particularly championed by Pakistani
scientists and is articulated in a paper presented to the Interna-

tional Conference on Science in Islamic Polity by Z. A. Hashmi of the Pakistan Academy of Sciences:

> A culture with such an exalted vision of man's role and responsibilities and with such a commitment to seek understanding, knowledge and truth through observation, reflection and reasoning (as Islam) provides the ideal motivation and environment for the cultivation of science. There is thus no reason at all to blindly follow the West (which faced a totally different situation) and divorce religion from the scientific and developmental activities in Muslim polity, for Islam does not constitute an impediment but is a source of strength for science . . .
>
> The renaissance of science in the Muslim *ummah* must thus be accomplished within the parameters of Islamic consciousness. There is a great challenge to reclaim and rehabilitate the elements of vitality and beauty from the treasure-house of our cultural tradition. Without this, the transfer of western science and technology would have highly disruptive consequences on the nature of our society and culture. While accepting modern science and technology, the Muslim *ummah* must arrange to carefully screen such transfer and eliminate the mechanistic, hedonistic and deterministic tendencies and the amoral stance of the West, which is accompanying the thoughtless and mechanical transfer of science and technology from Western societies.[20]

Hashmi argues that for Muslim scientists to be in position to eradicate the unwanted elements of Western science and technology, they must be trained in history and philosophy of science and have awareness of the future developments of science and technology. His goals for a science policy in an Islamic polity include improving the understanding and love of science among people, building adequate and effective natural science and technology systems, pooling of human and material resources of the Muslim world and ensuring that science and technology systems are 'directed towards the achievement of socio-economic goals, in particular the welfare of the people, economic growth, national security and cultural development'.

While 'science in Islamic polity' approach succeeds to a large extent in making science subservient to the goals and values of Muslim societies, it seriously underestimates the power of science to change society; indeed, change a polity beyond recognition. If one accepts the argument, based on Kuhnian analysis, that the entire system of science that exists today is so deeply entrenched in Western values and culture that, as Ravetz has argued and Mitroff has shown, even the experimental and quantitative techniques cannot escape the onslaught of these values, then the practice of this science in an Islamic polity, far from promoting the ideals and values of Muslim societies, would in fact completely undermine these values. Indeed, there will always be conflict and tension between the goals of this science and Islamic polity.

It has been argued by certain scholars that a science whose processes and methodologies incorporate the spirit of Islamic values, promote such ideals and goals of the world-view of Islam as brotherhood, social justice, adequate use of natural resources, remind man of his trusteeship of God and increase spiritual awareness, and serve the needs and requirements of Muslim societies, is quite a different entity in nature and style than modern science. As it is an embodiment of the values, culture and the intellectual tradition of Islam, it is most appropriately called Islamic science.

Islamic Science: the Emerging Paradigm

That there is an Islamic alternative to Western science was first pointed out by Seyyed Hossein Nasr in his brilliant study, *The Encounter of Man and Nature*.[21] Nasr's thesis, which he argues with powerful conviction, is simple: while science is legitimate in itself, the role and functions of Western science and its applications have become illegitimate and highly dangerous because it is completely divorced from a higher form of knowledge.

To make it explicit that other approaches to studying nature and material reality are possible, Nasr declares:

> The independent critical function which reason should exercise *vis-à-vis* science, which is its own creation, has disappeared so that this child of the human mind has itself become the judge of human values and the criterion of truth. In this process of reduction, in which the independent and critical role of philosophy has itself been surrendered to the edicts of modern science, it is often forgotten that the scientific

revolution of the seventeenth century is itself based upon a particular philosophical position. It is not *the* science of nature but *a* science making certain assumptions as to the nature of reality, time, space, matter etc. But once these assumptions were made and a science came into being based upon them, they have been comfortably forgotten and the result of this science made to be the determining factor as to the true nature of reality.[22]

The 'nature of reality' can also be described, quantitatively and objectively, by a science derived from a non-Western philosophical position which makes different assumptions about nature, time, space, matter, natural resources and the position and responsibility of human beings in creation.

Other scholars have argued for Islamic science from different perspectives. From a Kuhnian position, Glyn Ford states the case for Islamic science in its simplest form:

If science is not the unique intellectual construct which until so recently it was portrayed, if history of science is not the history of iterative movements towards the truth about the natural world but rather the history of various social constructions of reality mediated through science, scientists and society, then there exists the possibility of an Islamic science that will be one facet, or more likely a series of facets, of a multi-dimensional world of nature, all of which are imbued with the very essence of Islamic society. In this it only parallels those commonly accepted links between culture and society exclusive of science.[23]

Munawar Ahmad Anees sees the *raison d'être* of Islamic science in combating reductionism 'the central theme of modern science'. Anees states:

The argument that reductionism should be allowed to take its logical course is now dangerously untenable. Moreover, the stand that reductionism is by itself a good thing because the pursuit of knowledge can only bear beneficial fruits of mankind is naive—there is no indigenous self-correcting methodology in reductionism that will stop it from the path of oblivion. The alternative, and to my mind the only alternative, is to pursue science in a clearly defined framework of values. Islam provides both a system of enlightened coherent values as well as an example of how science can be pursued within the confines of these values. In the history of Islamic science and technology, there is a clear and distinct body of knowledge known as 'Islamic science'. We need to learn a great deal about the methodological content of Islamic science . . .

That Islamic science is no antithesis of reductionism is clear even from a casual perusal of the history of Islamic science. But what is unique about the methodological approach of Islamic science is that it emphasises balance, synthesis, treats reductionism not as an ideology but only as one method amongst a whole array of methods and it is essentially self-correcting. The inherent control mechanism of Islamic science is to develop and sustain a variable approach that neither sacrifices means for the sake of ends nor curtails the end to develop the means. The pursuit of 'objectivity' is not a forbidden fruit in Islamic science for it promotes rationality. What Islamic science does is to harmonise this objectivity with a value structure and thus it creates a world-view where human activity is viewed and experienced in its totality and not read through bits of behaviour as manifested by guinea pigs. In so doing, psychological as well as biological alienation is brought to an end. Development and evolution become synchronous with the *actual* human behaviour and biology and the social disruption concomitant with the *reductive* science disappears.[24]

While philosophically and sociologically, Anees' argument cannot be faulted, is there any evidence from the history of Islamic science and technology to suggest that it had a distinct identity which differed radically from the content and style of science as it is practised today? Much of the history of Islamic science and technology has been studied from the Western perspective where the main assumption has been that Islamic science was a single element in the long and linear development of science from the Greeks onwards to our own epoch. In this linear theory of the history of science and technology, Muslim civilization is often portrayed as a 'conveyor belt' which preserved the 'Greek heritage' and passed it on to its rightful owner, the European civilization. That approach, however, is now slowly giving way to more enlightened historical scholarship and analysis;[25] but we are still a long way from a corpus of material that specifically analyses Islamic science in history to bring out the *difference* of nature and style between it and modern science.

Only Hossein Nasr tries to bring out the difference and provides an overall glimpse of what Islamic science was possibly like in history and may look like in the future. In *Islamic Science: an Illustrated Study* [26] he argues convincingly that Islamic science had a distinct identity and tries to illustrate its uniquely Islamic character. However, he errs by overemphasizing the metaphysical aspects of Islamic science at the expense of its quantitative aspects. Moreover, Nasr's particular band of Sufism leads him to focus on such areas as astrology, alchemy and 'occult science' which were certainly there but cannot by any stretch of imagination be considered part of the Islamic tradition of science since they are explicitly forbidden by the Prophet Mohammad. Nevertheless, Nasr manages to convey the feel of an alternative science in action: a science that is just as 'objective' and 'rational' as Western science, but draws its legitimacy and its philosophical and sociological framework from the all-encompassing epistemology of Islam. Indeed, as Nasr argues, Islamic science in history was so deeply immersed in the world-view of Islam that it could synthesize and transform any ideas coming from outside, such as the Greek scientific heritage, and bring it in line with its own world-view. The strength of Nasr's analysis is that he explicitly shows the prominence of certain values in shaping the scientific enterprise in Islam.

Indeed, unlike Western science which tries to ignore all questions of values, Islamic science, as its history demonstrates, explicitly seeks to serve and promote the values of the world-view and civilization of Islam. The unique character of Islamic science stems from its all-embracing emphasis on the unity of religion and science, knowledge and values, physics and metaphysics. It is its insistence on multiplicity of methods and the use of enlightened means in the pursuit of enlightened goals which gives Islamic science its characteristic style with synthesis as its main feature. As I have said before,

> this unique nature and characteristic style means that while Islamic science values systematic, rigorous search for truth, it is not 'objective' in a clinical sense—it does not kill off all it touches. Concerns for social welfare and public interest, promotion of beauty and a healthy,

natural environment as well as systematic observation and experimentation and rigorous mathematical analysis are hall marks of Islamic science in history. As such Islamic science is *subjectively objective*: that is, it seeks subjective goals within an objective framework. The subjective, normative goals include seeking the pleasure of Allah, the interests of the community, promotion of such eternal Islamic values as *adl* (justice), *ibadah* (worship) and *khilafah* (man's trusteeship). This contrasts sharply with naive inquiry which is based on emotions, dogma, bias and prejudices. Islamic science has nothing to do with magic and occult: it does not seek to introduce anarchy and dogmatism into the pursuit of knowledge, neither does it seek to impose the method of one discipline on to another. It simply seeks to give equality to all methods of inquiry, and promote research and development within a framework of ethics and values which by nature are subjective. It therefore also contrasts radically with western science which excludes all other branches of knowledge and is based on a single Method which is considered to be outside human values and societical concerns. Islamic science, on the other hand, seeks a total understanding of reality. It is thus a very holistic enterprise.[27]

The rediscovery of the nature and style of Islamic science in our time is one of the most exciting and intellectually essential challenges facing Muslim societies. Indeed, the emergence of an independent, viable Muslim civilization of the future depends on how contemporary Muslim societies cope with this challenge.

The first steps towards meeting this challenge is to examine modern science and science policy within a framework of concepts that shape the goals of Muslim society. This exercise was attempted at a seminar on 'Knowledge and Values' held under the auspices of the International Federation of Institutes of Advance Study (IFIAS) in Stockholm during September 1981.[28] The seminar isolated ten Islamic concepts which embrace and describe the nature of scientific inquiry in its totality: *tawhid* (unity), *khilafah* (man's trusteeship), *ibadah* (worship), *ilm* (knowledge), *halal* (praiseworthy), *haram* (blameworthy), *adl* (social justice), *zulm* (tyranny), *istislah* (public interest) and *dhiya* (waste). The positive values act as guiding principles for scientific activity and science policy in Muslim cultures, while the negative values of *haram*, *zulm* and *diya* act as indicators which point out that the legitimate boundaries of Islamic science have been over-stepped. The three central concepts of *tawhid*, *khilafah* and *ibadah* shape the paradigm of Islamic science. Within this paradigm, Islamic science operates through the agency of *ilm* to promote *adl* and *istislah* and undermine *zulm* and *dhiya*. The concepts of *adl*, *istislah* and *zulm* are very broad and take in economic, social, cultural, technological and psychological aspects of justice, public interest and tyranny. Moreover, they are not limited to human beings: they also apply to other creations of God as well as the environment. The concepts of *halal* and *haram*, operating on *adl* and *zulm*, determine the social responsiveness and non-utilitarian nature of science. All that is destructive, physically, materially, emotionally, culturally, environmentally and spiritually, is *haram*; while all that promotes these societical parameters is *halal*. Thus scientific activity that promotes social justice and considers public interest to be important is *halal*; while that science and technology which promotes alienation and dehumanization, consumerism and concentration of wealth in fewer and fewer hands, unemployment and environmental destruction is *zalim* and therefore *haram*. A major characteristic of *zalim* science is that it destroys human, environmental and spiritual resources and generates waste. Such science is therefore categorized as *dhiya* (wasteful). Scientific activity that promotes *adl* draws its legiti-macy from *istislah* or public interest, which is the chief sup-plementary source of Islamic law.

While this rather theoretical model of Islamic science needs much further work, it is clear that it can form the basis of a practical science policy for Muslim countries. Islamic concepts, as the early history of Islam demonstrates so brilliantly, do not only have analytical value: they are also intrinsically pragmatic. Without operationalizing these key concepts, it is difficult for a society, or a civilization, to claim that it is Islamic. Thus the model of Islamic science developed at the Stockholm Seminar has a strong practical value. Apart from shaping science policies of Muslim countries, it can also be used as a criteria for examining the nature and content of Western science and determining the value of its various components for Islamic societies. More gener-ally, it can be used as the framework of a critique of modern science—a critique that would highlight the fact that the inhuman rationality of modern science can be tamed, indeed synthesized, with a humane vision of knowledge to the benefit of all mankind.

Notes

1. Ziauddin Sardar, 'Islamic Science or Science in Islamic Policy: What is the Difference?', *MAAS Journal of Islamic Science*, **1** (1), 31–44 (1985).

2. J. R. Ravetz, 'Science and Values' in Ziauddin Sardar (ed.), *The Touch of Midas: Science, Values and Environment in Islam and the West*, Manchester University Press, 1984, pp. 52–3.

3. David Morley, *The Sensitive Scientist*, SCM Press, London, 1978, p. 1.

4. See Karl R. Popper, *Objective Knowledge*, OUP, 1972; and *Conjectures and Refutations*, R. and K. Paul, London, 1963.

5. T. S. Kuhn, 'The Historical Structure of Scientific Discovery', *Science*, **136**, 760–4 (1962).

6. Barry Barnes, *T. S. Kuhn and Social Sciences*, Macmillan, London, 1982, p. 44.

7. T. S. Kuhn, *The Structure of Scientific Revolutions*, University of Chicago Press, 1962; 2nd edn, 1972.

8. J. R. Ravetz, *Scientific Knowledge and its Social Problems*, OUP, 1971.

9. Paul Feyerabend, *Against Method*, NLB, London, 1975.

10. Hilary Rose and Steven Rose (eds), *Ideology of/in the Natural Sciences*, Macmillan, London, 1976 (2 vols).

11. Ian Mitroff, *The Subjective Side of Science*, Elsevier, Amsterdam, 1974.

12. For a survey of this literature, see I. Spiegal-Rosing and D. de Solla Price, *Science, Technology and Society: A Cross-Disciplinary Perspective*, Sage, London, 1976.

13. Mashhood Ahmed, 'Islamic Ethos and Muslim Scientists', *MAAS Journal of Islamic Science*, **1** (1), 56–68 (1985).

14. See Ziauddin Sardar, 'A revival for Islam, a boost for science?' *Nature*, **282**, 354–7 (1979).

15. Seghers, Paris, 1980.

16. *Ibid*. p. 7.

17. Shamsul Haq, 'The Qur'an and Modern Cosmology', *Science and Technology in the Islamic World*, **1** (1), 47–52 (1983).

18. M. Manzoor-i-Khuda, 'Creation and the Cosmos' in *Islamic Scientific*

Thought and Muslim Achievements in Science, proceedings of the International Conference on Science in Islamic Polity, Islamabad, 1983, Vol. 1, pp. 96–113.

19. Keith L. Moore, 'Highlights of Human Embryology in the Koran and the Hadith' in *Proceedings of the Seventh Saudi Medical Meeting*, Riyadh, 1982.

20. Z. A. Hashmi, 'Future opportunities and challenges for science and technology in the Muslim World', Document ICSIP-5, International Conference on Science in Islamic Polity, Islamabad, 1983, p. 4.

21. Allen and Unwin, London, 1968.

22. *Ibid*. pp. 23–4.

23. Glyn Ford, 'Rebirth of Islamic Science' in *The Touch of Midas*, *op. cit.* p. 34.

24. Munawar A. Anees, 'Islamic Science: An antidote to reductionism', *Inquiry*, **1** (2), 49 (July 1984).

25. Research on the history of Islamic science and technology has increased tremendously in the last decade. The weight of fresh scholarship from such scholars as Fuat Sezgin, Ahmad Y. Al-Hassan, Donald Hill, David King, David Pingree, E. S. Kennedy and A. I. Sabra has considerably changed our understanding of Islamic science in history. The arrival of the *Journal of the History of Arabic Science*, means that the discipline has now really 'arrived'.

26. World of Islam Festival Trust, London, 1976.

27. Ziauddin Sardar, *Arguments for Islamic Science*, Centre for Studies on Science, Aligarh, 1985.

28. The discussion of the Stockholm Seminar is reported in *The Touch of Midas*, *op. cit.*

8

Developing Technology with a Muslim Face

While the nature of science has received some attention from Muslim thinkers, technology seems to have escaped their attention almost completely. This neglect appears paradoxical when one considers the formidable technological needs of Muslim societies, the intellectual labour that has gone into closely associated fields such as Islamic economics, and the massive attempts to transfer technology that have taken place over the last decades. However, the paradox is only apparent. The lack of Muslim thought on the nature and role of technology in society stems from the firm belief that all technology is good, and should be acquired from the industrial societies by any means possible: bought, received as aid or, if necessary, simply stolen. And there is the complementary belief that technology *per se* will transform Muslim states, almost overnight, from poor underdeveloped societies to rich, industrialized ones. Thus the emphasis has been on acquiring all technology rather than on working out what exactly are the needs of Muslim societies and building indigenous capability of generating desired technological innovations.

The belief in the good nature of technology is so pervasive, so powerful, that even three decades of bad experience, repeated failures of technical aid programmes and disastrous outcomes of technology transfer projects has not shaken it. A perusal of the papers presented at the North American Association of Muslim Scientists and Engineers annual conferences, which invariably have such themes as 'Applied Science for Muslim World Development', will reveal that the confidence in the good character of all technology is still deeply entrenched. A casual conversation with a technologist in Malaysia or Bangladesh, Saudi Arabia or Egypt, will inevitably lead to the remark, 'only if we can acquire the technical knowhow of the West, will we be able to solve all our problems'.

Indeed, all learned inquiries into the 'technological backwardness' of Muslim societies eventually end with the plea that Muslim countries should take full advantage of transfer of technology. The best demonstration of this is provided by Waqar Ahmed Husaini who has given considerable thought to what he calls 'imitative-innovative patterns of technological modernisation'. In his painstakingly researched book, *Islamic Environmental Systems Engineering*, Husaini sets out to examine the nature of environmental engineering which evolved under Islam and show its connections with Islamic law, economics, politics and culture.[1] After a detailed exposition of Islamic jurisprudence and philosophy of knowledge, Husaini shows how a particular type of engineering, based on such notions of the Shariah as *istislah* (public interest), *istihsan* (equity) and *khilafah* (trusteeship), evolved in the Muslim society. Islamic environmental engineering and its associated technology, asserts Husaini, paid particular attention to the proper use of natural resources, fulfilling the rights of natural habitats and wildlife, and promotion of socially desirable activities and cultural flowering. All of which shows that 'Islamic environmental engineering' was something unique and distinctive to Islamic society and contrasted sharply with conventional, modern technological activities. But Husaini draws a diametrically opposite conclusion. His extensive discussion shows, he writes,

> the universality of the material or technological culture, and the relatively greater freedom of these *empirical* vehicles of socio-cultural systems from value-orientations unique to an ideology or value system. The medieval Muslim and modern Western, including the Communist, systems of science grew through selective borrowing and assimilations. The greater possibilities of their variation and cross-cultural borrowing suggests that Muslims can and should borrow and adopt

from contemporary developed non-Muslim nations the material and technological culture more thoroughly and with greater freedom from concern for compatibility with Islamic ideological culture.[2]

Husaini's naive and erroneous conclusion simply reinforces the belief of Muslim technologists, engineers, academics, decision-makers and intellectuals in the 'universality of technological culture'. However, the benefits claimed from borrowing and adopting this culture—increases in material well-being, health and welfare, growth in agricultural productivity and industrial output and independence from foreign domination—are nowhere to be seen in the Muslim world. In fact, the converse is much more evident. Borrowed technology, almost always, has been unsuitable for Muslim societies: in most cases not just the hardware, but also skilled manpower and spare parts have to be bought; thus making the purchaser completely dependent on the supplier. For example, to develop a heavy industrial base, Egypt simply imported entire factories using relatively advanced technologies. Clement Henry Moore, who made a special study of Egypt's attempt to industrialize by importing technology, notes:

> As these technologies did not evolve from Egypt's previous efforts to industrialize, few Egyptians, however advanced their theoretical qualifications, enjoyed a working familiarity with them. Egypt lacked the intellectual as well as industrial infrastructure capable of integrating them into its economy. The showcase industries, such as iron and steel or automobile assembly, tended to be enclaves in a modern sector largely centred on the construction, textiles, and food processing industries. By importing the new technologies, the state enhanced the status of the engineers and gave some of them an opportunity to acquire new experience, but it perhaps also increased their dependence on the foreigners who had masterminded it. Apparently, the experiences with new technologies were not generating applied research, adopting and integrating them to local conditions; rather the new forms of dependence on foreign experts were becoming self-perpetuating and were discouraging indigenous research.[3]

Technology transfer is not just making Muslim countries more and more dependent on industrialized states, but the impact of transferred technology on Muslim culture and environment have also been devastating. Consider, for example, the impact of borrowed technology on the holy cities of Makkah and Medina and the *hajj* environment. In the last decade, the *hajj* environment has been mercilessly destroyed, delinked from its historical roots, by a brutal technology based on demolition and environmental violence that shows scant regard for cultural values or spiritual concerns. Massive transfer of technology to the *hajj* environment has led to the place where we are confronting, for the first time in 1400 years' history of Islam, a situation where one of its most cherished institutions, the very symbol of its immutable values, is faced with *total physical destruction* (discussed in Chapter 13).[4] Elsewhere, the environmental havoc caused by the construction of dams such as Egypt's Aswan High Dam,[5] chemical plants (of which the Bhopal disaster is the most well known), high-technology agricultural projects (the Gezira scheme in Sudan is perhaps the most notorious) and industrial pollution (for example, the Gulf has become one large cesspool from receiving the industrial effluent from the surrounding countries) continue to be multiplied.[6]

Technology and Secular Societies

But all the evidence before their eyes seems to carry no weight with Muslim technologists and intellectuals. The arguments and experiences against technology transfer is simply swept away by citing the shining example of Japan. The implication being: if Japan can do it, so can we.

Indeed, the Japanese example of adoption of Western technology appears truly exemplary. In just about three generations (1880–1960), Japan has not only closed more than a 100-year gap, but has also overtaken the West in certain areas. But this simple observation hides two important facts. Firstly, while Japan appears culturally to be radically different from Western societies, there is considerable common ground between Japanese and Western world-views: both are secular and 'this-worldly'. Although it does contain elements of proper respect for the heaven, nature and tradition, Japanized Confucian thought conceives man essentially as a product of his immediate secular and cultural environment. In the absence of an ontological base, it portrays human nature as essentially good and seeks the supreme societal goal embodied in *li* or the harmony gained by each person performing his task according to his allotted role in society. Inherent in Japanese Confucianism is a doctrine of inequality and class: each member of society is under someone else's authority who has complete power over him. It stresses duties rather than rights; its chief virtues are obedience, contentment, patience and restraint. As Frank C. Darling argues so powerfully in *The Westernisation of Asia*,[7] these specific characteristics of Japanese world-view enabled Japan to absorb Western technology and accommodate the associated process of Westernisation without societal trauma.

Secondly, after the Meiji Restoration of 1868, Japan undertook to prepare itself for the task of adopting and integrating Western technology. A vigorous programme to build an indigenous infrastructure was launched. The important point to realize here is that Meiji Japan was already a highly advanced technological society. Its technological infrastructure was not being built from square one; it was simply being developed so that Japan could cope with the formidable process of assimilating Western technology. This development was based on an explicit science and technology policy incorporating six measures:[8]

1. The government carried out extensive land reforms to free agriculture from feudalistic constraints. This led to farmers introducing new methods of irrigation, increasing the use of fertilizers, and undertaking improvements of rice strains.
2. Model factories were established with official funds. They were operated by officials who demonstrated the viability of selectively imported European technology used in the factories. After 1880, three model plants were sold to individual entrepreneurs.
3. The government heavily subsidized industry, thus making industrial investment, compared to investment in land or commerce, a viable option.
4. Official purchase policy favoured indigenous over foreign

industries. Had there been no clear-cut official policy, most of the nascent Japanese industry would not have survived.

5. The government developed a network of industrial banks to provide low-interest loans to investors in industry.

6. A great deal of attention was paid to communication systems: financial and intellectual resources were poured into railways, telegraph, post and national press.

While these measures ensured that Japan, from a position of relative strength, was able to absorb and integrate Western technology, they did not enable the oriental power to completely escape the cultural impact of the imported hardware. Modern Japan bears little resemblance to its Meiji counterpart. Despite the rigorous policy of selective technology transfer, particularly at the initial stages, the imported technology has transformed Japan from an independent authentic, albeit a secular, culture to an extension of Western civilization. Modern Japan is a capitalist society *par excellence* where Western norms and behaviour are the vogue; traditional Japanese culture is marginalized to an exotic existence.

Apart from Japan, Taiwan, Hong Kong, South Korea and Singapore are also cited as examples of successful adaptation of borrowed and bought Western technology. Here again a secular world-view combined with a capitalist infrastructure has helped enormously. However, the success of these nations is limited to individual technologies such as electronics and the computer industry where the advantage of extensive cheap labour has been used to build a manufacturing base. However, these successes will erode away once the labour of the microchip becomes even cheaper than the labour of Taiwanese women. Moreover, the toll that this limited success has exacted from these countries in terms of cultural destruction and savage exploitation of the workers is truly horrific.

The key point is this. Secular world-views have an in-built mechanism for adopting Western technology; but 'sacred-orientated' societies, to use Darling's term, tend to have an inherent rejection mechanism. No matter how one imposes Western technology on these societies, it never takes social roots. This is the lesson of three decades of 'development'.

There is nothing wrong with conventional Western technology, if one accepts that it is a product of a deeply secular world-view and culture. If one has no regard for one's culture or if one is willing to accept its exploitative nature, then Western technology will submit, to a certain extent, to one's demands. However, societies that promote values which are opposed to the goals inherent in Western technology are likely to be consumed by it.

As such, there is nothing neutral, universal or value-free about technology: those who still cling to this notion are simply living on another world. Modern technology is the product of the particular history and culture of Western civilization, and it carries the seeds of its cultural origins wherever it goes. So potent and vigorous are these seeds that the culture or political persuasion of the society that has adopted Western technology inexorably generates similar social institutions and practices. But it does not stop here: the seeds go on to germinate and produce Western economic structures and associated 'imperatives' of growth of capitalism to the extent of producing the historical scars and class struggles of European society. When the seeds have fully grown and matured, as in the case of Japan, the society that has adopted that technology becomes an extension of European culture and Western civilization. Western technology, therefore, is not only an instrument of physical domination and dependency, it is also a tool of cultural imperialism.

While externally Western technology makes host countries into subject cultures and dependent people, internally it duplicates the same exploitative structures: it gives the ruling elite the power to treat the masses as their subjects, completely dependent on their whims and fancies. Transferred technology aggregates economic and political power in fewer and fewer hands and even deprives the people of their legitimate right to work. It does this by enabling the management to deskill workers, impose the discipline of wage-labour and extract more and more surplus value from fewer and fewer workers at lower and lower wages. Furthermore, it ensures that technologically deskilled labour has no chance of alternative means of survival by destroying traditional craft and cottage industries. In the rural area the peasants have to make way for big machinery and agribusiness. To ensure that landless peasants, deskilled labourers and out-of-work craftsmen are kept in their positions, Western technology places a formidable array of instruments of political control at the feet of the ruling elite. It is not an accident of history that a large proportion of the products of Western technology are designed to serve repressive ends: computers,helicopters, night-vision devices, riot-control gases, sensory deprivation devices, electronic surveillance apparatus, and techniques of behaviour control, are just a few examples.

Indeed, conventional technology is so immersed in values that Sri Lankan philosopher Susantha Goonatilake has compared the behaviour of technology to that of a social gene,

> a carrier of social relations from one society to another. In being transferred from the social system in which it originated to another social context, a particular technology in its role as social gene 'tries' to recreate aspects of the social system which produced it in the first place. Technology, therefore, is a transmitter of social relations between social systems. In being adopted by its new host, it 'takes' elements from its new environment—hardware and knowledge as well as human operators—and rearranges them so that not only does it perform its technological function but also recreates aspects of the social system of its place of origin. It is thus like a virus, which enters a host cell whose component material it uses for its food as well as to reproduce itself.[9]

In this process of being consumed, the society that has adopted Western technology has no real choices. Although certain types of technology may be more suitable for a particular society, all technology that is available in the technological supermarket has already been shaped by Western, capitalist priorities and carries its genes. For example, a factory installed in Kuala Lumpur or Karachi, Dammam or Tehran, even though it ostensibly uses local material and serves local population and indigenous goals, intrinsically serves Western interests and promotes capitalist objectives. This is because the way a factory is organized and functions in Western technology already incorporates the world-view and social and economic philosophy of the capitalist culture. The modern factory system, with its organizational and management structure, was formalized by Charles Babbage who based his ideas of engineering and manufacture on the economic philosophy of his contemporary, Adam Smith. Thus Adam Smith's concept of division of labour, his notion of a labourer 'whose life is spent in performing a few simple operations' and who 'generally becomes as stupid and ignorant as is possible for a human creature to become' were the basic bricks of Babbage's framework. As Susantha Goonatilake points out, in formalizing the factory system, Babbage transformed these social views into the factory technology. Babbage's work was further developed by F. W. Taylor in his *Principles of Scientific Management*.[10] Taylor brought the capitalist conception of the worker to its logical conclusion; his ideal worker is 'so stupid and so phlegmatic that he resembles an ox' and requires managing by a 'man who is more intelligent than him'.[11]

Such notions form the basis of modern factory technology. On these social concepts and metaphysical ideas is built the entire edifice of manufacturing and production-orientated technologies. It is important to realize that technologies develop, mature and proliferate within this framework. For example, in the late eighteenth century there were two types of technologies capable of sophisticated textile production in England. The first, perfected by the 1760s, was based on cottage industry and had one machine built round the spinning jenny. The second, introduced in 1770s, was factory-based, used steam power and utilized Watts engine and Arkwright frame. However, the cottage industry based machines, despite the fact that they were no less sophisticated than the steam-powered ones, did not permit the textile merchants to exercise the same control on the workers that the factory-based technology did. They were thus systematically eliminated: their manufacturers were denied raw materials and financing, their operations made illegal by law which, on various pretexts, outlawed home-production. Factory-based textile technology thus became the norm.

Since the industrial revolution, control of workers has been the basis for the evolution of Western technology. The worker has been progressively reduced to the status of a single component in the technological process. His status is not that of a human being but of a component that can be replaced or dispensed with as and when the management sees fit. The assembly line epitomizes the highest level of the dehumanization of the worker: complex skills are broken down into simpler tasks, which can be learned quickly and require little skill or knowledge. As the process continues, workers are replaced with more and more machines. To ensure a desired level of productivity, the factory has to conform to a rigid discipline. There is a strict hierarchy: the management and those who are managed. The onward march of Western technology, therefore, has not only led to the fragmentation and division of labour, reduction of complex tasks into simpler and simpler forms, and destruction of traditional skills and crafts, but also to loss of independence and autonomy, the subjugation of mass labour to the tyrannical discipline and authority of the factory. The whole process has been brought one step closer to its logical conclusion with computerization and office automation. Computerization of offices is a new version of Henry Ford's automotive assembly line. The one difference is that it enables greater centralization and allows greater control on office workers.[12]

Thus when a factory is installed in a developing country, no matter what kind of technology or manufacturing process it involves, it takes the ethics of worker exploitation, management control and maximization of profit with it. And these are only the more overt values.

There is simply no way a Muslim society can overlook or, indeed, escape the consequences of values inherent in Western technology. It may be argued that Muslim countries can escape the disruptive effects of Western technology by making the right choices; by choosing from the vast array of technologies that are available in the market-place those which were more relevant. This is a false argument because the choice of technology available to a developing country involves preferences and options that exclude alternatives. The vast array of conventional technologies available in the market-place are those which have survived the social and economic prejudices of the Western society. Even if it was possible to 'select' and 'choose' a truly mythical belief, the choice is still limited to capital-intensive technologies that are *designed* to promote the goals and objectives of Western culture and civilization. *All* technologies available to a developing country are designed to support the various keepers of power.

What's Alternative about 'Alternative Technology'

The argument for choice and selection of technology has been particularly used by proponents of alternative technology. For example, K. D. Sharma and M. A. Qureshi argue that the very notion of alternative technology is based on 'choice and selection of a technology or technologies from a set of given technologies to produce the goods and commodities to satisfy the same needs'. The alternative technology, selected from a spectrum of technologies in the market-place, has the following characteristics: (1) it can be 'primitive, low and high or anywhere between the primitive and high technologies'; it must suit the resource availability of a country and should be in 'consonance with its economic, social, cultural and political objectives; and it should be environmentally sound'.[13] Hamid Ayub also defines alternative technology as 'an intelligent choice of technology, that is the most suitable to the needs of the user and in harmony with the natural environment'.[14]

But how is the choice for alternative technology to be made? According to Sharma and Qureshi, the choice of alternative technology should be based on two criteria: social, economic and cultural; and national security and prestige. Under the first criteria the technologies likely to be preferred would be labour-intensive, small, simple and utilize local resources and skills, so that the cost of skill formation and their development is minimized. However, when it comes to national defence and prestige, Sharma and Qureshi see no alternative to competing with 'the industrialised societies in some of the areas of big and complex technologies and where mass production is important for achieving the political and stategic security objectives'.[15] Similarly, Ayub also sees no alternative to Western technology in such areas as defence, aeronautics, petrochemicals and electronics.

Thus the 'alternative' is rather limited: it is limited to rural development, certain kinds of cottage industries and specific forms of village technology. However, this solution of having one leg in low-impact, soft technology and another in production-orientated, runaway high technology is not much of a solution. For apart from the sheer philosophical contradiction of the two approaches, the questions of values inherent in imported high technology and what they may do to a Muslim society remain unanswered. Moreover, such an approach does not free Muslim societies from the risks associated with such manifestations of high technology as chemical plants, nuclear power stations and bio-engineering research centres—a problem that is now emerging as a field of inquiry in its own right.

While on the whole alternative technology experiments have been rather disappointing, they have increased our awareness of the relationship between technology and society in two ways. Firstly, they have proved that the only truly suitable technology for a society is one that it has generated itself and which it can develop without any outside assistance. The central lesson of the alternative technology movement of the last decade is that alternative technology *has* to be an indigenous creation of the developing countries themselves. Alternative technology products and skills developed in such places as London and California and then transferred to Kenya and India have seldom taken indigenous roots.

Secondly, alternative technology cannot be developed within the philosophical and intellectual framework of the Western civilization. If, for example, alternative technology reduces productivity to a second-order determinant, then Western economics which sees consumption as the end of activity must be replaced by a more enlightened alternative. As such, alternative technologies will be based not on the theories of Adam Smith, Malthus and Keynes, but on more liberating economic outlooks. Schumacher developed his framework for alternative technology on the basis of Buddhist economics: the difference between Western and Buddhist economics is that while the former tries to maximize human satisfaction by the optimal pattern of consumption, the latter tries to maximize consumption by the optimal pattern of productive effort. But economics is by no means enough: a coherent epistemology that produces a distinctively alternative mode of thought, a body of vibrant law that has as much regard for the needs and rights of the environment and the earth as for the poor and the oppressed, a dynamic culture that still draws its strength from traditional values—in short, a complete world-view is needed if *really* alternative styles and modes of technology are to be discovered and developed.

Working outside the dominant paradigm is a formidable task; and while many advocates of alternative technology have worked on the periphery of Western civilization, no one has really worked within a complete and coherent alternative philosophical framework. However, over a decade of thought and analysis, theoretical and practical work, which produced many inventions and working models, John and Nancy Todd have evolved a metaphysical framework that forms the basis of their work and is described in *Bioshelters, Ocean Arks and City Farming*.[16] This framework is based on nine precepts:

Precept One: The living world is the matrix of all design; stated differently, the earth and all its inhabitants have certain rights which have to be respected and certain requirements which have to be fulfilled.

Precept Two: Technological design should follow, and not oppose, the laws of life; or all technological activity should be modelled on biology.

Precept Three: Biological equity must be preserved. This means not just human beings, but technological activity and design should also consider the rights and needs of the vast diversity of non-human life-form.

Precept Four: Design must reflect bioregionality. Or diversity, in all its rich multi-dimensional facets, must be preserved.

Precept Five: Technological activity should be based on renewable energy sources.

Precept Six: Design should be sustainable through the integration of living systems. In other words, technological activity should preserve environmental integrity and promote ecological interdependence.

Precept Seven: Design should be co-evolutionary with the natural world. Or technological activity should grow at a natural pace and should not grow beyond its ecological limits.

Precept Eight: Building and design should help heal the planet.

Precept Nine: Technology and design should follow a sacred ecology. Or technological activity, development and growth should take place within the framework of an enlightened and enchanted world-view.

What type of technological products have been produced working within the universe of these nine precepts? One outcome of the work within this framework is an ocean-liner sized bioshelter. After observing what is happening in the Third World fisheries, John Todd argued that 'there must be a *contemporary* alternative to buying boats, engines, fuel, and gear from industrialised countries'. This contemporary alternative had to meet four objectives to be of any help to Third World fisherman: it had to be primarily wind-powered, but at the same time as fast as most of the motor boats it was to replace; construction technologies had to be suitable for building in the tropics, within the communities themselves; the primary construction material must be derived from fast-growing trees; and finally, imported materials had to be less than 20 per cent of the overall cost of the vessel. The Todds and their colleagues built the vessel with these design criteria and showed that it is not only more suitable for Third World fishermen, but would yield a greater profit.

The ocean ark is just one product of a mode of technology that is based on a radically different approach to life and thought. The New Alchemy Institute, which the Todds founded in 1969 in Massachusetts, has perfected a host of techniques for city farming, development of agriculture that puts power and control in the hands of the rural population, even a blueprint to redesign New York on more human lines. What all this work demonstrates is that it is not only possible to work in non-Western paradigms but also to technologies which are both *contemporary* yet very different from the products of conventional technology.

Towards Domestic Self-reliance

As an embodiment of culture, as accumulated hardware of historical experience, as a pragmatic instrument of a world-view, technology is the essential building block of a civilization. Without its own distinctive technology—a system for solving practical tasks that involves people and organizations, living things and machines—a civilization cannot survive let alone develop and prosper. The Muslim civilization cannot survive the future without evolving its own distinct technology based on the world-view of Islam.

But what does it mean to develop an alternative style and mode of thought that is an embodiment of the world-view of Islam? Is it something that can be done overnight, like the 'development' of Jeddah from a traditional, Islamic city to a modern, Western one? What do Islamic societies have to do to develop Muslim technology?

The first thing to realize here is that there are no short cuts to technological independence, no easy way of fighting off the onslaught of, and dethroning, the dominant style and mode of technology. Instant solutions, even when they work, only delay the inevitable. The second is that we must see the evolution of distinctively Muslim ways of solving technical problems within its broader context: it cannot be separated from the rediscovery of Islamic science, development of a viable theoretical and practical Islamic economics, and the development of contemporary methodologies for the study of Muslim societies and culture. These four areas are intrinsically interlinked and interconnected.

To a very large extent, the philosophical framework which will promote the evolution of Muslim technology already exists in the form of Islamic values and Shariah imperatives that dictate the characteristics of Muslim societies. Such concepts as *adl* (all pervasive justice), *istislah* (public interest), *khilafah* (trusteeship) and *iqtisad* (moderation) and Shariah injunctions, for example on environmental areas such as *ihya* (land reclamation), *harim* (conservation areas) and *hima* (public reserves), can accurately map the circumference of technological activity. In addition there are a host of negative values such as *zulm* (tyranny), *israf* (extravagance) and *iktinaz* (accumulation of wealth) which act as warning bells which announce that the boundaries of positive values have been overstepped. But these values and concepts, and dictates of the Shariah which apply to technology, have to be understood in a much broader, contemporary sense. Moreover, these values have to be given a concrete shape and incorporated in technological activity.

In *The Culture of Technology*, Arnold Pacey identifies 'virtuosity', profit, prestige and political control as the basic values of Western society.[17] Many otherwise thoroughly moral technologists are motivated by virtuosity to produce technological hardware that can only be put to evil ends. It was virtuosity which gave Edward Teller's passionate desire to explore to the end the thermonuclear technology that he had pioneered'. And it was the same value which led Oppenheimer, who was rather troubled by his work, to remark that one invention used in the hydrogen bomb was 'technically so sweet that you could not argue' against its adoption. It is the excessive pursuit of profits that motivates the production of consumer technology, environmentally degrading manufacturing processes and drugs whose curative powers are decisively less than their side-effects. Supersonic flight and space exploration bring prestige. And microelectronics and automation, techniques of torture and nuclear, chemical and biological weapons are part of an effort to control and dominte the mode of production and marginalized classes and societies. The product of technological activity that replaces the values of virtuosity, profit, prestige and political control with those of *adl*, *istislah*, *khilafah* and *iqtisad* ought to be radically different from what exists in the world today.

This difference, in value base and end products, dictates that the guiding principle for technological activity in the Muslim world should be domesticity. It should be an axiom of technology policy in Muslim countries that local products and raw materials, local processes and techniques, local talent and manpower, can provide the best answer to local problems. Here 'local' means local within the Muslim world. The principle of domesticity also demands sharing: members of a domestic household share common chores to ensure smooth functioning of the house. Similarly, Muslim societies need to pool their technical resources and talents to secure viable solutions to their common and not so common problems. Necessity, the saying goes, is the mother of invention; and self-sufficiency is obviously the grandmother. When pressed to the full, local ingenuity can produce all the technological answers that a society needs. Moreover, within the Muslim world there is enough technological diversity and ability to transcend any technical problem—it only has to be mobilized and given the repsonsibility that is its due. Finally, as a natural corollary, the principle of domesticity dictates that the notion of transfer of technology, including transfer of 'alternative technology', and reliance on foreign help and assistance, should be placed where it belongs: on the scrapheap of tried and discarded ideas.

The principle of domesticity, and the associated regional technological isolationism, is an essential prerequisite for the evolution of Muslim technology. There are, however, other steps that have to be taken to smooth the ground for the technological independence of the Muslim world. Traditional technologies, including crafts and medicine, have to be promoted and given due recognition in society. Many traditional crafts, from cloth and pottery to furniture and tools, adequately met the modest needs of self-contained communities in the Muslim world before they were destroyed by transferred technologies. Similarly, traditional medicine has served the needs of Muslim communities for over 1400 years: now that their superiority in meeting the health and hygiene needs of rural areas has become self-evident, they need to be upgraded and given the state support that they deserve.

Conventional Western technologies are normally designed to serve a single function and are applicable for one purpose only. Muslim technologists have to develop multi-purpose alternatives: tools and processes that can serve a host of functions. Only a handful of such devices exist at the moment; but as there is no market for them, it is unlikely that they will become generally available. The first candidate here is the multi-purpose factory, a multi-purpose plant that can produce several allied products: electrical plants that can switch to producing bicycles, furniture factories that can also produce household appliances. The concepts of *adl* and *istislah* dictate that all this is done at the community level so the community can understand the technology used, participate in the technological activity and control the processes involved.

All this is, of course, the bare minimum: and even achieving this is not going to be easy. However, once the principle of domesticity is accepted and set on its course it will generate its own momentum and lead into areas and generate processes and hardware that we cannot imagine at this stage. The important thing for Muslim intellectuals, scholars and decision-makers to realize is that conventional technology is up to its eyes in Western values, and its implantation in Muslim societies, in whatever form, will further increase the technological dependency of Muslim societies and encapsulate them within the dominion of Western civilization. Western technology does not come to solve the problems of traditional societies but to seek revenge for cherishing non-Western values. Only self-confidence in local ingenuity and technical sufficiency of the Muslim world can produce true self-reliance and technological independence. Those who do not respect themselves and their culture, are not willing to preserve the domestic integrity of their household and cannot construct the technological edifice of their civilization ought to be prepared for a marginalized existence on the periphery of sanity.

Notes

1. Macmillan, London, 1980.

2. *Ibid.* p. 165.

3. Clement Henry Moore, *Images of Development: Egyptian Engineers in Search of Industry*, MIT Press, Massachusetts, 1980, pp. 97–8.

4. See also Ziauddin Sardar, 'The Gretest Gathering of Mankind', *Inquiry*, 1 (4), 25–32 (September 1984).

5. For a full account of the havoc caused by the construction of dams in the Third World, see E. Goldsmith and N. Hildyard, *The Social and Environmental Effects of Large Dams*, Wadebridge Ecological Centre, Camelford, 1984 (2 vols).

6. For a detailed account of pollution in the Gulf see 'The Gulf: Pollution and Development', Earthscan Briefing Document No. 24, London, 1980.

7. G. K. Hall, Boston, 1979, Chapter 2.

8. See Manfredo Macioti, 'Technology and Development: the Historical Experience' in Jacques Richardson (ed.), *Integrated Technology Transfer*, Lomond Books, Maryland, 1979.

9. Susantha Goonatilake, *Aborted Discovery: Science and Creativity in the Third World*, Zed Press, London, 1984, p. 122.

10. Harper and Row, New York, 1947.

11. Both Babbage and Taylor quoted by Goonatilake, *op. cit.* p. 124.

12. See Ian Reinecke, *Electronic Illusions*, Penguin, Harmondsworth, 1984.

13. K. D. Sharma and M. A. Qureshi (eds), *Science, Technology and Society*, Sterling Publishers, Delhi, 1978, p. 208.

14. Hamid Ayub, 'Alternative Technology: A Cross-section', *The Muslim Scientist*, **8** (4), 1–6 (1979).

15. Sharma and Qureshi, *op. cit.* p. 209.

16. Sierra Club, San Francisco, 1984. The precepts are discussed in detail in Chapter 2.

17. Basil Blackwell, Oxford, 1983.

9

Islamic Economics:
From Partial to Axiomatic Approach

Over the last three decades, economics has received more attention from Muslim scholars and intellectuals than any other discipline. Numerous attempts to 'Islamize' economics has led to numerous international conferences and seminars and generated a vast body of literature on Islamic economics. Indeed, by the criteria of information science, Islamic economics has matured as a discipline and 'arrived': it has its own journal (*Journal of Research in Islamic Economics*), at least two research centres[1] devoted to the subject and is now being taught in economic departments of numerous universities both in the Muslim world and the West. In Muhammad Nejatullah Siddiqui, who won the Faisal Award for his contribution to the field, Islamic economics even has its equivalent of a Nobel Laureate!

On first sight, the intellectual and practical activity in the field of Islamic economics seems overwhelming. Siddiqui's highly praised survey of contemporary literature on the subject lists some 700 works in English, Arabic and Urdu.[2] A more recent work by Muhammad Akram Khan contains over 1500 citations.[3] Islamic banks are mushrooming and almost every Muslim state, from Sudan to Saudi Arabia, Iran, Pakistan, Bangladesh and Malaysia, has one or more Islamic banks. There is thus good reason to believe that Islamic economics has not only arrived, it is here to stay.

But what is Islamic economics? How does it differ from the

conventional capitalist and socialist models? What are its axioms and principles? How will Islamic economics replace the dominant economic orders in Muslim societies? Given the intellectual effort that has gone into the evolution of Islamic economics, one would expect ready answers to such questions. And, indeed, answers of a sort are given by the leading scholars in the field.

One of the first points emphasized by author after author is that Islamic economics is not capitalism minus interest plus *zakah* or socialism minus state control plus Allah. It is something unique and different and exclusive to Islam. How unique and how different is essentially the key issue.

The uniqueness of Islamic economics is brought about in attempts to define it. S. M. Hasanuz Zaman offers the following definition: 'Islamic economics is the knowledge and application of injunctions and rules of the Shariah that prevent injustice in the acquisition and disposal of material resources in order to provide satisfaction to human beings and enable them to perform their obligations to Allah and society.'[4] M. Akram Khan considers that 'Islamic economics aims at the study of human falah achieved by organizing the resources of earth on the basis of cooperation and participation'.[5]

The role of the Sharia, the notion of justice and *falah* (salvation), cooperation and sharing are central to Islamic economics and are considered to be the basis of economic philosophy of Islam. Siddiqui sums up this philosophy as follows:

The key to economic philosophy of Islam lies in man's relationship with God, His universe and His people, i.e. other human beings, and the nature and purpose of man's life on earth. Man–God relationship is defined by tawhid. The essence of tawhid is a total commitment to the will of Allah, involving both submission and a mission to pattern human life in accordance with His will. The will of Allah constitutes the source of value and becomes the end of human endeavour. Life on earth is a test, and its purpose should be to prove successful in the test by doing Allah's will. The entire universe with all the natural resources and powers is made amenable to exploitation by man, though it is owned by Allah and Allah alone. Life on earth being a test and all the provisions available to man being in the nature of trust, man is accountable to Allah and his success in the life hereafter depends on his performance in this life on earth.[6]

As *tawhid*, *akhrah*, equality, sharing and cooperation play such a strong role in Islam, it is not surprising that they are considered fundamental to Islamic economics. Indeed, emphasis on the ethics of *tawhid* and *akhrah* is so strong that the whole economic enterprise in Islam assumes the character of *ibadah* (worship).

But how is this economic *ibadah* performed?

The proponents of Islamic economics rightly argue that the basic set of Islamic economic injunctions have to be operationalized in society. The economic outlook of the Qur'an and the Sunnah are expressed in the Islamic injunctions which make *Zakah* (normally translated as the 'poor tax') a religious obligation, forbid all forms of *riba* (usury), permit the ownership of private property but also give the society right to redistribute private property, and prohibit the ownership of land beyond an individual's and his family's capacity to handle. These injunctions are undoubtedly unique to the world-view of Islam and when implemented would create a society which has all the hallmarks of justice and equity, sharing and cooperation, as well as economic dynamism and growth.

In addition there are a host of Islamic concepts and values which limit the extent and nature of economic activity. There are many positive values such as *iqtisad* (moderation), *adl* (justice), *ihsan* (kindness), *amanah* (honesty), *infaq* (spending to meet social obligations), *sabr* (patience) and *istislah* (public interest). Similarly, there are a number of values which are negative: *zulm* (tyranny), *bukhl* (miserliness), *hirs* (greed), *iktinaz* (hoarding of wealth) and *israf* (extravagance). Economic activity within the positive parameters is *halal* (praiseworthy) and *haram* (blameworthy) if it is within the circumference of negative values. These concepts have profound impact on such economic areas as consumption which has to be moderated, production which is regulated by the *halal–haram* code, and distribution which must adhere to the notion of *adl*. Collectively these values and concepts, along with the main injunctions of the Qur'an, provide a framework for a unique, just and contemporary economics.

So far so good. No Muslim would disagree either with the expression of Islam's economic outlook or with the ideal of implementing the key injunctions of the Qur'an and Sunnah in society. However, Islamic concepts are almost always stated but never really used as analytical tools or to develop policies that are original and different. Moreover, when it comes to the question of 'how it is to be done' and 'what exactly needs to be done' problems emerge and differences arise. How can *Zakah* be made the cornerstone of public finance in an Islamic society? What needs to be done to abolish interest from society? How can brotherhood be promoted; and what needs to be done to ensure equity? How can wealth be redistributed? What needs to be done to ensure that wealth does not accumulate in fewer and fewer hands. What consumer goods constitute *israf*? What types of industry would lead to economic *zulm*? What types of technologies negate *adl* and promote hoarding of wealth? How can Islamic injunctions on the use of land be introduced without the use of force? What needs to be done to break the feudal structure in Muslim society?

It is here, in attempting to answer the questions of how and what, that the proponents of Islamic economics have let their field, and Muslim society, down. Indeed, many 'how' questions are conspicuous by their absence in the literature and many strategies of what needs to be done are indistinguishable from capitalist or socialist approaches to economic thought and activity. The field has been led by scholars who have no awareness of the future, are too conservative and too deeply entrenched in Western paradigms to free their thought and develop a truly original economic system that is not just recognisably Islamic but is geared to meeting the contemporary and future needs of Muslim society.

Islamic Terminology, Western Analysis

In the fifties and early sixties when Muslim economists were rediscovering the principles of Islamic economics, their output was in many respects genuinely original. However, the modern research on Islamic economics, as Abdul-Hamid Ahmad Abu-Sulayman has pointed out, is concerned only with partial issues, patchwork and compromises with the philosophies and methods of contemporary economics. The major subject they have tried to discuss is bank interest. They have played around bank interest, and have come sometimes very close to thinking that if they could avoid dealing with bank interest and introduce another modern means to provide the same motivation in a different way they could solve the problem, and modern capitalist societies could be labeled as Islamic.[7]

Indeed, despite their repeated references to *tawhid*, *akhrah* and other fundamental Islamic concepts, Islamic economics is little more than one huge attempt to cast Islamic institutions and dictates, like *zakah* and prohibition of interest, into a Western economic mould. The dominant models guide the analysis and shape the inquiry: everything is compared and contrasted with capitalism and socialism, highlighting the fact that there is an underlying apologia at work. This attempt starts right from the statements that define the main objectives of Islamic economics.

Thus Muhammad Umar Chapra's 'objectives of Islamic economic order' are not much different from those of a Western welfare state:

(a) Economic well being within the framework of moral norms of Islam;
(b) Universal brotherhood and justice;
(c) Equitable distribution of income; and
(d) Freedom of the individual within the context of social welfare.[8]

Adam Smith also argued for 'economic well being for all' based on the moral framework which he borrowed from his friend and fellow countryman, David Hume. While Chapra obviously does not believe in the 'invisible hand' of Adam Smith, the ideas of free economic activity and social welfare are derived not from any Islamic injunctions, but from a Scottish economist and philosopher. Moreover, Chapra's values and norms, 'the unshakable foundation of spiritual values', is also reflected by Adam Smith: in the *Theory of Moral Sentiment* (1759), which contrasts with *The Wealth of Nations* (1776), he emphasizes that sympathy and human brotherhood rather than self-interest are the basic forces in human nature. So how does the objectives of Islamic economics differ from the goals of a caring, democratic welfare state? Not much as Chapra demonstrates: he proceeds to paint the picture of a welfare state with an Islamic gloss all of which begs the question—why bother with Islamic economics when Adam Smith will do?

Once objectives of Islamic economics have been stated in terms of the Western paradigm, it is a short step to accept the major institutions of the system and try to mould them into Islamic shapes. The most obvious example of this is banking: the institution as it has evolved in the West since the industrial revolution has been accepted, without criticism and question, in its totality. Nowhere in the vast literature on Islamic economics would one find any discussion of the question whether banks are really needed in an Islamic society or could some other form of institution perform the necessary functions. The necessity of banks is taken for granted and attempts to mould them into Islamic shape are made by purging them of interest and basing their actions on the priniple of *mudaraba* or profit-sharing. Of course, an institution that has evolved to suit the needs of a particular society and economic system is not going to yield easily to outside attempts to change it. As a result, the complex knot that Muslim economists have tied themselves in is truly amazing.

While the alternative suggested for interest, profit-sharing, reflects the true ideals of Islam, it cannot fit in an institution which has grown up solely on the basis of interest. Consider how Siddiqui, the arch exponent of Islamic banking, describes the function of a banking system based on *mudaraba*:

A large number of depositers enter into individual *mudaraba* contracts with a banking company, organised on the basis of share capital, the contracts stipulating the sharing of the profits on the 'business of banking'. The bank undertakes two kinds of business. Firstly, it offers banking services earning fees and commissions. Secondly, it assumes the role of financier–entrepreneur making judicious selection of businessmen who seek capital from it, stipulating that they share with it the profits of their productive enterprise. Liability to loss in a *mudaraba* contract attaches to the financier only, the working party bears no part of the loss accruing to capital extended by the financier ... It follows that the loss incurred by an individual entrepreneur working with capital advanced by the bank will be borne by the bank. The bank has, however, advanced capital to a large number of entrepreneurs, diversifying its investments as far as possible. Losses incurred on individual advances are likely to get absorbed by some of the profits accruing to the bank from the successful entrepreneurs. As long as the totality of profits accruing on banks' advances plus the fees and commissions earned by the bank remain a positive quantity . . . the despositers' interests are safe. But what if the new revenue of the bank is a negative quantity? This will mean a loss, to be distributed equally on share capital and *mudaraba* deposits.[9]

So the ordinary act of depositing money becomes a risk-taking exercise. How can one plan for the future if one is not sure what will happen to one's money at the end of the financial year? And the banks have no guarantee that they will get a return on their investments. Consider what will happen to a rural agricultural bank in a year of bad harvest when it has invested all its capital in the labour of the local farmers! If the financier is risking his capital, he is likely to demand a hefty share of the profit; so the poor entrepreneur ends up working for the bank instead of himself. And if the bank does not ask for a lion's share of the profit, how can it ensure that it covers for all those entrepreneurs who have lost its money? Perhaps both the bank and the entrepreneur are getting a bad deal? Perhaps this is why all the Islamic banks are losing their investments so rapidly?

The point of this criticism is not that the principles of *madaraba* do not work, but that the un-Islamic institution of banking is the wrong place to put an Islamic injunction into practice. Moreover, Western economic institutions do not come on their own: they bring the entire system with them. Banking as Alvin Toffler points out so powerfully in *The Third Wave*[10] is the central institution of the modern money system. Accept the banks and you accept the entire exploitative structure and theoretical framework that comes with it. The two are integrated and cannot be delinked.

And this is precisely what has happened. Along with the banks, Muslim economists have accepted the entire Keynesian and monetarist economics that comes with it. Nejatullah Siddiqui is a Keynesian *par excellence*: his understanding of economy and functioning of banks is based on the tool kit of Keynesian thought—productivity, capital, market operations, liquidity etc. are concepts and notions by which he analyses 'banking without interest' and the workings of an Islamic economy. Apart from its concentration on banking, over 80 per cent of the literature on Islamic economics is on monetarism in the classical European sense. An indication of how dependent contemporary Muslim economic thought is on monetarism is given by the fact that when Milton Friedman, the monetarist Nobel Laureate, suggested that indexation may be an answer to inflation, a host of papers appeared arguing that as price instability is a major goal of monetary policy in Islamic economics, indexation may be a good answer!

The over-emphasis on monetary and fiscal economics is justified by Munawar Iqbal and M. Fahim Khan by pointing out that 'the abolition of *riba* and the imposition of *Zakah* are the corner-stones of Islamic economic system'.[11] But the natural emphasis of a system that outlaws interest would be to play down the role of money not to raise it as the arch factor of economy. Muslim economists, like economists of all thought and persuasion elsewhere, whether Keynesian, neo-Keynesian, Marxist or monetarists, are hypnotised by money, and look only at those sectors of production and consumption that are monetised and involve cash transactions. The emphasis on the monetised economy has meant that Islamic economics has equated the monetised sectors of a country with the whole system of production, consumption and maintenance. This one-dimensional linear view has produced a rather fragmented and truncated discipline that has neither provided any answers to some of the most pressing economic problems of our time nor is aware of the more important non-monetary factors that shape an economy.

Consider, for example, the new study of Umar Chapra which sums up the debate on Islamic banking and monetary system.[12] After a thorough analysis of the inequities and injustices that exist in the world's banking and monetary institutions, Chapra suggests a package of reform which includes moderation in spending, elimination of hoarding, efficient use of savings, responsible government spending, increases in equity financing, reducing the powers of banks, and establishment of 'sane' stock markets. While these reforms are being implemented, steps have to be taken to eliminate *riba* from society. Chapra suggests that this ought to be done in an institutional setting which includes (1) a central bank, (2) commercial banks, (3) non-bank financial institutions, (4) specialized credit institutions, (5) deposit insurance corporations and (6) investment audit corporation. Once this institutional set-up has emerged, a step-by-step transition can be undertaken to an interest-free economy. The transition involves the declaration of interest as illegal, substantial increases in equity/loan ratio of Muslim countries, the reform of the tax system, mobilization of idle funds, and the gradual conversion of interest-orientated financial institutions into profit-sharing ones. Chapra clearly believes that a just society can be produced simply by modifying the monetary system. The fact that injustice is not part of the monetary system, but that it is the system, has escaped Chapra. He is quite happy to borrow all the institutions of the Western monetary system and hopes that by purging them of interest they will bloom into socially conscious institutions which will promote justice and equity. Furthermore, he makes no attempts to relate his monetary reforms to technology and energy policy. It is as though monetary policies exist in water-tight compartments unrelated to the factors that shape modern society.

Inflation and unemployment are two of the most hideous plagues of our tme. Yet on both these fronts, Islamic economics is silent. Despite the fact that every author starts off by stating that 'full employment' is a major goal of Islamic economics, no one discusses how this ideal can be achieved. Or, indeed, given the increasing population base in Muslim societies and changing mode of production, whether it is possible? Or even desirable? Given their concern with justice and equity, not many authors talk about poverty or how it can be eliminated, except perhaps indirectly by distributing *zakah*. With the exception of the sole essay by Khurshid Ahmad, which has been reprinted in numerous places, there is no awareness in Islamic economic circles of the role of development or the concern for the economic plight of the peasant.[13] There is not a single citation in Siddiqui's survey or Akram Khan's bibliography on technology (surely, the most important economic force in modern society?). Neither can one find any discussion of the type or nature of industry that must form the basis of an Islamic economic system; nor of the role of energy in an Islamic economic system. The relationship between production and consumption is nowhere discussed. And the role or mode of production in shaping a society, the psychological impact of the divorce—in time, space and social distance—between a producer and a consumer and the illusionary nature of paper money are all topics to which Muslim economists are completely oblivious. Their enterprise, like modern economics itself, bears no real relationship to reality.

All of this means that the linear, one-dimensional thrust of Western economic thought, which is based on the vision of eighteenth-century England, have kept Muslim economists on the straight and narrow path. Indeed, Muslim economists are deeply sunk in the quicksand of the Western economic paradigm. From the statements of objectives onwards, they have adopted the Western economic paradigm in its totality. The major, and not so major, themes of Western economics occur again and again in the literature on Islamic economics: 'productivity', 'macro consumption economics', 'full employment', 'economic growth', 'welfare programmes', 'cost-benefit analysis' and 'monetarism'. Because the main frame of reference is the Western economic paradigm, its tools, methodologies, issues and institutions are accepted and questions are always asked in relation to them. Thus we have numerous research papers asking such questions as 'what is the role of theory of profit in Islam?', 'what function does macro consumption perform in Islamic economics?' and (would you believe?) 'what is the Islamic perspective on the economics of discounting in project evaluation?'. In this way Islamic meaning and justification is sought from accepted Western modes of economic thought and analysis.

By drawing on Western economic thought, Muslim economists have unwittingly based their analysis on six metaphysical assumptions: first, that money is to be studied like a physical commodity; second, what needs to be done is to analyse how the money system of today actually works; third, that monetary problems can be solved by modifying the dominant institutions of

Western society; fourth, that the tools of modern economics, whose cultural impact is seldom appreciated by Muslim economists, can solve the problem of Islamic economics; fifth, that the economic environment is never depleted; and sixth that the goals of the Islamic economics system can be achieved without changing the energy base of Muslim countries.

These metaphysical notions, and the accompanying borrowing of institutions, ideas and tools of the Western economic system, are implicitly leading Muslim economists to produce policies that are hardly different from the capitalist and socialist alternatives. In the end they will lead Muslim countries to the same crisis that confronts industrialized societies. Hazel Henderson sums up the state of the affairs succinctly:

> The crises of governance in all industrial economies today are inseparable from the fact that too much of their national policy making and the modeling of their problems are reduced to the abstraction of 'managing their economies', using the monetised data and tools provided by economists and econometricians and the concept of macroeconomic management. This obscures the other dimensions of the reality of dynamic societies, structured in now unsustainable modes of interaction with their resources and energy and based on technologies and institutions that now must be redesigned to fit totally new situations.[14]

Indeed, there is no awareness in Muslim economic circles that methodology and tools of analysis are out of date and ideologically value laden and direct the results of inquiry into a particular direction. For example, M. Akram Khan, who never tires of talking about *akhrah*, readily concedes that 'Islamic economics may utilise the tools of analysis developed by modern economics' oblivious to the fact that the methodologies of Western economics were developed, and evolved, to solve problems that are particular to the system.[15] Moreover, he further argues that 'Islamic economics may adopt the findings of Western economics so far as they have a universal application', once again begging the question: if Western economics is value-free and universal, why should one bother with Islamic economics?

The intellectual situation of Muslim economists is so absurd, so poverty-stricken, that even those issues which have been ditched in Western economic circles are being hotly debated in Islamic economic circles. Thus M. A. Mannan, a leading member of the circle, is driven to argue that Islamic economics is more than a social science, more than a system; it is indeed a 'science' thus trying to relive the ridiculous sixties debate when 'economics' was aping 'physics' in the hope of upgrading its status![16]

As a result of all this, Islamic economics has not emerged as an independent, interdisciplinary approach to understanding and building economic structures of Islam, but as a sub-discipline of Western economics. Because Western economists can readily see the ideas, tools and modes of thought of their discipline dominate all that is happening in Islamic economics, they do not feel threatened by it. Indeed, witness the number of Western scholars who have taken the subject to their heart and are writing papers and acting as consultants to Islamic banks. The entire exercise is a process of assimilation. Both in terms of thought and practice, Islamic economics is already sucked into the money system. Western economics behaves, in theory and action, as an integrated system; and this system is a machine. A self-amplifying process is already in motion.

The Axiomatic Analysis

If Islamic economics, just like Islamic science, has any meaning it is purely in the context of Islamic society and Muslim civilization. In this context, Islamic economics has to rely not just on Islamic principles and injunctions, but must develop its own tools of thought and analysis and its unique institutions. Islamic economic institutions have to be rediscovered, evolved and invented on the basis of the needs of Muslim societies and the principles of Islam, not taken or adopted from what already exists in the market-place. To a very large extent, this means that Islamic economics must adopt an axiomatic approach, and construct a living dynamic Islamic economic system, concept by concept, institution by institution, operationalizing Islamic injunctions such as the prohibition of *riba* and introduction of *zakah* in a truly authentic manner. Such an approach is not likely to find favour with Western economists as it will strike at the heart of their system.

Fortunately, there are a few Muslim economists who appreciate the importance of the axiomatic approach. In the early seventies, in short paper, Abdul-Hamid Ahmad Abu-Sulayman demonstrated how the concepts of *tawhid* and brotherhood can be used as analytical tools to construct the basis of Islamic economic theory.[17] Although some of his conclusions were a little simplistic, his analysis forced him to tackle such issues as mode of production, role of technology and sharing of natural resources which has continuously escaped the attention of Muslim monetarists.

More recently, however, Syed Nawab Haider Naqvi in his *Ethics and Economics: An Islamic Synthesis*[18] has shown what can be achieved by the axiomatic approach. Naqvi argues that any set of axioms to be meaningful must satisfy four criteria: they must be adequate and legitimate representations of Islam's ethical views; they must form the smallest possible set; the elements of the set must be internally consistent; and the axioms must have predictive power. On this basis, Naqvi argues that Islam's ethical philosophy can be summarized by four axioms: unity, equilibrium, free will and responsibility. Unity, or *tawhid*, refers not only to the unity of God, but also the unity of human life and the healing of the 'current schism between ethics and economics'. Social justice is only one component of equilibrium which is derived from *adl*. Free will refers to human freedom in the realm on worldly affairs; but free will can also lead to the denial of unity and upset nature's equilibrium unless man is made responsible for his actions. All four concepts are interlinked and interrelated and cannot be isolated from each other; discarding any one of them would mean demolishing the entire framework.

Naqvi uses his four axioms to develop the basic policy objectives of the Islamic economic system. He isolates social justice, universal education, economic growth and employment generation as the key policy objectives of Islamic economics. These policies are to be met by limiting ownership of private property, 'direct and indirect controls to regulate not only the level but also the composition, production and consumption', development of an elaborate social security system, and economic growth. Naqvi takes care to define the type of growth he is seeking: he rejects growth policies which require excessively inequitable income distribution and argues for a pattern of growth which combines state control of means of production with policies which encourage private initiatives and aim at equalizing 'the competing claims of present and future consumption'.

The strength of the axiomatic approach, as Naqvi demonstrates so convincingly, is that it provides not just the tools for analysis and guides inquiry, but it also produces policies for action. However, despite the strength of his approach, Naqvi could not completely shed the influence of Western economic thought. While *riba* clearly contradicts the axiomatic framework he has set up, he is unable to conceive institutions which can thrive and promote unity, equilibrium, free will and responsibility while shunning interest. Hence his suggestion that *riba* can perform desirable functions in society and a 'useful role' for it should be accepted, albeit till such time as it can be replaced by Islamically-legitimate financial mechanisms and wide-ranging structural changes.

By not being able to cope with *riba*, Naqvi essentially undermines his own approach: the very objective of axiomatic analysis is not to compromise on principles, methods and institutions. His compromise is the result not so much of his approach but the paramount belief in his discipline: he describes his approach as one of 'scientific objectivism' and seems to have more faith in the theory of positive time preference than on the dictates of axiomatic framework. Those who seek to justify their analysis by invoking the higher deity of 'scientific objectivism' (whatever it may be: certainly not many self-respecting scientists believe in its existance as is evident from the vast literature on science, subjectivity and ideology) clearly do not have enough confidence in what they are doing.

Coping with Future Realities

Despite its obvious shortcomings, Naqvi's study clearly demonstrates the power of the axiomatic approach. If Islamic economics is to yield positive dividends for Muslim societies, axiomatic analysis must become the key to all work on the subject. Indeed, Muslim economists need to go much, much further than Naqvi. Although Naqvi is careful to define such notions of dominant economic paradigms as 'economic growth', 'means of production' and 'social security' in Islamic terms, original Islamic concepts and notions have to be dug out and used to express precisely what is meant. As I have argued repeatedly, language and concepts have a profound impact on our thinking and can take us unwittingly in strange directions. Indeed, the fundamental flaw with Naqvi's study is not that he was unable to cope with *riba*, but that he moved away from pure Islamic concepts such as *tawhid*, *adl*, *istislah* and *khilafah* to vague European notions of equilibrium and responsibility, thus limiting the richness of the original concepts. The axiomatic approach has to be based on conceptual analysis, with pure Qur'anic and Shariah concepts providing both the framework as well as the methodological tools for anlaysis. Furthermore, he arbitrarily limits them to four: while it may make one's life simpler, there is no universal law which states that axiomatic inquiry has to be based on a minimum number of concepts. The rich reservoir of concepts to be found in the Qur'an and Sunnah are not there to be ignored; our present intellectual and physical status is a direct outcome of the fact that for over 400 years we have chosen to ignore them. Each one tells us something about the world-view of Islam; and all of them must play their part in the axiomatic analysis that is to produce a contemporary system of Islamic economics.

Moreover, axiomatic economic analysis cannot be based on the outmoded linear, either/or logic of Western economics. This logic can neither cope with contemporary complex realities nor with the richness and multidimensional nature of Islamic concepts. How does one, for example, on the basis of linear logic, reconcile the idea that *zakah*, which involves subtracting from one's income, can actually lead to increase of wealth? Growth by subtraction is an idea that Western economics has no understanding of. As soon as one adds value and cultural criteria to conventional economic analysis, it ceases to make sense. Islamic economic analysis, therefore, has to be carried out at a higher level of logic, where options and cost–benefits are not measured in linear categories and policy measures are not seen in either/or terms.

The linear logic of Western economics is reflected in the present structure of the world. Economically and technologically, the globe is structured as though developing countries, including all Muslim countries, were colonies of the industrialized states. Colonialism is alive and well: and the US, EEC, Scandinavia, Switzerland and Japan are reaping its benefits. And Western economic theory provides the paradigm which has created this structure. There are metaphysical axioms at its base and its tools and logic have evolved to express these fundamental assumptions of Western civilization. Islamic economics is not going to break this structure if it freely borrows from this paradigm: on the contrary, it will become part of the structure. Thus, all those Muslim economists who argue that we should not hesitate to borrow the 'good' and 'neutral' bits of the Western economic theory are asking to be absorbed into the dominant paradigm. There are no 'good' and 'neutral' bits of Western economics: it is one vast, interlinked value-laden, self-perpetuating system that is taking linear logic to its ultimate conclusion. E. F. Schumacher often related that his conversations with leaders of many developing and socialist countries ended with those leaders telling him 'that the western capitalist countries are like express trains heading towards a precipice of self-destruction—and then they add: but we shall overtake them!'. The modern economic theories and tools of analysis are the engine that drives this train.

If Islamic economics is to move towards the ideals that its proponents express, than it must develop not just its own body of theories and models, but also its own tools and modes of logic and thought. In other words, it must assume a civilizational role and work towards laying the foundations and building the structures of a Muslim civilization of the future. It has to break the shell of an atomized discipline and become a multidisciplinary mode of inquiry, taking into consideration the social organizations, the political ideals, the environmental imperatives, and scientific and technological needs of Muslim societies. In the modern world, where complexity and complementarity are all too evident, isolated ideas and policies do not produce positive results. Islamic economics has to draw not just from Muslim history, and contemporary Muslim societies, but also from the future. Islamic economics has to develop a future consciousness or be ready simply to be swept away.

All this means that Islamic economics should not be the sole concern of the 'economists' but Muslim scientists, technologists and environmentalists must also make their contribution to the field. Moreover, Muslim economists themselves have to develop an interdisciplinary base with a clear vision of the future, be aware of the long-term trends and conscientiously direct Muslim societies towards the desired economic future.

In particular, there are a number of global trends that spell danger for Muslim countries and need serious examination from the proponents of Islamic economics.

(1) It is almost a truism now to state that the world is shrinking and becoming more and more economically interlinked and interdependent. In such an interconnected world, how would interest-free economies deal with a global system exclusively based on interest. As the process of interconnection speeds up, it will become even more difficult for interest-free economies to delink and survive. The only winners in this exercise, as experience so far has shown, is the Western banking system. Given this trend, the development of a functional alternative economic structure that is not plugged into the global system becomes a matter of survival. How to delink from the world's economic system must, therefore, become a major theme of Islamic economics.

(2) Electronic banking and funds transfer systems are giving money an unparallelled and dangerous importance. Because of the speed of electronic systems, the same amount of money now supports five times as many transactions as before. Thus the speeding up of information about money also increases its velocity of circulation. At a point not too distant in the future, when the speed of transactions reaches 'real time', that is there is no delay in transmission, money will acquire a strange new status:

> the velocity of the information about money flows would lose all relationship with the thermodynamic realities of the actual system (sub-

ject to natural cycles of crops, weather, friction, inertia, and human frailties), and the amount of money and capital available at any point in the banking system would tend towards infinity. As information about the money system became delinked from actual events, all manner of new ventures and schemes might be initiated by false promissory notes signaling capital availability with nothing more than an electronic impulse over a computer terminal.[19]

Moreover, computerization of stock markets throughout the world has blurred the distinction between investment and speculation; the entire system is moving towards becoming a worldwide gambling casino with no pretension to serving social needs.

Given these futuristic drops, the overemphasis on monetarist and fiscal policies of contemporary thought on Islamic economics is a dangerous trend. Muslim economists must be aware of the changing role of money and its implications for Muslim societies; and diversify the basis of Islamic economic thought towards non-monetarist and non-fiscal areas.

(3) Along with increase in the velocity of information about money, information itself is becoming a key commodity. Economic power in the future will be determined by ability to generate and having access to information. It will play the same role as energy is playing now. Thus Islamic economic theory must be developed to cope with non-material commodities like information and energy.

(4) The use of energy in a society is intrinsically tied with economics. The globe's energy resources are not finite; indeed, they are depleting at a rapid rate. Both inflation and employment are tied to the rate of depletion of energy sources. As it becomes more costly to extract energy sources, as they became more and more scarce, so does the cost of transforming it into usable commodities increases. Throughout the world, the price of basic human necessities—energy, food, shelter and health care—are tied to the costs associated with the exchange and transformation of energy. Unemployment is the other side of the equation: the faster conventional sources of energy run out, more and more people became unemployed and underemployed. Thus transformation to a renewable energy base is essential for the future survival of the Muslim world. This means that energy equations

must play a predominant part in any economic analysis. Indeed, Muslim economists ought to be working out how the transformation to a renewable energy base can take place and what it would mean for the conventional theories of Islamic economics.

(5) At present, Muslim countries are essentially consumer states relying exclusively on imported goods. This situation is likely to get worse and the associated ill-effects of the ever-increasing social, psychological and intellectual distance between producers and consumers will multiply at great speeds. Therefore, it must be a major task of Islamic economics to change the patterns of consumption in Muslim societies as well as to direct production towards directions which are more suitable to the needs of Muslim consumers. Islamic economics will ignore industrial and consumer policies at the expense of its ideals.

The ethics of Islamic economics have been stated and restated and are now abundantly clear. However, the formidable task of transforming this ethics into a dynamic economic system that has its individual identity with its own institutions and methodological tools and presents a real alternative to the dominant paradigm has only just begun. It is a long and arduous task with no short-cuts. As long as Muslim economists remain true to their world-view, each new idea, each new theory, each new innovation will take us that much closer to a dynamic, thriving Muslim civilization of the future.

Notes

1. These include International Centre for Research in Islamic Economics at the King Abdul Aziz University, Jaddah, and the Institute of Policy Studies, Islamabad.

2. *Muslim Economic Thinking*, Islamic Foundation, Leicester, 1981.

3. *Islamic Economics: Annotated Sources in English and Urdu*, Islamic Foundation, Leicester, 1983.

4. *Journal of Research in Islamic Economics*, **1** (2), 51–3 (Winter 1984).

5. *Journal of Research in Islamic Economics*, **1** (2), 55–61 (Winter 1984).

6. Siddiqui, *op. cit.* pp. 4–5.

7. 'The theory of the economics of Islam: the economics of tawhid and

brotherhood', in *Contemporary Aspects of Economic and Social Thinking in Islam*, MSA, Plainsfield, Indiana, 1970, pp. 27–8.

8. *In Islam: Its Meaning and Message*, ed. Khurshid Ahmad, Islamic Council of Europe, London, 1975; and numerous other places.

9. M. N. Siddiqui, *Issues in Islamic Banking*, Islamic Foundation, Leicester, 1983, p. 23.

10. Bantam, New York, 1980.

11. Munawar Iqbal and M. Fahim Khan, *A Survey of Issues and a Programme of Research in Monetary and Fiscal Economics of Islam*, Institute of Policy Studies, Islamabad, 1981, p. 7.

12. M. Umar Chapra, *Towards a Just Monetary Ssytem*, Islamic Foundation, Leicester, 1985.

13. Khurshid Ahmad's paper on economic development is discussed in Chapter 12.

14. *Politics of Solar Age*, Anchor, New York, 1981, p. 31.

15. See Note 5.

16. M. A. Mannan, 'Islamic Economics as a Social Science', *Journal of Research in Islamic Economics*, **1** (1), 49–61.

17. A. H. A. A. Sulayman, *op. cit.*

18. *Ethics and Economics: An Islamic Synthesis*, Islamic Foundation, Leicester, 1981.

19. Hazel Henderson, 'Post-Economic Policies for Post-Industrial Societies', *Revision*, **7** (2), 20–9 (Winter 1984).

10

Towards an Islamic Theory of Environment

Mankind's future is intrinsically linked with its attitude towards the environment. It is to our attitudes, which are ultimately shaped by our world-views, that we must look to discover the underlying causes of our current environmental predicament.

The Western scholars of contemporary human situation have traced the roots of our environmental crisis to the Judaeo-Christian attitude towards nature. It is this attitude, and the accompanying traditional and intellectual heritage, which is responsible for the seven impersonal threats that the human future now faces: a runaway, production-orientated technology, which has led to the depletion of earth's natural resources, post-critical total and per capita pressure on land and environment, ever-increasing output of wastes; stockpiles of enough nuclear, chemical and biological weapons to destroy the earth several times; the massive growth of human population and its accumulation in vast urban conurbations; and the alienation of man from his environment and from nature. Each one of these trends represents a major threat to our collective well-being and survival. Scholars like Fraser Darling, Theodore Roszak, Jerome Ravetz, Sir Geoffrey Vickers and Lynn White Jr argue that these threats are a product of the Western ethical system. The roots of our ecological crisis are axiomatic: they lie in our beliefs and value structures which shape our relationship with nature, with each other and the life-styles we lead.

The chief spokesman of this anaysis is Lynn White Jr who argues that this sort of mechanism for self-destruction is inherent in monotheistic religions. He sees the Judeao-Christian tradition as the source of all ecological evil. This world-view is centred around a divine being who is 'above all and beyond all' and who created man to have dominion over all the animals and the rest of creation. Some contemporary Christian scholars have argued that 'dominion' can mean responsible stewardship. But White asserts that no matter how one interprets the concepts of 'dominion', it is difficult to argue that it does not imply the right to exercise power and control over nature. He writes:

> Christianity is the most anthropocentric religion the world has seen. As early as the 2nd century both Tertrillian and Saint Irenaeous of Lyons were insisting that when God shaped Adam he was foreshadowing the image of the incarnate Christ, the Second Adam. Man shares, in great measure, God's transcendence of nature. Christianity, in absolute contrast to ancient paganism and Asia's great religions (except, perhaps, Zoroastrianism), not only established a dualism of man and nature but also insisted that it is God's will that man exploit nature for his proper ends.[1]

For White, the present increasing disruption of the global environment is the product of a dynamic science and technology which has its origins in the ethical base of Christianity. He considers modern science to be an extrapolation of Christian theology; and technology to be 'an Occidental, voluntarist realization of the Christian dogma of man's transcendance of, and rightful mastery over, nature'. White also believes that as 'science and our technology are so tinctured with orthodox Christian arrogance toward nature that no solution for our ecological crisis can be expected from them alone'. Moreover, White asserts, as 'Islam, like Marxism, is a Judaeo-Christian heresy', it is equally responsible for the 'monotheistic debasement of nature'.

White made these pronouncements in 1967. Since then these assertions have been repeated by scholar after scholar so that now they have become part of the Western paradigm of contemporary ecological crisis. This situation has arisen largely because Muslim scholars have never concerned themselves with ecological issues or formulated a coherent Islamic theory of environment. Recently, however, a number of studies have been published which when examined collectively lead us towards a systematic exposition of Islam's position towards contemporary ecological concerns.

What concerns a growing number of Western scholars is the clear dichotomy between our behaviour and life-styles, including the behaviour and life-styles of most Muslim societies, and what ecology teaches us. Earth's ecosystems are governed by a number of principles which we have come to appreciate only recently. If our life-style is in harmony with these principles, the argument goes, then we can develop an inherent resilience which will ensure our survival, allow our ecosystems to heal, replenish and begin the long road to restoration. Collectively, these principles provide an ethical framework for our attitudes towards nature and environment—an imperative for a sane future of mankind.

What are the ethical principles of ecology? There are seven such principles which have been derived from the study of living systems. The first and primary principles is that of holistic environment, with everything affecting everything else—directly or indirectly. Nothing operates in isolation: everything connects with everything else to perform the cosmic symphony of life. 'This principle of holocentric environment', writes Beatrice Willard, 'leads us to certain criteria for guiding human activities. It leads us to the practice of "looking before we leap", and inculcates the need for each individual and group to engage consciously or otherwise in "ecological reconnaissance". This involves analysing ahead of time the ramifications of potential activities upon our immediate habitat or our ecosystem, upon present and successive generations of the human race, and upon living resources of all kind.'[2]

The 'living resources' of the earth provide us with the second principle of ecology. The earth exhibits an incredible range of biological diversity as manifested in an almost limitless range of morphological and physiological variations in the plant and animal kingdom. This biological diversity is the most precious and irreplaceable heritage that the human race possesses for it ensures the perpetuity of life on earth. Within this vast array of ecosystems, each organism has a role to play—a 'niche' to occupy—no matter how insignificant it may seem to us. Our management and use of living resources should be based on a thorough understanding and appreciation of this.

Recycling and redistribution of resources constitutes the third great principle of ecological behaviour. All ecosystems continuously recycle waste, materials are used, discarded and picked up by other ecosystems for their use—on and on, in infinite cycles. Making recycling an essential part of human behaviour will have profound consequences. We will have to learn to use materials in a new way which does not deprive the future generations of their use while also allowing the present generations a reasonable possibility of disposition. We need to foster the flow of materials rather than their sinking and destruction. Willard gives an interesting example of how this principle would change our mining activities:

> we are mining nitrate and phosphate deposits that took many millennia to form. We are distributing them to agricultrual lands, increasing run-offs of nitrogen and phosphates into rivers, reaping crops and distributing them to people who use them for human food, etc., the waste of which in many Western countries goes into lakes, rivers and eventually the oceans. Thus it may be removed from ecosystem benefits for millennia, as much of it will not be recycled until new phosphate and nitrate deposits are formed on the ocean floors and ultimately elevated in continent rebuilding millions of years from now. We can assist the operation of ecosystems by facilitating recycling and avoiding those semi-dead-end pathways that keep materials cooped up for longer periods.

But recycling is not limited to grand activities like mining; it has to be introduced in almost every aspect of our lives from daily living to our way of thinking about the future.

The next two principles of ecological ethics have not been properly understood in terms of human behaviour. The fourth principle is that of limiting factors: certain environmental factors limit the functioning of living organisms within all ecosystems. These factors define the operating parameters of ecosystems and the living organisms within them. Often, it is not one but a host of physical and chemical factors in the environment which are interacting with a group of species to describe the limiting factors of the system. Associated with this principle is the capacity of the vast majority of the living systems to reproduce in excess of the support capability of the ecosystem in which they live. A possible reason for this, the fifth principle of ecological behaviour, is the fact that overpopulation ensures that some individuals survive to reproduce the species. But the two principles act together to keep the population of a particular species in equilibrium. We do not really understand and appreciate the interconnection of these two principles and frequently we are unaware of the fact that we may have significantly altered the equilibrium by a seemingly innocent action. For example, in the United States grazing sheep have been protected by poisoning or shooting coyotes. The effect of this action on the decline of grain crops is not obvious at first sight. But the drop in coyote population produced a sharp rise in rodent and bird population which in turn had its effect on grain crops. Thus isolated actions which ignore the principles of limiting factors and the prolific nature of biological reproduction can have serious consequences. How we shape human behaviour in the light of these two principles is a question that needs to be examined with some urgency. But it is obvious that the impact of these principles on our norms and behaviour can be profound.

All ecosystems have a definite capability of sustaining a given amount of life. This capability is often referred to as 'carrying capacity'. This carrying capacity, the sixth principle of ecology, has its counterparts in engineering systems and organizational behaviour. However, it has a more sophisticated aspect in ecology. Because of the greater diversity of living systems, their strong capability of reproduction, complexity and resilience, the carrying capacity of ecosystems is not easy to determine. Often the fact that carrying capacity of an ecosystem has been exceeded only comes to the fore when the actual point has been far exceeded in time, numbers and equilibrium. But a kind of 'domino' effect may have already been set in motion resulting in a chain reaction which produces dire consequences for the ecosystem. That carrying capacity has ethical lessons for human thought and action has been ignored by us for a long time. Yet, we have been well aware of this principle for decades; its importance for us extends to our urban, rural and agricultural activities alike. It even extends to the earth as a whole: it is now being forcefully argued, by James Lovelock and others, that the earth behaves as a single organism, even a living creature; and as a living system the earth has a definite carrying capacity.[3] The biosphere is put together by the totality of living systems to carry out certain necessary control and survival functions. The living matter, the air, the oceans, the land surface, are parts of a giant system which is able to control temperature, the composition of the air and sea, the pH of the soil and so on so as to be optimum for survival of the biosphere. All this means that the earth—or *Gaia* as it is called in this hypothesis—is a finite system with a limited carrying capacity which cannot be exceeded without introducing serious imbalances. The sub-systems of *Gaia*, including man as its central nervous system, have to perform a supportive role within this carrying capacity. Urban areas, grazing lands, forests, parks, open spaces, roads—all have upper limits to their capacity for providing services and desired resources and maintaining the delicate balances of *Gaia* and supporting life. Our thought and action, planning and building, use of resources and materials have to be dictated by this insight.

The seventh and last principle of ecological ethics concerns the development and stability of ecosystems. Ecosystems have developed over a long span of time, starting from simple systems and progressing to more complex, highly interconnected systems which are in equilibrium and stable. In this progression, natural processes have come into being which ensure the permanency of the system and protect it from disruption which may be caused by such incidences as fire, landslide and insect infestations. These processes are slow but nevertheless ensure that the system meets various perturbations and survives. However, if processes which are opposed to these natural processes are introduced in the system, they can have a toxic effect on the ecosystem. Criteria for human behaviour evolving from ecosystem development and stability are not obvious at first sight. But the ethic begins to surface when we realize the value of time in the development of an ecosystem. Soil, water and natural resources like oil have taken millions of years to develop; a rain forest takes tens of thousands of years to reach maturity. The emerging ethic guides us not to destroy natural systems by deforestation, mining, pollution and other human activities, and to spend considerable time and profits to restoring viable ecosystems.

All the principles outlined above define and dictate the choice of our activities; and limit our options for full benefit of all human beings and living systems into the distant future. Proponents of ecological ethics argue that human behaviour based on these principles would distinguish between human needs which have to be met for the entire population of the globe and human desires most of which need to be checked. It also distinguishes between what man *can* do to the environment; and what he *should* do. In directing man's action in meeting basic needs and ensuring the survival of all living systems, the argument goes, the ecological ethic forces us to rid ourselves of the nineteenth-century technocratic thinking and to reject the idea that human existence is necessarily a battle against nature. Spelled out in detail, the ethics of ecological behaviour form a new philosophy: eco-philosophy. The idea of eco-philosophy offers a new paradigm for our comprehension of reality, for our way of thinking and our norms and behaviour. If the vast array of human societies that inhabit the earth could achieve a consensus on this ethic, the survival of our environment and its ability to sustain life will be ensured.

Well, what is the Muslims' stand on these principles?

Within the traditional and intellectual heritage of Islam, reverence and respect for ecological principles is total. But the ethical system of Islam is not based solely on environmental criteria. Islam is concerned with the complete human being and, as such, it expresses the state of being characteristic of humans by offering an impressive repertoire of values: instrumental, ethical, aesthetic, eschatological—all of which reflect and recapitulate the variety of aspects of man's existence. Some of these values are codified in the Shariah (Islamic law) while others are inherent in a rich reservoir of concepts to be found in the Qur'an. When understood in an environmental sense, the Shariah and Qur'anic concepts provide a very effective ethical and pragmatic answer to our environmental crisis.

The fact that these values, in their environmental aspects, are nowhere to be seen in the Muslim world, where the environmental situation is just as acute as in the West, can be attributed to a very simple fact. Nowhere in Muslim societies is the Shariah adhered to in its totality or the Islamic way of life forms the basis of human action. Moreover, Islamic concepts and ethical precepts have been divorced from a pragmatic, living, dynamic form for the last 300 or 400 years, since the decline of the Muslim civilization and its eventual colonization by the Occident. It is because the dominant patterns of behaviour, development and thought in the Muslim world are Western that we see this environmental degradation and exploitative way of life. Muslim societies themselves need to appreciate the ecological principles of Islam and find practical routes for adopting and establishing them.

So, what is the environmental ethic of Islam?

Any discussion of ethics in Islam must, of necessity, start with an exposition of the concept of *tawhid*, the foundation stone of Islam. *Tawhid* exemplifies the unity of God: the recognition that there is one, absolute, transcendent Creator of the universe and all that it contains. Man is ultimately responsible for all his actions to Him. As an ethical rule, *tawhid* dictates the acceptance of God as the only source of all values: not to do this would lead to *shirk*, the negation of *tawhid*, which is the cardinal sin in Islam. As such, *tawhid* is the matrix for human thought and action, it is all-pervasive and penetrates every aspect of our endeavour. In the words of Ali Shariti,

> in the world-view of *tawhid*, man fears only one power, and is answerable before only one judge. He turns to only one *qibla*, and directs his hopes and fears to only one source. And the corollary is that all else is false and pointless—all the diverse and variegated tendencies, strivings, fears, desires and hopes of man are vain and fruitless. *Tawhid* bestows upon man independence and dignity. Submission to Him alone—the supreme norm of all being—impels man to revolt against all lying powers, all the humiliating fetters of fear and greed.[4]

Thus conceived, *tawhid* becomes all-pervasive, penetrating all aspects of human thought and behaviour. It is the guiding prin-

ciple of religion and ethics, politics and social behaviour, epistemology and science, and at the centre of Muslim's curiosity
regarding nature.

From *tawhid* emerge the concepts of *khilafah* and *amana*. The
entire rationale of an Islamic environmental ethics is based on the
Qur'anic concept of *khilafah*: man's viceregency of trusteeship.
Gaia is an *amana* trust from God and man is the trustee who has
the responsibility of looking after the vast panaroma of God's
creation. Man can use the trust for his benefit but has no absolute
right to anything: the trust must be preserved and handed back to
its rightful owner. Man is accountable for the misuse of his trust
and is liable to pay a price both in this world and the *akhrah*
(hereafter).

This denial of absolute sovereignty to man, writes Parvez
Manzoor,

> is tantamount to investing him with moral responsibility. As any kind
> of responsibility can, in the last analysis, only be personal, it is a
> natural corollary of man's acceptance of trust that he be born free and
> innocent. Man is thus in the Islamic tradition a creature unsullied by
> any ontological flaws. He bears no stigma of any 'original sin' that
> would make him a victim of his own humanity. From the Muslim
> standpoint, a 'fallen' humanity is commensurable neither with divine
> justice nor with human dignity.

Within this framework, nature becomes man's testing ground.
Man is enjoined to read its 'signs' which reflect both man's position in creation and the glory of God. As such, nature is created
orderly and knowable. Were it unruly, capricious and erratic,
morality would be impossible. It would be both oppressive and
degrading for man who would humble himself before its slightest
whim. Quite apart from praising God, an unruly and disorderly
nature would hide the manifestations of God. Man would thus
be left in darkness. As such, the orderliness of nature and its
amenability to rational enquiry are an essential prerequisite for
morality.

The concept that regulates the reading of 'signs' of nature is *ilm*
(knowledge). In Islam, the pursuit of knowledge cannot be separated from the concerns of morality. *Ilm* operates through the

agency of *tawhid*: knowledge is pursued for the glorification of Allah and to fulfil man's responsibility towards His trust. It follows then that the pursuit of that knowledge which gives man false notions of absolute sovereignty, or which harm God's trust, the terrestial environment, is not permitted in Islam. The concept of *tawhid*, *khilafah* and *ilm* are interconnected and shape the concerns and direction of rational enquiry. Islamic epistemology is therefore 'unreservedly and uncompromisingly holistic' and within this context 'fragmented knowledge or reductionist epistemology would be a contradiction in terms'.

The Islamic environment is controlled by two concepts: *halal* (that which is beneficial) and *haram* (that which is harmful). When closely examined, *haram* includes all that which is destructive for man as an individual, his immediate environment and the environment at large. The word destructive should be understood in the physical, mental and spiritual sense. All that is beneficial for an individual, his society and his environment is *halal*. Thus an action that is *halal* brings all-round benefits. The environment, therefore, plays a dominant part in the Islamic scheme of things: an action that may bring benefits to an individual may produce harmful effects on society or the environment. The environment, in all its kaleidoscopic richness, must be preserved.

Combine the concepts of *tawhid*, *khilafah*, *amana*, *halal* and *haram* with the words for justice (*adl*) and moderation, temperance, balance, equilibrium, harmony (*itidal*) and the concepts of *istihsan* (preference for the better) and *istislah* (public welfare) and one has the most sophisticated framework for an environmental ethic that one can possibly desire. 'Muslim societical ethic, nay the very basis of society itself, is but a quest for equilibrium, and hence felicity with God, nature and history. It entails submitting oneself to the will of God, accepting the mandate of trusteeship and striving to be a moderate community (*ummah wastah*)', writes Parvez Manzoor. The goals of justice, public interest, environmental equilibrium and harmony with nature, Muslim consciousness affirms, is reached by treading the path of moderation.[5]

The matrix of this conceptual framework—*tawhid*, *khilafah*, *amana*, *halal*, *haram*, *adl*, *itidal*, *istihsan* and *istislah*—constitutes a paradigm of the Islamic theory of environment. If this framework was fully operationalized in the Muslim *ummah* (community) it would revolutionize the behaviour and thinking of Muslim people. For incorporated in these concepts is a deep respect for nature, an appreciation of interconnectedness of all life, recognition of the unity of creation and the brotherhood of all beings, and that concerns of morality and other living systems must form the basis of any rational enquiry. It was a consideration of these concepts from an ecological perspective that led Parvez Manzoor to dismiss Lynn White Jr's assertion that 'Islam, like Marxism, is a Judaeo-Christian heresy' and, as such, is equally responsible for the 'monotheistic debasement of nature' as 'irreverent nonsense'. Indeed, to assume that Islam, like Christianity, marshalls an ethic of environmental domination is either simple ignorance or the height of arrogance.

But the conceptual framework is only the tip of the iceberg. The ecological concerns of Islam are given a practical shape in the Shariah, or Islamic law, which incorporates a whole body of environmental legislation. There is no division of ethics and law in Islam: once again, the framework of key Qur'anic concepts synthesizes the two aspects of human life which in the Western intellectual and religious tradition are isolated in separated water-tight compartments. The ultimate consequence of man's acceptance of trusteeship is the arbitration of his conduct by divine judgement. To be a Muslim is to accept and practice the injunctions of the Shariah. Thus, Shariah is both a consequence of one's acceptance of *tawhid* and a *path*. 'It is simultaneously a manifestation of divine will and that of human resolve to be an agent of that will.'

But Shariah is also a methodology for solving problems. To quote Parvez Manzoor again:

> by its application temporal contingencies are judged by eternal imperatives, moral choices are transformed into options for concrete action and ethical sentiment is objectified into law. It is in fact the *problem-solving* methodology par excellence of Islam. Any theoretical Muslim thinking, as for instance our search for an environmental ethic, must pass through the objective framework of Shariah in order to become operative and be part of Muslim history. Shariah thus provides both

the ethical norms and the legal structure within which Muslim state(s) may make actual decisions pertaining to concrete ecological issues. And not only is Shariah indispensable for decision making in an Islamic context, its moral realism also provides excellent paradigms for theoretical discussion of Islamic ecological philosophy.

Shariah, then, is a value-centred system; it exists to realize the values inherent in such key Islamic concepts as *tawhid*, *khilafah* *istislah*, *halal* and *haram*. The ultimate objective of this system is the universal common good of all created beings, encompassing both our immediate welfare and our future in the Here-after. The importance of the ultimate future dimension of the Shariah cannot be overstated for many immediate benefits could be ultimately unethical. The objective of universal common good is a distinctive characteristic of the Shariah and an important implication of the concept of *tawhid*: one can only serve the one Creator of all life by working for the universal common good of all beings.

Consider, for example, the injunctions of the Shariah concerning land. If land is a gift from God, how is a Muslim entitled to use this gift? While Islam allows the ownership of land, it is limited to that which can be cultivated by human skills and labour. There are four ramifications of this *amana* from God:

(1) That ownership signifies only the right to *use* and this owner-ship can be transferred.
(2) That the owner is entitled to 'private ownership' *only* as long as he uses it.
(3) That the owner who ceases to use his gift is induced, and in some cases even forced, to part with his idle possessions.
(4) That in no case is the owner allowed to charge rent for a free gift of God from another person who, in fact, has the equal right to its use.

These limitations on the use of land are enforced by a number of principles developed by Muslim jurists over the centuries. One of the most basic principles of the Shariah is the declaration of the Prophet Mohammad that 'there shall be no injury, and no perpetuation of injury'. Using this principle, Othman Llewellyn points out.

> Malik ibn Anas and Abu Hanifah formulated the principles that the exercise of a right is permitted only for the achievement of the purpose for which the right was created, that the exercise of a right is illegal where it results in excessive harm, and that the exercise of a right is illegal if used to bring injury to others rather than for benefit. Malik restrained land owners from any use of their property resulting in injury. Abu Yusuf restricted both the individuals' and the authorities' cases concerning neighbourly relationship, placement of windows, division of tenancy in common property, and ownership of uncultivated land, he imposed restrictions if necessary to prevent excessive injury. Abu Yusuf restricted both the individuals' and the authorities rights in cultivating virgin land where its exercise would result in excessive injury. Hanabali jurists reasoned likewise that since Allah is the real owner of all property, human rights of beneficial title must not be abused.[6]

These principles prohibiting undue injury and abuse of rights form the basis of a large part of Islamic resource law. Invaluable resources such as pasture, woodland, wildlife, certain minerals and especially water cannot be privately owned in their natural state or monopolized in Islamic law. They are managed publicly for the common good of all, and everyone has equal access to them.

Accordingly, writes Llewellyn,

> a farm beside a stream is forbidden to monopolize its water. After withholding a reasonable amount of water for his crops, the farmer must release the rest to those downstream. Furthermore, if the water is insufficient for all of the farms along a stream, the needs of the older farms are to be satisfied before a newer farm is permitted to irrigate. This precept safeguards from future injury the previous farmers' investment of labor and wealth in the reclamation of their lands. Moreover, it allows a limited number of farms in one watershed to florish, rather than encouraging a number beyond its carrying capacity, which would result in an injury to all alike, and a general failure of reclamation. According to jurists such as Malik and Ibn Qudamah, these same principles apply to the extraction of groundwater for a person has no right to adversely affect his neighbour's well by lowering the water table or polluting the aquifer.[7]

The Prophet Mohammad himself emphasized the importance of land reclamation in a number of his traditions. For example: 'whosoever brings dead land to life, for him is a reward in it, and whatever any creature seeking food eats of it shall be reckoned as charity from him'; 'there is no Muslim who plants a tree or sows a field for a human, bird, or animal eats from it, but it shall be reckoned as charity from him'; and 'if anyone plants a tree, no human nor any of the creatures of Allah will eat from it without its being reckoned as charity from him'.

The Prophet also prohibited his followers from harming animals and asked them to ensure that the rights of animals are fulfilled. It is a distinctive characteristic of the Shariah that all animals have legal rights which must be enforced by the state. Othman Llewellyn even argues that Islamic law has mechanisms for the full repair of injuries suffered by non-human creatures including their representation in court, assessment of injuries and awarding of relief to them. The classical Muslim jurist Izz ad-Din ibn Abd as-Salam, who flourished during the thirteenth century, formulated the following statement of animal rights:

> the rights of livestock and animals upon man: these are that he spend on them the provision that their kinds require, even if they have aged or sickened such that no benefit comes from them; that he not burden them beyond what they can bear; that he not put them together with anything by which they would be injured, whether of their own kind or other species, and whether by breaking their bones or butting or wounding; that he slaughters them with kindness when he slaughters them, and neither flay their skins nor break their bones until their bodies have become cold and their lives have passed away; that he not slaughter their young within their sight, but that he isolate them; that he makes comfortable their resting places and watering places; that he puts their males and females together during their mating seasons; that he not discard those which he takes as game; and neither shoots them with anything that breaks their bones nor brings about their destruction by any means that renders their meat unlawful to eat.[8]

Wildlife and natural resources too have rights in Islam. The Prophet established inviolate zones bordering water-courses, utilities and towns. Within these *haram* zones, the Shariah restricts or prohibits development to ensure that invaluable resources are protected. Thus such zones are maintained around wells to protect the well or aquifer from impairment, to provide room from the well's operation and maintenance, to safeguard its water from pollution, and to provide resting area for livestock and room for irrigation facilities; around canals and natural water-courses to prevent their pollution; and around towns and cities to ensure that their energy needs—forage and firewood—are fulfilled, their carrying capacity is not exceeded and to provide habitat for wildlife. Wildlife and forest come under the dictates of *hima* in the Shariah. *Hima* is a reserve that safeguards their rights: it is established solely for the conservation of wildlife and forest. The Prophet Mohammad reserved the surroundings of Medina as a *hima* for the protection of vegetation and wildlife. And he declared that private reserves for the exclusive use of individuals are *haram*. Thus reserves in Islam are public property and are managed by the state. Following the Prophet Mohammad, a number of caliphs established public reserves. Caliph Umar ibn al-Khattab, for example, established the *hima* of ash-Sharaf and the extensive *hima* of ar-Rabdah near Dariyah. Caliph Uthman ibn Affan extended the second *hima* which is reported to have carried forth 1000 animals every year. A number of the *hima* established in western Arabia have been grazed responsibly since early Islam and are considered by the Food and Agricultural Organization (FAO) to be the most longstanding examples of wise grazing management known in the world. There are five types of *hima* to be found in the Arabian peninsula today.

(1) Reserves in which grazing is prohibited.
(2) Reserves for forest trees in which woodcutting is prohibited or restricted.
(3) Reserves in which grazing is restricted to certain seasons.
(4) Reserves restricted to certain species and numbers of livestock.
(5) Reserves for beekeeping, in which grazing is prohibited during flowering.
(6) Reserves managed for the welfare of a particular village or tribe.

These injunctions concerning the use of land, the protection of water from pollution, the conservation of wildlife and forests are among the few ecological principles codified in the Shariah. They demonstrate the environmental awareness of the world-view of Islam which provides not just an ethic based on ecological concerns but also a body of legislation to give practical shape to ethical issues. But more than that: the legislative structure of the Shariah can be extended to cover new problems. And the conceptual framework of key Qur'anic concepts can be used to develop new theories and models of the Muslim environment.

This is exactly what Gulzar Haider has done in his conceptual formulation of an Islamic city and the design principles for Islamic environment. What is 'Islamic' about Islamic architecture and Islamic environment? This question is being hotly debated among Muslim intellectual circles—not least because in the name of Islam hideous structures have been erected and alienating environments have been created. However, in defining the Islamic nature of Islamic architecture and Islamic environment, much of the attention has been focused on form and structure. A mosque is a mosque because it has a minaret and a dome and wonderful mosaics and calligraphy inside. The geometrical form of Islamic architecture, for example, has been made an end in itself: the arches which conform to the 'square and root two system' and the 'golden ratio' and the geometric methods based on the circle and so on. Airports, universities and even city enclaves have been built using these rules and there is nothing, as all those who use them confirm, Islamic about them. The manic concern with the forms and structures of Islamic architecture is a great fallacy; it is propagated largely by Western architects, planners and consultants, not to mention scholars whose thinking is dominated by linear logic and outward forms. The fact that some of them build mosques, 'Islamic universities' and judge awards for Islamic architecture only adds insult to injury.

What is Islamic about Islamic architecture and Islamic environment is the atmosphere they create: an atmosphere that encourages the remembrance of Allah, motivates behaviour according to the dictates of Shariah and promotes the values inherent in the matrix of key Qur'anic concepts. Such an atmosphere is a living, dynamic entity whose force is felt and experienced by those who come within its purview. This atmosphere is created not just by outward forms, though they are important. It is created by the *totality* of the system that produces the built environment: the principles of design, the methodology of architecture, the materials used in the construction, the form and structure of the buildings and their relationship with the natural environment, and the attitudes, motives and the world-view of the people involved in the system. As such, Islamic environment cannot become a contemporary reality, if one were to rely on principles, methodologies and building technologies which have created the urban dystopias in the Occident and whose growing reflection one sees in Muslim cities. This system, as Alison Ravetz argues so forcefully in *Remaking Cities*, is completely bankrupt.[9] We need to reconceive and recreate the principles, methodologies and building technologies which will combine to produce an atmosphere which is instantly and instinctively recognized as Islamic.

Gulzar Haider's formulation of an Islamic City is based on the concepts of *tawhid, khilafah, khilqat* (nature), *jihad* (directed struggle), *adl, ibadah* (worship), *ilm* and *jamal* (beauty). *Tawhid* and *khilafah* dictate that the Islamic city be a city of trusteeship and accountability: 'there is individual freedom contained by responsibility to the collective *(ummah)*' and 'there is trust with answerability to God'. All this is done within the parameters of the Shariah: 'Islamic environment is to provide the support structure for Shariah and in turn be formed by it. There is to be a delicate equilibrium between the rights of the collective against those of the individual such that one is not antagonistic to the other. Such an environment will provide security and protection not so much by imposed controls as by social responsibility and mutual accountability.'[10] It is a city that nurtures the attitude that every act has consequences which could be harmful or beneficial, and it produces an environment that both by its morphology and institutions establishes *adl* in all aspects of human endeavour without imposing grey uniformity. It is a city of ecological harmony that reflects the beauty *(jamal)* of nature and promotes the awareness of nature *(khilqat)* as portents and signs *(ayat)* of God for man to reflect upon and enhance his faith *(iman)*, as a book of knowledge (*ilm*) to be understood and appreciated, and as a benevolent trust (*amana*) whose value is in its utilization towards the enhancement of the art of life within the coordinates of Islamic norms and values. Islamic city creates an environment that 'values simplicity as economy of means towards generosity of ends', promotes problem-solving attitudes and values skills, hard work and ingenuity, and where 'creativity and craft are a manner of worship, a homage by the believer to the Creator of all the man's abilities'. Islamic environment is 'a sense of order that inspires aesthetic response, a beauty that is hidden, elusive, transcendental—a beauty beyond our sense bound and fashion dependent normative tastes'. And finally, Islamic city promotes an active, dynamic, goal-orientated environment which maintains a sustained struggle (*jihad*) for values inherent in the matrix of concepts that give it its unique character.

Identifying the basic characteristics of an Islamic city is the first step in constructing a viable theory of Islamic urban environment. These ethical coordinates not only delineate the principles of design and development but also describe the options available—in terms of materials, technologies, building techniques, forms, structure and limits to growth—for achieving the final goal. Gulzar Haider argues that the design principles which amalgamate the ideals of an Islamic environment are based on three formative values: environmental sensibility, morphological integrity and symbolic clarity.

Environmental sensibility implies that the design of Islamic environment must show respect for natural topography such as land form, water bodies and woodlands and climate to which it must respond in the same manner as 'sand dunes respond to wind'. It must not deprive the human psyche of the experience of nature and ensure a balance between the organic and the inert. And it must be sensitive to the nature of tools and materials: building technology is far from value-free and requires a strict value discipline within which it is selected, developed and deployed.

Morphological integrity requires a sensitivity towards size, scale and quality, maintenance of private and public intimacy and an appreciation of human scale both in social systems and physical environment. Moreover, it dictates spatial integrity where 'form follows space and space is adopted to function'; and it should show a labyrinthine continuity in both its purpose and form: while physically bounded, the Islamic environment must give an impression of infinite continuity. And, finally, morphological integrity dictates that Islamic architecture achieves its integratedness and ultimate sense of unity and purpose 'through the search for mutually sympathetic orders of function, meaning, symbol, geometry, gravity, energy, light, water, movement' and by characterizing 'parts to whole and whole to parts relationship—simultaneously differentiated and integrated'.

Symbolic clarity requires respect for tradition and culture as well as for traditional metaphores, allegories and symbols without which Islamic architecture cannot 'encourage full expression of selfhood and identity without damaging the pervasive unity of *ummah*'. It also requires the creation of a relevant language of elements as well as exploration of their compositional rules which achieve an environmental syntax with a socially relevant meaning. It therefore constitutes a challenge to create an urban environment that 'provokes experiences and phenomenon that constitutes an Islamic expression of life'.

Implementing such a sophisticated set of design principles would not be easy. It requires the development of a whole set of new methodologies and building technologies as well as rediscovering traditional techniques and crafts. More generally, the environmental dictates of the Shariah need to be given a living form and extended to cover contemporary and future problems. The work of Gulzar Haider, Othman Llewellyn and Parvez Manzoor has demonstrated that the most viable solution to our ecological crisis is to be found within the world-view of Islam. Drawing from a purely conceptual matrix of Islamic concepts, the rich legal inheritance of the Shariah, and the history of Islamic architecture and urban planning, they have laid the basic foundations of a comprehensive Islamic theory of environment. It is an exciting challenge for other scholars to develop this theory further and demonstrate how it provides pragmatic solutions to today's and tomorrow's problems. The challenge of conceiving and creating methodologies and technologies and adopting appropriate Islamic legislation to meet the contemporary environmental crisis lies with Muslim societies. It is a challenge that has to be met, for the only other option is to permit our natural and built environment to lead to an ecological catastrophe.

Notes

1. Lynn White Jr. 'The Historical Roots of Our Ecological Crisis', *Science*, **155**, 1203–7 (1967).

2. This and subsequent quotations from Beatrice Willard, 'Ethics of Biospheral Survival' in Polunin, N. (ed.), *Growth or Ecodisaster?*, Macmillan, London, 1980.

3. The *Gaia* hypothesis first appeared in James Lovelock and Sidney Epton, 'The Quest for Gaia', *New Scientist*, **65**, 304–6 (1975).

4. Ali Shariti, *On the Sociology of Islam*, trans. by Hamid Algar, Mizan Press, Berkeley, California, 1979, p. 87.

5. This and subsequent quotations from Pervaz Manzoor are from his paper, 'Environment and Values: The Islamic Perspective' in Sardar, Z. (ed.), *The Touch of Midas: Science, Values and the Environment in Islam and the West*, University of Manchester Press, Manchester, 1984.

6. Othman B. Llewellyn, 'The Objectives of Islamic Law and Administrative Planning', *Ekistics*, **47**, 11–14 (1980).

7. Othman B. Llewellyn, 'Desert Reclamation and Islamic Law', *The Muslim Scientist*, **11**, 9–30 (1982).

8. Quoted by Llewellyn, 'Desert Reclamation and Islamic Law', *op. cit.*

9. Alison Ravetz, *Remaking Cities*, Croom Helm, London, 1980.

10. This and other quotations from Gulzar Haider, 'Islam and Habitat: a Conceptual Formulation of an Islamic City', *The Touch of Midas, op. cit.*

Part Three

Saving the Immediate Future

I I

Rewriting the Seerah:
Future Significance of the Life of Mohammad

Earlier, I discussed the emerging intellectual ideas which will collectively lead to the establishment of a pragmatic foundation for a dynamic, thriving future civilization of Islam. However, all these ideas, from the development of an Islamic theory of environment to the rediscovery of Islamic economics, Islamic science and Islamic epistemology, will require constant and continuous effort over several decades. Meanwhile, can Muslim cultures survive the time required for these ideas to mushroom and bear fruit with their sanity and identity intact?

At present, Muslim societies are being relentlessly pulled in two opposite directions. On the one hand, the onslaught of culturally destructive 'modern' trends, for example in high technology and urban planning, threaten to decimate Muslim cultures en masse. On the other hand, the inertia of ossified traditionalism threatens to suffocate Muslim societies. The tension generated by these inimical life-styles is now affecting the very being of Muslim personality. Indeed, the strain has now reached such a pitch that it has become a matter of urgent priority for Muslim intellectuals to take steps to preserve the Muslim personality and save the immediate future. In particular, there are four tasks which urgently need the attention of Muslim scholars:

(1) The Seerah, the life of the Beloved Prophet Mohammad, has to be made more meaningful and significant to Muslim individuals and societies.

(2) Muslim societies have to be liberated from 'development' and other similar mind-enslaving concepts so they can be intellectually free to explore alternatives within the purview of Islam.

(3) The environment of the Hajj—which includes the holy cities of Makkah and Medina as well as Muna, Arafat and Muzdalifah—has to be saved from total destruction and preserved, in an enlightened way, to accommodate the needs of a growing number of pilgrims. The hajj is the microcosm and heart of the Muslim world; when the environment of the hajj suffers degradation and abuse, the whole of the Muslim world is affected.

(4) Islamic studies have to be delivered from the narrow confines of 'religious studies' and Islam has to be taught as a universal world-view, complete with the apparatus to build a dynamic civilization, so that the future generations of Muslim intellectuals and scholars can cope with the diversity and interconnectedness so inherent in Islam and so much needed to survive the future.

Development, hajj and Islamic studies are explored in Chapters 12, 13 and 14 respectively. Here, I would like to discuss the important issue of making the Seerah relevant to contemporary needs and future possibilities.

The Contemporary Approach to the Seerah

The Seerah literature is a unique institution of Islam. Seerah, the life of the Prophet Mohammad, is both history and biography. But more than that: it is a source of guidance as well as of law. It is in the Seerah that Muslims seek inspiration for their behaviour and understanding of the Qur'an. As such, the Seerah is an integral part of the Shariah or Islamic law. Thus the Seerah is biography, history, law and guidance all integrated together. It therefore transcends time and has eternal value as a model of ideal Muslim behaviour and a practical demonstration of the eternal principles and injunctions of the Qur'an.

The Seerah has always been written in a standard form. Literary biography was a particular strength of Arab literature and it was almost natural for writers who lived a few years after the death of the Prophet Mohammad to throw themselves wholeheartedly into writing his Seerah. Indeed, a massive attempt was made not just at writing the biography of the Prophet, but also of his companions as well as the narrators who related various traditions of the Prophet and formed a key link in the transmission of the narration going back to the Prophet himself.

The classical studies on the Seerah approached the subject chronologically. This is hardly surprising, as in that period biography was valued largely as chronological history. Thus the celebrated work of Ibn Ishaq,[1] published in the middle of the eighth century, starts with a description of life in Arabia before the birth of the Prophet (the period of Jahiliyah or Ignorance), and continues to describe his birth, childhood, first marriage, first revelation, the migration from Makkah to Medina, the battles of Badr, Uhad and Trenches, various expeditions following these battles, the Treaty of Hudaibiya, the conquest of Makkah, the farewell pilgrimage, the Prophet's death and the election of Abu Bakr as the first Caliph of Islam. As many of the battles of the Prophet marked a turning point in the story, Ibn Ishaq gives a great deal of emphasis to them. But the emphasis on the battles was also due to the influence of a literary form very popular in Arabia during that period—the Maghazi, or the literature of the military expedition. Thus biography written as chronological history and the Maghazi literature became the main models for writing the Seerah. For classical biographers like Ibn Ishaq, Ibn Hisham, Ibn Sa'd, Waqidi and a multitude of other scholars, this was the simplest and the most accurate way of furnishing the Muslim community with the basic details of the life of the Prophet. The accent was on what the Prophet did, and the overall emphasis was on providing as detailed information as possible on his actions so that individual Muslims can follow his examples. And this is precisely what they did with a comprehensiveness and scrupulous care that is unique in the annals of history. The classical biographers were indeed very successful in achieving their objectives. They not only provided a reliable body of basic data but because the cultural and technological milieu in which they were writing was not much different from the time of the Prophet Mohammad, they made his life relevant to the minutest elements of the community. Thus for the Muslim communities of early Islam, the Prophet was not just a fact of immediate history, but a living presence whose every action shaped their own behaviour.

However, the classical Seerah literature, cast as it is in an idiom which is over 1200 years old, does not have the same impact on a modern mind as it had on the early Muslims. Facts of biography, as indeed of history, make sense when an individual can relate to them and when avenues for assimilating these facts into the individual's life are clear. One would expect the contemporary writers of Seerah to cast the life of Mohammad in an idiom that is instantly recognizable and relates to modern living. Unfortunately, modern authors, for some strange but compelling reason, have stuck to the classical method of writing the Seerah. The result is that the life of Mohammad, which is the paradigm of Muslim behaviour, *uswa hasna*, makes no real sense to the vast majority of contemporary Muslims.

Thus most modern studies of the Seerah relate the life of Prophet Mohammad as a chronological story adding no new facts and emphasizing exactly the same points once emphasized by the classical authors for a community whose priorities and mode of production were radically different from those of contemporary Muslim societies. The widely read *Muhammad: The Holy Prophet* by Ghulam Sarwar,[2] for example, presents a collection of facts from 'The Age of Ignorance' to 'The Eleventh Year of Hegira'. Apart from the fact that much of the book is quite unreadable, written as it is in an over-the-top subcontinental version of Victorian English, the author makes no attempt to explain any of his facts, or to put the Prophet's action in some sort of context, or indeed draw any lessons from the narrative. Quite often he is simply content to list things; as if knowing the fourteen chiefs of the Quraish who conspired to kill the Prophet in Makkah is an end in itself!

Modern biographers of the Prophet are also plagued by another serious shortcoming: the reaction syndrome. Many contemporary studies of the Seerah amount to little more than benign apologia written in answer to various orientalist accusations. There are many orientalist studies of the Seerah from Andrae to Boswell, Carlie, Goldziher, Margoliouth, Muir, Noldeke, Sprenger, Watt and Weil, full of various allegations and insinuations. Much of orientalist writings about the Prophet

Mohammad, as Tibawi and Said have pointed out so forcefully, were designed to prove that the Muslims are an inferior people and turn the imperial and political conquest into an intellectual and religious victory.[3] The Christian missionaries, in their crude way, and the orientalists in a more subtle way, singled out the personality of the Prophet Mohammad for attack and ridicule. The Muslim scholars responded by presenting the Seerah in an apologetic mould. Whether they were denying the accusations of the missionaries and the orientalists or simply justifying them, they were, at best, wasting scholarly energy which could be better utilized in analysing the biographical narrative and, at worst, actually producing apologia. Thus the two most respected studies of the Seerah, Shibli Numani's massive six-volume study in Urdu, *Seerat un Nabi*,[4] and Muhammad Husain Haykal's *Hayat Muhammad*[5] in Arabic, are seriously marred by the author's obsessions with orientalist acusations.

Shibli Numani's *Seerat un Nabi*, undoubtedly the best contemporary study of the Seerah in any language, is still incomplete, but the first two volumes give the complete life of the Prophet. Shibli wanted nothing less than to take every orientalist who had written on the Prophet since the days of Hal de Bert, who flourished around the twelfth century, to task. He planned to devote an entire volume to the work of orientalists but was unable to finish his task. That, to some extent, is unfortunate, for Numani is a powerful writer who does not mince his words in dissecting the studies of the orientalists. For example, of Margoliouth's work he writes:

> in all the written record of the world, his biography of the Prophet stands unsurpassed for lies, calumnies, misinterpretations, and biased expressions. His sole excellence lies in the art of giving, by dint of his genius, the ugliest colour to the plainest and cleanest incident in which it is not possible to discover the tiniest black spot.[6]

Despite devoting a great deal of time and energy to taking orientalists apart, Numani managed to produce a monumental, balanced and guidance-orientated study of the Seerah. He was able to do this largely because he relied exclusively on classical Muslim authors. The second half of the first volume which presents a chronological account of the Prophet's life, and the second volume which is concerned with battles of the Prophet, are almost entirely based on classical sources. Numani keeps the orientalists' allegations separate from his main biography and takes their arguments apart elsewhere. But, while Numani relies on the traditional sources, he also breaks from tradition in that he devotes separate volumes to discussing such aspects as the social organization, forms of worship and methods of inviting people to Islam and the organization of the state. In this respect, Shibli Numani's *Seerat un Nabi* is almost unique. When one considers its authenticity and wealth of detail it provides, his study stands out as a true giant among contemporary works on the Seerah.

However, Haykal is all too willing to concede authority to orientalist scholars and consequently is always forced to justify his arguments in their terms. The net result is an overtly apologetic biography of the Prophet. He is concerned with writing 'a scientific study, developed on the western modern method'. Indeed, he is so obsessed with 'scientific objectivity' that he considers his approach to the Seerah almost at par with that of the 'researcher in the natural sciences'. However, the motivating force behind Haykal's Seerah is his anger at the 'slanders', 'false charges' and the 'hostility' of the orientalists. And often he judges the particular events of the Seerah by the stand that an orientalist may have taken on them. For example, his obsession with Muir forces him to take a defensive attitude to the story of Prophet Ibrahim's attempt to sacrifice his son. Similarly, it is not enough for Haykal to state that the story of angels cleaning Mohammad's chest during his childhood is dismissed by no less an authority than the classical scholar al-Tabari; he has to bring Muir into the equation and use his authority, which he disputes elsewhere in the book, to justify his claim that the story should not be given undue weight. The whole of Haykal's *Hayat* is enveloped in this type of apologia. Indeed, in his preface to the first and second editions and concluding essay, 'Islamic civilization and western orientalists' (what is it doing in a book on Seerah?) he launches a fully-fledged attempt to justify Islam and Muslim civilization—almost as though he was pleading for his right to exist.

Both Haykal and Numani are products of a colonial age: they

were writing from a defensive position in an era when Western intellectual domination went unchallenged. Given these circumstances, one must acknowledge that their studies of Seerah, as well as Syed Amir Ali's *The Spirit of Islam*,[7] had a major impact on Muslim minds. Although their writings are undoubtedly apologetic, they were brave endeavours of their time—and, indeed, their works have not been surpassed in scholarship, clarity and the force of argument.

More recent biographers of the Prophet have achieved even less. Thus Abdul Hamid Siddiqui[8] sets himself the same goal as Numani and Haykal. But instead of following the standard chronological pattern, Siddiqui, rather bravely, abandons the chronological order of events and gathers 'interrelated thoughts and events' in one place so they can be discussed more easily. However, while Haykal takes an apologetic stance towards the orientalists, Siddiqui takes a more aggressive one. But by choosing to fight the accusations of one orientalist by quoting another, Siddiqui effectively undermines his case. We are thus treated to the spectacle of a chronicle of quotations whereby the views of one orientalist are refuted by authority to the second; and sometimes the opinions of the second, whose views on some other issue were considered inappropriate, are refuted by invoking the authority of the first. Beyond this maze of quotations there is nothing really new; after spending all his energies arm wrestling with the orientalists, the author has no energy left for analysis of making Seerah relevant to contemporary life.

And this is precisely the point. The orientalists and missionary scholars have tied down Muslim authors with a number of bogies—'Prophet's marriages', 'he was vengeful and full of hate', 'that he was a poet and Qur'an is his composition' etc.—which have no basis in historical reality but nevertheless serve a very good purpose: they pin down Muslim biographers of the Prophet Mohammad to narrow confines, sap their energies and keep them from addressing relevant issues. The state of contemporary Serrah literature, to some extent, proves that the orientalists have succeeded in achieving this goal.

Recently, however, there has been a move to leave the orientalists aside and present the Seerah by relying exclusively on classical sources. Abul Hasan Ali Nadwi,[9] Muhammad Hamidullah[10] and Martin Lings[11] have used traditional sources to different, and distinctive, effects.

Apart from the Qur'an and Hadith from which all three authors quote generously, Nadwi bases his *Muhammad Rasulullah* on the works of Ibn Hashim, Ibn Kathir and Ibn Qayyim. Lings relies on Ibn Ishaq, Ibn Hashim, Ibn Sa'ad and Waqidi. In terms of actual content, there is hardly any difference between Nadwi and Lings. Both present the Seerah as chronological history, with the same stories making an appearance in both texts. But here the similarity ends. Nadwi makes no real attempt to explain the events of his narrative; Lings uses the literary device of weaving relevant and explanatory quotations from the Qur'an and the Hadith into the narrative, thus increasing its informational content. Lings is a master story-teller whose prose and style is well suited to both the grandeur of the subject and the sublime personality which is the focus of the narrative. Nadwi is awkward (which is probably the fault of the translation), repetitious (probably because he dictated most of the book) and somewhat pedestrian in prose and style. The difference between Nadwi and Lings is not of scholarship or approach or the fact that either of them have come up with something new: they are both story-tellers, essentially telling a story. The difference is in the style and the power one of them gives to his narrative. Lings' study has been described as the Seerah 'par excellance'[12] and a 'work of art . . . a modern English classic'.[13]

If the art of the story-telling is the criteria by which Seerah literature is judged, Lings certainly has produced a masterpiece. But if insight, analysis and contemporary relevance are the indicators of quality, then Hamidullah's *Muhammad Rasulullah* would easily prove to be a superior work. Hamidullah, who bases his study on Ibn Ishaq, Ibn Hisham, ash-Shami and al-Maqrizi, has tremendous problems with style. Indeed, his style is stilted, clumsy and extremely difficult to read. But unlike Lings and Nadwi, Hamidullah is not telling a story. He wants to emphasize that on which 'the classical biographers have not cared to lay much emphasis'. He therefore reorganizes the 'raw material' furnished by the traditional scholars to focus on: 'politics, state administration, social institutions, economics, methods of creating inter-racial concord, blending of the spiritual and the material in a single and balanced whole, where no aspect of human life is sacrificed and nothing is left to prosper at the expense at something else'.[14] The end result is that the guidance elements of the Seerah which emerge are not restricted to personal piety and historic warfare. It is worth noting that while all the essential events of the life of the Prophet Mohammad are in Hamidullah's study, he does not, for example, fill pages and pages with the battles of the Prophet. While the techniques used for defence and warfare are fully described, what is actually emphasized is the relationship between the Prophet and his enemies. Considering that Hamidullah is the only contemporary scholar who has tried to produce an 'integrative' study of the Seerah, it is a pity that his techniques of anlaysis are not very refined and that he does not pursue his arguments to the required level of depth and analysis. But he certainly indicates the direction that the contemporary Seerah literature should take.

Seerah and the Future

The conventional method of writing the Seerah has provided us with a vast body of reliable facts and information, what Hamidullah calls 'raw material', about the life of Prophet Mohammad. However, while this approach to the study of Seerah has been invaluable in the past, it has serious shortcomings which must now be supplemented by new and more innovative methods of studying the paradigm of Muslim behaviour.

Even from the viewpoint of modern writers, it should be obvious that the story-telling approach to writing biography or history is not going to break any new ground. Besides, if all one needs to do is to relate the story of the Prophet, then why is it necessary for new authors to relate the story over and over again? Whatever their individual merits and shortcomings, there is no recognizable difference, narratively speaking, between the studies of Ghulam Sarwar, Muhammad Husayn Haykal, Abdul Hamid Siddiqui, Abul Hasan Ali Nadwi and Martin Lings. Moreover, the story-telling approach has the tendency of inducing intellectual and stylistic laziness in the writer. Thus many facts of the Prophet's life are narrated with hardly any variation of style and words. Sometimes expressions that were used by Ibn Hasham or Ibn Ishaq or Ibn Qayyim or even by Shibli Numani are reproduced verbatim by contemporary writers. What makes Lings' Seerah stand out so much from the pedestrian works is the simple fact that he has his own distinctive style. It has nothing to do with originality or scholarship.

But there are a number of other more pressing reasons why the conventional approach to writing the Seerah is now inadequate. While the conventional Seerahs furnish Muslim individuals and societies with facts, these facts by themselves are not enough to motivate individuals or solve societal problems. Knowing that during the Battle of Badr, 317 ill-equipped Muslims fought and defeated a well-equipped army of one thousand Quraysh warriors, does tell us that the Muslims fought very bravely. But is the only lesson to be drawn from the Battle of Badr that Muslims should be brave? Or can the Battle of Badr also tell us something about the conduct of war, treatment of enemies, when spying on others is justified, who can and cannot be killed during war, what can and cannot be destroyed, what action can one take from harming that which should not be harmed, and how international relations should be pursued during hostilities? If the Battle of Badr is to have some meaning for us today and in the future, its lessons must be shown to be relevant to contemporary situations. The facts of the Seerah cannot just be stated; they have to be integrated, synthesized and analysed, turned into principles and models, so that they can be absorbed into contemporary and future life.

Moreover, the conventional approach emphasizes certain elements of the Seerah which the classical authors saw as the main events of the Prophet's life. After the Qur'an and the Hadith, the main important source for the biographies of the Prophet, as I mentioned earlier, were the journals of the battles fought by the Prophet, the *maghazi*. Written mainly to record the events relating to expeditions and battles, the *maghazi* furnish incredible wealth of detail. It is not surprising, then, that the classical authors gave so much emphasis to the battles of the Prophet in the studies of the Seerah. However, when one considers that the main battles of his life, the Battles of Badr and Uhad, which followed in quick succession, did not last more than a day, and that at the longest battle, the Battle of Trenches which lasted a month, no fighting took place because the enemy could not cross the trench and was forced to retreat by a sandstorm, and that at the conquest of Makkah, the Prophet's biggest military triumph, no blood was shed, one realizes that in an extremely hectic and busy life spanning sixty-three years, Prophet Mohammad did not spend more than a few months, perhaps a year, in actually fighting battles or holding his enemies under siege. Yet, almost two-thirds of Martin Lings' *Muhammad*, the most modern of conventional Seerahs, deals with the battles of the Prophet. What happened to the rest of his life? The excessive emphasis of the traditional studies, and the modern works which draw from them, on warfare, apart from doing injustice to the subject of the study, also fixes the life of the Prophet to a particular historic epoch when that type of warfare had some meaning.

Furthermore, because the emphasis in the conventional approach is on description, often static description, it fails to distinguish what is particular and what is eternal in the Seerah. Consider, for example, this particular tactic of the Prophet to deceive his enemy mentioned by Imam Ibn Kathir:

When the Messenger of God, peace be upon him, arrived at Makkah, he and his companions had suffered badly from Yathrib's (Medina's) fever and it had exhausted them. The Mushrikin (the non-Muslims) said that the People (the Muslims) who would be arriving here were people who were exhausted from Yathrib's fever and, as a result, in bad conditions. The Mushrikin were seated near the (Black) Stone (of the Ka'aba) (in the Sacred Mosque). God made known to His Prophet what the Mushrikin had said. The Prophet ordered his companions to walk half-running (in the area where the Mushrikin could see them) in the first three circumambulations (of Kaaba) to show the Mushrikin their endurance, and ordered them to walk between the two corners where the Mushrikin could not see them. The prophet spared his companions half the running in all the circumambulations in his fear for their exhaustion. The Mushrikin said, 'Are these the people whom we thought the fever had exhausted? These are stronger than so and so.[15]

This particular tactic of the Prophet, clearly designed to deceive the ever-ready enemy waiting to attack and destroy the Muslim army at every opportunity, has in fact become an eternal practice. Muslims walk half-running in the first three rounds of the Ka'aba in Makkah whenever they perform the circumambulations. However, the Prophet was actually responding to circumstances around him and a mere simple static description does not allow for differentiating between those actions of the Prophet which are to serve as signposts for guidance and those which are in response to particular historic situations.

The fact that the conventional methodology of studying the Seerah does not even recognize the problems of space and time is its fundamental shortcoming. Moreover, it traps the modern writer into a certain field of facts and does not allow him to look elsewhere apart from the classical biographies and *maghazi* literature. For example, the excessive reliance on Ibn Ishaq and Ibn Hashim has meant that other historical literature of the period, which describes the social and economic life in Makkah and Medina, has been overlooked. There is considerable literature based on the chronicles of Makkah and Medina which gives details of life in Arabia in general. Al-Azraqi's *Akhbar-i-Makkah* and Umar bin Shaiba's *Akhbar-e-Medina* are perhaps the best known of these; but there are many others which could provide new insights into the cultural and technological milieu within which the Prophet moved. Even the *shamail* literature, which focused on the morals, character and habits of the Prophet, has been largely ignored by the modern biographers writing in traditional grooves.

The major instrument of conventional methodology is static description and is therefore only interested in answering one question: what the Prophet did. As Hamidullah points out, classical biographers were not interested in cause and effect. However, if the contemporary Muslim scholars are to make the Seerah relevant to the present and the future, they have no choice but to tackle the supplementary questions: how did he do it? And why did he do it?

These two questions demand that the Seerah is subjected to searching analysis to discover the explanations behind the facts. And that requires going beyond the handful of traditional sources which have hitherto dominated the Seerah. The life of Prophet Mohammad has to be written as living history, not as a distant, historic biography. As analytical history, Seerah is the understanding of the life of Mohammad as it shapes and motivates the behaviour of contemporary Muslim individuals and societies. Analytical Seerah aims at discovering and synthesizing general principles from historical situations—principles with strong contemporary relevance which would enable modern Muslim societies to make moral and value judgements in the face of complex reality.

In trying to answer the questions of how and why, analytical Seerah has to focus as much on ideas and concepts as on the actions of the Prophet. The guidance aspects of the Seerah can best be brought to the fore by examining how the Prophet operationalized key Islamic concepts in his life. In trying to establish how the Prophet put certain ideas and concepts into action, the logic of detailed questioning often yields more productive results than simply examining anecdotal evidence. In a short essay on how the Prophet implemented the idea of shura (consultation), Tayeb Abedin provided more answers than many fully-fledged biographies of the Prophet.[16] Starting from the premise that shura is obligatory on Muslims, Abedin asks: (1) Who is to be consulted—all the people, or only a small section? (2) On what issues does consultation become essential? and (3) Is the outcome of the shura binding on the leader?

Studying the Seerah in relation to the idea of shura provides the answers to all three questions. The Prophet practised consultation throughout his life as described by Abu Hurairah: 'I have never seen any one more consultative with his companions than the Prophet.' But who did he consult? Once on a certain issue the Prophet asked the opinion of all the men concerned, after the Taif battle when the defeated tribe accepted Islam. The Prophet was not happy about taking the booty, especially after they had become brothers in faith. He asked his soldiers whether they would give back what they took from their brothers. The soldiers agreed. But the Prophet was not happy with the general answer of 'yes'. So he said: 'We do not know which one of you has agreed and which one has not, go back till your heads bring us your answers.'

On another occasion the Prophet decided to take action against the Quraish. Two of his companions, Abu Bakr al-Siddiq and Al-Miqdad ibn Umar, agreed with him. But the Prophet sought out other representatives of the community and specifically asked for their opinion. On yet another occasion the Prophet wanted to make a truce with Gatafan (a tribe living near Medina) so as to induce them not to fight with other pagan tribes. He thus called for the opinions of Sa'ad ibn Mu'adh and Sa'ad ibn Aubadh who were the heads of al-Aus and al-Kharzraj, the two dominant tribes at Medina.

From these incidents, Abedin concludes that 'the ruler should obtain the approvals of individuals when the issues concern their right to property'.[17] In matters of special experience and knowledge, a Muslim leader has to consult those who possess it irrespective of their representative power.

But what issues are to be put to consultation? Abedin argues that the whole of the Seerah is full of illustrations showing that the Prophet consulted the community on every problem which affected them. However, he cannot find any examples where the Prophet consulted his followers when appointing leaders of armies, district governors or judges. From this he concludes: 'perhaps such consultation would develop ill-feelings in the Muslim community, or possibly it should be a prerogative of the ruler to choose his subordinates'.[18]

And finally: is the outcome of the consultation binding on the leader? Abedin notes that there is not one single case when the Prophet consulted his people and did not accept the opinions to which they agreed. However, there are at least three incidents where the Prophet submitted to the people's opinions which differed from this own. Abedin writes:

> On two of these occasions it was without any indication of his being convinced by what had been said. The first was when al-Hubab ibn al-Munzir told him to change the army camp before the battle of Badr.

The Prophet agreed and changed the camp. The second case occurred when many Muslims expressed their wish to fight the Quraish outside Medina at the battle of Uhad. The Prophet's opinion was to wait for the Quraish inside the town so that they would have cover against them, and that women and youngsters participating in the battle could disturb the attackers' approach. But the others gave no other argument than they would be called cowards if they waited inside the town. The third situation is when Sa'ad ibn Nuadh and Sa'ad ibn Aubadh opposed the Prophet's decision to make a truce with Gatafan. The truce was written but never signed and when the Ansar chiefs opposed it because they would not accept its conditions, the Prophet told them to tear up the treaty.[19]

The over-riding conclusion: consultation is binding on a leader whatever his own opinion.

Even a simple ideational interrogation of the Seerah, as Tayab Abedin's analysis shows, can yield rich rewards. The answers to each of his three questions are based on strong evidence and can be translated into, for example, public policy legislation which makes public consultation mandatory on important issues, or for placing constitutional limitations on a government. If Seerah is the paradigm of Muslim behaviour, then it is the only place for seeking understanding of Islamic ideas and concepts.

What is important about the Seerah of the Prophet Mohammad are the causes and principles for which the Prophet lived and the operational form he gave to the basic concepts and ideas of Islam. The Muslims are not obliged to do, even if it was possible, what the Prophet did. But they are required to promote the norms of behaviour and the principles of life which are the *raison d'être* of the Seerah. Only studies of the Seerah from the perspective of ideas and concepts, seeking to answer the questions of why and how, can turn the life of Mohammad into a living reality. And only by turning the Seerah from a historical narrative into a contemporary map of guidance can Muslims fully appreciate the future significance of the life of Mohammad.

Notes

1. Ibn Ishaq's *The Life of Muhammad*, trans. by A. Guillaume, OUP, Oxford, 1955. Guillaume's translation is unreliable and contains many

256 Saving the Immediate Future

distortions. See the classic review of A. L. Tibawi, 'The Life of Muhammad: A Critique of Guillaume's English Translation' originally published in the *Islamic Quarterly* and reprinted in his *Arabic and Islamic Themes*, Luzac, London, 1974. Tibawi's conclusion: the translation 'cannot be accepted as a reliable reproduction on the received Arabic text of the Sira'.

2. Ashraf, Lahore, 1961.

3. See the brilliant analysis of A. L. Tibawi, *English Speaking Orientalists*, Islamic Cultural Centre, London, 1965; and Edward W. Said, *Orientalism*, R. and K. Paul, London, 1978.

4. Translated by Tayyid Bakhsh Budayuni, Kazi Publications, Lahore, 1979, vols 1 and 2. The original Urdu is in six volumes and was published in 1936.

5. Translated by Ismail Ragi al-Faruqi, American Trust Publications, Plainsfield, Indiana, 1976. The first Arabic edition was published in 1935.

6. Shibli Numani, *Seerat-un-Nabi*, vol. 1, p. 85.

7. Christophers, London, 1922; Methuen, London, 1967.

8. *Life of Mohammad*, Islamic Publications, Lahore, 1969.

9. *Muhammad Rasulullah*, trans. by Mohiuddin Ahmad, Academy of Islamic Research and Publications, Lucknow, 1979.

10. *Muhammad Rasulullah*, Huzaifa Publications, Karachi, 1979.

11. *Muhammad: His Life Based on Earliest Sources*, George Allen and Unwin, London, 1983.

12. Khurram Murad reviewing Lings in *Impact*, 23 December–12 January 1984.

13. Maryam Jameelah in *Muslim World Book Review*, 4 (4), 43–4 (Summer 1984).

14. *Muhammad Rasulullah*, *op. cit.* p. ii. Repeating Shabli Numani almost verbatim: Numani, *op. cit.* p. 53.

15. Quoted by A. H. A. Abu-Sulayman, 'The Islamic Theory of International Relations: Its Relevance, Past and Present', unpublished PhD thesis, University of Pennsylvania, 1973. Abu-Sulayman provides an excellent analysis of how space-time dependent studies of the Seerah canot help the development of a contemporary Islamic theory of international relations.

16. 'The Practice of Shura', *The Muslim*, 7, 159–61 (April 1970).

17. *Ibid.* p. 160.

18. *Ibid*.

19. *Ibid*, pp. 160–1.

12

Tazkiyah
The Islamic Alternative to Development

Along with the urgent task of rewriting the Seerah of the Beloved Prophet Mohammad, the Muslim intellectuals also face the equally important and no less urgent task of rescuing Muslim societies from the suffocating hold of ·certain dominating concepts. Perhaps no other concept has a greater grip on the minds of Muslim people than the concept of development.

Development attained notoriety in the late fifties and early sixties when it was synonymous with 'progress' and 'modernization'. The basic assumptions were those of a linear teleology *vis-à-vis* the industrialized countries of the West. These countries were considered to be 'developed', industrially, economically, technologically, institutionally and culturally; others were considered to be progressing along a straight incline with the goal of becoming 'developed' on the Western model. To become developed, it was assumed, one had to abandon one's cultural and traditional heritage, religious and other values which interfered with progress and modernization.

Modernization was defined as the process by which a society comes to be characterized by a belief in the rational and scientific control of man's physical and social environment and the application of technology to that end. Urbanization was one of the main indicators of modernization. In a noted study of the late fifties, Daniel Lerner used urbanization as 'an index of development' to construct a matrix containing data on urbanization, along with literacy, voting and media participation and used it to calculate the modernization state of the Middle East countries. The higher the level of urbanization, the more 'modern' the society. Lerner's analysis led him, and many others to conclude, that the traditional society was dead.[1]

Much of the development work done in the sixties, and the strategy set by the UN for the First Development Decade (1960–70), was largely based on this kind of thinking and analysis. The concept of development was equated with modernization and it was argued that the only way for nations to modernize and hence achieve economic growth was through industrialization. The proposed goals of the First Development Decade were industrial growth, economic diversification, expansion of trade and, in a minor vein, modernization of agriculture. Aggregate growth target was a moderate 5 per cent annual increase, a target widely met and bettered by some Third World countries.

However, at the end of the sixties it was obvious that the Muslim countries had not improved their lot after a decade of development and modernization. In fact, their situation had definitely become worse. Poverty had increased, distribution of wealth became more unequal, agriculture—this, despite the efforts of the Green Revolution—was in ruins. The little industry that was established in the Muslim world was facing immense production problems. The machinery, the spare parts, the skilled staff and sometimes even the raw materials had to be imported. Unemployment was rising rapidly. The experience of the Muslim countries, indeed the Third World itself, of its formal 'independence' largely consisted of a cruel joke for it enjoyed neither the sovereignty nor the equality promise by decolonization. Instead, it found to its own cost and dismay that it remained dependent upon, and discriminated against by, the industrialized countries.

When industrialization and urbanization in the Muslim world made the problems of poverty, unemployment, shelter and food even worse and ushered in a set of new ones—violence, alienation and cultural dislocation—aware authors were forced to acknowledge that the costs of modernization can be heavy and the comcept of development may be suffering from malaise. While the strategy for the Second Development Decade (1970–80) was not all that different from its predecessor and still focused on economic growth, it did manage to provide a more social statement of the concept of development. Its preamble stated that the ultimate objective of development must be to bring about sustained improvement in the well-being of the individual and bring benefits to all. If undue privileges, extreme of wealth and social injustices persist, then development has failed in its essential purpose.

However, the model that was followed was still that of the industrial development of the West; and modernization was still a major goal and progress the key word.

When the concept of unchecked technological progress began to be challenged in the West in the early seventies, development entered a new phase. As *The Limits to Growth*[2] and other studies of the Club of Rome pointed out, the contemporary rate of technological development has brought mankind face to face with six impersonal threats: a runaway, production-orientated technology, which has led to the depletion of natural resources (such as energy, food and water), a post-critical total and per capita pressure on land and environment, ever-increasing output of waste; nuclear, chemical and biological weapons; and the growth and distribution of world population.

The main thrust of the environmental criticism concerned the intrinsic connection between development and industrialization. Industrialization, the argument goes, has not freed Western societies from injustice and oppression; it is unlikely to do so for the developing countries. A comparison between the results of contemporary technological progress with feudal societies of the 'Dark Ages' brings the point home. As an hierarchical society of classes, feudalism had its lords and its common people at the two extremes with a military caste in the middle, all living in a security which was relative. The principal mode of production was the productive power of man himself, and the creative initiative was all the more common for it lay in the hands of a great body of craftsmen who not only developed their skills and artistic sense but also met the utilitarian needs of the community. In contrast, the industrial society too has its lords and common people as well as its military caste, and the feeling of insecurity was never so profound. But the lords of today tend to rule the entire globe, the military caste think out strategies that could easily destroy the entire planet several times, and the craftsmen have passed on to become scientists, engineers and technologists who every day surpass man's enterprise in work subject to the ascendancy of the machine. The final product of the technological society is a man who is less free, less able to think, alienated from other fellow men as well as nature and his environment, living with a permanent and increasing feeling of insecurity. Perhaps the Western society is not, after all, the prototype for the developing countries to imitate.

The rapid industrialization and technological development of Western society is the basic cause of the problems which have become preoccupying for the whole of humanity. Ever greater alienation of individuals living in permanent conflict with each other and with the natural environment whose equilibrium is threatened forced many to think of alternative development strategies for the Third World societies which are not yet under the all-pervasive tyranny of applied knowledge and crystallized technological power. Aware authors and groups who could see the weight of technology crumbling the Western civilization in front of their own eyes began to talk about the social, environmental and even cultural dimensions of development. A strange creature called 'the people' began to emerge in the development literature; and what's more, people began to matter.[3] Development theoreticians began to argue that the transfer of technology not only causes cultural and social dislocation in the Third World societies, but it also aggregates power in fewer and fewer hands and increases despotism, dictatorship and domination of the people. Development now emerged in a new form.

The essence of the new concept of development is best expressed by the five value dimensions that are stated in a paper presented to the UN Conference on Science, Technology and Development (UNCSTD) in 1979 by the Washington-based Centre for Concern:[4]

(1) Human dignity—Each and every person, male and female, adult and child, has basic rights and needs which are to be

respected and satisfied. Each person is to be given the opportunity to develop to her or his full potential. And each culture, with its own particular traditions, symbols, religious expressions, social organizations and modes of behaviour, is to be respected and its heritage perserved.

(2) Social involvement—Each person should be given the freedom to be an active participant in the planning and decision-making process which directly affects him or her. This requires social structures which provide interested persons with access to information that allows them to enter into the process as equals. Moreover, income-generating employment is a key element in the development process.

(3) Social justice—All people and nations are interdependent and should share fairly in the fruits of the earth and the development process. No economic or political structure or ideology should be allowed to oppress or marginalize individuals or groups within societies or nations within the international arena.

(4) Ecological sustainability—There is a bonding between humanity and the physical environment which is to be respected. This requires a recognition of the finiteness of resources and the fragility of the global system. The future impact of actions taken today should be weighted.

(5) Self-reliance—Nations and people should have the capacity for autonomous decision-making and implementation in all aspects of the development process. This is opposed to all forms of dependency. It recognizes that the main responsibility for solving the problems of the Third World countries lies with these countries themselves. This is not, however, autarky, and it requires new modes of incorporating the developing countries into the international order.

Other authors and groups have broadened the concept of development even further. For example, Joao Frank da Costa, Secretary General of UNCSTD, in his 'consolidated discussion paper' to the Conference, characterized development with twelve points:[5]

(1) Development should be comprehensive.

(2) Development should have endogenous roots and should not merely imitate a (Western) model.

(3) Development should be self-determined and self-generated.

(4) Development should be approached co-operatively and collectively.

(5) Development should be integrated.

(6) Development must respect the natural and cultural integrity of the environment as well as the traditional social structures of a country, which are necessary for the preservation of its cohesion.

(7) Development should be planned and requires constant attention from, and intervention by, national authorities without, necessarily, the exclusion of private interests and free-market mechanisms.

(8) Development needs to be directed towards the establishing of a just and equitable social order.

(9) Development must be democratic and respond to the choices made by the population as a whole.

(10) Development must be competitive and not insulate less developed countries or regions to such a degree that they are, in fact, 'enclaves', where they would barely survive and lead a marginal life far from the main flows of growth and dynamism.

(11) Development should be innovative.

(12) Development planning should be based on a realistic definition of needs and on consumption models that are consistent with the national characteristics of a country including its resources, gross national products, capability for capital formation and effective interaction of science and technology with the productive sectors.

More recently, the Brandt Commission report, *North–South: A Programme for Survival*, argued that 'development involves a profound transformation of the entire economic and social structure. This embraces changes in production and demands as well as improvements in income distribution and employment. It means creating a more diversified economy, whose main sectors become more interdependent for supplying inputs and for expanding markets for output'.[6] The report identified poverty, housing, education, population, energy, disarmament, commodity trade, and the world monetary order as the main 'dimensions of development'.

In all these attempts to define and redefine development, broaden the concept, incorporate the embarrassing bits, lasting over three decades, the underlying axiom has remained unchanged: development is necessary, relevant and desirable. Moreover, development refuses to be identified with anything else but economic activity, pure technology and naked industrialization no matter how much concerned groups, scholars and development theorists talk about environmental and cultural dimensions of development. Whether one follows the recommendation of radical Christian groups like the Centre for Concern, or the recommendations of UNCSTD, or the dictates of the Brandt Commission, the end product of development is always the same—it is always perceived *à la occident*: the Western civilization is the frame of reference and the ultimate goal of development.

Moreover, there are very strong forces working to ensure that the classical notion of development continues to dominate the minds and attitudes of intellectuals, decision-makers and politicians of the Third World. There is, of course, the need of the industrialized countries to sell technology and arms to the Third World nations. There is the Global Economic System, maintained by such institutions as the International Monetary Fund (IMF) and transnational corporations, whose very survival depends on the promotion of conventional development strategies. And there are the elites of the Third World who are content with their work, their positions and their comfortable standard of living—and the only way for them to preserve this is to promote Westernised development schemes. But these are the obvious and natural allies of classical development; the motives and actions of people and institutions are not too difficult to grasp. More subtle, and hence more difficult to appreciate, are the conceptual forces.

The most formidable of these forces is the ideology of science and technology. Western science and technology, as I discussed in Chapter 7, is a rationality of domination. The intention of such seventeenth-century thinkers as Descartes and Bacon, the fathers of modern science, was to investigate external nature while leaving to religion the task of specifying the rules of social conduct. But through Comte and others, scientific method became absolutized as the basis for social reconstruction in a 'positive' manner. By basing social reconstruction on scientific certain grounds, it raised science and technology to the level of absolute utopia, perfect fusion of unlimited power and good to which all willingly submit, hence reconciling cultural and social conflicts. Although science and technology remain limited by real interests and structures of power, they claim to be an overarching power. They thus take on the classical form of ideology, being an inversion of reality. Scientific and technocratic consciousness maintains the *status quo* and legitimizes the present structures within nations and between nations. It does not project a future time when men's hopes will be fulfilled. Rather, it tells us that the future is already here in essentials, if not in full maturity. The future comes, then, as incremental addition of the products of science and technology rather than a structural transformation. It is the end of transcendental hope. The only course open is development along the well-trodden path of the industrialized countries.[7]

Another major conceptual force that promotes orthodox development is the idea of interdependence, a tool of intellectual terrorism that is both an approach and an ideology.[8] As a doctrine, it is the major responses of the industrialized countries to the demands of a New International Economic Order, significant changes in the global political economy, and the reduction of the power of the transnational corporations. Advocates of interdependence have tried to revive flagging faith in orthodox development theory and strategies by proposing further integration of the Third World countries into the world system and increases in capital flow as the catalyst of growth. Within the interdependence perspective, global change and inequality are interrelated with the benefits accruing largely to the already rich and advantaged, thus reinforcing the relative (and, in many cases, absolute as well) deprivation of the poor: interdependence and inequality go hand in hand. Third World nations may become more and more integrated into the Global Economic System, but the result will only be increasing inequality.

Interdependence, particularly the use of ecological notion in economic thought, is an attempt at mystification and disguises the causes of uneven growth and lack of national autonomy in the majority of Third World states. As such, interdependence is only a cant word that serves to rationalize the relationship between industrialized nations and the developing countries and promotes strategies of development that enforce that relationship.

With such conceptual allies, it is no wonder that orthodox development has such a hold over Muslim intellectuals and decision-makers. But Muslim countries trying to telescope decades of development into a few years and industrializing their economies along the lines of Western states are chasing a dead concept. No Muslim country should harbour hopes that it can reach the material abundance that has existed in the United States and Europe for the past few decades. The dream is in fact a nightmare simply because even if there were a complete redistribution of world's resources, it would physically be impossible to realize such a desire. As Gandhi put it so aptly, if England had to exploit half the world to develop, how many globes would India need to exploit to become another England? To erect industrialized infrastructures at a time when the world is running out of non-renewable resources is a cruel hoax. Muslim states like Saudi Arabia, Algeria, Nigeria and Malaysia, who are trying to build a massive infrastructure by the year 2000, are writing their own national and cultural obituaries.[9] Even if they succeed in creating such an infrastructure, and the evidence so far is unfavourable, they will find that they can no longer secure adequate amounts of non-renewable energy to keep the economic machinery running.

Moreover, development along the classical route of industrialization has become even more remote with the advent of microelectronics. Whatever industry Muslim countries may develop, micro-electronics will ensure that they become obsolete even before they become operational.[10] Chasing industrialization, therefore, is like the donkey chasing a carrot, hanging from a stick tied to his back. Furthermore, micro-electronics will replace the only comparative advantage many Third World countries have over the industrialized nations: cheap labour. Labour-intensive goods account for a sizeable percentage of total exports and constitute an important source of employment and foreign exchange in the Third World. For the newly industrializing countries, labour-intensive goods account for over 40 per cent of manufactured exports from South Korea, Taiwan, Hong Kong and Singapore, and over 20 per cent for Brazil, Argentina and Mexico. For the less industrialized nations, the majority being Muslim states, the percentages are even more dramatic, accounting for 73 per cent of manufacturing exports in Egypt, 79 per cent in Pakistan, 97 per cent in Bangladesh, 71 per cent in Iran and 61 per cent in Morocco. This comparative advantage in Muslim and other developing countries of cheap labour will be eroded by the labour of the microchip: the chip is more efficient, much faster and much cheaper. The three crucial areas of export for the Third World—clothing, textiles and electronics—will soon be lost to the industrialized countries.

So, as far as Muslim states are concerned, development, particularly development *à la occident*, is truly dead. Muslim societies are now revolting against the notion with increasing militancy—the Islamic revolution in Iran is only one, but an obvious, manifestation of this revolt.

If the concept of development continues to exercise an all-pervasive hold on Muslim societies, the consequences for Muslim people will be dire. If policies of Western-style progress continue, 'instant under-development' will become the norm. That is to say, Muslim societies will become poorer and poorer as development continues. The reasons for this are not very profound. Industrial development favours cities over rural areas, and highly centralized, energy- and capital-intensive production over human labour. As Muslim nations seek to industrialize, jobs will diminish more and more because production will become more and more automated. At the same time, mechanized agriculture, which was introduced in the Muslim world in the form of the notorious Green Revolution, will force more and more peasant farmers off the land. All this will force urbanization at even greater speeds. As forced urbanization proceeds, greater and greater poverty will ensue, and this is already happening.

Moreover, high-energy industrial development will destroy

what is left of the cultural and environmental heritage of the Muslim world. High-energy technology brings its own ideology of contempt for culture, tradition and environment. So Muslim societies stand not just to become poorer and poorer, but also alienated from their traditions and cultural roots and, to add salt to the wounds, they may even lose the physical environment which sustains their populations.

The cultural, environmental, ecological and human costs of orthodox development are well known, yet it still holds a singular fascination as the paradigm of progress. No matter how one redefines development, industrialization remains firmly entrenched as its only goal. Any vocabulary is itself a system of analysis. As long as development remains the catchword for the dreams of Muslim societies, orthodox models of economic growth will be pursued without consideration for Islamic tradition and culture or the wishes of the Muslim people. As long as Muslim countries seek to 'develop', Western logic and social grammar will continue to dominate Muslim societies.

Muslim Response to Development

Muslim authors have tried to undermine the Western connotations of development by hedging it with Islamic terminology and ideas. To some extent, this approach has been productive if only it has led to the realization that Western development planners, advisers, even in Muslim garb, are in no position to devise development strategies for Muslim societies. But, on the whole, the introduction of Islamic vocabulary in discussions of development does not really dethrone the Orthodox concept.

However, the ideas of Jafar Shaykh Idris and Khurshid Ahmad have given the notion of development within an Islamic framework a completely new meaning. Idris, for example, equates development with 'service to God' and describes it as a category of man's existence and life. For Islam, the essence of man is a faculty with which everyone is naturally endowed: to be a complete human being, man must direct all his activities towards the service of God. This internal reality of man must be reflected, argues Idris, in the external organization of human society, the pursuit of which is seen by Idris as development.[11]

Within this framework of the Islamic way of development, material and spiritual aspects of life are complementary. 'To be able to live the good life of devotion to God, we have, therefore, to make the best use of the material resources of our world.' Talking about development without considering the spiritual side of man is meaningless; development must preserve the essence of man:

> The qualities which make men human are the cement which binds them together in a human society, and which keeps them wholesome as individual persons. Once they are lost, the individual starts to disintegrate, and the disintegration of society follows as a matter of course. When the individual finds no meaning to his life, when he loses his sense of purpose, when individuals become alcoholics, drug-addicts and promiscuous, when the family ties are weakened or broken and everyone lives by himself and for himself, then the society of which those individuals are members is sure to decline and fall. Why should one who does not care for his own, care for others? Why should one who sees no meaning in life defend the people to whom he happens to belong?[12]

Thus, for Idris, development is the pursuit of meaning in an individual's life as well as the pursuit of material benefits—for him, the two go hand in hand. This approach to development, he argues, will free Muslim societies from being an annex of western civilization where they have to borrow everything they have including 'the worms in their intestines' and allow them to flourish with their own identity and culture intact.

Khurshid Ahmad's analysis is much more conceptual.[13] He argues that the philosophic foundation of the Islamic approach to development is based on four fundamental concepts: *tawhid* (the unity of God); *rububiyyah* (divine arrangements for nourishment, sustenance and directing things towards their perfection); *khalifah* (man's role as the trustee of God on earth); and *tazkiyah* ('purifi-cation plus growth'). *Tawhid* and *khalifah*, as we have seen in previous chapters, are two of the fundamental concepts of Islam and define the basic relationship between God and man, man and man, as well as man's relationship to nature and his terrestrial environment. *Rububiyyah* is 'the divine model for the useful development of resources and their mutual support and sharing'. *Tazkiyah* is the concept that relates to the growth and development of man in all its relationships: the ultimate goal of *tazkiyah* is to purify and mould an individual, that holistic aggregate of individuals which form a society, and the envelope of material things and products that constantly interact with the individual and collective elements of society.

Ahmad's definition of *tazkiyah* focuses on individuals and relationships. *Tazkiyah* in all its dimensions, he writes, 'is concerned with growth and expansion towards perfection through purification of attitudes and relationships'. In an earlier essay,[14] he isolated six 'instruments' of *tazkiyah*: *dhikr* or remembrance of God; *ibadah* or acts of servitude to God; *tawbah* or seeking the forgiveness of God; *sabr* or the spirit of perseverance; *hasabah* or criticism and self-criticism; and *dua* or supplication. All these instruments of *tazkiyah* essentially operate on the individual leading to his/her *falah*—prosperity in this world and the hereafter. Apart from simply stating that 'the mission of all prophets of God was to perform the *tazkiyah* of man in all his relationships—with God, with man, with the natural environment, and with society and state', Ahmad does not elucidate the role *tazkiyah* plays in man's relationship to material goods and products. Nevertheless, his understanding of *tazkiyah* leads him to identify five essential features of development within an Islamic framework which he compares and contrasts with the contemporary understanding of the concept:

(a) The Islamic concept of development has a comprehensive character and includes moral, spiritual and material aspects. Development becomes a goal- and value-orientated activity, devoted to optimisation of human well-being in all these dimensions. The moral and the material, the economic and the social, the spiritual and the physical are inseparable. It is not merely welfare in this world that is the objective. The welfare that Islam seeks extends to the life (in the) hereafter and there is no conflict between the two. This dimension is missing in the contemporary concept of development.

(b) The focus for development effort and the heart of the development process is man. Development, therefore, means development of man and his physical and socio-cultural environment. According to the contemporary concept it is the physical environment—natural and institutional—that provides the real area for developmental activities. Islam insists that the area of operation relates to man, within and without. As such human attitudes, incentives, tastes and aspirations are as much policy variables as physical resources, capital, labour, education, skill, organisation, etc. Thus, on the one hand, Islam shifts the focus of effort from the physical environment to man in his social setting and on the other enlarges the scope of development policy, with the consequent enlargement of the number of targets and instrument variables in any model of the economy. Another consequence of this shift in emphasis would be that maximum participation of the people at all levels of decision-making and plan-implementation would be stipulated.

(c) Economic development is a multi-dimensional activity, more so in an Islamic framework. As effort would have to be made simultaneously in a number of directions, the methodology of isolating other key factors and almost exclusive concentration on that would be theoretically untenable. Islam seeks to establish a balance between the different factors and forces.

(d) Economic development involves a number of changes, quantitative as well as qualitative. Involvement with the quantitative, justified and necessary in its own right, has unfortunately led to the neglect of the qualitative aspects of development in particular and of life in general. Islam would try to rectify this imbalance.

Among the dynamic principles of social life Islam has particularly emphasised two: First, the optimal utilisation of resources that God has endowed to man and his physical environment, and secondly, their equitable use and distribution and promotion of all human relationships on the basis of Right and Justice. Islam commands the value of *shukr* (thankfulness to God by availing of His blessings) and *adl* (justice) and condemns the disvalues of *kufr* (denial of God and His blessings) and *zulm* (injustice).[15]

These essential features of development in an Islamic framework lead Ahmad to define six goals of development policy in an Islamic society: human resources development, expansion of useful production, improvement of the quality of life, balanced development in different regions within a country, evolution of indigenous technology and reduction of national dependency on the outside world and greater integration within the Muslim world.

Ahmad's appreciation of *tazkiyah* is rather limiting. He has confined *tazkiyah* to the role of personal piety and individual salvation: in his scheme, development is achieved through personal salvation rather than societal transformation. The focus of *tazkiyah* is not just man; Islam does not only insist that 'the area of operation is man' but it also seeks to build a society which enables its various elements and components to practice *tazkiyah* in a positive atmosphere. Ahmad believes that if people's attitudes, character and personality—the main concern of his goal of human resource development—are correct, then they will, almost by magic, produce a righteous and just society. It is his over-emphasis on individual salvation, the zealous evangelical approach to Islam, that stops Ahmad from seeing the social dimensions of *tazkiyah*.

However, because Ahmad's analysis is based on pure Islamic concepts, he offers the best elucidation of 'the Islamic concept of development' and the goals of a 'development plan for a Muslim society'. Most enlightened Western scholars and concerned groups will appreciate his emphasis that for Muslim societies development must mean meeting the basic needs of the *ummah* and shaking off their dependence on the non-Muslim world.

The trouble is that there is no such thing as an 'Islamic' concept of 'development'. Development cannot be 'Islamized' any more than alcohol can be declared an Islamic beverage. Development *per se* is a Western concept: it cannot be applied to Muslim societies, no matter how the coy academic redefines it to placate his own susceptibilities, without placing them in a linear teleology *vis-à-vis* the industrialized countries of the occident.[16] It represents an ethnocentric view of the world, with the developed countries on top of the development pyramid, down through less-developed and underdeveloped to undeveloped to the lowest possible level. A typical basis for characterization would involve (1) per capita income, (2) ability to produce capital goods, (3) per output energy consumption, (4) literacy rates, (5) productivity, (6) general consumption, and (7) defence capabilities—the very criteria which form the basis of Ahmad's 'Goals of Development Policy'.

In a classical study, Lucian Pye defined development as being a multi-dimensional process of social change.[17] The idea of social change, of movement of a society from one state of organization, one system of ideas, beliefs and traditions and one stock of equipment to another, is central to the concept of development. Thus to ask or motivate Islamic societies to develop is to ask them to leave their system of ideas, beliefs and traditions for another system that is perceived to have a higher status of development. Of course, Khurshid Ahmad or any other Muslim scholar would not even contemplate that Islamic societies should modify let alone abandon their cherished system of beliefs and ideas and fourteen centuries of tradition. But concepts have a particular way of working their way through a society. It is the end result of development that counts and not the anodyne assurances and good intentions of development economists. Development will always be wholly identified with Western capitalists, economics and profit-motivated technology; and any attempt to rescue it from the clutches of the framework originally devised by Rostow and Lerner, broaden its scope and get cultures, people and environment involved in the whole process is, as is evident from three decades of history, doomed to failure. It is self-defeating to devise Islamic strategies for development as the concept, even if it is hedged with an Islamic vocabulary, ensures that the decision-makers see it only in terms of the classical industrialization strategies which 'developed' the West.

Thus, as far as Muslim societies are concerned, development is a dead concept. Muslim societies have no need to 'develop'; they do, however, need to operationalize *tazkiyah* in all its multi-dimensional facets.

Growth Through Tazkiyah

The literal meaning of *tazkiyah* is purification. It is a process of purification that all Muslim individuals and societies have to apply if they seek to be in a constant state of Islam. However, *tazkiyah* is not a static state of purification: it is a dynamic concept that seeks to motivate individuals and societies to grow by a constant process of purification. The Islamic institution of *zakah*, purification of one's earnings by giving a fixed proportion of it to the less fortunate members of society or by using it to promote works of public benefit, which is regarded as the third pillar of Islam and is a religious duty encumbent on every Muslim, is etymologically derived from *tazkiyah*. The idea is that the very act of purifying one's earnings increases one's wealth. In the Qur'an, *tazkiyah* has been given the connotations of growth:

> He is successful who grows,
> And remembers the name of his Lord, so pray.
> (87:14–15)

And again:

> He is indeed successful who causes it to grow
> And he is indeed a failure who corrupts it.
> (91:9–10)

The idea of growth through purification is particularly unique to Islam. The process of purification acts as a rein on unchecked growth which could indeed make it impossible for societies and individuals to practise the instruments of *tazkiyah* so clearly described by Khurshid Ahmad. On the other hand, static or declining societies which could not even meet their basic needs would be unable to practise *tazkiyah* in its totality. *Tazkiyah*, therefore, demands that individuals and societies should grow within particular limits which provide them with time, ability and the environment for self-reflection and introspection, criticism and self-criticism, promotion of values and cultural authenticity—the societal elements that give a living form to the process of purification.

Tazkiyah, then, is that quality in an Islamic society which ensures that it maintains critical variables within limits acceptable to its social and cultural values and organizational and institutional structures. It is a steady, selective growth that requires Muslim societies to maintain their fundamental, internal balances while undergoing various processes of change. It requires Muslim societies to grow as far as it is necessary to meet their basic requirements but it also demands a pace of change that makes it possible for people to match genuine needs with available resources and potentials and find acceptable means for the realization and implementation of feasible alternatives. *Tazkiyah* applies growth with the consensus of the people (otherwise it will be 'corrupt') allowing no change without full backing from the entire society and with firm conviction of its necessity. It requires perservation of the natural and cultural heritage of Muslim societies as a living, dynamic environment from which they can draw their sustenance and aesthetic pleasure: this is purification in total action.

Essentially, the concept of growth promoted by *tazkiyah* is very similar to patterns of growth we find in eco-systems. A tree, for example, conforms well to the dictates of *tazkiyah*. Muslim societies could well see themselves as trees, and various societal activities—scientific, technological, economic, educational, managerial, organizational—as so many branches of a single tree, which grows and sends forth leaves and fruits in conformity with the nature of the tree itself. However, branches of a tree do not continue to grow indefinitely; and so a particular activity of the society should not be pursued beyond a certain limit or at the expense of other activities. If a branch of a tree grew indefinitely, it would certainly end up destroying the whole tree. Similarly, indefinite technological growth would eventually destroy the society which is the basis of its nourishment. If organizations continue to grow they would develop inertia which would suffocate them. And so on. However, if a society cannot meet its basic needs, it must pursue economic growth vigorously just as a sapling needs to grow to become a tree. However, once a sustainable stage is reached, further economic growth can lead to self-destruction. Brakes must now be applied.

Growth through *tazkiyah* demands that preservation of moral and environmental integrity, cultural strength and the practice of such vital Islamic concepts as *ijma* (consensus of the people), *shura* (cooperation for the good) and *istislah* (public interest) must be the corner-stones of science, technology and economic policy. The practice of *tazkiyah* on a national level dictates that growth policies must have four basic components: self-reliance, self-sufficiency, social justice and cultural authenticity. It is not possible for a society to 'purify' its wealth unless it is equitably distributed within the various segments of society. Neither it is possible for a society to operationalize one of the main instruments of *tazkiyah*, *mahasbah* (criticism and self-criticism), if it is economically or technologically dependent on outside powers. Similarly, the whole practice of *tazkiyah* makes no sense unless a society is true to its cultural and traditional roots.

In the Muslim world, self-reliance and self-sufficiency make particular sense at the level of the *ummah*. Muslim countries suffer from what is known in development circles as a 'small country problem'; that is, they are so small that it is not viable for them to be self-sufficient and self-reliant on their own; Tunisia, Mali and Mauritania are good examples. Other countries lack certain basic resources such as manpower and technological skills but possess excess capital; Saudi Arabia, Kuwait and Algeria are the obvious examples here. Still others have excess manpower and a certain amount of technological capability—Pakistan, Turkey and Egypt lead to *ummah* here. Thus Muslim countries can work together to overcome their deficiencies and cooperatively to become self-sufficient and self reliant. Essentially, self-reliance and self-sufficiency require making do with what one has and developing one's own skills and efforts, including humble, less pretentious styles of science and technology. Social justice and equal distribution of wealth necessitate a struggle against political despotism and tyranny, illiteracy and run-away industrialization. Cultural authenticity requires emphasis on indigenous growth based on rural areas and the protection of traditional cultures from the onslaught of Western patterns of consumption and those consumer goods that represent the omnipotence of technology.

All this means that the prime goal of growth through *tazkiyah* is meeting the basic needs of Muslim societies. Essentially there are five such needs which are intrinsically linked to the practice of *tazkiyah* in Muslim countries:

(1) Physical and mental health: the former is that need of the individual which keeps his body functioning normally, and free from any discomfort, illness and disease; the latter permits the individual an open perception of reality, an open interaction with other people and produces an optimum benefit from group and individual activity.

(2) Shelter and housing: both for physical well-being—warmth, safety, protection—and emotional satisfaction—privacy, maintenance of family bonds.

(3) Recreation and community involvement: *tazkiyah* aims at a level of recreation that provides maximum possible opportunity for physical and intellectual growth for the individual and society as well as a community spirit and involvement that ensures that the individual has a sense of responsibility to the community and its members.

(4) Security, dignity and freedom: the security of the individual from external threat; equality of all before the law; equal respect and dignity and protection of all cultural and ethnic minorities; and freedom of expression, communication and peaceful assembly.

(5) Education and training: growth through *tazkiyah* aims at providing facilities and resources necessary for the provision of essential community and individual skills and for the full flowering of the individual and community talents. Here, four particular types of skills are needed:

(a) Social and political skills—that quantity and quality of information and skills necessary for the members of a society to understand the political and social process, imperatives and pressures on groups and individuals in a contemporary society, and to develop alternatives and choose from among them for themselves, among themselves for their community and country.

(b) Cultural and communication information and skills—that quantity and quality of common history, rituals, symbols and values which are essential for an individual's self-identity made equally available to a people, and the skills to appreciate it for oneself and one's groups, and to re-express and re-create it, and to communicate with a sense of dignity and respect on all questions of cultural, political, social and economic import.

(c) Cultural heritage and skills—the level and quality of knowledge of one's heritage, and the level and quality of skills necessary for learning, transformation and re-creation of culture.

(d) Production and service skills—the level and quality of skills for production and services available and disseminated in a society that gives everyone a socially useful and creative task and role, backed by the necessary skills.

Growth through *tazkiyah* aims to create an infrastructure to meet the above basic needs. However, once such an infrastructure is created, *tazkiyah* is then concerned with maintaining a dynamic equilibrium between infrastructure and the society. Essentially, the creation of a suitable infrastructure to meet the dictates of *tazkiyah* can be resolved into four basic components:

(1) Sustaining the society in dynamic equilibrium: pursuing policies of conservation, fuller utilization of resources, recycling of 'waste', controlling and avoiding pollution, and providing facilities and regulations for health and safety.

(2) Support system: providing social, cultural, educational and informational support systems that are adequate for the achievement of the goals of *tazkiyah*, generate a community feeling and a sense of dignity and protect and stimulate cultural creativity and responsibility.

(3) The political environment: growth through *tazkiyah* aims at creating political stability, increasing quantity and quality of participation in decision-making and the degree of accountability of political office-bearers, improving efficiency of administration of public programmes, and improving planning and allocations of social capital and resources.

(4) The economic environment: growth through *tazkiyah* is based on technological activity that can be easily controlled and provides employment and does not present an environmental and cultural threat: it aims at equality in the distribution of resources, optimum use of natural and human resources, adequacy in the quantity and quality of goods and services without undue waste, including administration and working conditions and the distribution system; improvements in the level and quality of accountability of the economic system to the community and political authority for its planning, efficiency, administration and allocation of resources.

Both these objectives of *tazkiyah*-orientated growth—meeting basic needs and creating an adequate infrastructure—are best sought in a framework of economic and technical cooperation within the Muslim world. The pursuit of *tazkiyah*, unlike the pursuit of development, dictates that the Muslim world looks for its strength within its own circumference. The choice between 'development' and the operationalization of *tazkiyah* is a choice between human, cultural, environmental and economic survival, and external dependency and decay. Only through working together under the guidance of the action-orientated ethics at *tazkiyah* can Muslim societies fight conceptual slavery and avert the associated suffering and successfully make the transition to a rewarding future of selective growth.

Notes

1. D. Lerner, *The Passing of the Traditional Society*, New York, 1958.

2. D. Meadows *et al.*, *The Limits to Growth*, Potomac Associates, New York, 1972.

3. People really began to figure in development literature after the publication of an anthology of celebrated essays by E. F. Schumacher, *Small is Beautiful: Economics as if People Mattered*, Blond and Briggs, London, 1975.

4. Centre for Concern, UNCTAD Memorandum No. 9, Washington, 30 July 1979.

5. Speech of the Secretary General, Joao Frank da Costa, to the United Nations Conference on Science and Technology for Development, Vienna, August 1979; see also the Vienna Programmes of Action on Science and Technology for Development, UN, New York, 1979.

6. *North–South: A Programme for Survival*, Pan, London, 1980.

7. For a detailed account of the impact of the ideology of science and technology on Muslim societies, see Ziauddin Sardar, *Science, Technology and Develoment in the Muslim World*, Croom Helm, London, 1977.

8. See Ziauddin Sardar, 'Development: Interdependence and Terrorism', *Geographical Magazine*, **54** (1), 608 (1982).

9. For a really crude example of how Westernized patterns of development are promoted, see J. P. Cleron, *Saudi Arabia 2000: A Strategy for Growth*, Croom Helm, London, 1978.

10. See the excellent paper by K. Hoffman and H. Rush which spells out the likely impact of micro-electronics on the developing countries: 'Micro-

electronics, industry and the Third World', *Future*, **12** (4), 289–302 (1980).

11. Jafar Shaykh Idris, 'The Islamic way of developing nations' in *Proceedings of the Eighth Annual Convention of the Association of Muslim Social Scientists*, Plainsfield, Indiana, 1982.

12. *Ibid.* p. 16.

13. Khurshid Ahmad, 'Economic Development in an Islamic Framework' in Khurshid Ahmad (ed.), *Studies in Islamic Economics*, Islamic Foundation, Leicester, 1980.

14. Khurshid Ahmad, 'Some aspects of character building', *The Muslim*, **8** (1), 9–15 (1970) and **8** (2), 39–42 (1970).

15. Khurshid Ahmad, 'Economic development . . .', pp. 179–80.

16. For an analysis of how development is always perceived *à la occident*, see Ziauddin Sardar and D. G. Rosser-Owen, 'Science Policy and Developing Countries' in I. Spiegal-Rosing and D. de Solla Price (eds), *Science, Technology and Society: A Cross-Disciplinary Perspective*, Sage, London, 1977.

17. L. W. Pye *et al.*, *Aspects of Political Change*, Little Brown, Boston, 1966.

13

Can the Hajj Survive the Future?

The most destructive manifestation of 'development' in the Muslim world is undoubtedly the environment of the hajj. Just fifteen years of development have changed the holy areas beyond recognition and eradicated fourteen centuries of history from the noble and blessed cities of Makkah and Medina. Indeed, the situation is so critical that if the present pace and policies of development are continued, there is a real possibility that the performance of hajj will become not a spiritual exercise but a deathly struggle with pollution and traffic congestion, deafening noise and alienated environment where the pilgrims will need all their wits to survive.

The pilgrimage to Makkah is the zenith of a Muslim's spiritual experience. It is a living, dynamic, operational form of the command of God: 'Perform the hajj and *umra* for Allah'. As such, the hajj is performed not because the believers in Islam seek inspiration, but because they are inspired. It is an expression and not a search for belief.

The hajj is the supreme expression of the belief in one God, the Beneficent, the Merciful, the First and the Last. It is a practical demonstration of the beliefs that He has honoured the ancient Ka'abah by calling it 'His own House' and by fixing it as the goal and destination of His servants, thus rendering sacred the territory surrounding the House, that He has designated the locality called Arafat to be the channel for the outpouring of His mercy. And that, to enhance further the sacred nature of this territory,

He forbade the hunting of game or felling of trees within its borders. For the believers, this territory is a Divine Audience Hall: a place to come from far and near to seek His Divine presence—in all humility, covered with the dust of travel, bowing low before the Creator of all that is in the heavens and the earth. It is in this territory that they seek refuge from the material world, abandoning all bodily desires, abstaining from pleasure and luxury, giving themselves entirely to God during both the active life of the day and the hours of rest and quietness. Standing before His majesty and power, seeking forgiveness and knowing full well that God is too pure to be contained in a building, or limited to one place or territory. And all this symbolizes the expression of their faith and personifies their complete submission to the Commands of God.[1]

Apart from the expression of the faith of the believers, the hajj is also an expression of the universal brotherhood of Islam.[2] Here, in the Divine Audience-Hall, men and women of all races, colour, languages and countries of origin stand in complete unity and equality. All social categories, financial status, worldly power and authority evaporate. There is nothing: only His divine presence and His worshippers, all assimilating their beings with the will of God; all wearing the most simple of garments: the *ihram*. The *ihram* consists of two unsewn sheets of cloth, a loin cloth and a shoulder cover with which the pilgrims cover themselves. It is the physical expression of the unity of Muslims and equality of all before God. In their simple white *ihrams*, the pilgrims move as one from Makkah to Muna to Arafat to Muzdalifah and back to Muna and Makkah. Submerging their worldly identities, the pilgrims move as one creation from one holy area to another, acknowledging the command of God in unison:

Here I am O Lord, in answer to your call!
What is thy call, here I am!
What is thy call, here I am!
What is thy call, here I am!
Thou art without companion!
What is thy call, here I am!
Praise and blessing are thine, and Dominion!
Thou art without Companion!

The hajj is also an expression of the simplicity of Islam. Conventionally translated as pilgrimage, hajj, like most Qur'anic words, is far richer and signifies much more. It means 'to direct oneself towards one God', to endeavour to overcome one's ego and earthly desires; and this effort, indeed it is a great Effort, leads to the point where oneself is forgot entirely and annihilated and becomes one with the will of God. It is this one, all-encompassing goal that manifests the spiritual simplicity of Islam. The pilgrims repeat again and again: 'O Lord! I seek Thy protection against every doubt, against all forms of polytheism, against all division, against all hypocrisy, against all unworthy behaviour, against all misfortune . . .' Their spiritual desires are simple: to seek refuge from all doubt. The *ihram* gives a physical form to their spiritual simplicity. And in this complete state of simplicity, the pilgrims acquire the *rahmah* (bounty) of their Creator. At Arafat, during the ritual of *wquf* (standing), the pilgrims in all their humility and simplicity ask for forgiveness. Already, they have experienced a brotherhood, universality, and spiritual enlightenment the like of which they have never known before. Here in the valley of Arafat, the Magnificent, the Beneficent, the Merciful, will send down his forgiveness on those whom He will—and they feel His presence. Universality and brotherhood of Islam reaches its zenith—but the overriding experience is personal. It is I, and my Creator; and the noblest hours of my life. I am as pure and simple as the day I was born.

This is why the hajj signifies a new birth; and, its natural corollary, the death of the old self. And this is why the classical Muslim scholars have often referred to the hajj as 'the completion of religion'. It was during the hajj that Prophet Mohammad gave his Farewell Sermon containing that simple truth that Islam is universal and all mankind is equal before God. And it was also in this connection that the Qur'anic verse, 'this day have I perfected for you your religion. . .' (5:3) was revealed. The hajj, therefore, is the seal of a Muslim's spiritual quest; it is the last of four fundamental and essential elements of Islam. Historically, it was the final commandment to be laid down as the religious duty of the believer: the Prophet began his mission by declaring the Oneness of God and instituting the daily prayers; fasting and *zakah* followed in turn with the hajj coming at the end. From a purely devotional perspective, the daily prayers constitute an ascension towards God, while the hajj is a rite which is carried out within the territory declared by God to be sacred and on the very threshold of the House which God Himself has declared to be His House. As such, the hajj is a veritable Resurrection, a resurrection on this earth. The Day of Arafat has often been compared to the Day of Resurrection: 'Whose is the Kingdom today? It is God's, the One, the Ruler of all!' (40:16).

Such sublime experience of Divine Presence, universality and simplicity cannot be an everyday occurrence. Moreover, it is an occurrence that a Muslim cannot be without. It is therefore an obligation on all Muslims to perform hajj at least once in their lifetime if their circumstances permit. This obligation is so important that if a Muslim dies before accomplishing it, then this duty becomes incumbent on his heirs, who take his place. Because of its spiritual importance, it is an obligation that requires tremendous preparation on the part of the believers who come to Makkah for a rebirth; the desire to perform the hajj in its complete, pristine form—just as the Prophet himself performed this vital spiritual ritual.

The Ideal Hajj

The pilgrims come to Makkah with certain desires and expectations. They expect to perform the hajj according to the Sunnah. They desire spiritual enlightenment for which they abandon worldly luxuries and pleasures and are willing, indeed all too willing, to exert themselves physically to annihilate their egos and become one with the will of God. They expect the environment of hajj to be pure and simple and soaking with the rich history of Islam. Their goal is Makkah, the 'mother of cities' (*Um-ul Quarra*) within which lies the House of God (*Bait Allah*). Makkah! The City of Allah upon earth. The Birthplace of Prophet Mohammad. Makkah, the enlightened; the 'Barren Valley'. For devout Muslims, Makkah is not just a geographical location. Its sacred territory, its living, thriving history, its spiritual dynamic make it one of the Gardens of Paradise. It is a sanctuary; a frame of mind; a profound experience. Pilgrims, therefore, expect Makkah to be Beautiful; and Timeless.

The ideal hajj, for a pilgrim, is the one that is performed according to the Sunnah in the beautiful and timeless city of Makkah in the barren and simple environment that is the sacred territory.

The Beloved Prophet only performed one pilgrimage and two *umrahs*: the Farewell Pilgrimage was in fact the only one performed by the Prophet and it laid down the procedure to be followed during the ritual. On the 25th Dhul al Qidah of the tenth year of the *hijra*, the Prophet set off towards Makkah. He was accompanied by all his wives and an estimated 90,000 to 114,000 Muslims. The entourage reached Dhu al Hulayfah at the end of the day and spent the night there. On the following morning the Prophet went into *ihram* and the Muslims followed his example. When the caravan reached the town of Sarif, halfway between Makkah and Medina, the Prophet said to his companions: 'those of you who do not have any sacrificial animals with you may perform the lesser pilgrimage. But those who do, must perform the complete ritual.' On the 4th Dhu al Hijjah, the procession reached Makkah. According to the Egyptian scholar, Muhammad Husayn Haykal,

> upon arrival, the Prophet, followed by the Muslims, hastened to the Ka'abah. There, the Prophet went to the Black Stone and kissed it. Then he circumambulated the holy sanctuary seven times, the first three of which he did at a trotting pace, just as he had done in the lesser pilgrimage. He then proceeded to the Sanctuary of Ibrahim where he performed a prayer. Returning back to the Black Stone he kissed it once more and then left the temple area for the Mount of al Safa, and from there performed the *Sa'y* between that mount and the mount of Marwah.[3]

On 8th Dhu al Hijjah the Prophet went to Mina and spent the day and night in the valley. The following day, at sunrise, he moved to the plains of Arafat. He asked some of his companions to put up a tent for him at a spot called Namirah. When the sun passed the zenith, the Prophet had his camel saddled and rode on it until he reached the valley of Uranah. And it was here that the Beloved Prophet delivered his Farewell Sermon. Haykal continues:

> The Prophet left Arafat and spent his night at Muzdalifah. In the morning, he visited first the santuary of al Mashar, and then Mina on the road to which he threw pebbles against the symbol of Satan. When he reached his tent, he sacrificed sixty-three camels, one for each year of his life. Ali sacrificed the rest of the animals which the Prophet has brought with him from Madinah. The Prophet then shaved his head and declared his pilgrimage completed.[4]

Most pilgrims would like to perform the pilgrimage strictly according to the Sunnah. Moreover, they would like to perform the hajj in an environmental atmosphere that is similar to the one that existed during the Farewell Pilgrimage. This desire of most pilgrims is the result of their devotion to the last Messenger of Allah and their perception as acquired through the traditional works of Islamic theology and history. But can the desire of pilgrims to perform the Ideal Hajj be accommodated with contemporary reality? And, indeed, with future trends?

Ideals and Reality: the Inverted Cone Model

It is obvious that some aspects of the perceived Ideal Hajj are not easy to perform today. It is practically impossible for some pilgrims to kiss the Black Stone once, let alone twice, during the performance of *tawaf* and *Sa'y*. And if every pilgrim sacrificed one camel for each year of his/her life, the beast would be extinct within a few years. Moreover, if one were to be strict about the Sunnah one would have to ride a camel during the entire performance of the hajj. But the hajj today does not only ask the pilgrims to sacrifice the minor aspects of their vision: unfortunately, it destroys their vision completely.

This destruction of the Ideal Hajj is brought about by an acute imbalance in the environment of hajj caused by, among other factors, an unhindered invasion of inappropriate technology in its rapidly changing structure. We can best understand the dichotomy between an idealized vision and present-day reality in terms of a model.

The journey towards the spiritual realization of hajj, the assimilation with the will of God, leads through the physical process of hajj. All rites of hajj require a certain amount of physical exertion: the *tawaf* requires going round and round the *ka'aba* seven times: the *Sa'y* requires running between the hills of Safa and Marwah seven times; the *wquf* requires standing in the plains of Arafat under the burning sun; and the *nafrah*, the mass exodus of pilgrims from Arafat to Muzdalifah, requires the pilgrims to run the distance. The pilgrims expect to suffer these physical discomforts of hajj—for these are the rites that the Beloved Prophet himself performed. However, man's physical capabilities are limited and the natural boundaries of physical exhaustion are easily reached. If 'noise'—that is, discomfort—that does not belong to the natural environment of hajj is introduced into the system, it will quickly take the physical discomfort of the pilgrims beyond the God-given limits. The hajj now becomes much more of a physical experience than a spiritual one. If the physical discomfort is further increased, the spiritual experience of hajj diminishes proportionally. There is a hypothetical point at which the spiritual aspect of hajj is altogether removed by the overpowering physical discomfort. When this point is reached, the hajj is reduced to a set of mechanical actions—a tragedy of unparalleled magnitude.

The relationship between physical discomfort and spiritual realization can be demonstrated if we imagine the entire process of hajj as an inverted cone (Figure 6).[5] The upper lip of the cone, extending towards infinity, represents the spiritual dimension of hajj. The base of the cone (in fact, the inverted apex) signifies the physical dimension of hajj. In an Ideal Hajj, that is a hajj performed according to the Sunnah within the structure and environment at the time of the Beloved Prophet, the physical experience of the pilgrim will be significant compared to his spiritual experience. In the present-day hajj the pilgrim spends most of his time fighting the physical discomforts which have taken a formidable form. He has little time left for reflection, prayer and meditation (the dotted cone).

In this model we also have a third type of hajj experience: the technological hajj, which deprives the pilgrims of all physical

Spiritual dimension

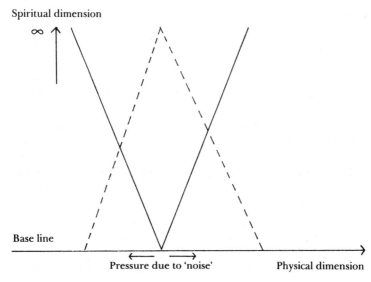

Figure 6. *The Process of Hajj*

exertions and hence reduces their spiritual enrichment to nothing. This is the non-experience hajj (the base line of the cone).

Most of the changes in the environment of hajj are recent. Up to a few decades ago the hajj environment was similar to the one in which the Beloved Prophet performed his Farewell Pilgrimage. It was as though time had left Makkah and the holy areas untouched; and the vast majority of pilgrims performed their rites as pilgrims had always done: on foot or on beasts of burden. The physical discomforts were all due to the natural causes: the heat and the harshness of the environment. The spiritual realization of the pilgrims was enhanced by the knowledge that they are walking on the very mud and rock where the Prophet himself walked.

The spiritual dimension far, far outweighed the natural physical discomfort.

However, within the last few decades the environment of the hajj has been changed beyond recognition.[6] Makkah has been transformed to a modern city: its traditional character has been displaced with all the main characteristics of the contemporary Western city. Dual carriageways, concrete tower blocks with the accompanying pollution and the problems of dislocation are all there. Other holy areas such as Muna and Medina have also experienced similar transformations. It was inevitable that time and modern civilization would make its mark on the holy environment.

Moreover, to cope with the pressures of increasing numbers of pilgrims, a whole host of technological solutions have been tried. Bridges have been built, tunnels have been dug, high-mast lighting has been introduced, and extensive provisions have been provided for pilgrims to drive everywhere. From the moment he arrives at the ultra-modern King Abdul Aziz Airport in Jeddah, the pilgrim moves on to the conveyor belt of modern technology that carries him to all the ritual points and brings him back. As is the way with modern technology, each solution has generated a whole host of new problems. Instead of reducing the physical exertion of the pilgrims, these solutions have aggravated the physical discomfort to such a level that it now becomes the predominant experience for many pilgrims.

This situation arises because elements alien to the environment of the hajj interfere with the pilgrims' quest for assimilation with the will of God. We have already argued that physical discomfort natural to the environment acts as a catalyst in the spiritual realization of the pilgrims. However, anything that is alien to the environment and that interferes with the spiritual development of pilgrims is 'noise'. In modern-day hajj, a whole range of noise is generated that constantly detracts the pilgrims from their primary goal. Elsewhere, I have described how noise debases the hajj environment:

> The dominant theme during hajj, as noted, is the assimilation of the
> pilgrim with the will of God. This assimilation results, in part, from

prayer, inner reflection and meditation. The major requirement for prayer and reflection is peace: peace within and peace without, peace with Allah and peace with one's soul, peace with one another and peace with the environment, peace with birds, animals and even with insects. This is why *all* form of aggression is forbidden during hajj. The state of *ihram* is a state of peace. However, it is difficult, nay quite impossible, to be in a constant state of peace amidst the automative nightmare: the perpetual noise of motor vehicles, helicopters and aeroplanes; the ear-piercing shrieks of horns and sirens; the continuous chants of competing loudspeakers; the horrific music of the transistors and the pungent smell and suffocating effect of the exhaust fumes.

One of the aims of Hajj is to acquaint the pilgrims with the historical and the spiritual environment of the Prophet—peace be upon him—so that they may derive inspiration and strengthen their faith. Walking on the pathways used by the Prophet can be phenomenally uplifting. Driving through formidable traffic jams, or plodding on concrete roads, dodging cars and human waste and debris generates only fatigue. In present-day Muna what is experienced is not the environment of the Prophet, but the surroundings of Manhattan; and there are no spiritual gains to be made by experiencing the urban dystopia.

Cleanliness is part of the faith says the tradition. It is certainly a requirement for any part of spiritual experience. Yet the environment of the hajj is indescribably wretched and insanitary. This is partly due to the lack of adequate toilets (in number and in design); partly due to urban pressure on its environs; and partly due to the unhygienic habits of some pilgrims. The end result is that many pilgrims spend much of their time during hajj avoiding filth and debris rather than in prayer and supplication.[7]

It is clear that while the Ideal Hajj cannot be realized in its totality in today's circumstances, the present-day hajj, with all the problems that the introduction of inappropriate technology has generated, is also untenable. We cannot go back in time. Neither can we stand still: change is now the only constant. But more: it is not just that things are changing, but the rate of change is itself changing. Managing the hajj environment under these circumstances requires a formidable dimension of research and effort.

Given this all-too-dominant rate of change, the interconnected and complex nature of contemporary problems of hajj and the desire of pilgrims to perform the Ideal Hajj, what can we expect for the future? Can we plan for a hajj environment that fulfils some aspects of pilgrims' desires and the dictates of contemporary reality?

Two Scenarios

We can envisage one possible scenario based on the present trend. This scenario takes the present development to its absurd, but logical conclusion. The holy city of Makkah continues to see development until every segment of the city is transformed: two-thirds of the city consists of roads saturated with traffic, the remaining part has tower blocks, each one higher than the next. The same developments happen in Muna. The mountains surrounding Makkah and Muna are flattened and given over to highways. To cope with the increasing traffic congestion during hajj, a whole complex of flyovers and spaghetti junctions are built. Consumer shops, fast-food dispensers and petrol pumps occupy every inch of available space. Exhaust fumes in the air make it very difficult to breathe. Lead from the polluted air ensures that even the hardy date palm cannot grow. Makkah and its environment is now transformed into a perpendicular metropolis; it is a city like any other American city: say, like Columbus, Ohio.

An alternative scenario is presented by the work of the Hajj Research Centre (HRC) of Umm al-Quarra University, Makkah.[8] Several years of research has convinced the HRC that the automobile is the prime cause of the destruction of the hajj environment. The Center has argued to ban the car from the hajj environment and to persuade the pilgrims to walk on specially constructed pedestrian routes. Furthermore, high technology should also be banned and only low-impact, 'soft' technological solutions to the problems of hajj should be sought. Traditional architecture should be rediscovered and conservation should become the norm. What would the future hajj environment look like if these policies were followed?

Within a few decades the entire environment of Makkah will be transformed. The old city will return to its former glory. The *mashrabias* will return; the traditional housing will become the dominant mode of living in the city. A whole host of pedestrian walkways, surrounded by lush trees and shaded areas, will connect Makkah to Muna, Arafat and Muzdalifah. Pilgrims will walk everywhere, performing the rituals at their own pace, resting in the shaded areas and soaking in the historic environment. Makkah will regain some of its uniqueness and beauty.

Both of these scenarios are equally possible. If the present trends continue, Makkah and the environment of the hajj will resemble an American city within the next ten years. If the Hajj Research Center succeeds in pushing its policies through, some of the richness and beauty of the natural environment of the hajj can be restored by the end of the century. However, while the Hajj Research Center scenario is infintely more acceptable than the logical outcome of the present trends, it lacks a futuristic base. To some extent the scenario contains elements of regression rather than moving forward. The HRC's approach is focused on returning to a static past rather than moving to a dynamic future based on alternative development solutions that bring out both the uniqueness of the hajj environment and the specific Islamic character of the solution.

On what bases can we study the future of the hajj? How can we plan to secure the unique character of the 'Barren Valley' and ensure that the solutions to the contemporary problems of hajj do not generate noise and are flexible enough to accommodate changing needs? The solutions to the problems of hajj have to be sought within the framework of two criteria: the determinants such as demographic trends and evolution of technology that will shape the future; and the physical and spiritual limits of the hajj environment. We will examine each of these criteria separately.

The Limits of Hajj

The spiritual limits of the hajj are sacred: they cannot be transgressed. Any solution to contemporary problems of hajj must preserve the sanctity of these limits.

Earlier, we argued that the hajj is an expression of the ultimate spiritual quest of the Muslim: the assimilation of the self with the will of God. Only an environment that is ecologically balanced can facilitate this sublime desire of pilgrims. The first spiritual limit to the hajj environment is, therefore, *ecological harmony*. Ecological harmony dictates that the environment is in a symbiotic, mutually enhancing relationship with nature. The basic values are to conserve, not to waste; to enhance the art of life rather than entropic decay; and to nurture the attitude that the environment that has produced the problems also contains the seeds of solution. The Makkan environment has a delicate ecological balance. For example, the spring of Zamzam, a place of religious attachment from which the pilgrims quench their thirst after performing the *tawaf* and the *S'ay*, receives its water from Precambrian basement rocks through three sets of fractures which are extending from Ka'aba in the direction of Safa and Marwah, intersecting at the well. Almost any ecological violence suffered by the mountains and plains in Makkah can move these faults and close the spring. Alternatively, new faults and fractures may be created causing leakage of sewage systems and other underground water into the Zamzam spring. Preserving the delicate ecological harmony of the natural environment of hajj is therefore paramount: it is a spiritual necessity.

The hajj is also an expression of the universalism of Islam. This is the second spiritual limit of hajj. *Preserving universalism* means that any Muslim, rich or poor, from whatever background, cannot be stopped from performing the hajj if he fulfils the basic criteria. Solutions to the problems of increasing pilgrims have to be based on policies of equal opportunities for all: local as well as foreign pilgrims. It also means that the environment of hajj is equally accessible to all pilgrims: segments of the holy areas cannot be cordoned off for the privileged few: the rich and the powerful. And, preserving universalism also means acknowledging diversity—the pilgrims come from every corner of the globe, from every social background, communicating in hundreds of different languages. Solutions to the problems of hajj must take into account this rich diversity: in community information, the language differences; in designing toilets, the sanitary behaviour; and in performing of rituals, their individual preferences and peculiarities.

The third spiritual limit concerns the fact that the hajj is also an expression of the simplicity of Islam. *Simplicity* must be the essence of all technological solutions to the problems of hajj.[9] Simplicity must be the theme of the total hajj environment. Such an environment would value simplicity as economy of means towards the generosity of ends. It would stress avoidance of arrogance and extravagance and encourage graciousness and sensitivity. It would be an environment that creates a sense of place that though being of this realm is continuously indicative of responsibility towards the hereafter through highlighting our duties to God and fellow man. The built form celebrates the rituals of man's subservience to God and supports the social acts of service to fellow man.

The special role and functions of the holy city of Makkah produce the fourth spiritual limit: Makkah is *umm al-Qurra*, mother of cities.[10] It is the spiritual focus of the Muslim world. Makkah, more than any other city in the world, possesses an intense sense of history: it was there that Prophet Ibrahim and his son Ishmael erected the first House for the worship of One God, the Ka'aba. It is the city of birth of Mohammad, the last Messenger of Allah. It was here that Divine Revelation began and was finalized. Makkah is the holiest sanctuary of Islam—one of the Gardens of Paradise. It is therefore like no other city on earth—and should resemble none. Makkah exists in the fourth dimension: time. This quality of timelessness is sacred: Makkah is the Beginning, the Present and Forever. The other sacred quality of Makkah is beauty: it is the city of God on earth and the Prophet in glorifying God tells us that He is Beautiful and loves beauty. Beauty is an intrinsic dimension of Truth. But the beauty of Makkah is not an ordinary beauty. It is hidden, elusive, transcendental—a beauty beyond our sense, not bound on fashion-dependent normative tastes. It is a beauty generated by the natural environment, by great architecture and philosophical integrity, by technological insight that compliments the creation of Allah. It is a beauty generated by ecological harmony and simplicity. The qualities of timelessness and beauty make sense of the words of the Prophet: 'it is not man but God who has made Makkah sacred'. And: 'what a splendid city thou art. If I had not been driven out of thee by my tribe, I would dwell in no other place but thee.'

These four limits form a spiritual cordon that maps out the

boundaries within which the solutions to contemporary and future problems of hajj have to be found. In addition to these four limits, there is one characteristic of hajj that puts a physical limit on our search for solutions.

The basic unit of hajj is the pilgrim: a devout Muslim with natural limits, some desires and some expectations. We have already stated that the desire of most pilgrims is to perform the Ideal Hajj: a hajj based on their interpretation of the Sunnah in an environment that reflects authenticity and the feeling of the time of the Beloved Prophet. But what are the main expectations of a pilgrim? At the very least the pilgrim expects that his basic needs will be fulfilled and that he will be able to perform the hajj with some dignity. Bodo Rasch has described the basic expectations of a pilgrim as follows:

(he needs) good, clean food, fresh water for drinking and his ritual ablution, a shaded place for sleeping, a warm blanket for the cool hours of the night, as well as privacy for his personal needs. He needs shade where he spends the longer periods of his time because the majority of pilgrims are not used to the burning sun of Makkah. He needs paths on which he can go barefoot to the various Holy Places, should he have lost his sandals in the crush. He needs resting places, and water again and again so that he does not get dehydrated and suffer a heatstroke. If he is old, handicapped or weak, he needs . . . to be driven or carried and should he fall ill or meet with an accident, he needs medical help and care, he needs reliable information about all questions of religion and orientation. He needs a person he can turn to with all questions during the hajj, one who recognizes him, one who cares. He requires a bed in Makkah and Muna, although he only needs shade from the sun and a makeshift camp in Arafat, and the bare essentials to sleep in Muzdalifah . . . the pilgrim has a right to get a healthy and high quality animal for slaughter, if he buys it in the holy region. . .[11]

These then are the bare essentials that a pilgrim expects. The fulfillment of the basic needs of the pilgrim is one aspect of the physical limit of hajj. This physical limit has a second component which relates to the sheer physical battering a pilgrim can take. If the pilgrims are too densely packed at various ritual points they will either be unable to move or be injured. In principle, a density of four to six pilgrims per square metre cannot be exceeded, especially at *tawaf*, *S'ay* and the Jamarat area.

Pilgrim density is directly related to their movement. If they are too tightly packed they will be unable to move and cause congestion as well as injury to themselves and others. Optimum pilgrim density will also allow the pilgrims to move at their natural pace and conserve their energy as and when they need to. Moreover, it integrates well with the physical limits of the *tawaf* and *Sa'y* areas: in principle, it is difficult for more than 50,000 pilgrims to perform *tawaf* and more than 80,000 to perform *Sa'y* at the same time. But if the pilgrims move at their natural pace, at optimum density, they move in and out of *tawaf* and *Sa'y* areas without exceeding these physical limits. We can best understand the movement of pilgrims by the use of an analogy.

Consider the totality of pilgrims to be a mighty river. Each pilgrim is like a drop of water, flowing, meandering, moving towards its natural goal. But the flow of water in a river can be gentle and streamlined—what is sometimes called lamina flow; or it can be fast with rapids—turbulent flow. When the river flows on an even sandy bed, lamina flow dominates; when it flows on an uneven, rocky surface with boulders in its path, rapids are produced and turbulence results. If there is a sharp and violent break in the river bed, waterfalls are generated. Similarly, if the pilgrims are allowed to move at their natural pace with optimum density, lamina flow will result. They will move from one holy area and from one ritual point to another like a gently flowing river. However, if boulders are placed in their path in the form of vehicles, or if the river bed is changed violently by the introduction of bridges or tunnels, or if their natural flow is speeded up or slowed down by allowing the use of the car and by traffic congestion, turbulence will be produced, rapids will be generated and even waterfalls could emerge.

The river analog is a powerful model for studying the movement of pilgrims. That pilgrims behave like a river can be easily demonstrated by time-lapse photograpy of the *tawaf* area or by slow-motion films of the pilgrim movement at the Jamarat. It also gives us an insight into how the physical limits of a pilgrim and of the hajj environment can be used to find a solution to a particular problem of modern hajj: the movement of the pilgrims.

The spiritual and physical limits of hajj, then, perform two functions. They map out the boundary within which solutions have to be found and they act as signposts and indicators for solution. They enable us to preserve the authentic character of the hajj environment and move forward to meet the challenge of the future.

Future Determinants of Hajj

The future challenge to the hajj environment would come largely from two directions: demographic and technological changes.

There are approximately 1000 million Muslims in the world today[12] and this figure is doubling every twenty-five years.[13] There is no reason for us to believe that this rate of growth will not continue. In the last few years the hajj has been performed regularly by over 2 million Muslims. There will be a natural increase of about 50,000 pilgrims every year for the foreseeable future. Up to now, pilgrims from behind the Iron Curtain have been in hundreds. This will change considerably: by 1986, the Russian race will be a minority in their own country and will have to concede certain ground to the Muslims who dominate the southern part of Russia.[14] Similarly, other Communist countries with large Muslim populations, such as China and Yugoslavia, will find that their Muslims will not only grow in numbers but also in articulation. We can thus expect a substantial increase in pilgrims from the Communist bloc. All this means that by the year 2000, an average of 3 million Muslims will be performing hajj every year.

It is not always wise to conceive of the future as a mere extension of the present: trends, no matter how powerful, do not always continue in linear fashion. But we have seen a tenfold rise in pilgrims since the Second World War. And, given the present growth rates, we can reasonably ancitipate a 3 million hajj by the turn of the century. Unless, of course, an unexpected phenomenon makes an appearance.

However, the problems associated with the accommodation,

food and water needs, toilet requirements, transportation facilities and the impact of such large masses of people on the hajj environment are not as formidable as they seem at first sight. Accompanying the demographic changes will be a number of profound changes in all intellectual, scientific and technological fields that will enable us to meet the challenge of the future hajj.

Conventionally, the problems of hajj have been tackled by two means: various problems of hajj are isolated into individual components and then these specific components are tackled with the help of imported technology. This approach has two fundamental drawbacks. Isolationist and reductionist methodology does not look at the hajj in its totality, as a complete, dynamic system. Problems of accomodation are solved in one way and the developments and construction in Makkah are allowed to continue in another way. The problem of pilgrim movement is seen as a problem for the discipline of transportation engineering and not as a systems problem that must be tackled within an holistic framework. Masterplans have concentrated on buildings and roads as though the spiritual significance of the hajj environment was irrelevant. While solutions to individual problems were indeed found, they could not be integrated with the entire system of problems or with spiritual, cultural and religious concerns. The whole exercise is like the random walk of a disorientated man who continues to walk but gets nowhere.[15]

We are realizing that reductive methodologies have an inherent weakness: they cannot solve problems with several interacting factors, especially if some of these factors—like culture, transcendental concerns—cannot be quantified. We have now discovered that the obsession of our tools and methods with quantified detail without context, with finer and finer measurements of smaller and smaller problems, leaves us, to use an often-quoted phrase, 'knowing more and more about less and less'. We are now returning to holistic thinking and synthesis.

The second drawback has been the technology we have imported. First of all, along with the imported technology, a whole set of values and cultural assumptions have been introduced in the hajj environment. It is these alien values and cultural assumptions that have generated the noise we have identified earlier. Technology is a human activity: there is nothing neutral or value-free about it. It develops in a society according to its needs and requirements, social pressures and political priorities. It solves the problems that it is designed to solve. For example, the contemporary building technology with steel, glass and concrete as its raw materials has developed out of social and material concerns of Europe and America.[16] They have evolved to build a typical, standardized Western city. It is unrealistic to expect modern building technologies to produce something else. One would need a totally different kind of building technology, based on different social assumptions and using different materials, to produce a different kind of city. Technologies developed to build airports cannot be used in a conservation area for it will end up resembling an airport. The evidence, and the supporting literature, for the social and cultural bias of technology is now so strong that we can ignore it only at our peril.[17]

Moreover, the technology we have imported to tackle the problems of the hajj environment, even when perceived to be the latest, have normally been out of date. The contemporary rate of change is such that by the time a particular technology has developed it is already out of date: both the problems and the ways of looking at them have changed. The only way to keep up with technology is to plan into the future.

We have been importing, to use the analogy developed by Alvin Toffler, the second-wave technology. This technology is characterized by its excessive use of non-renewable energy sources. These technologies are directly linked to the mass-production system of Western civilization. In this civilization, energy-intensive technologies have played a useful role; and the second-order determinants have taken many decades to come to the fore. In traditional societies, a heavy dose of such technologies produces almost immediate side-effects. And in an environment that is characterized by sensitivity, spiritual concerns and cultural authenticity, such technologies can cause havoc. This is what is happening in the environment of hajj.

There is considerable evidence for Toffler's assertion that we are on the verge of a great synthesis—the Third Wave; 'in a great historical confluence, many raging rivers of change are running together to form an oceanic Third Wave of change that is gaining momentum with every passing hour'.[18] The Third Wave civilization will have many unique characteristics, but what concerns us here is its technological base. Toffler writes:

> Third Wave civilization will rely on a far more diversified technological base as well, springing from biology, genetics, electronics, material science, as well as on outer space and under-the-sea operations. While some new technologies will require high energy inputs, much Third Wave technology will be designed to use less, not more, energy. Nor will Third Wave technologies be as massive and ecologically dangerous as those of the past. Many will be small in scale, simple to operate, with the waste of one industry predesigned for recycling into primary materials for another.
>
> For Third Wave civilization, the most basic raw material of all—and one that can never be exhausted—is information, including imagination. Through imagination and information, substitutes will be found for many of today's exhaustible resources. . .[19]

With information as the most important raw material, the Third Wave civilization, Toffler argues, will restructure education, scientific research and priorities and modes of communication. Toffler describes the future earth as an 'electronic cottage' where the micro-computer provides access to information and distributes technological power to ordinary people.

Whatever our reservations about Toffler's vision, Third Wave technologies will be a major determinant in shaping the future environment of hajj. Such technologies will enable us to meet the problems produced by an increasing number of pilgrims within the spiritual and physical limits of hajj. However, Third Wave technologies tailor-made for the environment of hajj will not emerge from within the Western social and cultural milieu. While we may be able to borrow certain Third Wave technologies which can be proved by assessment to be appropriate, in the long-term future we will have to create and develop a Third Wave technological base for the environment of hajj. This is the only viable, sane and futuristic solution to the complex, interconnected hajj *problematique*.

Third Wave Solutions

The future solutions to the problems of hajj begin with an acknowledgement that we cannot go back to the time of the Beloved Prophet and create conditions and an environment in which he performed the Farewell Pilgrimage. Certain aspects of the Sunnah have to be seen in a spiritual rather than pragmatic sense. While we cannot go back in time, we can, nevertheless, preserve for future generations and for spiritual reasons, the cultural property, historic sites and natural environment of the holy areas in a living, dynamic form. Moreover, we cannot allow ourselves to become a victim of our present: we cannot permit Second Wave technologies, which are rapidly becoming obsolete, to destroy our traditions and history and the natural environment of Makkah. This will cut the environment of hajj from its spiritual and historic roots. A future that is deprived of a sense of history is no future at all.

A futuristic technological base for the hajj environment has to be developed within the boundaries set by the physical and spiritual limits of hajj. In this framework the individual pilgrim becomes the basic unit of energy; and any hardware developed must relate in a direct, simple and human level to this basic unit. It has to enhance the ecological balance of the environment and complement the natural creation of God. It should promote universalism by acknowledging the diversity of the pilgrims; it should promote simple, yet elegant, innovations that can easily be understood and used by pilgrims. The building technology evolved for this technological base should use local materials that blend in with the natural environment. The Third Wave technological base for the environment of hajj should, above all, promote peace: there should be no conflict or unrest.

In the development of this technological base we have to anticipate the new Third Wave technologies which are likely to emerge in the developed countries. Some of these may be synthesized with the technologies developed locally. Such a process of synthesis would require:

(1) An awareness of the trends in technologies that are appropriate and relevant to the environment of hajj.

(2) An awareness of the value systems inherent in these technologies.

(3) An assessment to ensure that the technologies selected do not transcend the limits of hajj by examining the likely secondary and tertiary consequences of their application.

(4) Continuous monitoring if these technologies are introduced in the hajj environment.

Some contemporary technologies identified by Toffler as Third Wave technologies may be examined in this way. For example, micro-computers are considered by Toffler to be one of the main Third Wave technologies of the future. The information needs of the pilgrims are extensive: pilgrims need information on religious matters, directions, meeting basic needs and a host of other issues. Can an information system be developed which can meet the information needs of the pilgrims, communicate the information in their own languages and even communicate information to unlettered pilgrims, extremely simple to use and physically accessible to all pilgrims? Will such a system transcend the spiritual and physical limits of hajj? Can it be integrated with the natural environment? What will be the system's secondary and tertiary consequences? Such questions as well as modern microprocessor technologies need urgent attention.

In today's hajj the sacrifice meat is almost totally wasted. It is either left to rot or is buried in large holes or finds its way to incinerators, thus debasing a holy and sacred institution. Conventional factories are designed to mass-produce and operate the whole of the year. Can a Third Wave factory be designed to operate only during the hajj season, use little energy, waste little of the carcass, employ a few components and store the meat and end products until it can be distributed to the needy? Can the simple, age-old tent, so useful in Muna, Muzdalifa and Arafat, be improved? Can a special hajj tent be devised which can better protect the pilgrims from the heat of the mid-day sun and cold of the desert night, that is easy to assemble and reassemble and is so light that it can easily be carried by an individual pilgrim using the pedestrian walkway? These and countless similar questions are awaiting serious investigation and study in a Third Wave framework.

The hajj is the microcosm of the Muslim world. Makkah, and the environment where the hajj is performed, is the prime focus of the global Muslim community, the *ummah*. Thus the problems of Makkah and the hajj are the central Muslim problems of our time. Their solution is a matter of concern for every Muslim; it is a matter of integrity and cultural survival. Under such circumstances, hasty and expedient solutions could spell disaster. The future of hajj is intrinsically linked to the future of the Muslim *ummah*.

Under these circumstances we must seek long-term, futuristic solutions to the problems of hajj and the holy areas. Such solutions will have to look at the hajj as a holistic system, every component of which is intricately connected to every other. They will have to be sought within the spiritual and physical limits of hajj, taking the individual pilgrim as the unit of operation. Finally, they have to be implemented by conceiving and developing a Third Wave technological base for the environment of hajj. Only such Third Wave solutions can meet the ever complex needs to today's hajj and the challenges of the future.

Notes

1. For a profound account of the spiritual significance of hajj, see Ahmad Kamal, *The Sacred Journey*, Allen and Unwin, London 1961. See also, M. Valiuddin, 'The Secrets of Hajj (Pilgrimage)', *Islam and the Modern Age*, **2** (4), 42–70, and Abul Hasan Ali Nadwi, 'The Spirit of Hajj', *Journal of the World Muslim League*, **1**, 4 (January 1974).

2. See Eshraf Edib, 'The Universality of the Institution of Hajj—the Pilgrimage to Mecca', *Muslim Digest*, **18** (7), 2–9 (February 1968).

3. M. H. Haykal, *The Life of Muhammad*, trans. by Ismail Ragi A. al Faruqi, American Trusts Publications, Indianapolis, 1976, p. 484.

4. *Ibid.* pp. 487–8.

5. This model was first reported in my article, 'The Spiritual and Physical Dimensions of Hajj', in Z. Sardar and M. A. Zaki Badawi, *Hajj Studies*, Croom Helm, London, 1979, pp. 27–38.

6. The literature monitoring this change is considerable, most of it produced by the Hajj Research Center. See Z. Sardar, 'The Hajj: a Select Bibliography', *Muslim World Book Review*, **3** (1), 57–66 (1982).

7. Z. Sardar, 'The Spiritual and Physical Dimensions of Hajj', *op. cit.*

8. The Hajj Research Center was started in 1975 by Sami Angawi at the King Abdul Aziz University in Jeddah. It moved to Umm al-Quarra University in Makkah in 1983.

9. The exposition of the concept of simplicity and ecological harmony is taken from Gulzar Haider, 'Habitat and Values in Islam: a Conceptual Framework of an Islamic City', in Z. Sardar (ed.), *The Touch of Midas: Science, Values and the Environment in Islam and the West*, University of Manchester Press, Manchester, 1984.

10. For an understanding of the importance of Makkah to Muslims and its role in Islamic history, see Al-Azarqi, *Akhbar Makkah*, 2nd edn, Makkah, 1933–8; M. T. K. al-Makky, *Authentic History of Mecca and Holy House of God*, al-Mahdah Library, Makkah, 2 vols., 1965; and F. al-Sibai, *Tarikh Makkah, 2nd edn, Cairo*, 160–2.

11. Bodo Rasch, *The Tent Cities of the Hajj*, IL 29, University of Stuttgart, Stuttgart, 1980, p. 160.

12. The Muslim population of the world is a hotly disputed figure. Most estimates ignore the Muslims of India, the Soviet Union, China, Eastern Europe and Muslim minorities in the West. This figure takes the Muslim minorities into account and is from *The World Muslim Gazeteer*, Ummah, Karachi, 1979.

13. Marvin Cetron and Thomas O'Toole, *Encounters with the Future: a Forecast of Life into the 21st Century*, McGraw-Hill, New York, 1982, p. 168. Cetron and O'Toole faithfully reproduce the figure of 450 million for the Muslim population of the world—this figure has been quoted by several Western writers since the early 1950s! They estimate that by the year 2000 there will be 1000 million Muslims; and Muslims performing the hajj will continue to increase by 100,000 every year.

14. *Ibid.* p. 298.

15. Reductive methodologies have been the corner-stone of a host of masterplan studies done by various consultants. For example, *The Hajj Special Action Area Study*, 1972, and the *Special Action Area Study—Holy Area of Muna, Aziziah and al Adl*, 1975, both by Robert Mathew, Johnson, Marshall and Partners, suffer from this and have aggravated the situation rather than improved it.

16. See Alison Ravetz, *Remaking Cities*, Croom Helm, London, 1980; T. L. Blair, *The Poverty of Planning: Crisis in the Urban Environment*, Macdonald, London, 1973; and the devastating criticism of Jane Jacobs, *The Death and Life of Great American Cities*, Random House, New York, 1961.

17. The fifteen articles in Ina Spiegal-Rosing and Derek D. Solla Price (eds), *Science, Technology and Society: a Cross-Disciplinary Perspective*, Sage, London, 1979, examine the social and cultural bias of science and technology from a number of different angles; each article gives an extensive bibliography. See also J. R. Ravetz, *Scientific Knowledge and its Social Problems*, Oxford University Press, Oxford, 1971.

18. Alvin Toffler, *The Third Wave*, Bantam Books, New York, 1980, p. 349.

19. *Ibid.* p. 351.

14

The Future of Islamic Studies

Our efforts to save the future have also to be focused, along with rewriting of the Seerah, dethroning the concept of development and rescuing the hajj environment, on discovering new and innovative approaches to the teaching of and research on Islamic studies. Up to now, Islamic studies has been approached as though it was an independent discipline with no connection with any other discipline, or worse, it was a sub-discipline of 'religious studies' or 'comparative religion'. From a futuristic perspective, this approach is untenable. There is now an urgent need to place Islamic studies within a conceptual framework and approach the subject from the much wider perspective of the world-view of Islam.

Muhammad Iqbal, the most outstanding Muslim philosopher of the twentieth century, argued that Islamic studies had four basic objectives. In a letter written in June 1925 to the Secretary of 'All India Muhammadan Educational Conference', which was then developing a curriculum for the Islamic Studies course at the Aligarh Muslim University, he wrote that the purpose of Islamic Studies is 'to educate and train well-qualified theologians'; 'to produce scholars who may, by their researches in the various branches of Muslim literature and thought, be able to trace genetically the continuity of intellectual life between Muslim culture and modern knowledge'; 'to turn out Muslim scholars well-versed in the various aspects of Muslim history, art, general culture and civilization'; and 'to produce scholars who may be fitted to carry on researches in the legal literature of Islam'.[1] Iqbal had obviously given the matter some thought, and he elaborates each objective.

The training of well-qualified theologians, he argues, is necessary to satisfy the spiritual needs of the community. 'But the spiritual needs of a community change with the expansion of that community's outlook on life. The change in the position of the individual, his intellectual liberation and infinite advance in natural sciences have entirely changed the substance of modern life so that the kind of scholasticism or theological thought which satisfied a Muslim in the Middle Ages would not satisfy him today.'[2] Therefore Iqbal was looking for a new and more innovative way of teaching Islam. He dismissed the syllabus suggested by the Conference: 'it is perfectly useless to institute a school of Muslim Theology on older lines unless it is your objective to satisfy the more conservative portion of our community,'[3] he wrote. What is needed, he argued, 'is intellectual activity in fresh channels and the building of a new theology and *kalam*.'[4] Iqbal was too far ahead of his time. In the event, the 'conservative' forces had their way.

However, the move to reform the syllabus of Islamic studies at the Aligarh Muslim University was not without significance. It was the academic expression of a growing concern amongst Indian Muslim scholars that Islamic studies needed a fresh breath of life. In the same letter, Iqbal suggests that students of Islam should be persuaded to study science and mathematics, economics and sociology, while students of natural sciences should attend such courses as 'Science in the Muslim World'. He and other intellectuals of his time were firm, on the one hand, that Islamic studies should not be the sole preserve of 'Muslim theologians' and, on the other, that Muslim students of natural and social sciences should be exposed to Islamic studies.

The idea that modern Muslim universities should have departments, schools or institutes of Islamic studies has its roots in the revivalist movements of India and in the thoughts of such reformers as Iqbal.[5] Indian universities such as Aligarh, Osmania and Allahabad established departments of Islamic and Arabic

Studies which awarded graduate and postgraduate degrees early in the twentieth century. Thus 'Islamic Studies' as a discipline received its first, to use Mohamed Mackeen's words, 'academic, though somewhat inarticulate, formulation as a university grouping' in India.[6] This 'formulation' has had considerable impact on the evolution of the discipline.

Islamic Studies in the Muslim World

In the 1950s when some Muslim countries obtained their independence, old universities were expanded and a number of new ones were established. Islamic studies received a new impetus: the departments were broadened and somewhat 'modernised'. Along with the traditional subjects of *tafsir, fiqh*, Arabic, etc., new courses such as 'Islam in the Modern World' and 'Contemporary Revivalist Movements' began to be taught. A great deal of emphasis was beginning to be laid on the traditional/modern dichotomy, and issues such as birth control, 'Islam and science', Islam and modern ideologies, came into the syllabus. The universities of Cairo, Dacca, Karachi and the Punjab and the 'Universited Islam' in Djakarta all updated their Islamic Studies courses in this way. The new universities of Malaya, Ibadan and King Saud in Riyadh adopted the more up-to-date version of the discipline.

However, not all universities acquired separate departments for Islamic Studies. In some universities like those of Alexandria, Damascus, Rabat and Baghdad, Islamic Studies was integrated within the departments of faculties of Art or Humanities and disciplines such as literature, languages, history, law and so on, had various courses dealing with Islamic aspects. For example, the Department of Law would offer a course of Islamic law. In certain other universities, like those of Ankara and Tehran, 'Islamic studies were incorporated within the university structure under a more specific classification as faculties or department of theology based on the Western models of the faculties of divinity and theology'.[7] Thus the Istanbul University established a School of Divinity in 1949 'to study religious principles in the light of scholarly principles'.[8]

Only at the University of Cairo did Islamic studies have a unique status: the discipline had a whole faculty to itself. The *Dār al-'Ulūm* was named after an institute founded in 1871 for studies on religion, language, literature and engineering. In 1946 this institute was brought within the university and given the status of a faculty which ran courses on a whole range of Islamic topics.[9]

While the discipline of Islamic studies was going through these changes, the old-established Islamic universities of al-Azhar in Cairo, Qarawiyyin in Fez, and Zaytunah in Tunis, with their roots going back to over a thousand years of history and tradition, continued to teach Islam in the traditional manner. Only al-Azhar went through a radical change. In 1961 it was transformed into a 'modern university' with constituent colleges for Islamic Studies, Arabic Studies, management and administration, engineering and industry, agriculture and medicine.[10] However, the traditional al-Azhar became the prototype of the Islamic University of Medina which was founded in 1960.

The emergence of the more modern courses of Islamic studies, however, has not radically changed the contents of the discipline. Both in the traditional institutions of Islamic learning such as al-Azhar, Deoband and Medina universities, and the modern universities, Islamic studies are essentially theological studies of defined purpose and content. The objective, as Iqbal pointed out, is still to produce well-trained scholars of Islam. The syllabus in both types of institutions is based on the classical Muslim tradition which has evolved through centuries of growth and reform. It consists of the Qur'an and Hadīth which occupy a central position, while Shariah, scholastic theology and Arabic grammar, rhetoric and logic play a supporting role.[11] Modern universities would, of course, add courses which would touch on contemporary issues and controversies.

There are strong reasons why the classical approach to Islamic studies is concentrated on this framework. Mackeen, for example, argues that this framework

> owes its origin and structure to the political, social and intellectual patterns in the expansion of Islam and, above everything, to orthodoxy, the master criterion of Muslim thought and practice. But

this range of studies is not totally different from that which obtained in medieval Europe, where the trivium—namely, grammar, logic and rhetoric—formed the basis of a system in which Biblical studies, scholasticism, theology and law figured prominently. The grammar was Latin, the universal language of the all-powerful Church. Logic furnished the weapon for argument as well as a convenient method of escape to erudite obscurities. Rhetoric provided the foundation necessary for disputation and oratory in an era of the spoken word. A fact which is not often realised even by the Muslims themselves is that the major disciplines like scholastic theology and law were the ultimate outcome of a genuine urge to pin down with precision the terms of a civilization and were not in themselves wanting in intellectual content and value. There were centuries of hard thinking and application behind them. Scholastic theology (*'ilm al-kalām*), for example, is an independent scientific discipline based on rational concepts and the use of scientific tools, namely, logic and physics.[12]

While the critics of the classical methods of teaching Islamic studies are right in pointing out that this curriculum is somewhat out of touch with contemporary reality, the reforms they have introduced have been hardly innovative. Modern universities may not teach rhetoric and logic, but they retain the bulk of the classical syllabus. Moreover, the new courses that have been introduced do not form an integrated part of the whole syllabus, but are always an appendage to the classical syllabus. Mackeen himself has nothing to add to the classical contents. He suggests that Islamic studies should 'spread over' to the following fields: religion, philosophy and ethics, ṣūfism and music, literature, art, archaeology and history. While these subjects may expose the students of Islamic studies to topics that are outside the classical syllabus, the discipline itself benefits little. Adding such subjects to the periphery of Islamic studies would hardly give the discipline an integrated, coherent and contemporary structure. The modernist criticism of the syllabus and contents of classical Islamic studies is devoid of philosophical content and systematic analysis of contemporary reality.

Both the classical and modern approaches to Islamic studies concentrate on Islam as a religion and culture. Whether it is memorizing the Qur'an or Hadīth, mastering the opinions of the classical jurists or learning Islamic history, the emphasis is on rote learning and collecting facts. Islamic studies essentially amounts to a vast storehouse of facts and opinions which the student accumulates during the course of his or her study. No wonder then that the contemporary *ulama* and scholars of Islam are noted for a conspicuous absence of the ability to analyse, argue and appreciate contemporary issues.

Islamic Studies in the West

In the West, Islamic studies followed a somewhat different course. The roots of Islamic studies in the West lie deep in the colonial history. Marshall Hodgson argues that Western scholarship came to Islamic studies through three paths.

> First, there were those who studied the Ottoman empire, which played so major a role in modern Europe. They came to it usually in the first instance from the viewpoint of the European diplomatic history. Such scholars tended to see the whole of Islamdom from the political perspective of Istanbul, the Ottoman capital. Second, there were those, normally British, who entered Islamic studies in India so as to master Persian as good civil servants, or at least they were inspired by Indian interests. For them, the imperial transition of Delhi tended to be culmination of Islamicate history. Third, there were the Semitists, often interested primarily in Hebrew studies, who were lured into Arabic. For them, headquarters tended to be Cairo, the most vital of Arabic-using cities in the nineteenth century, though some turned to Syria or the Maghrib. They were commonly philologians rather than historians and they learned to see Islamicate culture through the eyes of the late Egyptian and Syrian writers most in vogue in Cairo.[13]

Hodgson considers other Western paths to Islamic studies—the Spanish and some Frenchmen who were interested in studying Muslim Spain and the Russians who were preoccupied with studying northern Muslims—as less important.

Whatever the path, the objectives of Islamic studies in the West were simple and direct: to understand the Muslim mind and culture so as to facilitate colonization and to meet the demands of the growing colonial civil service. These objectives ensured that Islamic studies in the West was a problem-oriented discipline—how could Islam be shown to be inferior? how could

Muslims be persuaded to accept their fate as subject people? how could they be made intellectually and hence physically insular? etc.—that was pursued within the framework of Western values and cultural systems. It was this framework that produced orientalism, the approach and methodology of studying Islam that has been analysed so penetratingly by, among others, Edward Said.[14] The major function of the centres of Islamic studies at Cambridge, Oxford, Leiden, Sorbonne and Berlin Universities was to produce civil servants trained in the art of colonial administration, to arm Christian missionaries with arguments for conversion, and to produce a body of scholarship that justified European domination of Muslim lands.

The colonial legacy is evident in most current Islamic studies courses in Western universities. They are taught with a blend of zealous philanthropy and latent self-interest. The links with foreign policy are never far away. However, Islamic studies in the West do have a distinct advantage: because Islam is studied as a 'problem', albeit from the perspective of Western values and culture, there is a strong emphasis on analysis. Best works of oriental scholars, for example, Hodgson's *The Venture of Islam* and D. M. Dunlop's *Arab Civilization to A.D. 1500*,[15] are works of analysis.

Moreover, with the partial shift in the global power structure and the newly acquired economic wealth of certain Muslim countries, Islamic studies has received a more sympathetic attention. What that actually means is that in their analysis orientalist scholars now tend to treat the values and culture of Islam on their own terms. Islamic studies courses now include works by Muslim scholars and Islam is studied as a civilization.

Perhaps no one has done more in presenting Islam as a civilization than Hodgson. His work entitled *The Venture of Islam*, a systematic and penetrating three-volume study of the civilization of Islam from its beginning to the twentieth century, is now used as a standard text in most Islamic studies courses in Western universities. Hodgson has even developed his own terminology of analysis: 'Islamdom' and 'Islamicate' are two of many important terms in his work. 'Islamdom', by analogy with Christendom, is used to describe the society in which Muslims and their faith are predominant—it does not refer to an area as such but to 'a complex of social relations' which are territorially reasonably well defined. While 'Islamdom' does not describe a civilization or a specific culture, 'Islamicate' is used to describe just such a culture, historically distinct from Islamdom, the society which has been shaped both by Muslims and non-Muslims. Using such distinctions, Hodgson wants Islam to be studied and taught from the perspective of 'exceptionalizing' historians. That is to say he wants to highlight, emphasize and analyse what is unique in 'Islamdom' and 'Islamicate' system. Only by concentrating on what is exceptional in the totality of experience that is Islam, Hodgson maintains, can we increase our understanding of 'Islamdom' and provide an objective framework for Islamic studies. In Hodgson's own words:

> for an 'exceptionalising' historian . . . it is Islamdom as a morally, humanly relevant complex of traditions, unique and irreversible, that can form his canvas. Whether it 'led to' anything evident in modern times must be less important than the quality of its excellence as a vital human response and an irreplaceable human endeavour. In this capacity, it would challenge our human respect and recognition even if it had played a far less great role than, in fact, it did play in articulating the human culture nexus in time and space and in producing the world as we find it now.[16]

The notion that Islam should be studied and taught from the perspective of an 'exceptionalizing' historian is a powerful one. Hodgson is concerned primarily with the exceptional character of Islamic society, culture and civilization. But what is really unique and exceptional about Islam is not just the society and civilization that it has produced, which have reached the zenith of human achievements and declined, but its world-view. And it is this world-view that should be the prime focus of Islamic studies, both in the Muslim world and the West.

Islamic Studies: A Futuristic Perspective

Despite the fact that Muslim scholars unanimously agree that Islam is not just a religion, but a complete way of life as well as a sophisticated culture and civilization, Islam, as we have seen, is never actually studied or taught in its totality. In Muslim universities, Islamic studies seldom transcends the boundaries of religion and culture. In the Western academia, as indeed in the occident civilization itself, there is a pathological obsession for treating 'religion', 'philosophy' and 'science' as three different realms of the mind, each with its own methods, laws and truths. In such a milieu, Islamic studies, whether studied within the perspective of an exceptionalizing historian or simply as an exotic discipline, can never really acquire a status greater than that of religious studies. Yet, there are obvious insights to be had if the method of Islamic studies was tackled with the methods of 'philosophy' and 'science'.

Let us make the naive assumption that the purpose of Islamic studies in the West is to increase the *understanding* of Islam, its people, culture, society and civilization in the developed world. Taking our cue from Iqbal, the objective of Islamic studies in the Muslim world is to produce well-versed scholars who can tackle, and perhaps solve, some of the formidable problems that face the Muslim societies. Can one suggest a new, radically different approach to Islamic studies that takes full account of contemporary technological and political realities and serves both objectives? What factors and trends should such an approach take into consideration?

To a very large extent, universities in the West and the Muslim world have, up to now, sheltered themselves from the vast complex web of social and cultural problems in the real world outside. However, it is no longer possible to ignore these problems simply because they have acquired a momentum of their own and now threaten to engulf the entire planet. We all recognize these problems and we all know that somehow they are interlinked and cannot be separated from each other. Each one of them—nuclear warfare, demographic trends, depletion of resources, energy problems, global unemployment, environment problems—is linked to every other problem and the whole set together forms what the Club of Rome has called the world *problematique*.[17] In this vast complex of problems, any single problem is itself complex. One may think, for example, that the population problem is very simple. A closer look, however, will reveal that the issues go much beyond birth control to age structure of a population, how fast it is growing, the rate of material progress, the availability of food and so on. All these problems are not just technical problems but they also have important ethical components: and their ultimate individual, social and societal solutions must be based on ethical criteria.

Furthermore, these problems are changing and becoming more and more complex day by day. What is more, the *rate of change* itself is changing. Society, therefore, is constantly adjusting and readjusting to change. Developments in microtechnology and genetic engineering now threaten to introduce fundamental changes in society. Cybernetics and artificial intelligence are poised to introduce even more basic changes in our lives. And the process continues.

With such a futuristic backdrop, we cannot afford to pretend further that what we learn at university has no bearing on our personal and societal environment and its future. We cannot now easily assume that our problems can be solved in isolated linear cause–effect sequences. We need to deal with the world in a more profound manner, going much deeper, where all our actions could have serious side-effects and produce a whole lot of interactions and non-linear effects. Thinking in terms of old-fashioned logic and cause and effect is totally inadequte to our present situation. Most young people, both in the West and the Muslim world, realize that what they are being taught does not prepare them for the complex decisions and ethical choices they have to make in their daily lives. They require newer methods of dealing with these problems but these methods do not fit any standard syllabus or curriculum.

The future scholars of Islam face a formidable responsibility. If they are to play an active role in raising the consciousness of the *ummah*, in solving some of its most pressing problems, in helping it to adjust to change, then they have to be trained by newer methods that are radically different from the classical approach.

There are two sharp breaks from the conventional approach to Islamic studies that we need to make. First, the picture of Islamic studies as a rigid discipline and sub-disciplines in neat little boxes marked 'the Qur'ān', 'Hadīth', 'Islamic law', 'Islamic history', etc., must be abandoned. Let the author hasten to add that this does not mean that the traditional content of Islamic studies should be dropped; rather it should not be taught as isolated components divorced from reality. Moreover, the traditional emphasis is no longer necessary: for example, it is not necessary to memorize all the authentic traditions and the opinions of the classical jurists on which the students spend much time and energy. For even in the poorer Muslim countries, scholars would be able to obtain these, at the touch of a button, from their personal micro-computers. The emphasis on memory and learning facts is now dangerously obsolete. The new emphasis has to be on analysis, solving ethical and moral problems—in short, thinking within Islamic paradigms. Islamic studies, therefore, must touch all contemporary problems, no matter how irrelevant and remote they may seem in the classical framework. The growing understanding of the linkages and interactions between diverse fields of learning and approaches to discovery of new knowledge that we have acquired suggests the need to adopt a devoted and dynamic approach: in some sense a return to the reality of the unity of all knowledge which was the foundation stone of the classical theory of Islamic education. This then is our link with tradition.

Islamic studies, therefore, must be taught and researched from multi-disciplinary and inter-disciplinary perspectives. Multi-disciplinary approach uses various disciplines to study a particular subject and attempts to create an overall comprehensive picture. For example, studying the Medina State of Prophet Muhammad using the theories and tools of social anthropology, political science and history of technology would yield much greater insights than one would find in a standard book of *Sīrah*. The inter-disciplinary approach uses a number of disciplines to explain particular events and situations and attempts to produce a synthesized perspective. The Hijra, for example, could be studied by examining the historical processes of social change, by a sociological and psychological analysis of Makkan society and of the specific reasons that persuaded Prophet Muhammad to migrate to Medina. Once more the end result would be far more penetrating than one is likely to find in the works of modern scholars. Only students trained in the multi- and inter-disciplinary approach to Islamic studies can tackle and study the complex, multi-dimensional contemporary and future problems of Muslim societies.

If Islamic studies is to evolve as a multi- and inter-disciplinary subject, then Islam cannot be taught as a religion or culture or even a civilization. And this is the second sharp break with the conventional approach. Islam must be presented as a world-view—only as a world-view does it solves the problems of its adherents and only as a world-view does it provide a unique, 'exceptionalising' perspective on the political, economic, scientific, technological, social, cultural and spiritual problems of man. And as a world-view it is open to examination by tools and methods of any discipline that can increase our understanding of the problems of mankind. Moreover, as a world-view it is as relevant for Muslims as it is for the West which is crying out for alternative ways and means for solving its problems of alienation.

The basic components of world-views are concepts. It is concepts that shape society, culture and civilizations. The framework of concepts on which the world-view of Islam depends provides the civilization of Islam with its bearings as well as its methods for solving ethical, moral, social and practical problems. It is these concepts that provide the Islamic society with policy guidelines and make sense of its actions. The successes and failures of particular Muslim societies in a given space–time location have depended on their abilities to operationalize and understand these concepts anew in the face of historical events, new social situations and new discoveries and innovations. It is these concepts that make Islam both universal and eternal.

Islamic studies then should essentially expose the student to a core of Qur'anic concepts—such as *tawhid, risalah, din, akhirah, ibadah, ilm, jihad, ijtihad, istihsan, shura,* brotherhood, *ummah, muhasabah, hudud, hisbah, islah, hikmah, haya, tazkiyah, waqf*—that are studied from multi- and inter-disciplinary perspectives. The world-view of Islam is presented as a country to be mapped. Qur'anic concepts form the basic grid of the map, and the Qur'an, the Sīrah, Shariah and Islamic history, the tools of understanding that are essential for mapping this country. Making a map of a country, like learning to deal with concepts, is essentially a process of becoming more self-conscious of one's environment. We may live in a country and know the mountains and rivers and our way around it. But we may not be objectively conscious of it in the way that one needs to if one is going to make a map of it. We can find our way from one town to another and know the green areas and the desert patches, but we cannot sketch it out on paper with any accuracy, because we do not know the country in *that particular way*. The student is asked to become self-conscious of concepts he may have taken for granted in multi- and inter-disciplinary frameworks. He learns to relate these concepts not just to history but to contemporary reality. He learns to deal with concepts and think within the world-view of Islam. He begins to shape Islamic perspectives on the issues of development, food problems, technological adjustment and other contemporary problems.

As an example, consider the concepts *din, mu'min, ummah, khilafah, shura, ita'at, Shari'ah, jihad* and *amwal* which must form the basis of any creditable Islamic political theory.[18] The student first discovers what the Qur'an has to say about these concepts and how Prophet Muhammad materialized them in the Medina State. He then discovers what the imaginative and thinking men of Islam have said about these concepts and how they were operationalized by other Islamic societies in history. He finally studies how the tools and methodologies of contemporary political science and other disciplines can be used to gain a fresh understanding of these concepts and how they can form the basis of a contemporary theory of Islam. Thus the student learns the Qur'an by becoming familiar with its basic concepts, he learns the *Sirah* by discovering the role these concepts played in the life of the Prophet, and he learns Islamic history not as a collection of dead and distant facts presented in a chronological fashion from pre-Islamic Arabia to the twentieth century but in terms of how these concepts were operationalized by previous Muslim societies. Multi- and inter-disciplinary analysis provides him with a contemporary insight into these concepts that he needs if he is to tackle the problems of his society. He feels the whole force of Islamic history as a living, dynamic reality. The process forced him to think and seek solutions from within the world-view of Islam.

It is clear that such an approach to Islamic studies cannot be divorced from research. The totalistic and dynamic approach of conceptual and multi- and inter-disciplinary analysis demands continuous research. In this framework learning is no longer a one-way traffic between authoritarian teachers and the taught. Teachers have to learn from learners. And research is the only criterion for teaching. The ideal place for Islamic studies in a university, therefore, is in an independent institute where research and teaching go hand in hand.

Theories, models, analysis—the characteristics that give a living form to a discipline—are conspicuous by their absence in contemporary Islamic studies. Concepts are the smallest units of theories and models. As terms combine to form sentences so concepts combine to form theories. To acquire a concept is primarily to learn, and to possess a concept is primarily to know. Moreover, to learn and possess a concept is to be able to *do* something—to develop a theory, devise a model, solve a problem. Both study and research are therefore important for conceptual analysis. By rooting Islamic studies firmly in multi- and inter-disciplinary conceptual analysis we can provide the future scholars of Islam with the essential mental furniture they need to serve the *ummah*. The challenges that await them cannot be underestimated. Conceptual analysis will give Islamic studies a meaning and provide it with a framework for thinking that might otherwise get lost under the weight of dead facts and meander indefinitely and purposelessly among the vast marshes of theological disputes.

Notes

1. Allama Muhammad Iqbal, 'Some thoughts on Islamic Studies' in *Thoughts and Reflections of Iqbal*, ed. by Syed Abdul Vahid Ashraf, Lahore, 1964, pp. 103–10.

2. *Ibid*. p. 105.

3. *Ibid*. p. 106.

4. *Ibid*.

5. A. M. Mohamed Mackeen, 'Islamic Studies as a University Disci-

pline', *Islamic Review*, **57** (5), 13–18 (May 1969).

6. *Ibid*. p. 15.

7. Nuri Eren, *Turkey Today and Tomorrow*, London, 1963, p. 201.

8. *Ibid*. p. 202.

9. Mackeen, *op. cit.* p. 16.

10. For an account of the history and modernization of al-Azhar, see Bayard Dodge, *Al-Azhar: A Millennium of Muslim Learning*, Middle East Institute, Washington, 1974.

11. For this development of the classical theory of Islamic education, see M. Nakosteen, *History of Islamic Origins of Western Education*, University of Colorado, Colorado, 1974; A. L. Tibawi, *Islamic Education*, Luzac, London, 1972, Chapters 1–3; and S. Waqar Ahmed Husaini, *Islamic Environmental Systems of Engineering*, Macmillan, London, 1980, Chapter 3.

12. A. M. Mohamed Mackeen, 'Islamic Studies as a University Discipline: Part 2', *Islamic Review*, **57** (6), 36–8 (June 1969), p. 36.

13. Marshall G. S. Hodgson, *The Venture of Islam*, University of Chicago Press, Chicago, 1974, vol. 1, p. 39.

14. Edward Said, *Orientalism*, R. and K. Paul, London, 1980. But see also the critiques of A. L. Tibawi, 'English Speaking Orientalists', *Islamic Quarterly*, **8** (3–4), 23–45 (1964) and 73–88 and **23** (1), 3–54 (1979) and 'On the Orientalists Again', *The Muslim World*, **70** (1), 56–61 (1980). See also the analysis of Abul-Hasan Ali Nadwi, *Western Civilization, Islam and Muslims*, Lucknow, 1974. For a list of references, see M. M. Ahsan, 'Orientalism and the Study of Islam in the West: A Select Bibliography', *Muslim World Book Review*, **1** (4), 51–60 (Summer 1981).

15. Longman, London, 1971.

16. Hodgson, *op. cit.* p. 26.

17. The Club of Rome has been responsible for a number of reports on the world *problematique*. The most famous is, of course, D. Meadows *et. al.*, *The Limits to Growth*, Potomac Associates, New York, 1972, which has been called 'the most important book of the twentieth century'. But a more enlightened work is by M. Mesoranic and E. Pestal, *Mankind at Turning Point*, Hutchinson, London, 1974. See also the two works of C. H. Waddington, *Man-Made Futures*, Croom Helm, London, 1978, and *Tool for Thought*, Jonathan Cape, London, 1977. Stephen Cotgrove has summarized the current 'futures' thinking in *Catastrophe or Cornucopia*, Wiley, Chichester, 1982. For a Muslim perspective on the future, see the present author's book, *The Future of Muslim Civilization*, Croom Helm, London, 1979.

18. In *The Nature of Islamic Political Theory*, Ma'ārif, Karachi, 1975, Muhammad Aziz Ahmad tries to develop an Islamic political theory based on the concepts of *din*, *mu'min*, *millat*, *mulk*, *khilafat*, *shūra*, *ita'at*, *shari'at*, *jihād*, *amwāl*, *amwal* and *khair*. This is as penetrating a conceptual analysis as one finds in contemporary Islamic scholarship. However, he could have gone much further by placing his study firmly within an inter-disciplinary perspective.

15

The Emerging Intellectuals

Apart from the fact that numerous new ideas have emerged from the political and cultural unrest that has become the characteristic feature of contemporary Muslim world, a whole new generation of young intellectuals have also recently appeared on the scene. The new intellectuals are a breed apart from the modernist scholars, who are mostly the product of the colonial period, and the traditionalist *ulama* who, on the whole, appear to be left over from a bygone age. What distinguishes the younger intellectuals, from their older contemporaries is their approach to Islam and their attitudes towards the West.

The traditional scholars have completely shunned the West. They regard the Western culture and mores as antithetical to the spirit of Islam. During the colonial period, they fought, physically and intellectually, for keeping the values and culture of Islam intact. But in the post-independence period, with the sole exception of Iran, the role of the *ulama* has been limited to making declarations against the West, issuing trivial *fatwas* (religious rulings) which have no bearing on contemporary reality, and generally wallowing in a nostalgia for the glorious Muslim past. In most countries, the *ulamas* have actually collaborated with the ruling powers to perpetuate the systems of injustice. What Ibraheem Sulaiman says of the *ulamas* in Nigeria is in fact true of *ulamas* throughout the Muslim world:

The *ulama* in Nigeria, being the symbol and conscience of a large proportion of the Nigerian population, hold the key to the future of the country. Are they up to this gigantic but noble task of inspiring this teeming multitude to take control of their destiny and thereby create the nation anew? Now given the propensity of the *ulama* to revel in conflicts and squabbles and to fight, even to the point of violence, over non-issues, and given their general inclination—with a few notable exceptions—towards oppressors among rulers and business communities; their lack of concern for the poor and the dispossessed as well a their aloofness from politics and social matters in general, one fears that the *ulama* are not equipped to play their rightful role in society.[1]

Unlike the *ulama*, modernist scholars do not shun the West. In fact, they embrace the West in its totality, warts and all. While the traditional scholars sit on the crest of contemporary times perpetually looking back into history, modernist intellectuals place no real value on Muslim tradition and history. Their basic function has been that of a traffic warden: directing the traffic of ideas, technology and cultural artifacts, without subtracting or adding an iota to it, into Muslim societies (see Figure 15.1). Intellectually, they have been responsible for the introduction of poor replicas of Western educational systems, the imposition of alienating high technology, rampant consumerism and vast destruction of cultural property in Muslim societies. The past three decades of development in the Muslim world have been years of modernism and its Muslim apologists. It is not surprising that they have led to revolution in Iran and upheavals in Pakistan, Egypt, Sudan and Turkey.

The modernist scholars fight for power and influence with Marxist intellectuals. They too serve as the preservers of European values in Muslim societies, although they have borrowed ideas not from the mainstream of the West, but from the Eastern bloc and radical Western groups. Intellectuals who use Marxist credit cards in Muslim establishments tend to be middle-class academics, teaching social sciences and liberal arts, sometimes specializing in Islamic studies and history of science; they tend on the whole to be social activists rather than ideologues. In the sixties and seventies they contributed some original insights into Muslim societies, but for the last decade or so, they have been trapped in a vicious methodology which leads only to political slogans and empty rhetoric. Moreover, Marxist intellectuals in Muslim societies have served as imposers of Western values and norms and conservers of exploitative structures because despite all the apparent concern for values in Marxist ideology, its methodology allows no room for the issues of and concerns of transcendental values and morality. In fact, the main impact of Marxist intellectuals in Muslim universities has been to strip the body politic of Muslim societies from all moral concerns. And where the Marxists have come into prominence, as for example in Pakistan under Zulfiqar Ali Bhutto, or acquired outright power, as in Algeria, they have abused power and shown themselves to be just as exploitative as modernist intellectuals.[2]

The fact that a large segment of the young generations of Muslims are completely disenchanged with the *ulamas*, modernist scholars and Marxist intellectuals is hardly surprising. This disenchantment has produced a new type of intellectual: deeply committed to Islam and appreciative of Muslim history and tradition, he is neither afraid of the West or Marx, nor does he regard them as a panacea for all ills. He is ready to see good in other systems of thought and action, and even ready to borrow those ideas which he can synthesize within the world-view of Islam. But his main concern is to develop a contemporary, integrated Islamic system of thought and action that presents a genuine alternative to the dominant system.

The new intellectual can be seen teaching and learning, arguing and discussing, at university campuses in Kuala Lumpur and Islamabad, Tehran and Damascus, Cairo and Khartoum, Rabat and Lagos, Aligarh and Ottawa, London and Chicago. Although this group is predominantly young, it is not exclusively so. After seeing what their thought and policies have done to Muslim societies in the last thirty years, some modernist scholars have shed their Western garments and begun to address themselves to the questions frequently raised by the new intellectuals. Similarly, a few Marxist Muslims, disillusioned with the confines of Marxist ideology and methodology, have joined the ranks of the emerging intellectuals. Even some traditional scholars are beginning to take account of the new thinking.

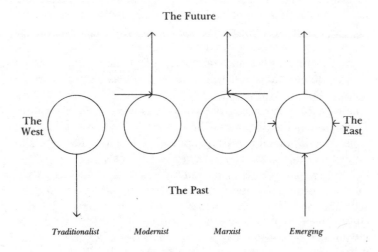

Figure 7. *Intellectuals in Muslim Societies*

While most modernists and Marxist scholars find the discussion on Islamic economics, Islamic science and 'Islamization of knowledge' quite bewildering, for the emerging intellectuals it is the starting point for developing a truly contemporary Islamic intellectual tradition and hence laying the foundations for a true resurgence of Islam. Their style is uncompromisingly Islamic, even aggressive, intellectually bold and without a trace of apology.

Many of the ideas discussed in this book are at an embyronic stage. While the establishment of an Islamic state has been the cherished goal of Muslim groups throughout the Muslim world, the political theory behind the concept of Islamic state has not yet fully evolved. Various attempts at 'Islamization of knowledge', while opening the whole area to new analysis and discussion, have achieved little so far. The discussion on the style and nature of contemporary Islamic science started just over a decade ago: enormous philosophical, sociological and practical work needs to be done before we can see the result of Islamic science policies. While work on Islamic economics has been going on for almost thirty years, the basic problems of the field, as we saw in Chapter 9, are still to be tackled. Islamic banks have not evolved alternative and viable structures; and Islamic economics has still not solved the problems of inflation and interest-free economies. An Islamic theory of environment is clearly emerging; the next step is to consolidate the ground and turn the emerging ideas into outline policies which can be promoted in Muslim countries. Most of the theoretical loose ends in these areas of epistemology, statehood, science, technology, economics and the environment can be solved if the Shariah can be developed as a problem-solving tool.

It is my belief that these problems will be solved, and the new ideas given concrete and practical shape, by the emerging group of young Muslim intellectuals. The thoughts and ideas of the more senior members of this group (albeit not a coherent one) have been quoted and mentioned throughout this book. Their strength lies in their ability to perceive Islam not as a mere religion but as a dynamic world-view, to synthesize the historical and the modern, and to appreciate the concerns of the traditional sectors of the Muslim population while possessing the intellectual apparatus to communicate with the modernists. This is a sharp departure from the isolated, fragmented and alienated intellectuals who have dominated the Muslim world since the colonial period. As the new thinkers are products of an age where borrowed ideologies and ideas have clearly been shown to be bankrupt, their confidence in Islamic alternatives is deep rooted: they are intellectually bold and have visions to match.

On the surface the contemporary Muslim world presents a bewildering array of stigmas and problems. But from the unrest and the accompanying social and political upheaval have emerged a host of ideas which collectively present a practical route to a Muslim civilization of the future. The unrest has also produced a new kind of scholar and intellectual who is not afraid to travel on that route. It is the fusion of new ideas and their practical implementation that will shape the destiny of the *ummah*. And it is this fusion which makes the immediate future such an exciting and challenging time to be a Muslim.

Notes

1. Ibraheem Sulaiman, 'Will the Nigerian Ulama Please Stand Up?', *Inquiry*, **2** (2), 45–7 (February 1985).

2. For a more detailed discussion of the plight of Marxist Muslim intellectuals, see my 'Victims of Methodology', *Afkar: Inquiry* **1** (3), 44–8 (August 1984).

Appendix

Islamic Council's Model of an Islamic Constitution

There have been surprisingly few efforts to give the Shariah a contemporary form. Where this exercise has been attempted, as for example in Pakistan, the emphasis has been on specific rules rather than general principles, imposing certain elements of the Shariah while violating certain others (see Chapters 4 and 5). The end results, not surprisingly, have produced confusion and belittled the Shariah.

The 'model' Islamic constitution developed by the Islamic Council, with the efforts of an international group of Muslim scholars, concerns itself primarily with integrating the essential principles of the Shariah into a contemporary constitution which any Muslim country can adopt easily. It emphasizes the equality of all men and women before the Creator, insists on strict observance of the Islamic code of human rights which regard 'human life, body, honour and freedom as sacred and inviolable', and reminds the Muslim countries of the world that they are part of one *Ummah*, one civilization. The model builds a constitutional structure around the Islamic concepts of *khalifa* (trusteeship of man), *adl* ('justice tempered with mercy') and *shura* (consultation in governance, policy formulation, decision making and exercise of authority). The general Shariah principle of 'promoting what is right and forbidding what is wrong' is introduced through the historic Islamic institution of *hisbah*; although the model constitution limits *hisbah* to the investigation of complaints against the State and its organs and the protection of individual. rights, it can be clearly extended to cover preservation of the environment and cultural property, industrial safeguards and protection of workers' rights, and many other areas.

Within the framework of this model, power cannot be acquired except through the consensus, or *ijma*, of the people (and that means elections), the Judiciary is completely independent, and basic human rights, including the rights of the minorities, are guaranteed. Moreover, a Muslim state is required to stand up for the rights of other countries and oppose power blocs seeking the exploitation and domination of weaker nations.

A study of the Islamic Council's 'Model Islamic Constitution', one of the best examples of recent efforts to contemporize the Shariah, clearly demonstrates that the behaviour of most Muslim countries is violently at odds with the ideals and norms of Islam.

Preamble

WHEREAS Islam is a complete code of life suitable for all people and all times, and Allah's mandate is universal and eternal and applies to every sphere of human conduct and life;

WHEREAS every individual has his own personal dignity;

WHEREAS all capabilities, individual and collective, and all power are a trust to be discharged within the terms laid down by the Shariah, to qualify for fulfilment of the Divine promise of a life free from want and oppression, and blessed with harmony, plenitude, security, health and fulfilment;

ACKNOWLEDGING that the setting up of a society based on Islam and its principles requires the complete application of the Shariah in the constitution and in the law, and that every individual under this order is able to undertake and fulfil his duty to himself, to his country and to all humanity;

We, the people of ...., commit ourselves to make the following the prime values of our socio-political order:

    (i) submission to Allah alone
   (ii) freedom governed by responsibility and discipline
  (iii) justice tempered with mercy
  (iv) equality strengthened by brotherhood
   (v) unity in diversity
  (vi) *shura* as the method of governance

We, the people of ...., therefore, hereby, by means of a referendum[1] held for this purpose on ...., assent to

1. Or by a resolution of a parliament or other competent body.

adopt this constitution, committing ourselves to the above principles and to a covenant to do our utmost to faithfully discharge our duties in accordance with them. And Allah is our witness.

Foundation of Authority and Basis of Society

Article 1
(a) Sovereignty belongs to Allah alone, and the Shariah is paramount.
(b) The Shariah—comprising the Qur'an and the Sunnah—is the source of legislation and policy.
(c) Authority is a trust which the people exercise in accordance with the Shariah.

Article 2
.... is part of the Muslim world and the Muslim people of .... are an integral part of the Muslim Ummah.

Article 3
The State and society are based on the following principles:
(a) The supremacy of the Shariah and its rules in all walks of life;
(b) *Shura* as the method of governance;
(c) The belief that everything in the universe belongs to Allah and is a blessing from Him to mankind, and that everyone is entitled to a just share in this Divine bounty;
(d) The belief that all natural resources are a trust (*amanah*) from Allah and that man is individually and collectively custodian (*mustakhlaf*) of these resources. Man's economic effort and its reward are determined within the framework of this trust;
(e) Inviolability of the Islamic code of human rights and obligation to support and defend the oppressed anywhere in the world;
(f) The paramount importance of inculcating an Islamic personality in the individual and in society, through Islamic education, cultural programmes, the media, and other means;
(g) Provision of opportunities for work to all able-bodied members of society and guarantee of the provision of the necessities of life for the disabled, the sick and the old;
(h) Provision of public services for all: health, education, cultural and social;
(i) Unity of the Ummah and unceasing efforts for its realization;
(j) Obligation to engage in *da'wah islamia*.

Obligations and Rights

Article 4

(a) Human life, body, honour and freedom are sacred and inviolable. No one shall be exposed to injury or death, except under the authority of the Shariah.

(b) As in life, so also after death, the sanctity of a person's body and honour is inviolable.

Article 5

(a) No person shall be exposed to torture of body, mind or threat of degradation or injury either to himself or to anyone related to him or otherwise held dear by him; nor shall he be made to confess to the commission of a crime, or forced to act or consent to an act which is injurious to his or another person's interests.

(b) Torture is a crime and shall be punishable irrespective of the passage of time.

Article 6

(a) Every person is entitled to the protection of his privacy.

(b) The right to privacy of home, correspondence and communication is guaranteed and cannot be violated except through the judicial process.

Article 7

Every person has the right to food, housing, clothing, education and medical care. The State is to take all necessary steps to provide the same to the extent of resources available.

Article 8

Every person has the right to his thoughts, opinions and beliefs. He also has the right to express them so long as he remains within the limits prescribed by law.[2]

Article 9

(a) All persons are equal before the law and are entitled to equal protection of the law.

(b) All persons of equal merit are entitled to equal opportunity, and to equal wages for equal work. No person may be discriminated against or denied the opportunity to work by reason of religious beliefs, colour, race, origin or language.

2. It is forbidden according to this constitution for any law to be contrary to the Shariah. Thus, wherever reference is made to 'law' it means the Shariah, or that which is permitted by the Shariah.

Article 10

(a) Every person shall be treated in accordance with the law and only in accordance with the law.

(b) All penal laws shall apply prospectively and shall not have retrospective effect.

Article 11

(a) No act shall be considered a crime and no punishment awarded therefor unless it is stipulated as such in the clear wording of the law.

(b) Every individual is responsible for his actions. Responsibility for a crime cannot be vicariously extended to other members of his family or group, who are not otherwise directly or indirectly involved in the commission of the crime in question.

(c) Every person is presumed to be innocent until finally adjudged guilty by a court of law.

(d) No person shall be adjudged guilty except after a fair trial and after reasonable opportunity for defence has been provided to him.

Article 12

(a) Every person has the right to protection against harassment or victimization by official agencies. No one is liable to account for himself except for making a defence to charges made against him or where he is found in a situation wherein a question regarding suspicion of his involvement in a crime could be reasonably raised.

(b) No person shall be subjected to any form of harassment while he is seeking to defend personal or public rights.

Article 13

(a) Every Muslim is entitled to found a family through marriage and to bring up children in conformity with the Shariah.

(b) Every husband is obliged to maintain his wife and children according to his means.

(c) Motherhood is entitled to special respect, care and assistance on the part of the family and the organs of State and society.

(d) Every child has the right to be maintained and properly brought up by his parents.

(e) Child labour is forbidden.

Article 14

(a) Citizenship shall be determined by law.

(b) Every Muslim has a right to seek citizenship of the State. This may be granted in accordance with law.

Article 15

Without any restriction unless imposed by law, every citizen has the right to freedom of movement to and from and within the country, and to stay within the country. No citizen shall be expelled from the country or prevented from returning to it.

Article 16

(a) There is no compulsion in religion.
(b) Non-Muslim minorities have the right to practise their religion.
(c) In matters of personal law the minorities shall be governed by their own laws and traditions, except if they themselves opt to be governed by the Shariah. In cases of conflict between parties, the Shariah shall apply.

Article 17

Every citizen over the age of ...... years has an obligation and a right to participate in the public affairs of the State.

Article 18

(a) Citizens have a right to assemble and to form groups, organizations and associations—political, cultural, scientific, social, and other—as long as their programmes and activities are consistent with the provisions of the Shariah.
(b) The formation and activities of such groups, organizations and associations shall be regulated by law.

Article 19

The State shall grant asylum to persons who seek it, in accordance with the law. The State shall extend security, protection and hospitality wherever necessary to those given asylum and the facility of safe passage if requested.

Majlis al Shura

Article 20

(a) There shall be a Majlis al Shura consisting of ...... members directly elected by the people.
(b) The term of the Majlis shall be ...... years.
(c) The qualifications for membership to the Majlis shall be established by law.

Article 21

The functions of the Majlis al Shura shall be:

(a) To legislate promoting the objectives of the Shariah, seeking the opinion of the Council of Ulema as necessary;
(b) To enact laws proposed by the government and by members of the Majlis al Shura;

(c) To approve the financial programmes and budgets and accounts of the government and public bodies receiving or using state funds;

(d) To review policies of the government and its different departments, by questioning and interpellation of the respective Ministers; and to investigate or authorize investigation of departments and institutions established under law;

(e) To authorize the declaration of war or peace or national emergency;

(f) To approve treaties and international agreements and undertakings.

Article 22

Members of the Majlis al Shura are free to express their views during the execution of their duties, and may not be arrested, prosecuted harassed or removed from membership of the Majlis al Shura for so doing.

The Imam

Article 23

(a) The Imam[3] shall be the Chief Executive of the State, who shall be elected by an absolute majority of the country's voters[4] for a term of ...... years, commencing from the date the *bay'ah* is offered to him by the Majlis al Bay'ah.

(b) The Imam shall be accountable to the people and to the Majlis al Shura, as stipulated by the law.

Article 24

A person qualified for election to the office of Imam shall be:

(a) A Muslim not under ...... years of age;

(b) Of unblemished character;

(c) Known to be following the injunctions of the Qur'an and the Sunnah, committed to Islam and knowledgeable in the Shariah;

(d) Physically, mentally and emotionally fit to discharge the obligations of the office;

(e) Of courteous bearing and balanced behaviour.

Article 25

Before taking office, the Imam shall make a declaration of commitment, before a National Assembly (Majlis al Bay'ah) consisting of members of the Majlis al Shura, the Council of Ulema, the Supreme Constitutional Council, the higher judiciary, the Election Commission, and the Heads

3. The Imam could be called by any other appropriate title, such as Amir, President, etc.
4. Direct election is suggested here, but indirect election through elected representatives of the people is also possible.

of the Armed Forces, to follow the Shariah in letter and in spirit, to uphold the message of Islam at all costs, to obey the mandate of the constitution and to defend the territorial, ideological, political and economic independence of the State, and the rights of the people, and to ensure justice to all members of the society without discrimination, and without fear or favour, and be available to them directly or through appropriate agencies for the redress of their grievances. On his making this commitment, all the participants shall offer him *bay'ah* on the above terms on their own behalf and on behalf of the people.

Article 26

The Imam is entitled to obedience by all persons even if their views differ from his. There is, however, no obedience if it involves disobedience of Allah and His Prophet (peace be upon him).

Article 27

The Imam shall enjoy the same rights as other citizens. He is subject to all the obligations of law, without any special immunity or executive privilege.

Article 28

(a) The Imam shall not purchase or hire any state property, nor shall he rent or sell his own property to the State, nor shall he engage himself in any business within the country or outside.

(b) Gifts presented to the Imam and his family or to other officials of the State in their official capacity shall be treated as public property.

Article 29

The Imam shall have no power to overrule the decision of a court, or to change or annul or delay the punishment a court has resolved against anyone guilty of the *hudud*, *qisas* or *diyah*. He may, however, exercise his power of clemency in all other cases.

Article 30

The Imam or his duly authorised representative shall enter into pacts, conventions, treaties and other agreements negotiated by them with other governments and with international organizations.

Article 31

The Imam shall assent to legislation passed by the Majlis al Shura and then forward it to the concerned authorities for implementation. He shall not have the right to veto legislation passed by the Majlis; however, he may refer it back to the Majlis only once, within 30 days from the date of receipt, for reconsideration with his arguments. On return of the legislation after reconsideration, if passed by a two-thirds majority of the members of the Majlis al Shura, he shall assent to the legislation.

Article 32

The Imam shall appoint adivsors, ministers, ambassadors and the heads of the Armed Forces.

Article 33

(a) The Imam shall be impeached if he intentionally violates the provisions of the constitution, or for wanton violation of the Shariah, by a resolution to that effect by a two-thirds majority of the members of the Majlis al Shura, and, if it is found that he has violated the *bay'ah*, the *bay'ah* would be annuled by approval of a two-thirds majority of the Majlis al Bay'ah.

(b) Rules and procedures to govern the impeachment and removal of the Imam shall be determined by law.

Article 34

(a) The Imam may resign his office under his own signature by submitting his resignation to the Majlis al Shura.

(b) In case of vacancy of the office of the Imam, the Speaker of the Majlis al Shura shall act as Imam until elections for filling the vacancy are held, within a maximum period of ...... days from the date of vacancy.

(c) In case of disability of the Imam, the Speaker of the Majlis al Shura shall act as Imam until the Imam resumes his duties within ...... days. Otherwise, the office of the Imam shall be considered vacant.

Judiciary

Article 35

Everyone shall have the right to present a case before the courts.

Article 36

(a) The judiciary is independent and free from all influence of the executive and is responsible for the administration of justice and the protection of the rights and obligations of the people.

(b) The judges are independent and there is no authority above them except the authority of the law.

Article 37

Dispensation of justice shall be free and the law shall protect this dispensation from misuse.

Article 38

All court proceedings shall be in public and not in camera except when sanctions by the court for protection of personal secrets or honour or out of consideration of national security or public decency.

Article 39

(a) The establishment of special courts or tribunals is not permitted.

(b) However, military courts shall be established to try members of the Armed Forces for acts which constitute offences only under military law. They shall be tried in the civil courts for all other offences.

Article 40

Implementation of court decisions is the duty of every concerned person exercising public authority, and slackness or failure to implement them is an offence liable to punishment, according to law.

Article 41

In consonance with the principles contained in this constitution, the organizational structure of the judiciary, qualifications of the judges and procedures for their appointment, transfer and removal, relationships with the executive and legislature and related matters, shall be established by law.

Article 42

There shall be an establishment of *Hisbah* for:

(a) The promotion and protection of Islamic values with a view to establishing what is right and forbidding what is wrong;

(b) The investigation of complaints by individuals against the State and its organs;

(c) The protection of individual rights;

(d) The review of the work of officials of the State, and rectification of cases of maladministration, neglect or dereliction of duty on their part;

(e) Monitoring and examining the legality of administrative decisions.

Article 43

There shall be a Muhtasib Aam as the head of the organization of *Hisbah* in the country assisted by muhtasibs at provincial and lower levels, and the rules and procedures relating to this office shall be established by law.

Article 44

The muhtasibs shall be able to act on their own initiative or on application or information received from others. They shall have the power to obtain relevant information and records from any government department or public agency, and officials shall be obliged to respond promptly and affirmatively to their demands.

Article 45

If the Muhtasib Aam considers a law or regulation oppressive or unreasonable, in that it causes difficulty or undue hardship in obedience, or if it appears to be unconstitutional, he shall have the power to refer to law or regulation in question to the appropriate judicial authority for its annulment or amendment.

Article 46

A muhtasib shall not take cognizance of a case of which cognizance has already been taken, or is being taken, by a court of competent jurisdiction.

Economic Order

Article 47

The economic order shall be based on the Islamic principles of justice, equity, human dignity, freedom of enterprise, balanced relationships and prevention of extravagant spending. It shall seek to mobilize and develop the human and material resources of society, in a planned and harmonious manner, to satisfy the spiritual, material and social needs of all members of the community.

Article 48

It is the duty of the State to develop all sources of energy and wealth and to put them to optimum use, and to ensure that they are not hoarded, wasted or kept idle. Individuals shall be permitted to participate in this process within the limits prescribed by law.

Article 49

(a) All natural and energy resources belong originally to the society as do enterprises and institutions established through the public exchequer.

(b) Private ownership of wealth is lawful and protected provided that it is acquired by means that are held legitimate and is retained and used for purposes allowed by the Shariah.

(c) No publically owned property or interest can be liquidated except in cases of necessity to the interests of the society; and no privately owned property or interest can be expropriated by the State except in cases of necessity to the public interest and on prompt payment of fair and adequate compensation.

Article 50

(a) Freedom of enterprise is guaranteed within the limits prescribed by law.

(b) All kinds of profit or spending contrary to the Shariah are forbidden.

(c) Confiscation of any legally and legitimately gained profit or entitlement is forbidden.

Article 51

Money being a medium of exchange and a measure of value, no monetary or fiscal policy is legitimate which destabilizes the value of money or contributes to its erosion.

Article 52

All wealth and property not owned by private individuals or organizations shall vest in the State.

Article 53

Riba, monopoly, hoarding, profiteering and exploitation, and other such anti-social practices are forbidden.

Article 54

The State shall take all such measures as may be necessary to terminate and prevent foreign economic domination.

Article 55

There shall be an Economic and Social Council consisting of persons specializing in socioeconomic affairs and the Shariah, which shall:
(a) participate in the economic decision-making in the country for the realization of the socio-economic obligations stipulated in this constitution;
(b) advise the government and the Majlis al Shura on economic and social planning and budgeting and other socio-economic matters.

Article 56

The composition of the Economic and Social Council, its rules and procedures shall be established by law.

Defence

Article 57

(a) *Jihad* is a perpetual and inalienable duty.
(b) It is incumbent on every Muslim to defend the Land of Islam and the Islamic order.

Article 58

(a) The State shall be responsible for building viable Armed Forces consistent with its resources and capable of fulfilling the demands of *jihad*.
(b) The State shall take all necessary steps to enable the people to perform the duty of *jihad*.
(c) In addition to military training there shall be a programme of Islamic education and training to inculcate in the Armed Forces the concept of *jihad*.

Article 59
(a) The Imam is the Commander-in-Chief of the Armed Forces.
(b) He is empowered to declare war or peace or a national emergency on authorization from the Majlis al Shura.

Article 60
A Supreme Jihad Council shall be established to formulate the strategy for war and peace. The composition of the Council, its rules and procedures shall be established by law.

Supreme Constitutional Council

Article 61
There shall be a Supreme Constitutional Council—an independent judicial body—which shall be the guardian of the constitution and of the Islamic character of the State.

Article 62
The Council's functions shall include:
(a) Ruling on any question which arises of a law being repugnant to the Shariah;
(b) Interpretation of the constitution and the law;
(c) Deciding cases of conflict in jurisdiction;
(d) Hearing and ruling on complaints against the Election Commission.

Article 63
(a) Rules and procedures for the composition of the Supreme, Constitutional Council, qualifications of its members, terms of their appointment, removal or retirement, and related matters, and the mode of operation of the Council shall be established by law.
(b) The afore-mentioned law shall be passed or amended by a two-thirds majority of the members of the Majlis al Shura.

Council of Ulema

Article 64
The Council of Ulema shall comprise persons well-versed in the Shariah, who are known for their piety, God-consciousness and depth of knowledge and who have deep insight into contemporary issues and challenges.

Article 65
The functions of the Council of Ulema shall be:
(a) The application of juridical *ijihad*;

(b) To explain the stand of the Shariah on various legislative proposals before the Majlis al Shura;

(c) To fulfil the Islamic obligation of declaring the truth and pronouncing judgement without procrastination on issues affecting the Muslim Ummah.

Article 66

Rules for the formation of the Council of Ulema, its composition, qualifications of its members and other relevant matters shall be determined by law.

Election Commission

Article 67

There shall be an independent permanent Election Commission consisting of .... members.

Article 68

The functions of the Commission shall be:

(a) To organize, supervise and hold elections to the office of the Imam and to membership of the Majlis al Shura and other offices in accordance with the law;

(b) To organize, supervise and hold referenda;

(c) To ensure that candidates for elective offices fulfil the conditions stipulated by law.

Article 69

(a) Members of the Commission shall be appointed from amongst the sitting members of the senior judiciary of the State.

(b) Any person while a member of the Election Commission shall be ineligible for any other post.

Article 70

The rules and procedures concerning appointment to the Election Commission and other allied matters shall be provided by law. This law, while making provisions for organizing, supervising and holding elections, shall: determine the qualifications of the electors and assure fair delineation of constituencies, filing and determining of nominations, voting procedures, declaration of election results and assure secrecy of ballots.

Article 71

All public authorities and public servants shall act in aid of the Election Commission to enable it to discharge its constitutional obligations, and obey its commands directly and promptly without leave or consent of any other authority.

Unity of Ummah and International Relations

Article 72

It is the duty of the State to strive by all possible means to seek the unity and the solidarity of the Muslim Ummah.

Article 73

The foreign policy of the State and the conduct of its international relations shall be based on the principles of freedom, justice and peace in the world and shall strive to attain the welfare and well-being of mankind.

Article 74

The State is opposed to all actions, policies and programmes based on inequality, and is committed to strive actively against them to the best of its capabilities.

Article 75

In addition to the above, the State is duty-bound to fulfil the following obligations deriving from the principles and injunctions of Islam:

(a) To protect the freedom of man throughout the world;

(b) To struggle and to strive to end oppression and persecution of the people wherever and whenever it occurs in the world;

(c) To protect and observe the sanctity of all places of God's worship.

Article 76

(a) The State is obligated to refrain from engaging in wars on grounds of difference in religious belief, or for the exploitation of other people's resources and to control their economies.

(b) War is permitted to defend the faith, the territorial and ideological integrity of the State, to defend the oppressed and persecuted of the world, to protect the honour, dignity and freedom of man, and to preserve peace in the world.

Article 77

The State shall oppose power blocs and groups seeking the exploitation and domination of weaker nations.

Article 78

The State shall not allow the establishment of foreign military bases or the provision of military facilities to foreign powers which might in any way impinge on the sovereignty of the State or be prejudicial to its interests or to the interests of other Muslim states.

Article 79

The State shall honour and implement international treaties, pacts, agreements and obligations in letter and in spirit.

The Mass Media and Publications

Article 80

The mass media and publications have full freedom of expression and presentation of information so long as they respect and adhere to facts and to the norms and values of Islam. The freedom to publish newspapers and journals shall be permitted within these limits and the closing or censuring of the news media shall be through judicial procedure, except in times of war.

Article 81

The mass media and publications are obliged to:

(a) Expose and protest against oppression, injustice and tyranny, regardless of whomever is guilty of such acts;

(b) Respect the privacy of individuals and refrain from prying into their personal affairs;

(c) Refrain from inventing and circulating slander, calumny and rumour;

(d) Express the truth and scrupulously avoid spreading falsehood or mixing the truth with falsehood or knowingly concealing the truth or distorting it;

(e) Use decent and dignified language;

(f) Promote the right conduct and ethical values in society;

(g) Strictly refrain from the dissemination of indecency, obscenity and immorality;

(h) Avoid condoning or glorifying crimes or acts repugnant to Islam;

(i) Refrain from suppressing evidence except in so far as it might cause harm to the interests of society;

(j) Avoid becoming instruments of corruption of any kind.

Article 82

The executive organs of the State shall have no authority to take any administrative action against or to penalize the media or publications in any way except to prosecute violations in a court of law. Similarly, media and publications' personnel are protected in the performance of their professional duties.

General and Transitional Provisions

Article 83

Hijrah is the official calendar of the State and the offical language is .... If Arabic is not the official language, it shall be the second official language.

Article 84

(a) The Imam or the Majlis al Shura may propose amendments to this constitution. Amendments may only be made if approved by a two-thirds majority of the members of the Majlis al Shura.

(b) Any amendment which might endanger the Islamic character of the State, or which violates the tenets of the Shariah, would be void.

Article 85

(a) The legislative, executive and judicial authorities and all bodies, institutions and organizations existing at the time of the coming into effect of this constitution shall continue to exercise their functions and activities until the establishment of substitutes in accordance with the provisions of the constitution and the assumption of functions by such substitutes.

(b) All laws, regulations and decrees in operation at the time of the coming into effect of this constitution shall continue to be in operation until annulled or amended in accordance with the provisions set out in this constitution.

(c) After the adoption of this constitution, and in keeping with the provisions of this constitution, the existing legislative authority shall, through an appropriate law, take necessary steps to establish the first Majlis al Shura, the first Election Commission and the first Supreme Constitutional Council.

Article 86

There is an imperative obligation on everyone concerned to ensure that the provisions of this constitution are implemented effectively and without delay so that the constitution becomes effective in its entirety as soon as possible after its adoption.

Article 87

This constitution is applicable from ...., the date on which the results of the referendum were published (if adopted by means of a referendum) or the date it was adopted by the country's constitutional body.

Glossary

Amanah	A trust from God.
Bay'ah	The pledge of allegiance to the ruler of a Muslim community within the framework of the Shariah.
Da'wah Islamia	The call to Islam.
Diyah	Compensation paid according to law or mutual agreement in cases of murder or physical injury.

Hijrah	The migration of the Prophet and his companions from Makkah to Madina in 622. The Muslim lunar calendar is dated from this event.
Hisbah	The institution for supervising and safeguarding the fulfilment of right norms of public behaviour. Its purpose is to enforce what is right (*Maruf*) and forbid what is wrong (*Munkar*).
Hudud	(Plural of *Hadd*). The specific penalities prescribed by the Qur'an and Sunnah for certain specified crimes.
Ijtihad	The exercise of independent judgement to ascertain the appropriate Shariah ruling.
Imam	Leader of the Muslim community or head of a Muslim state.
Jihad	Literally striving and struggle: mental, moral or physical. It has come to mean engaging in a just war for the defence of the faith, of the Islamic state, or of the rights of oppressed people.
Khalifa	Representative. In the Qur'an (2:30) the title *Khalifa* has been given to Adam and by extension to all mankind, and signifies that God has made mankind His representative or vicegerent on earth with limited authority to fulfil His will. (Spelled *Khilafah* in the text.)
Majlis al Bay'ah	The body which, representing a Muslim community, formally offers the oath of allegiance to the ruler.
Majlis al Shura	Consultative Assembly.
Majlis al Ulema	Council of religious experts.
Muhtasib	In charge of Hisbah.
Muhtasib Aam	Chief Muhtasib.
Mustakhlaf	Khalifa.
Qisas	Just retribution in cases of crime against person.
Riba	Usury. Fixed interest.
Shariah	Islamic law governing all aspects of human life.
Shura	Decision making through consultations.
Sunnah	The traditions of the Prophet, comprising what he said, did and approved.
Ulema	Religious experts.
Ummah	The Muslim community.

References

Foundation of Authority and Basis of Society
1. Qur'an Yusuf *12:67*
   Qur'an Al-Jathiyah *45:18*
   Qur'an An-Nisa *4:58*
   Hadith narrated by Bukhari, Muslim,
   Abu Daud, Tirmidhi, Nasai
2. Qur'an Al-Muninun *23:52*
   Qur'an Al-Hujurat *49:10*
   Qur'an Al-Anfal *8:72*
3. Qur'an An-Nisa *4:105*
   Qur'an Al-Jathiyah *45:18*
   Qur'an Al-Maidah *5:44, 45, 47*
   Qur'an Ash-Shura *42:38*
   Qur'an Al-Maidah *5:120*
   Qur'an At-Tawbah *9:105*
   Qur'an Al-Hadid *57:7*
   Qur'an An-Nisa *4:75*
   Qur'an At-Tawbah *9:122*
   Qur'an At-Tawbah *9:105*
   Qur'an Al-Imran *3:103*
   Hadith narrated by Bukhari, Muslim
   Hadith narrated by Ibn Majah
   Qur'an Al-Maidah *5:67*
   Qur'an Yusuf *12:108*
   Qur'an An-Nahl *16:125*
   Hadith narrated by Bukhari

Obligations and Rights
4. Qur'an Al-Isra *17:33*
   Qur'an Al-Maidah *5:32*
   Hadith narrated by Muslim
   Hadith narrated by Bukhari, Muslim,
   Abu Daud, Tirmidhi, Nasai
   Hadith narrated by Bukhari
5. Qur'an Al-Ahzab *33:58*
   Hadith narrated by Ibn Majah
   Hadith narrated by Bukhari, Muslim,
   Abu Daud, Tirmidhi, Nasai

Bibliography

Abdalla, I. S., *et al. Images of Arab Future*, Frances Pinter, London, 1983.

Abdalla, A. *Iran's Revolution: Causes and Consequences*, Tanzeem Publishers, Karachi, 1979.

Abu Lughod, I. (editor). 'The Islamic Alternative'. Special Issue, *Arab Studies Quarterly*, **4** (1–2) (Spring 1982).

Ahmad, Anis. 'The future of the jihad movement in Afghanistan: a review', *Al-Ittihad*, **17** (3) 23–9 (1980).

Ahmad, Khurshid (editor). *Islam: Its Meaning and Message*, Islamic Council of Europe, London, 1975.

——— 'Some aspects of character building in Islam', *The Muslim*, **8** (1) 9–15 (1970) and **8** (2) 39–42 (1970).

——— 'Economic development in an Islamic framework', in *Studies in Islamic Economics*, edited by Khurshid Ahmad, Islamic Foundation, Leicester, 1980.

——— 'What an Islamic journey!' *Muslim World Book Review*, **2** (3) 13–22 (Spring 1982).

——— 'What is wrong with western perception of Islamic resurgence?' *Muslim World Book Review*, **5** (2) 3–6 (Winter 1985).

Ahmed, Mashhood. 'Islamic ethos and Muslim scientists', *MAAS Journal of Islamic Science*, **1** (1) 56–68 (1985).

Ahmad, M. *Islamic Political System in the Modern World*, Saad Publications, Karachi, 1983.

Ahmad, M. A. *The Nature of Islamic Political Theory*, Maaref, Karachi, 1975.

Ahmad, Rais and Ahmad, S. N. (editors). *Quest for New Science*, Centre for Science Studies, Aligarh, 1985.

Ahsan, Manazir. 'Islamic resurgence—an unbroken thread', *Inquiry*, **1** (4) 53–5 (1984).

——— and Anees, M. A. 'Contemporary Islamic resurgence—a select bibliogrpahy', *Muslim World Book Review*, **2** (4) 55–67 (1982).

Algar, Hamid. *Religion and State in Iran, 1785–1906*, University of California Press, Berkeley, 1969.

——— 'The oppositional role of the ulama in twentieth century Iran', in *Scholars, Saints and Sufis*, edited by N. Keddie, University of California Press, Berkeley, 1972.

——— *The Roots of Islamic Revolution*, Open Press, London, 1980.

Al-i-Ahmad, Jalal. *Occidentosis: A Plague from the West*, translated by Hamid Algar, Mizan Press, Berkeley, 1984.

Amilcar, O. H., *et al. Catastrophe or a New Society?* International Development Research Centre, Ottawa, 1976.

Anees, M. A. 'Islamic science—an antidote to reductionism' *Afkar/Inquiry*, **1** (2) 49 (July 1984).

——— 'Brave new DNA—Is man playing God?' *Inquiry*, **1** (6) 45–8 (November 1984).

——— 'Cloning better futures?' *Inquiry*, **2** (5) 48–51 (May 1985).

——— 'Islamic values and western science: a case study of reproductive biology', in *The Touch of Midas*, edited by Ziauddin Sardar, *op. cit.*

——— and Athar, A. N. 'Development of higher education and scientific research in the Arab World', *Journal of South Asian and Middle Eastern Studies*, **2** (3) 93–100 (Spring 1979).

——— and ——— 'Significance of scientific, technical and social information in the Muslim World', *Al-Ittihad*, **17** (1) 46–52 (1980).

Ansari, M. A. H. 'The future of Islamic mission', *Islam and the Modern Age*, **13** (1) 56–9 (1982).

Asad, Muhammad. *The Principles of State and Government in Islam*, Dar al-Andalus, Gibraltar, 1980.

——— *Islam at the Crossroads*, Ashraf, Lahore, 1940.

Asaria, M. I. 'Tabung Hajji—the Malay way to Mecca', *Inquiry*, **2** (1) 26–31 (January 1985).

——— 'Constructing the edifice of homo Islamicus', *Inquiry*, **2** (4) 28–33 (April 1985).

Askari, H. *Society and State in Islam*, Progressive Books, Lahore, 1979.

al-Attas, S. M. N. *Islam, Secularism and the Philosophy of the Future*, Mansell, London, 1985.

Audah, A. Q. *Islam Between Ignorant Followers and Incapable Scholars*, IIFSO, Kuwait, 1971.

Ayoob, M. *Arabism and Islam: The Persian Gulf in World Politics*, Australian Institute of International Affairs, Canberra, 1980.

——— (editor). *The Politics of Islamic Reassertion*, Croom Helm, London, 1981.

Ayub, Hamid. 'Alternative technology—a cross-section', *The Muslim Scientist*, **8** (4) 1–6 (1979).

Azzam, A. R. *The Eternal Message of Muhammad*, Quarter, London, 1979.

Azzam, Salem (editor). *Islam and Contemporary Society*, Longman, London, 1982.

Badawi, M. A. Z. *The Reformers of Egypt*, Croom Helm, London, 1979.

Barnes, B. *T S Kuhn and Social Sciences*, Macmillan, London, 1982.

Barnett, A. *The Gezira Scheme—An Illusion in Development*, Frank Cass, London, 1977.

Behbehani, K., Girgis, M. and Marzouk, M. S. (editors). *Proceedings of the Symposium on Science and Technology for Development in Kuwait*, Longman, London, 1981.

Blake, G. H. and Lawless, R. I. (editors). *The Changing Middle East City*, Croom Helm, London, 1980.

Bolitho, Hector. *Jinnah—Creator of Pakistan*, John Murray, London, 1954.

Bloor, D. *Knowledge and Social Imagery*, Routledge and Kegan Paul, London, 1976.

Blunt, W. C. *The Future of Islam*, London, 1882; reprinted by Sind Sagar Academy, Lahore, 1975.

Braibanti, R. 'The recovery of Islamic identity in global perspective', in *The Rose and the Rock: Mystical and Rational Elements in the Intellectual History of South Asian Islam*, edited by Bruce Lawrence, Carolina Academic Press, North Carolina, 1979.

Bucaille, Maurice. *The Bible, the Qur'an and Science*, Seghers, Paris, 1980.

Cetron, M. and O'Toole, T. *Encounters with the Future*, McGraw-Hill, New York, 1982.

Chapra, M. U. *Towards a Just Monetary System*, Islamic Foundation, Leicester, 1985.

Cleron, J. P. *Saudi Arabia 2000: A Strategy for Growth*, Croom Helm, London, 1978.

Cotsgrove, S. *Catastrophe or Cornucopia? The Environment, Politics and the Future*, Wiley, Chichester, 1982.

Council for Science and Society. *Superstar Technologies*, Barry Rose, London, 1976.

——— *The Acceptability of Risk*, Barry Rose, London, 1976.

—— *Scholarly Freedom and Human Rights*, Barry Rose, London, 1977.

Cudsio, S. A. and Dessouki, A. E. H. (editors). *Islam and Power*, Croom Helm, London, 1981.

Daghestani, F. A., Qasim, S. and Sakat, B. (editors). *Science and Technology for Development: Jordan's Science Policy Conference*, Royal Scientific Society, Amman, 1981.

Dar. B. A. *Qur'anic Ethics*, Institute of Islamic Culture, Lahore, 1960.

—— *Religious Thought of Sayyid Ahmad Khan*, Institute of Islamic Culture, Lahore, 1971.

Darling, F. C. *The Westernisation of Asia*, G. K. Hall, Boston, 1979.

Davies, Merryl Wyn. 'Towards an Islamic alternative of Western anthropology', Inquiry, **2** (6) 45–51 (June 1985).

De Jouvenel, B. *The Art of Conjecture*, Basic Books, New York, 1967.

De Kmejla, R. H. 'The anatomy of Islamic revival: legitimacy, crisis, ethnic conflict and the search for Islamic alternatives', *Middle East Journal*, **34** (91) 1–12 (Winter 1980).

Dessouki, A. E. H. (editor). *Islamic Resurgence in the Arab World*, Praeger, New York, 1982.

Donohue, J. and Esposito, J. H. *Islam in Transition: Religion and Sociopolitical Change*, Syracuse University Press, 1982.

Earthscan. 'The Gulf: pollution and development', Briefing Document No. 24, London, 1980.

El-Awa, M. S. *On the Political System of the Islamic State*, American Trust Publications, Indianapolis, 1980.

Enayat, Hamid. 'The resurgence of Islam. the background', *History Today*, **30**, February 1980, 16–22.

—— *Modern Islamic Political Thought*, Macmillan, London, 1982.

Esposito, J. L. (editor). *Islam and Development: Religion and Sociopolitical Change*, Syracuse University Press, 1980.

El-Fandy, M. G. 'Islam and science', *Journal of World Muslim League*, **1** (8) 39–40 (1974).

Faruki, K. A. *Islamic Jurisprudence*, Pakistan Publishing House, Karachi, 1962.

—— *The Evolution of Islamic Constitutional Theory and Practice from 622 to 1926*, National Publishing House, Karachi, 1971.

Al-Faruqi, I. R. 'Science and traditional values in Islamic society', *Zygon*, **2** (3) 231–46 (1967).

—— *Islamisation of Knowledge*, International Institute of Islamic Thought, Washington, 1982.

—————— and Naseef, A. O. (editors). *Social and Natural Sciences: The Islamic Perspective*, Hodder and Stoughton, London, 1981.

Faruqi, N. A. *Early Muslim Historiography*, Idarah-i Adabiyat-i Delli, Delhi, 1979.

Fathy, Hasan. *Architecture for the Poor*, Chicago University Press, Chicago, 1973.

Ford, G. 'A framework for a new view of Islamic science', *Adiyat Halab* **4/5** 68–74 (1978/79).

—————— 'Rebirth of Islamic science', in *The Touch of Midas, op. cit.*

—————— 'Liberating science with Islamic values', *Afkar/Inquiry*, **1** (2) 50–1 (July 1984).

Feathers, Frank. (editor). *Through the 80s: Thinking Globally, Acting Locally*, World Future Society, Washington, 1980.

Feyerabend, Paul. *Against Method*, New Left Books, London, 1975.

Funston, N. J. *Malay Politics in Malaysia: A Study of the United Malay National Organization and Party Islam*, Kaula Lumpur, 1980.

Gauhar, A. *The Challenge of Islam*, Islamic Council of Europe, London, 1978.

Al-Ghazzali. *The Book of Knowledge*, translated by Nabih Amin Faris, Ashraf, Lahore, 1966.

Gilsenan, M. 'The spectre of Islam', *Issues*, April 1980.

Goldsmith, E. and Hildyard, N. *The Social and Environmental Effects of Large Dams*, Wadebridge Ecological Centre, Powys, 1984 (2 vols.).

Goonatilake, Susantha. *Crippled Minds: An Exploration into Colonial Culture*, Vikas, Delhi, 1982.

—————— *Aborted Discovery: Science and Creativity in the Third World*, Zed Press, London, 1984.

Goulet, Denis. *The Cruel Choice*, Atheneum, New York, 1973.

Haddad, Y. Y. *Contemporary Islam and the Challenge of History*, State University of New York Press, Albany, 1981.

Haider, Gulzar. 'Habitat and values in Islam: a conceptual formulation of an Islamic city', in *The Touch of Midas*, edited by Ziauddin Sardar *op. cit.*

—————— 'Heritage and harmony', *Inquiry*, **2** (2) 39–44 (1985).

—————— 'The city never lies', *Inquiry*, **2** (6) 38–44 (1985).

Hamidullah, M. *The First Written Constitution in the World*, Ashraf, Lahore, 1970.

—————— *Introduction to Islam*, Islamic Cultural Centre, Paris, 1970.

—————— *Muhammad Rasulullah*, Huzaifa Publications, Karachi, 1979.

Hanafi, H. *The Origin of Modern Conservatism and Islamic Fundamentalism in Egypt*, Amsterdam, 1979.

Haq, S. 'The Qur'an and modern cosmologies', *Science and Technology in the Islamic World*, **1** 47–52 (1983).

Hasan, A. *The Doctrine of Ijma in Islam*, Islamic Research Institute, Islamabad, 1978.

Hasan, Ibnul (editor). *In search of An Islamic Economic Model*, New Century, London, 1983.

Hashmi, Z. A. 'Future opportunities and challenges for science and technology in the Muslim World', Document ICSIP-5, International Conference on Science in Islamic Polity, Islamabad, 1983.

Hassan, M. K. *Muslim Intellectual Response to 'New Order' Modernisation in Indonesia*, Kuala Lumpur, 1980.

Haykal, M. H. *The Life of Muhammad*, translated by I. R. al-Faruqi, American Trust Publications, Indianapolis, 1976.

Henderson, Hazel. *Creating Alternative Futures*, Berkley Publishing, New York, 1978.

—————— *The Politics of the Solar Age*, Anchor, New York, 1981.

—————— 'Post-economic policies for post-industrial societies', *Revision*, **7** (2) 20–9 (Winter 1984).

Hodgson, M. G. S. *The Venture of Islam*, University of Chicago Press, 1971 (3 vols).

Hoffman, K. and Rush, H. 'Microelectronics, industry and the Third World', *Futures*, **12** (4) 289–302 (1980).

Husaini, W. A. *Islamic Environmental System Engineering*, Macmillan, London, 1980.

Hussain, Asaf. *Islamic Movements in Egypt, Pakistan and Iran: An Annotated Bibliography*, Mansell, London, 1983.

Hussain, M. H. and Kamali, A. H. *The Nature of the Islamic State*, National Book Foundation, Karachi, 1977.

Idris, G. S. *The Process of Islamization*, Muslim Students' Association, Plainsfield, Indiana, 1977.

—————— 'The Islamic ways of developing nations', in *Proceedings of the Eighth Annual Convention of the Association of Muslim Social Scientists*, Plainsfield, Indiana, 1982.

Inquiry. 'Pakistan: a blueprint for return to civilian rule', **1** (1) 13–15 (June 1984).

Iqbal, Sir Muhammad. 'Some thoughts on Islamic studies', in *Thoughts and Reflections of Iqbal*, edited by Syed Abdul Vahid, Ashraf, Lahore, 1964.

—— *The Reconstruction of Religious Thought in Islam*, Ashraf, Lahore, 1971 (reprint).

Iqbal, M. and Khan, M. F. *A Survey of Issues and a Programme of Research in Monetary and Fiscal Economics of Islam*, Institute of Policy Studies, Islamabad, 1981.

Interfutures. *Facing the Future: Mastering the Probable and Managing the Unpredictable*, OECD, Paris, 1979.

International Organisation of Islamic Medicine, *Islamic Code of Medical Ethics*, Kuwait, 1981.

Impact of Science on Society. 'Science and the Islamic World', Special Issue, **26** (3) (May–September 1976).

Ismael, S. 'Thoughts for the education of Muslim planners of the future', *Ekistics*, No. 28, 428 (1980).

Ibn Ishaq. *The Life of Muhammad* translated by A. Guillaume, OPU, Oxford, 1955.

Islamic Council of Europe, *The Muslim World and the Future Economic Order*, London, 1977.

—— *Universal Islamic Declaration*, London, 1980.

—— *Universal Islamic Declaration of Human Rights*, Paris, 1981.

Jacobs, Jane. *The Death and Life of Great American Cities*, Random House, New York, 1961.

Jafary, S. M. *Shi'ite Islam*, Longman, London, 1979.

Kamal, Ahmad. *The Sacred Journey*, Allen and Unwin, London, 1961.

Karr, Malcolm. *Islamic Studies: A Tradition and its Problems*, Undena Publications, Malibu, California, 1980.

Khan, A. U. 'Islam and Science', *Journal of Research Society of Pakistan*, **7** (4) 15–20 (1970).

Ibn Khaldun. *The Mugaddimah*, translated by Franz Rosenthal, Routledge and Kegan Paul, London, 1967.

Khalifa, M. *The Sublime Qur'an and Orientalism*, Longman, London, 1983.

Khomeini, Ayatollah Ruhullah. *Islamic Government*, translated by Hamid Algar, Mizan Press, Berkley, 1982.

—— *Islam and Revolution*, European Islamic Cultural Centre, Rome, 1983.

King, Alexander. *The State of the Planet*, Pergamon, Oxford, 1980.

King, P. (editor). *The History of Ideas*, Croom Helm, London, 1983.

Kirmani, Zaki. 'New ideologies on science', *MAAS Journal of Islamic Science*, **1** (1) 69–74 (January 1985).

—— 'On the parameters of Islamic science', in *Quest for New Science*, edited by Rais Ahmad and Naseem Ahmad, *op. cit.*

Kizilbash, Hamid H. 'The Islamic conference—retrospect and prospect', *Arab Studies Quarterly*, **4** (1–2) 138–157 (1982).

Koestler, A. and Smythies, J. (editors). *Beyond Reductionism*, Hutchinson, London, 1969.

Kuhn, T. S. 'The historical structure of scientific discovery', *Science*, **136** 760–4 (1962).

—— *The Structure of Scientific Revolution*, University of Chicago Press, 1962; second edition, 1972.

Kurdi, A. A. *The Islamic State*, Mansell, London, 1985.

Kushner, D. *The Rise of Turkish Nationalism*, Frank Cass, London, 1977.

Lacoste, Y. *Ibn Khaldun: The Birth of History and the Past of the Third World*, Verso Editions, London, 1984.

Laszlo, E. (editor). *Goals for Mankind*, Hutchinson, 1977.

Leontief, W., *et al. The Future of World Economy*, OUP, Oxford, 1977.

Lerner, D. *The Passing of Traditional Society*, The Free Press, New York, 1958.

Lings, Martin. *Muhammad: His Life Based on the Earliest Sources*, Allen and Unwin, London, 1983.

Llewellyn, Othman B. 'The objectives of Islamic law and administrative planning', *Ekistics* **47** 11–14 (1980).

—— 'Desert reclamation and Islamic law', *The Muslim Scientist*, **11** 9–30 (1982).

Lovelock, J. E. *Gaia: A New Look at Life on Earth*, OUP, New York, 1979.

Macioti, M. 'Technology and development: the historical experience', in *Integrated Technology Transfer*, edited by Jacques Richardson, Lamond Books, Maryland, 1979.

Mackeen, A. M. M. 'Islamic studies as a university discipline', *Islamic Review*, **57** (5) 13–18 (May 1969).

MacRobie, G. *Small is Possible*, Jonathan Cape, London, 1981.

Mannan, M. A. 'Islamic economics as a social science', *Journal of Research in Islamic Economics*, **1** (1) 49–62 (1983).

Manzoor, S. P. 'Environment and values: the Islamic perspective', in *The Touch of Midas*, edited by Ziauddin Sardar, *op. cit.*

——— 'The power of faith', *Muslim World Book Review*, **4** (1) 3–13 (1983).

——— 'The future of ethics: an agenda', *Afkar/Inquiry*, **1** (1) 40–4 (June 1984).

——— 'World order: visions of faith', *Afkar/Inquiry*, **1** (2) 42–6 (July 1984).

——— 'Islam and the challenge of ecology', *Inquiry*, **2** (2) 32–8 (February 1985).

——— 'Cultural autonomy in a dominated world?' *Inquiry*, **2** (6) 32–7 (June 1985).

Al-Makky, M. T. K. *An Authentic History of Mecca and the Holy House of God*, Al-Mahdaa Library, Macca, 1965 (2 vols).

Masud, M. K. *Islamic Legal Philosophy: A Study of Abu Ishaq al-Shatibi's Life and Work*, Islamic Research Institute, Islamabad, 1977.

Maududi, Abul Ala. *Birth Control*, Islamic Publications, Lahore, 1978.

——— *Islamic Law and Constitution*, Islamic Publications, Lahore, 1955.

Maula, E. 'On the impact of the past upon the future of Islamic science', Journal of Central Asia, **3** 77 (1980).

Meadows, D., *et al. The Limits to Growth*, Potomac Associates, New York, 1972.

Mehden, Fred R. von der. 'Islamic resurgence in Malaysia', in *Islam and Development*, edited by J. Esposito, *op. cit.*

Mendelsohn, E. 'Should science survive its success?' *For Dirk Struik*, edited by R. S. Cohen, *et al.*, Reidel, Dordrecht, 1974.

——— 'The social construction of scientific knowledge', in *Social Production of Scientific Knowledge*, edited by E. Mendelsohn, *et al.*, Reidel, Dordrecht, 1977.

Mendelsohn, K. *Science and Western Domination*, Thames and Hudson, London, 1976.

Mesarovic, M. and Pestel, E. *Mankind at the Turning Point*, Hutchinson, London, 1975.

Mitroff, Ian. *The Subjective Side of Science*, Elsevier, Amsterdam, 1974.

Moraze, C., *et al. Science and the Factors of Inequality*, UNESCO, Paris, 1979.

Moore, C. H. *Images of Development: Egyptian Engineers in Search of Industry*, MIT Press, Massachusetts, 1980.

Morley, D. *The Sensitive Scientist*, SCM Press, 1978.

Moore, Peter. 'Science and technology in traditional Islam and in the modern world', *Studies in Comparative Religion*, **11** (1) 37–52 (1977).

Moore, K. L. 'Highlights of human embryology in the Koran and the hadith', in *Proceedings of the Seventh Saudi Medical Meeting*, Riyadh, 1982.

Moorehouse, W. 'Confronting a four-dimensional problem: science, technology, society and tradition in India and Pakistan', *Technology and Culture*, **8** 363 (1967).

—— (editor). *Science and the Human Condition in India and Pakistan*, Rockerfeller University Press, New York, 1968.

Murad, K. *Islamic Movement in the West: Reflections on Some Issues*, Islamic Foundation, Leicester, 1981.

—— 'On arms race and nuclear armageddon', *Muslim World Book Review*, **4** (4) 3–8 (Summer 1984).

The Muslim. 'Science and Values', **15** (5) 99 (1979).

Nadvi, A. H. A. *Muhammad Rasulullah*, translated by Mohiuddin Ahmad, Academy of Islamic Research and Publications, Lucknow, 1979.

Naqvi, S. N. H. *Ethics and Economics: An Islamic Synthesis*, Islamic Foundation, Leicester, 1981.

—— *et al. Principles of Islamic Economic Reform*, Pakistan Institute of Development Studies, Islamabad, 1984.

Naqvi, S. H. Z. 'Islam and the development of science', *Nigerian Journal of Islam*, **2** (1) 11–20 (1971–2).

Nasr, S. H. *Islamic Studies*, Librairie du Libon, Beirut, 1967.

—— *Science and Civilization in Islam*, Harvard University Press, Cambridge, Massachusetts, 1968.

—— *Encounter of Man and Nature*, Allen and Unwin, London, 1968.

—— *Islam and the Plight of Modern Man*, Longman, London, 1975.

—— *Islamic Science: An Illustrated Study*, World of Islam Festival Publishing Company, London, 1976.

—— with W. C. Chittick and P. Zirmis, *An Annotated Bibliography of Islamic Science*, Tehran, vol. 1 (1975), vol. 2 (1979).

Nature, 'Pakistan needs indigenous medicine', *Nature*, **275** 1 (7 September 1978).

—— 'Development in the Muslim World', *Nature*, **272** 195 (16 March 1978).

Nowotny, H. and Rose, H. (editors). *Counter-movements in Science*, Reidel, Dordrecht, 1979.

Numani, Allama Shibli. *Sirat-un-Nabi* translated by M. T. B. Budayuni, Kazi Publications, Chicago, 1979. (2 vols)

Nyang, S. 'Islam and the technological man', *Journal of World Muslim League*, **3** (6) 16–17 (1976).

Pacy, Arnold. *The Culture of Technology*, Basil Blackwell, Oxford, 1983.

Popper, K. *Conjecture and Refutation*, Routledge and Kegan Paul, London, 1963.

—— *Objective Knowledge*, OUP, Oxford, 1972.

Qadri, A. A. *Islamic Jurisprudence in the Modern World*, Ashraf, Lahore, 1973.

Quddus, S. A. *Pakistan: The Task Before the Nation*, Gillani, Lahore, 1980.

Qureshi, I. H. 'Islam and the west: past, present and future', *The Challenge of Islam*, edited by Altaf Gauhar, *op. cit.*

—— *Education in Pakistan*, Ma'aref, Karachi, 1975.

—— *Ulama in Politics*, Ma'aref, 1975.

Qutb, Sayyid. *This Religion of Islam*, Al-Manar Press, Palo Alto, California, 1967.

—— *The Religion of the Future*, IIFSO, Kuwait, 1975.

—— *Milestone*, IIFSO, Kuwait, 1977.

—— *Social Justice in Islam*, American Council of Learned Societies/ Octagon Books, New York, 1970.

Rahman, Fazlur. *Islamic Methodology in History*, Central Institute of Islamic Research, Karachi, 1965.

—— 'Roots of Islamic neo-fundamentalism', in *Change and the Muslim World*, edited by Philip H. Stoddard, *et al.*, *op. cit.*

—— 'Islamic studies and the future of Islam', in *Islamic Studies: A Tradition and its Problems*, edited by Malcolm Karr, *op. cit.*

—— *Islam and Modernity: Transformation of an Intellectual Tradition*, Chicago University Press, Chicago, 1982.

Ramadan, Said. *Islamic Law: Its Scope and Equity*, Geneva, 1970.

Rasch, B. *Al-Hajj: Tent Cities*, IL29, Institute of Lightweight Structures, University of Stuttgart, Stuttgart, 1980.

Ravetz, Allison. *Remaking Cities*, Croom Helm, London, 1980.

Ravetz, J. R. *Scientific Knowledge and its Social Problems*, OUP, 1971.

—— 'Science and values', in *The Touch of Midas*, edited by Ziauddin Sardar, *op. cit.*

—— 'Marxism and the history of science: Bernal's Marxist vision of history', *ISIS*, **72** (263) 393–402 (1981).

Rehman, M. K. 'The Islamic renaissance and the contemporary problems of Islamic science', in *Quest for New Science*, edited by Rais Ahmed and S. Naseem Ahmed, *op. cit.*

Reinecke, Ian. *Electronic Illusions*, Penguin, Hammondsworth, 1984.

Rifkin, J. and Howard, T. *Entropy: A New Worldview*, Viking, New York, 1980.

Roberts, H. *An Urban Profile of the Middle East*, Croom Helm, London, 1979.

Rosenthal, F. *Knowledge Triumphant*, Brill, Leiden, 1970.

Rose, H. and Rose, S. (editors). *Ideology of/in the Natural Sciences*, Macmillan, London, 1976 (2 vols).

Roszak, T. *Person/Planet: The Creative Disintegration of Industrial Society*, Gollancz, London, 1979.

Saad, E. N. *Social History of Timbuktu*, CUP, Cambridge, 1983.

Sadr. M. H. 'An Islamic view of science', *The Muslim Scientist*, **8** (2–3) 1–7 (1979).

Said, Edward. *Orientalism*, Routledge and Kegan Paul, London, 1978.

―――― 'Islam through western eyes', *The Nation*, **230** (6) 488–92 (1980).

―――― 'Inside Islam', *Harper's*, **262** (1568) 25–32 (January 1981).

Saiyid, M. H. *Mohammad Ali Jinnah: A Political Study*, Elite, Karachi, 1962.

Sadar, Ziauddin. *Science, Technology and Development in the Muslim World*, Croom Helm, London, 1977.

―――― (editor). *Hajj Studies*, Croom Helm, London, 1978.

―――― *Muhammad: Aspects of A Biography*, Islamic Foundation, Leicester, 1978.

―――― *Islam: Outline of a Classification Scheme*, K. G. Saur, London, 1978.

―――― *The Future of Muslim Civilization*, Croom Helm, London, 1979.

―――― *Science and Technology in the Middle East*, Longman, London, 1982.

―――― (editor). *The Touch of Midas: Science, Values and the Environment in Islam and the West*, University of Manchester Press, Manchester, 1984.

―――― *Arguments for Islamic Science*, Centre for Science Studies, Aligarh, 1985.

―――― 'Science in Turkey: choosing the wrong priorities', *Nature*, **282** 354–531 (1979).

―――― 'Scientific thinking behind Khomeini', *Nature*, **282** 439–41 (1979).

―――― 'Inculcating an appropriate sense of confidence', *Nature*, **280** 530–1 (1979).

———— 'A revival for Islam, a boost for science?' *Nature*, **282** 354–7 (1979).

———— 'Where will we be in the year 2000?' *al-Muslim al-Ma'asir*, **5** (19) 29–49 (1979) (in Arabic).

———— 'Islamic Awakening', *Resurgence*, No. 83, 26–7 (1980).

———— 'The fight to save Malaysia', *New Scientist*, **87** 699–703 (1980).

———— 'Can science come back to Islam?' *New Scientist*, **88** 212–16 (1980).

———— 'Islamic Science', *British Journal for the History of Science*, **14** (48) 285–6 (1981).

———— 'Integrated technology transfer', *Technology and Culture*, **22** (3) 683–6 (1981).

———— 'The day the Saudis discovered technology', *New Scientist*, **90** 481–4 (1981).

———— 'Between GIN and TWIN: meeting the information needs of the Third World', *Aslib Proceedings*, **33** (2) 53–61 (1981).

————'What does the Third World really want? Expectation and reality in the North–South dialogue at UNCSTD', in *World Interdependence and Economic Cooperation among Developing Countries*, Centre for Applied Studies in International Negotiations, Geneva, 1981.

———— 'Last chance for world unity', *New Scientist*, **91** 334–41 (1981).

———— 'Development: who benefits?' *Geographical Magazine*, **54** (5) 246–7 (1982).

———— 'Development: is it so desirable?' *Geographical Magazine*, **54** (7) 367–8 (1982).

———— 'Development: interdependence and terrorism', *Geographical Magazine*, **54** (1) 608 (1982).

———— 'Why Islam needs Islamic science', *New Scientist*, **94** 25–8 (1982).

———— 'The Hajj: a select bibliography', *Muslim World Book Review*, **3** (1) 57–66 (Autumn 1982).

———— 'Science and technology in the Muslim world: a select bibliography', *Muslim World Book Review*, **4** (3) 58–65 (1984).

———— 'Intellectual space and western domination: abstracts, bibliographies and current awareness', *Muslim World Book Review*, **4** (2) 3–8 (1984).

———— 'Islamic science or science in Islamic polity?' *Pakistan Studies*, **2** (3) 3–16 (1984).

———— 'The need for Islamic science', *Afkar/Inquiry*, **1** (2) 47–8 (July 1984).

———— 'Victims of methodology: Marxism and Muslim intellectuals', *Afkar/Inquiry*, **1** (3) 44–8 (August 1984).

———— 'Hajj: the greatest gathering of mankind', *Afkar/Inquiry*, **1** (5) 75–6 (September 1984).

———— 'Laying the foundation of intellectual revival', *Afkar/Inquiry*, **1** (5) 75–6 (October 1984).

———— 'Development: who's afraid of population?' *Geographical Magazine*, **56** 506 (1984).

———— 'Making history', *Inquiry*, **2** (1) 7 (1985).

———— 'Pakistan: a state of borrowed ideas', *Inquiry*, **2** (3) 39–45 (1985).

———— and Rosser-Owen, D. G. 'Science policy and developing countries', in *Science, Technology and Society: A Cross-Disciplinary Perspective*, edited by L. Spiegal-Rosing and D. de Solla Price, Sage, London, 1977.

Sayigh, Y. A. *The Economies of the Arab World*, Croom Helm, London, 1978.

———— *The Determinants of Arab Economic Development*, Croom Helm, London, 1978.

Schumacher, E. F. *Small is Beautiful*, Blond and Briggs, London, 1975.

Sharma, K. D. and Qureshi, M. A. (editors). *Science, Technology and Society*, Sterling, Delhi, 1978.

Shariati, Ali. *On the Sociology of Islam*, translated by Hamid Algar, Mizan Press, Berkeley, California, 1979.

Sharif, M. M. (editor). *A History of Muslim Philosophy*, Otto Harrassowitz, Wiesbaden, 1963 (2 vols).

Sherif, M. A. 'Re-examining scientific knowledge', *The Muslim*, **16** (94) 82–3 (1980).

Siddiqui, M. N. *Muslim Economic Thinking*, Islamic Foundation, Leicester, 1981.

———— *Issues in Islamic Banking*, Islamic Foundation, Leicester, 1983.

Stoddard, P. H., Cuthell, D. C. and Sullivan, W. (editors). *Change and the Muslim World*, Syracuse University Press, New York, 1981.

Sulaiman, Ibraheem. 'Will the Nigerian ulama please stand up?' *Inquiry*, **2** (2) 45–7 (February 1985).

Sutcliffe, C. R. 'Is Islam an obstacle to development: ideal patterns of belief versus actual patterns of behaviour', *Journal of Developing Areas*, **10** (1) 77–82 (1975).

Technical University of Istanbul, *Proceedings of the First International Conference on the History of Turkish–Islamic Science and Technology*, Istanbul, 1981 (4 vols).

Tibawi, A. L. *English Speaking Orientalists*, Islamic Cultural Centre, London, 1965.

—— *Islamic Education*, Luzac, London, 1972.

—— *Arabic and Themes*, Luzac, London, 1976.

Tinbergen, Jan (editor). *Reshaping the International Order*, Hutchinson, London, 1977.

Todd, N. and Todd, J. *Bioshelters, Ocean Arks and City Farming: Ecology as A Basis of Design*, Sierra Club, San Francisco, 1984.

Toffler, Alvin. *The Third Wave*, Bantam Books, New York, 1980.

Toprak, B. *Islam and Political Development in Turkey*, Brill, Leiden, 1982.

Valaskakis, K. 'Eclectics: elements of a transdisciplinary methodology for future studies', in *The Future as an Academic Discipline*, Ciba Foundation Symposium 36, Elsevier, Amsterdam, 1975.

Valiuddin, M. 'The secrets of hajj', *Islam and the Modern Age*, **2** (4) 42–70 (1971).

Umma. *The World Muslim Gazeteer*, Karachi, 1979.

University of Aleppo. *The Second International Symposium for the History of Arabic Science*, Aleppo, 1979.

University of Riyadh. *Islamic Solidarity Conference in Science and Technology*, Riyadh, 1976.

Walgate, R. 'Science in Islam and the west: synthesis by dialogue', in *The Touch of Midas*, edited by Ziauddin Sardar, *op. cit.*

White, Jr., Lynn. 'The historical roots of our ecological crisis', *Science*, **155** 1203–7 (1967).

Willard, Beatrice. 'Ethics of biospheral survival', in *Growth or Ecodisaster?* edited by N. Polunin, Macmillan, 1980.

Wise, G. S. and Issawi, C. (editors). *Middle East Perspectives: The Next Twenty Years*, Darwin Press, Princeton, N.J., 1981.

Wolpert, S. *Jinnah of Pakistan*, OUP, New York, 1984.

Index

Footnotes and bibliographical references have not been indexed. Alphabetization is word by word; in the arrangement of subheadings, prepositions, etc., are ignored. Arabic names: 'Abu' and 'Ibn' are entered directly; the prefix 'al-' is ignored in filing.